"The cold zero is the one shot you get at finishing a job. It means truth. Finality. You can practice until your barrel glows red hot, but the cold zero—that first, irrevocable pull of the trigger—is the only statement anyone will remember."

PRAISE FOR *COLD ZERO*

"Compelling. . . . Whitcomb offers the unadorned reality . . . a brave book, an intensely personal look at a career of awesome responsibilities."
—Men's Journal

"A gripping read . . . an authentic, thrilling, gritty account of life in a dangerous field. . . . Whitcomb's behind-closed-doors account is a fascinating glimpse into the FBI's training, team-building, and sanctioned killing, as well as into the personalities of those who pull the strings and those who pull the triggers."
—Portland Oregonian

"Whitcomb does a superb job of putting us in his shoes. . . . [His book] is full of adventure [and] it is timely." **—Charleston Post & Courier (SC)**

"A vivid first-person account . . . fascinating . . . a well-written, informative, revealing, and gripping book."

COLD ZERO

INSIDE THE FBI HOSTAGE RESCUE TEAM

BY SPECIAL AGENT

CHRISTOPHER WHITCOMB

WARNER BOOKS

An AOL Time Warner Company

WARNER BOOKS EDITION

Cover design by Jerry Pfeifer
Cover photo by Deborah Feingold

Warner Books, Inc.
1271 Avenue of the Americas
New York, NY 10020

Visit our Web site at
www.twbookmark.com.

 An AOL Time Warner Company

Printed in the United States of America

Originally published in hardcover by Little, Brown & Company
First Paperback Printing: October 2002

10 9 8 7 6 5 4 3 2 1

To Rose

CONTENTS

AUTHOR'S NOTE

At the FBI's request, all names have been changed, except those of widely known public figures. Some events and details have been slightly altered to protect sensitive investigative techniques. The opinions and observations expressed in this book do not necessarily reflect those of the FBI.

COLD
ZERO

PROLOGUE

The world looks different through a rifle scope. Even here, in this dark jungle, where the moon peeks through the double canopy in slivers, I can feel the power of holding life and death at the pull of a trigger. The smells of damp steel and leather fill my nose as I tuck the stock into my shoulder. My eye hovers behind the reticle, searching the distance for just the right combination of windage and elevation. My index finger rests lightly on the trigger guard, conditioned not to reach past the safety until it's time to kill.

"Sierra One to TOC. I have subject movement on the white-blue corner. Copy?"

Light drifts off the green Birdsong finish of my barrel as I collect information through a Unertl ten-power scope, one observation at a time.

"Copy, Sierra One."

Radio traffic. People talk differently with a microphone to their lips.

Sierra One, in our language, means sniper position one — the highest observation post on this dank mountainside. From here, I can look down with anonymity on our "subjects" and gather information about all aspects of their day-to-day lives. I can observe the color of their hair, whether they shaved this morning, what they ate for breakfast. Sometimes I get so close, I can almost smell the cologne on their neck and the garlic on their breath. That's the irony in long-range surveillance: intimacy. Even at 300 yards, you learn things about your subjects that no one else gets to see.

Sniping is a lonely, intrusive business built on long hours of boredom and rare moments of epiphany and thrill. For every shift wasted in tedium, you might get a single moment's adrenaline — maybe a passing glimpse of a fugitive you've hunted for weeks, or a clear shot at a hostage taker that negotiators have written off as rabid. These moments come quickly, at the margins of a mission; sometimes just a face in a window, or a figure shuffling through a passing crowd.

You study him, the man in the scope, scouring his habits, his environment, for bits of information the street agents haven't discovered. Watch carefully and he'll offer you a small gesture — that intimacy we trust when we think we're alone. Sometimes he'll dance to music on the car radio. Sometimes he'll catch his reflection in a store window or a mirror and make faces at himself, imagining how he'll chat up a pretty woman or respond to a rival's taunt. People let their guard down when they think no one is watching. They'll show you what's inside, next to their thoughts.

Tonight, I lie beneath the heavy first drops of a tropical squall, waiting for opportunity. The air tastes moldy.

"D'ya ever try to run a dado blade through longleaf pine?"

Bobby Metz, my Chicago-bred partner, tries to get comfortable on a poncho in a makeshift tent behind me. This is downtime for him, but sleep comes hard out here, and he wants conversation. We rotate shifts "on target" every two hours, trying to stay focused.

It's hot. Even at 2:07 A.M., the air feels rheumy against my skin. The sounds of dancing women filter up through the trees, coloring the jungle with energy, calling us down.

There are other distractions. An iguana the size of a Chesapeake retriever sidles through the ground cover just off to my right. I heard him coming a few minutes ago and trained my night vision goggles on his vicinity just to make sure of his intentions. I don't mind lizards, but the rats he's sniffing out make my skin crawl.

"I pay a dollar ninety-five a linear foot for that stuff when I can find it," Bobby says. "I get the shakes every time I think about trying to make a cut."

I don't know much about longleaf pine. I've never even heard of a dado blade.

"What you making?" I ask.

These are the courtesies we extend each other on surveillances, during the long stretches of quiet between moments. I listen to him, then he listens to me in a sort of reciprocal tolerance. I don't give a shit about woodworking. The only thing I know about pine is how good it would feel, right now, carved into an Adirondack chair.

"Sierra Two to TOC. We got a vehicle passing the checkpoint. White sedan, three to four occupants."

I pan right, about ten degrees, trying to pick up a shadow moving along the narrow street below us. Cars always kill their lights at the checkpoint. That makes discerning things like license numbers and faces more difficult.

"Box," Metz says.

"What kind of box?"

"Just a box. You know, to hold all that crap in your top drawer. A man needs a box."

Bobby loves tools: big Shopsmith power saws with turning lathes and automatic air filtration systems, Matco hex drivers with Day-Glo handles, box sets of ¾-inch sockets. He can't pass a tool store without dragging the rest of the team in for a look.

"Sierra Two to TOC. We just lost them around the corner. Looks like subject Carlos, returning."

Bobby's voice trails off into the jungle as I concentrate on the scene down below.

"Hold it, buddy, I've got traffic," I say.

Bobby's off his radio. He can't hear Sierra Two's assessment of the only significant movement we've seen in the last two hours.

"What's the situation?" he asks.

The situation, to be precise, involves eight Hostage Rescue Team snipers and a hyperviolent Puerto Rican street gang responsible for supplying the eastern half of the island with everything from Jamaican sinsemilla to black tar heroin. Agents working the case out of the San Juan office have tagged a half-dozen main subjects with a string of carjackings, gang murders, and drug-related hits that would have made Tupac jealous. While they work up search warrants and indictments through the court system, we sit up here, gathering intelligence that will help facilitate the assault. The rest of the team is coming at dawn.

From here, I can look 257 yards due east down into a ragged suburb called Villa Pilar. Mountains surround the village, choking all traffic through a small one-lane road. Buyers must pass through armed sentries at the gate. That makes security easy on the dealers and hard on us. Previous attempts at search warrants have produced nothing. By the time the cops get through the gate, all the drugs have disappeared into the jungle.

"Sierra One to TOC. I have a white Mercedes sedan — four door — with three adult males stopping in front of Building One."

I whisper the intelligence update into the bone mic resting against my jaw. Party noise echoes through the hills. Dogs bark at the shadows. There's no way anyone down in the village can hear my voice, but whispering is a tough habit to break. Something about sneaking around and spying on people makes you want to talk in hushed tones.

I roll away from my rifle, a .308-caliber thunderstick custom built by FBI gunsmiths on a Remington Model 700 bolt-action receiver. It holds five match-grade 168-grain boattail hollow-point bullets in a spring-loaded magazine. The jeweled trigger is tuned to break at two and a half pounds of pressure. The leather cheek pad on the stock is stained dark with sweat.

Just to my right, less than a foot from my rifle, sits a forty-power Burris spotting scope mounted on a camouflage tripod. This rubber-coated optic provides four times the magnification of my rifle scope and allows me to zoom in on small details that could make a difference when the rest of the team executes the arrests. We've brought along a complete package of night vision equipment, too, but the streetlights and porch lamps down below render it useless.

Things look much clearer through the Burris scope. I recognize two of the men immediately. We've already nicknamed the driver Gene because of an uncanny resemblance to Gene Gene the Dancing Machine on the old *Gong Show*. I almost expect him to start some goofy shuffle as he pushes open his door and extricates his floppy gut from behind the steering wheel. His true name is Julio Aquirre, but assigning him a handle is easier because we invariably run into three or four Johns or Franks, or Julios. Nicknames help avoid confusion.

The two passengers step out into the light of a streetlamp: we've named them Slick and Carlos. No one has identified Slick, but Carlos is a bona fide executioner, born Juan Miguel Salinas. If everything goes right, he'll wake up later this morning facing charges in four gang-related murders. Our case agent seems particularly interested in finding a Glock 9mm pistol used in three of the homicides. It looks like Carlos has it tucked in his belt.

"Sierra One to TOC. Carlos and Slick just exited the vehicle. Appear to be armed."

Despite their well-documented provenance, these men don't look dangerous from up here. The pistols under their T-shirts are no match for our rifles. They look small, almost trivial.

Metz shuffles around behind me.

"Don't those people ever sleep?" he asks. The tent ruffles over his head as he tries to find a comfortable position.

This mission began four days ago with a mile-and-a-half stalk into our mountainside sniper lair. We arrived early, in the shifting light just before dawn, moving slowly in ominous-looking ghillie suits. The burlap and Cordura garments meld us with the surrounding jungle so effectively, local vermin sometimes slither in to hide from the sun. My four-year-old ghillie looks decayed and rancid like the jungle floor. The thought of crawling into it would make most people ill, but I find its utility comforting. Nature rots. If you want to blend in, you have to rot right along with it.

Everything we need to do our job came with us in backpacks. We lugged enough food and water for a week's stay, along with bivouac equipment (a foam sleeping pad), weapons, ammunition, and optics. The standard kit weighs about seventy-five pounds but offers lean accommodations.

A poncho stretched between two trees serves as a pup tent. Two quarts of water and one MRE (military ration) have to last a full day.

This job isn't about comfort, it's about mission: ours centers on learning the patterns, behaviors, and weaknesses of the gang members. FBI commanders want to know where they hide the drugs, who comes in to buy them, what weapons they carry, how sophisticated their own surveillance might be. Armed with this information, the arrest teams can sweep through the village in a couple of hours and shut the place down. Murder, drug trafficking, armed robbery, assault — the charges go on and on. All we care about is making sure our fellow agents can move in to make the hit without stumbling over outside variables.

"You got something?"

Metz peeks out of the tent, sensing a priority spike. Surveillance is a lot like fishing. As soon as someone feels a bite, everyone else in the boat wants to join the angle.

"Looks like the boys are back," I tell him.

The gang leader left just before ten o'clock with three of his men. The San Juan office attempted a loose ground surveillance of its own, but lost them in traffic.

"Sierra One to TOC. Carlos, Slick, and Gene just exited the vehicle. They're moving around to the trunk."

Metz lies beside me and stares down the barrel through the scope.

"New shipment, you think?" he asks.

That would make the case agent very happy. These guys have been selling dope out of the same stash for three days, and traffic has been heavy. We've counted an average of forty-three sales per hour, twenty-four hours a day. Wal-Mart would be happy to turn these numbers. Unfortunately, they're selling off all their stock. If we don't get a new shipment in the next few hours, the agents might as well leave their search warrants in the car.

Metz and I train our optics on the Mercedes sedan with its gold hubcaps and chain-link license plate frame. Three Puerto Rican males climb out, look up into the surrounding hills, then move to the trunk.

We stare silently into our optics, hoping for a glimpse that will help us identify their cargo. Big square bales will be pot: anticlimax. Small parcels mean crack, heroin, coke, meth . . . the kind of drugs worth waiting for. These guys are going away for a long time on the murder charges, but tacking on an extra decade for quality pharmaceuticals wouldn't hurt.

"Holy shit," I say out loud. There's no mistaking the package they pull out of the trunk. "That's a body."

Gene and Slick shuffle away from the car, trying to maintain their grip on the corpse. Gene has the feet; Slick, the shoulders.

Carlos yells something up to the house and several people emerge excitedly.

"Cover the front door, Bobby," I say. Suddenly, it looks like the entire place is emptying out to meet them. A short, stocky kid of about nineteen holds a Ruger Mini-14 assault rifle, scanning for trouble. I can hear his voice above the music, but it fades into that muffled, run-together din that comes with distance. He talks all high-pitched and quick, full of adrenaline.

"You know him?" Metz asks. The dead guy.

Unfortunately, his head hangs forward on his chest. I can't see his face.

"Check with Sierra Three. Maybe they can make him."

I key the radio transmitter with my left hand, still trying to improve the focus on the spotting scope.

"Sierra One to TOC, Sierra Three. Subjects carrying unknown male from trunk of car . . . appears dead or seriously injured." His shirt is soaked in blood. There's no way to tell if it's a bullet hole or some broader wound.

I wait through a long pause. No one expects any significant intel this time of night, and I wonder if Sierra Three has nodded off in the thick air.

"Sierra Three to TOC. We have no eye from this position." Guess not.

Gene and Slick lead a growing crowd of onlookers up the stairs to the house. A hand grenade wouldn't have created much more havoc. People materialize out of the jungle, out of the side buildings, the main house. Two or three others dash up the street, yelling. Everyone converges in a flurry of activity unlike anything we've seen yet.

"Must be one of theirs," Metz says.

And they're gone. The whole crowd darts inside the house, leaving the kid with the Ruger perched outside, waiting for trouble. He looks serious, focused, too present for his age.

I can see inside the house through the side door where they've stretched the body out on the floor. One of his shoes is missing, leaving a crumpled sock hanging from his right foot. The others dance around him, trying to figure out what the hell to do, but he lies still on the tile, staining the white squares dark under the fluorescent ceiling light.

The kid with the Ruger reaches to pull the door closed, and the night settles back into the same empty rhythm I've grown used to. It's quiet again.

"What the heck?" Metz mumbles. He rarely swears.

"Yeah," I answer. "What the heck."

Just before dawn, Bobby kicks my boots to wake me for my shift. A gentle Caribbean rain taps against the poncho over my head. The music has stopped.

"You up?" he asks.

"Up?" I wonder. I haven't slept more than two hours at a stretch in four days. I don't even know exactly what "up" feels like.

"We got a half hour before they hit the gate. Better get your stuff together."

I know the drill. Though we last briefed this operation almost a week ago, the plan seems simple. Charlie, Echo, Golf, and Hotel assault teams will storm through the gate with specially equipped Suburbans. As they race up to the four primary search sites, Zulu and Yankee snipers will lie in wait just inside the jungle to cut off any "runners." Whiskey and my own X-ray snipers will provide long-range cover should gang members opt for violence.

Officers from the Puerto Rican National Police will secure the gate and form a loose perimeter, but none of us expects this raid to come as a surprise. The local gendarmes' track record for operational security leaves a lot to be desired. As with most operations, however, politics plays a considerable role. This is their turf, and despite our considerable jurisdiction, we can't keep them out.

"How's business?" I ask Bobby, pulling my rifle out of its Cordura travel case. The day's first sun begins to lighten the jungle behind me, leaving us prone to silhouette.

"Slow. Business basically stopped at four."

Roosters start to crow in the new day. Lights dot the valley as some of the households wake for school or work. Not everyone earns a living in the drug trade. Some want these thugs gone as much as we do.

I slide out the front of our tent with my rifle in my lap. Metz has already laid claim to the surveillance spot as his forward firing position (FFP). Mine lies ten yards off to the left on a sloping ledge protected by needle ferns. Though not the best-camouflaged position on the hill, it does offer a pristine view of all Villa Pilar. In flat wind like this, my rifle will drive tacks.

My watch reads 5:37 A.M., but I don't try to rationalize time anymore: I'm either awake or asleep, period.

"They back yet?" I ask. I ruffle through my pack looking for a fresh radio battery and a canteen of water.

Recollection comes slowly through sleep deprivation, but I remember enough. Just after three o'clock, as my shift ended, Slick and the others hurried out the side door with the body hanging limp between them. His head fell to the side, lifeless, bobbing up and down as they walked, like one of those little dogs people stick in the rear windows of their cars. I've handled enough death to know he isn't part of this problem anymore. He's gone.

Metz radioed the movement into the Tactical Operations Center, and the San Juan Special Operations Group (SOG) followed the car. After that I handed the surveillance back to Metz and caught a little sleep. Though the whole thing seemed interesting at the time, it had no bearing on the job at hand. We're here for the drugs.

"Twenty minutes ago. Either they dumped the stiff someplace in the jungle or they still have him in the trunk," Metz said. "You got any Pop Tarts?"

I wonder about who he was and why someone killed him. He's the only mystery left in this village. After four days up here, we know who is sleeping with whom, how they hide the dope in hollow fence posts, beneath garbage cans, in the rain gutters. There's nothing sophisticated about this enterprise. If not for their proclivity for violence, this group would look like a bunch of kids playing post office.

"We running on schedule?"

I toss Metz two blueberry pastries, still in the silver foil wrapper.

"The assault teams just left the staging area. Be about ten minutes."

I pull my radio headset over my right ear and adjust the mic. "HR-28 to TOC. Radio check."

"Copy, HR-28. I've got you five by five."

I stop just short of my forward firing position and look down into the valley. The sun is rising fast over my left shoulder. The roosters are dancing now. Kitchens and bathrooms and bedrooms light up in dull yellows and orange, as the normal people start their day.

The first voices of H-hour cackle in my earpiece as the other sniper teams call in from their firing positions. Radio silence among the assault teams means they are moving toward us. They won't break squelch again until they reach the forward rallying point — Yellow.

My game day routine seldom changes. First priority is always to make sure I have a clear, unobstructed view of the target. The smallest twig between my barrel and the target could create enough deflection to make me miss, or worse, to hit someone else.

Next, I slide the rifle out in front of me, emerging precariously from a eucalyptus thicket as I work my way into position. I low-crawl, following my rifle across an exposed section of flat rock, breathing shallow, measured breaths like they taught us in sniper school. A brown gecko darts out in front of me, inured to my smell and demeanor at this point. We're part of the jungle, now, Metz and I. Even the rats accept us.

The tiny lizard leads me into position behind a tuft of razor grass. The sun glints off a dew-covered leaf to my right. I lay my right cheek against the cool rock slab, forcing myself to slow movement and to exercise discipline.

"Sierra Three to TOC. HR-44 and -76 in position."

That would be Junior and Trask. They lie in the shadows

down below us, just off one of two trailheads the dopers might use as escape routes. Others call in to the TOC, advising of their readiness. Everyone's gearing up for the hit, working on their game plan.

Discipline, I tell myself. This is the most exposed position on the mountain. No need to hurry.

I slowly lift my head to confirm the shot. Even without optics, I can see his face: 252 yards from the tip of my barrel. The sentry waits outside the side door with his Ruger. Drug sales ended abruptly fifteen minutes ago without resupply. They know we're coming.

I reach forward and flip the spring-loaded bipod into position, giving my rifle legs. A heavy weapon like this is pretty much useless off-hand at 250 yards. The bipod steadies my aim, offering benchrest stability with the wide range necessary to track "movers."

My setup is ritual. First I place a small beanbag under the stock to support the weight of my upper body as I settle into position. My left arm folds up under me, elbow forward, fingers pinching the beanbag to adjust the aim. My right hand caresses the pistol grip, thumb loosely opposite my index finger, squeezing just enough to feel its pebbled texture.

Working from my head south, I set my cheek weld against the stock, finding the eye relief necessary to center the crosshairs in the scope tube. I align my body with the recoil path to minimize muzzle jump when the round kicks out at 2,700 feet per second. I press my hips against the ground, spread my knees shoulder-width for stability, and lower the heels of my boots to minimize profile. From down below, I'll look like a thin black shadow.

"Hotel One to TOC. We're at Yellow."

The assault teams have arrived. No time to look for their caravan of Suburbans on the horizon. I'm still not ready for my shot.

"Copy, Hotel One. I have you at Yellow. Stand by."

Slowly, I tell myself. *Don't push it.* Good position means little without the proper calibration. A rifle does what its operator tells it, period. Without dialing in the correct settings, a sniper can expect nothing more of his $2,500 instrument than he could of a homemade slingshot.

I dial 200 yards into the elevation turret of my bullet drop compensator, then add an extra two half-minute clicks. This will accommodate the acute angle of incidence and high humidity. With air this still, I need no left or right windage at all. It seems like a simple shot. If this guy turns the Ruger on members of the arrest teams, I feel confident in my ability to put a .308-caliber round right where the crest of his nose bisects his dark Latin eyes.

"Sierra One to TOC. We're in position."

There. Time. All the countless hours of investigation, all the undercover dope buys, the Title III wiretap affidavits, the interviews, the paperwork, come down to this. I know these agents, their families. It's my job to protect them.

I pull the stock into my shoulder and exhale a long, slow breath.

"HR-1 to all units. You have compromise authority and permission to move to Green."

The crosshairs in my scope dance slightly as the final traces of adrenaline ebb from my muscle. I settle the thin black sighting lines on the sentry's face. They trained us to take out the brain stem, where the spinal cord attaches to the skull.

I visualize the assaulters sitting in the Suburbans with their breaching rams in their laps, running mental checklists as the drivers hold the brakes, awaiting the order to execute. I've been there before, too, concentrating on how the door opens, who goes in first, how to say "Drop the gun" in phonetic Spanish.

"HR-1 to all units. Stand by . . . I have control . . ."

Here it comes. That infinite pause before all hell breaks loose.

I'm thirty-six years old. A nine-year veteran of the FBI. This is my fourth year on the Hostage Rescue Team. In some ways I feel like I've been training for this all my life. In some ways I feel like I have no idea what the hell I'm supposed to do next. That's the dilemma you juggle in a shooting situation: No matter what they tell you, pulling a trigger is a personal decision. Once you make it — right or wrong — the consequences never go away.

"Five . . ."

The HRT commander's voice rings in my ear as he counts down the launch sequence. I think back over shots I've taken. You slide the first bullet into battery with your index finger so you can feel it seating.

"Four . . ."

You think back on all the thousands and thousands of rounds you've run down the barrel, learning the rifle, the way it reacts to heat and wind and weather. The first shot is called a "cold bore" — that unpracticed, leap-of-faith imprint on a fresh target. If your aim and your calibrations are true, the point of aim and point of impact align. That is your "zero."

"Three . . ."

On a good day, when everything spins just perfectly, they come together, the cold bore and the zero. Cold zero. All outside influences fade off into the subconscious. The rest of the world turns someplace else without you, oblivious to the intricacies that govern trajectory. Here, the entire universe boils down to a rifle and a human being working in concert to throw a tiny slug 250 yards with no error.

"Two . . ."

The cold zero is the one shot you get at finishing a job. It means truth. Finality. You can practice until your barrel glows red hot, but the cold zero — that first, irrevocable pull of the trigger — is the only statement anyone will remember.

"One . . ."

And this is mine.

BOOK
ONE

What lies behind us
and what lies before us
are tiny matters compared
to what lies within us.

OLIVER WENDELL HOLMES

1

ENTRANCE ON DUTY

The only thing the FBI ever promised me was that I'd get the opportunity to prove myself. I was working in Washington, D.C., as speechwriter and press secretary for Congressman Silvio O. Conte of Massachusetts when an FBI applicant coordinator named Wayne called in March 1987 to offer me a job.

"Chris," he said, with the assurance of a man who knew virtually every detail of my twenty-seven-year life, "we have a New Agent class scheduled to start in two weeks. Can you make it?"

My heart stopped in my chest. It had been more than a year since I'd mustered the courage to fill out a preliminary application for the Federal Bureau of Investigation. Though I met the basic requirements, the notion that I might have the chops to join the world's most prestigious law enforcement agency seemed just a bit presumptuous.

As Wayne's voice rang in my ear, my mind raced back

over the months and months of waiting for this one moment. I drifted to a quiet evening in 1986 when I sat at the dining room table of my basement apartment and started to fill out the initial application. The two-page form asked for basic things like my full name, date and place of birth, Social Security number — the kind of information most people assume the FBI already knows. It outlined the applicant criteria: All prospective agents had to be U.S. citizens between the ages of twenty-four and thirty-five, with at least a bachelor's degree and three years of work experience, or a graduate degree.

It all sounded simple enough back then, but after more than a year of testing, hoping, interviewing, waiting, and enduring their faceless form letters, I wondered how anyone ever got in.

"I have been given authorization to offer you a position, if you think you can make the time constraint," Wayne said. "If not . . . well, I can't make any guarantees."

He struck me as a cross between a fraternity rush chairman and the caller at a bingo match. The last time I'd seen him was at the Washington Field Office three weeks earlier, where he handed me an old Smith and Wesson Model 10 revolver with a red pistol grip.

"This is the trigger pull test," he told me. "You have sixty seconds to cycle the hammer as many times as possible. This is designed to predict how well you will perform with an actual weapon."

He showed me how to hold the gun at arm's length and pointed me toward a silhouette target taped to the wall. I didn't really get the part about cycling the hammer, but the drill seemed simple enough. I held the small dark weapon out in front of me and waited for him to hit the stopwatch.

"Go!" he said. And I pulled for all I was worth.

No one ever explained the correlation between finger endurance and accuracy with a live weapon, but I asked no questions. I wanted the job, and if that meant playing shoot-out with the wall, using a fake gun, well, that was okay by me.

"Can you get away in two weeks?" Wayne asked, drawing me back into the job offer.

He sounded impatient with the task, as if it were keeping him from something more important. I could picture him sitting at a steel gray government-issue desk with a No. 2 pencil in his hand. I was just another name on an endless list of applicants, and he had slots to fill. If he called enough numbers, he'd eventually close out his card.

Two weeks? I thought. The room around me started to spin.

I felt ready, in most ways. I had become a zealot for the cause, working out twice a day for the past year, preparing for the worst they could throw at me during New Agent Training. Each day started with a four-mile run through the streets of Southeast Washington. At night, I took my lumps, sparring at Finley's Boxing Gym, up above the 10th Street Body Shop, where the smells of paint solvent and Krylon lacquer cleared my head between beatings.

Every set of push-ups ended with three extras for the F-B-I. Every round of sit-ups included an exhaustion marathon in homage to J. Edgar Hoover. Though the Director's taste for madras sundresses and suede pumps hadn't leaked out yet, it wouldn't have mattered. I worked each day with crystalline ambition. I absolutely willed acceptance.

"Can I pencil you in?" Wayne asked, again, unaccustomed to vacillation.

I leaned back in my chair and tried to focus. Overwhelming excitement threatened to boil out of my gut and erupt into a banshee wail. My heart started to beat again, then pound, throbbing so hard I worried that people in the next room might hear.

I started to answer, but the words caught in my throat. The thought of breaking the news to my boss, a senior member of the United States Congress, and giving up my office on Capitol Hill seemed anathema itself. Only one person on the staff knew of my undercover job hunt, and he'd sworn himself to the kind of secrecy he suspected my new life in the FBI might require. Accepting this offer meant turning my back on a promising writing career built at a California magazine and two of New England's finer unknown newspapers. I could kiss good-bye my hopes of moving over to a speechwriting gig at the White House.

On top of that, my wife, Rose, enjoyed her staffer job with Representative David Dreier of California, we'd just bought an 1880s brownstone, and our four-month-old son, Jake, was not quite ready for travel. The FBI wanted investigators, not writers. This kind of career move seemed ill-conceived.

"Chris?" Wayne asked. "You still with me?"

What the hell was I doing?

❖

The road to a Special Agent badge runs pretty much the same for everyone. Just about a month after submitting the initial application, you receive a Xeroxed form letter from an applicant coordinator. Mine came from Wayne. It listed a time and date for the entrance examination and stated that I should report to the Washington Metropolitan Field Office if I wanted to continue the process. If I scored high enough in comparison to other applicants from around the country, I would be "afforded the opportunity" to continue the application process.

So, on April 10, 1986, I scheduled a day of annual leave

and traveled a little more than a mile from my Capitol Hill apartment to a gray, sagging office building in South East Washington, appropriately named Buzzard's Point. Inside, a receptionist greeted me through a wall of bulletproof glass and pointed me to a windowless waiting room full of like-minded applicants. I counted twenty-six other people. None of them said a word.

I looked the room over, trying to assess my chances. The group included men and women of all different sizes, ages, and colors. Some of them held their form letter in their hands as if the document might be checked for authenticity. One man fidgeted in his chair so overtly, I began to feel self-conscious myself. He kept staring up at the ceiling, as if looking for the cameras he assumed they'd use to record our behavior. He crossed and uncrossed his legs half a dozen times, then exhaled deeply, stood up, and left without explanation.

The man sitting next to me tapped me on the arm and said, "He ain't coming back. I seen him in here before." He wore a lime-green leisure suit and white patent leather zipper boots. The pants had hung so long on the hanger, they showed fade lines across his knees. Fashion sense probably wouldn't appear on the exam, I guessed, but basic decorum had to figure in to the equation somewhere.

I just nodded and tried to relax until a repressed-looking GS-6 clerk entered with an armful of examination booklets.

"How many of you have taken this before?" she asked.

Three people raised their hands.

"We have your names on record, and we'll check," she prodded without expression. "Now, how many of you have taken this test before?"

Twelve more people, including my new pal in the double knit, raised their hands.

I knew very little about the FBI or their admissions procedures, but I figured that lying this early in the process had to be a bit risky.

My instinct proved true. A couple of months after the entrance exam, I received another form letter notifying me that my score had placed me high enough above the guys in leisure suits to warrant an interview. It was written with all the personality of a road sign, but it meant that this whole idea of reaching out to federal law enforcement might not be so preposterous after all.

On June 3, 1986, I took my second of five vacation days and headed back to Buzzard's Point for a little palaver. Two men and a woman, all very professional looking, entered a small conference room overlooking the Potomac and triangulated me.

"I imagine you feel a little nervous," the taller man said. I sat at the business end of a ten-foot conference table surrounded by people who knew more about me than my mother did. "A little nervous" seemed just a bit understated.

I adjusted my posture in the slippery naugahyde chair and tried to breathe normally.

"Let me start out by asking if you remember a November day in the mid-nineteen seventies," one of the men began, "when three agents came to interview your father about a shooting."

Nineteen seventies? I was just a teenager then.

"As I understand it, your father had some involvement in the untimely death of one of Mr. Hoover's top aides. Perhaps you could tell this panel how you think that will affect your chances of becoming an FBI agent."

The room began to spin. This was one of those moments in life when you can feel the current of manifest destiny switching polarity. My mind shot back to a sunny November morning in New Hampshire more than twenty years earlier, when three men dressed in business suits and long faces showed up at my house to share a few words with my old man.

❖

"Hello, I'm Special Agent Michael Donelly with the Federal Bureau of Investigation," one of them said. He carried a cordovan briefcase and a small gold badge worn black around the edges.

The formality of his presentation stood out from everything around our house on Profile Road. FBI agents didn't visit northern New England very often. In fact, other than the official FBI briefcase–machine gun I'd received for my eighth birthday, I knew almost nothing about J. Edgar Hoover's intractable G-men.

Franconia, New Hampshire, is a small mountain village halfway between Boston and Montreal. A steep notch pinches travel to the south with cliff walls that reach 1,000 feet straight up on both sides of the road, offering local boys such as myself a granite security but narrow horizons. The "Great Stone Face," a natural profile strong enough to inspire a poem by Daniel Webster, stands watch over the valley. His eye wanders south with a strange remorse, as if he stopped for a rest and lost his way.

Robert Frost, the town's most famous denizen, had lived out on the Easton Road, in a small meadow overlooking the Kinsman range. He spent several years walking the white birch forests and maple groves, resting on stone walls and marveling at the snows. If I ascribe the place immodest beauty, don't take my word for it. Read "The Road Not Taken" or "Mending Wall." Franconia swelled with meter and grace, from the deep beds of fall foliage to the understated truth of sunrise over a millpond. All a poet ever needed there was a pen and the audacity to call the words his own.

The only things even vaguely federal about the tiny village of 250 people boiled down to the Presidential Mountain Range, which filled the dining room window of our house on the Gale River, and an occasional Farm Bureau inspector. Our sole resource in the way of law enforcement was Police Chief Dunne, a spare, weary man who spent most of his time working a pint bottle of Old Granddad and plinking rats with Eddie Splude at the town dump. Crime — at least the sort of crime worthy of FBI intervention — just didn't roll through very often.

"Nice to meet you, sir," my dad said, reaching for Agent Donelly's hand. He wore that awkward grin he showed around the time report cards came out. "I'm sorry to hear about your boss."

Agent Donelly reached into his pocket for a notebook. My father stood firmly at the bottom of our front stairs with both hands in his pockets. If he felt any embarrassment over the fact that a local man had just shot and killed a former Assistant Director of the FBI, he didn't show it. The killing bore no signs of malice. Marty Corliss, the soft-spoken son of a New Hampshire state trooper, simply mistook the Assistant Director for an eight-point buck on the back side of Sugar Hill. Though it was just a tragic accident, Corliss shot him as neatly as any Mob hit man ever could have.

The story made the front page of the *Littleton Courier* and sent shock waves through the North Country. Marty wasn't the first overzealous hunter to whack a fellow woodsman, but no one else had ever drawn a bead on one of the country's top crime fighters. Washington apparently took the news hard, suspecting everyone from the Luchese family to Russian cold warriors of the hit.

Rumor held that the agents sent in to investigate the killing had driven all the way from St. Johnsbury, Vermont, a considerable distance by local standards. The plates on their car said Massachusetts, though, scarring their reputation before they said a word. I felt bad enough for my dad as it was, without thinking about the possibility that he'd have to undergo interrogation from a carful of marble-mouthed flatlanders.

Whatever their origin, three men showed up dressed for a funeral in dark wool suits and white shirts. The one who took my dad out of sight into our garage looked enough like Efrem Zimbalist, Jr., that I started humming the theme song under my breath. His buddies stood there as I rocked my new Schwinn Stingray back and forth in the driveway. Maybe they'd like to see the new fly rod my Uncle Gary just bought me, I wondered.

One of the men tucked his hands in his pockets and leaned against the car, dissuading me from such intimacies until my dad emerged from the garage unhurt. These guys investigated matters of international intrigue in places I'd never been. They might know torture, too.

I decided to stick around, just for protection.

"Hey, Mister. You ever kill anybody?" I asked the shortest, least intimidating of the three. I guess that question just naturally pops into people's minds when they meet someone who packs a tommy gun on TV.

The man looked down at me over the tops of his wire-rimmed glasses and squinted. He seemed a little uncomfortable with the question, which surprised me, considering his occupation. I saw it on television all the time — run-and-gun battles between the forces of good and evil. *The FBI* aired every Tuesday night on Channel 3. But this guy didn't impress me as the television type. He stared back as if he wanted to blab but couldn't hack up the words.

"Nice bike," he said. "Can you ride a wheelie?"

Could I ride a wheelie? A smile exploded across my face as I dropped the stick shift into first gear and jumped up on the right pedal for my patented high-torque takeoff. I could actually get a little rubber if the driveway was dirty enough.

I rode fast down the road, pulling on the handlebars and lifting the front wheel into the air like a seasoned veteran. The agent with the glasses watched me with the discriminating eye of a man who appreciated danger. I cocked the front wheel to the right like all the great motocross riders and concentrated so hard on my stunt that I barely noticed my dad and Agent Donelly emerging a short time later from the garage.

Everything looked all right on the surface, but for one very long moment, I searched in panic for my dad's hands, hoping Efrem Zimbalist hadn't cuffed him. Growing up in a small town left me with plenty of time to guess at how things happened in the outside world, but I'd never contemplated a scene like this. The thought of seeing these men shackle my personal hero and drag him away in shame almost shook the wind out of me.

The panic passed, however, when my dad slapped Agent Donelly on the back and laughed at some remark I couldn't hear. I locked up my brakes and just sat there at the side of the road as all three agents climbed into their blue Plymouth Fury, nodded in unison, and steered the big car past me on their way back to St. Johnsbury or Boston or wherever the hell they came from.

My buddy, the wheelie aficionado, looked up at me as they passed. He tossed out a wink and a smile in acknowledgment of my riding ability. He lifted his right hand, pointed his index finger at me in that universal sign of a fully cocked revolver, and dropped his thumb. I could almost hear the shot going off as he drove away to someplace a whole lot more exciting than Franconia, chasing spies or fugitives or bank robbers.

Every time I tested my balance from that day on, I wondered if the look on that agent's face came from a desire to protect my youthful innocence or a need to make it go away.

❖

My God, they're good, I thought, staring across the table at my interviewer. That day in Franconia swelled up inside me as if I were still standing astride my Stingray, watching my dad emerge from the garage.

How did they know about this? I wondered. I had filled out the comprehensive background questionnaire detailing my life history all the way back to grade school. I had listed everyone I'd ever lived with, every address, every school I'd attended, references, social contacts, foreign travel in twelve countries. I'd admitted to "experimental drug use" in college, conceded a traffic violation, detailed the most intimate secrets of my first twenty-seven years. But how the hell did they know this?

I stared at the man, frozen with self-doubt. *Get a grip,* I argued with myself. I didn't kill any FBI agent and neither did my dad. Shit, I'd never even met Marty Corliss.

The three members of the blue-suit inquisition stared back stone-faced, waiting for an answer.

"That was a long time ago, sir," I said. "My father had nothing to do with that shooting, and I can't imagine how it would affect my ambitions now."

"Good," he said, "because if you make it through the background check, you're going to be the fourth person from Franconia, New Hampshire, to become an FBI agent."

Suddenly a broad smile cracked his face. He stood up, leaned forward and shook my hand.

"Relax, kid. I'm Bernie Pierce . . . grew up on Sugar Hill, about five miles from your old house. Just busting your balls about the shooting thing."

He laughed a good-natured chuckle, introduced me to the

other two agents and pulled out a notebook. I tried to regain my composure. Years come back fast with the right suggestion.

"Four agents out of a town of two hundred and fifty people," he said. "Must be something in the water, huh?"

I nodded politely.

"Now, Chris," he said, "why don't you tell us just what it is that makes you want to become an FBI agent."

I just sat there, drifting, as a year's worth of ups and downs filtered through my mind the way life passes before you during a fall. In that one moment, I tried to assess the biggest career move of my young life.

Working in the Nation's Capital brings a certain flavor and excitement you can't find anywhere else. Nationalist pride consumes the place, and you gain a taste for the tremendous complexity and commitment that make this country great. Washington presented a richness of experience that transcended money. It was that twenty-four-hour vibe politicians exude: power, huge power, and that musky, intoxicating smell of cold cash and decaying ideology.

My wife, Rose, and I had come to Washington, D.C., two years earlier, at the invitation of U.S. Representative Silvio O. Conte, an old-school Yankee best known for his colorful well speeches. His administrative assistant had called Rose, and she tracked me down in the Hanover, New Hampshire, public library where I sat writing a freelance piece on something important enough to appear in the *Valley News.*

Conte's A.A. told me, in an inclusive voice, that a story I'd written a year earlier on the Congressman's trip to Moscow had caught his eye and that he just happened to have an opening for a speechwriter and press secretary. Would I be interested?

I pressed the phone against my ear and wondered for a moment if I was hearing things. Since college I had traipsed around the country working as a bartender, a features free-lancer for *Orange Coast* magazine in Southern California, an English teacher at a boarding school, and a newspaper reporter at the *North Adams Transcript* in the Berkshire Hills of Massachusetts. I was two things in 1985: hungry and mobile.

"Sure," I said. "I think this might be an appropriate time for a career move."

That was on a Friday. The following Monday morning, I knocked on the double doors outside room 2300 in the Rayburn House Office Building and introduced myself. A warm and kindly grandmother named Franny McGuire ushered me into the reception area and welcomed me aboard.

"Pat!" she yelled over her shoulder. "Chris is here!" She smelled of Youth Dew and cherry cobbler. It just felt like home.

Silvio Conte served as ranking member on the House Appropriations Committee, and after nearly thirty years in office had become one of the most powerful men in Congress. He walked with an endearing limp and had a grip that seemed to fit, in strength and character, the hand of everyone he ever met. His office suite, overlooking the front of the U.S. Capitol, boasted one of the finest views on Independence Avenue. He also kept a Capitol office just off the viewers' gallery above the House floor that was so well located and appointed, first ladies from Mamie Eisenhower to Nancy Reagan used it as a green room prior to their husbands' State of the Union addresses.

That's where the path to the FBI first started to appear before me. One afternoon in January, Mr. Conte took me aside and offered me a ticket, big as a postcard. It read "State of the Union," and promised a front row seat to one of the grandest nights in America.

"Can't buy one of these at Ticketmaster," the Congressman said, waving the green gem in my face. "I want you to go and see how the big boys do it. Maybe you can pick up some new material." He handed it over with one of his grandfatherly winks. "And don't try to scalp this thing, pal. That's a federal offense."

On the evening of February 4, 1986, I closed the door to my Capitol Hill row house and walked ten blocks through a pristine winter chill. Mist rose from my mouth like taffeta curtains at the edges of a frosted window. I walked past the Library of Congress and the Supreme Court and the motorcades and black limousines toward a Capitol building that seemed to pulse with energy.

I walked past news cameras and bomb dogs and SWAT teams and Secret Service snipers on the roof with scoped rifles. I gawked at the ambulances in the parking lot and the helicopters on the east lawn and the satellite dish–topped TV production trucks up and down a barricaded Independence Avenue. The hair on the back of my neck stood straight up. The ticket felt heavy as a Gale River rock in my overcoat pocket.

The viewers' gallery above the House floor is steep and shallow. My seat looked down over the Republican side of the aisle just to the left of where Nancy Reagan would sit among the seats traditionally held for first ladies and their attendants. She was still sipping tea in Mr. Conte's office when I arrived, but she would soon emerge and make an entrance, waving down to Republican friends and savoring her husband's American transformation. There was no talk of "voodoo economics" or the "Teflon president" or of a somewhat befuddled actor playing a role that night. There was just an overwhelming sense of pride and a tangible awe for the pageantry of it all.

I watched with a lump in my throat as the sergeant at arms welcomed the Senate, the Joint Chiefs of Staff, twelve of the thirteen Cabinet secretaries, and the Supreme Court. They walked slowly, nodding and shaking hands as they went. It was all done with great respect and tradition that I'd never read about in civics texts.

Chanel No. 5 and Aramis mingled in the air as a thousand voices echoed off the mahogany Speaker's chair, the marble columns and gold-leaf frescoes. Light fell from recessed fixtures in the ceiling near carefully hidden security cameras. Reporters peered down from the press gallery, sharpening their pencils for the sage articles and editorials that would flow out with the applause to editors crowding midnight deadlines.

"Mr. Speaker!" A hush fell over men and women who made their living by flapping their gums.

"The President of the United States!"

The House of Representatives erupted in bedlam.

And then I saw him: the Great Communicator taking the floor, his right hand raised above that shock of G.I. Joe hair and the little-boy smile.

He walked toward the dais, home triumphantly from his trip to the Soviet Union with an olive branch in one hand and a steel hammer in the other. Vice President George Bush and House Speaker Tip O'Neill rose and clapped. The Joint Chiefs followed suit, as did the entire Senate and the Cabinet and all 435 members of the home team. This was an amazing moment in American history and in my life.

To stand there in that room, with my hands trembling between claps as the entire executive, judicial, and legislative branches of the United States government assembled below me, felt absolutely stunning.

I knew then, as if by epiphany, that what I wanted to do with my life was to help protect it all. Suddenly it wasn't enough to craft speeches that braced its facades or to play knight's second to a man who waged its battles. It no longer interested me to be Holden Caulfield standing quietly among them, waiting to catch the symbolism as it jumped into the rhetorical rye. I wanted to make a difference in society, to wake up in the morning with a cause. Justice.

I wanted jurisdiction.

And so it came down to agency. I had a friend in the Secret Service, but he had burned out on the idea of throwing himself in front of a bullet for a complete stranger. The DEA (Drug Enforcement Administration) was still pretty much unknown in those days, and the ATF (Bureau of Alcohol, Tobacco, and Firearms) — well, they were pretty quiet too. That left the FBI. They were the biggest and the best, according to everyone I talked to. And they were hiring. Maybe I had a chance.

After a sleepless night wondering how I could best serve my country, I decided to take a stroll down the road less traveled by. The next day, I pulled out a D.C. phone directory and called the FBI's Washington Field Office for an application.

What the hell? I thought. Who'd ever believe I could have found my way into this never-never land from the wooded slopes of New Hampshire to begin with?

Something in my answer must have struck Bernie Pierce and his interview team as genuine, because a short time after our little talk, another letter arrived in my mailbox.

"Your combined test and interview scores have made you eligible for further consideration for the Special Agent position," it read. "A thorough review will be made of your application and dependent upon the needs of this Bureau, you will be considered for further processing."

If the language seemed dry, I didn't notice. Joining the FBI had become an obsession at that point, and "further processing" sounded like an invitation from the Director himself.

I completed the final steps in the hiring process within a couple of weeks. Wayne drove me from Buzzard's Point to FBI Headquarters in his Bureau car for a physical fitness test, which he held in the basement parking garage. Five other candidates and I ran a mile and a half for time at 4:30 in the afternoon as the car pools emptied out around me. I finished in just under nine minutes, despite the course, which required that I dodge a motorcade of government Chevys while sucking exhaust fumes and weaving my way through a labyrinth of concrete pillars.

After the fitness test came the comprehensive physical examination at Walter Reed Army Hospital. They checked everything from hearing and vision to lung capacity and heart rate. No problems.

"Sure, Wayne," I said, finally finding the words that would change my life forever. "Two weeks will work just fine."

I hung up the phone and stared out at the Capitol as it glowed in the brilliant crimson sunset that old-timers refer to as "red weather." The future seemed absolutely incandescent as I contemplated three months of training at Quantico and thirty years sporting a gold FBI badge. Becoming a G-man had seemed impossible for so long, and now the prospect danced coyly in front of me like a debutante at a spring cotillion.

2

THE ACADEMY

Two weeks later, on March 27, 1987, after offering the Congressman my notice, I said my good-byes, packed the last of my office clutter into a leather briefcase, and bade farewell to America's legislative branch. A thin piece of paper rested in my breast pocket. On it, someone at FBI Headquarters had typed the blueprint for my foreseeable future.

"You are offered a probationary appointment in the Federal Bureau of Investigation, United States Department of Justice," it read, "as a Special Agent, Grade GS-10, $24,732 per annum less the necessary deductions for retirement and Social Security purposes."

These tersely worded orders stipulated that acceptance to the Academy for thirteen weeks of New Agent Training meant almost nothing. If I failed two academic exams with scores of 85 or lower, they'd bounce me. If I failed to shoot a qualifying score of 80 with a handgun, they'd show me the door. If I failed to score a minimum of 80 percent in the physical fitness program or in the defensive tactics program, I was gone. Other grounds for dismissal included conduct unbecoming an agent, poor attitude, "incompatibility" (whatever that meant), lack of candor, and general absence of aptitude.

"This appointment is subject to cancellation or postponement at any time prior to your entry on duty," the letter said. "Inasmuch as this appointment is probationary for a period of one year, it will be necessary for you to demonstrate during your probationary period your fitness for continued employment in the Federal Bureau of Investigation, including successful completion of New Agent Training, Quantico, Virginia."

Should I have found anything vaguely exciting about this dispassionate welcome, I couldn't share it with a soul. "This appointment letter," the personnel officer wrote, "should be considered strictly confidential and given no publicity."

Wait a minute, I thought, trying to mine congratulations from somewhere in this bureaucratic slag. Rose and I had just sold our newly refurbished Capitol Hill brownstone, given up our jobs, health insurance, Smithsonian concerts, our friends. We had a new baby and another on the way. Everything we had vested our lives in hung on a very thin line of civil service string, and if I failed, we were in for a real tumble. The road back to any sort of self-esteem would surely include some long nights of introspection and a steady diet of crow.

Whatever the odds of success, I left Capitol Hill on the first Sunday in April with a black garment bag and a lump in my throat so big I could just barely breathe. I drove south along I-95 until a small sign near exit 132 pointed me due west. Five miles from the highway, in the middle of the Quantico Marine Corps base, I found the FBI Academy. It simply appeared out of the forest as I turned a bend in the narrow two-lane road.

Whatever I expected in the way of armed guards, gatehouses, and hidden surveillance cameras evaporated into the loblolly pines. I saw no fleets of unmarked police sedans, no doors marked "Top Secret" or fenced-in buildings sprouting ominous-looking antennas. With the exception of a fairly elaborate firearms range complex, the rambling 480-acre campus of brown brick and glass looked more like a well-kept community college than G-Man U.

A plaque just inside the main entrance explained the Academy's ascetic charm. J. Edgar himself had this complex built in the early 1970s as a national academy for law enforcement executives. By the time I arrived it had been expanded to accommodate both FBI and DEA recruits, but there was no mistaking the place's pedigree. Law enforcement is the business of discipline. The Academy wasted nothing on frills.

It was late afternoon when I arrived. I found my name on a list of recruits at the front desk, and followed directions to my new residence on the sixth floor of the Madison dormitory. Accommodations looked spartan, like the rest of the facility. All thirty-eight members of New Agent Class 87-10 lived on the same floor in two-bedroom suites connected by a common bathroom. Each new agent got a desk, a dresser, and a single bed. We brought our own towels.

Most of the group had already arrived when I got there. We introduced ourselves with perfunctory acquaintance: handshake, name, home town, marital status, number of kids, former profession. Everyone wore their sternest game face, trying to convey confidence. I did the same, though any sense of belonging had deserted me somewhere just south of Alexandria. The swell of personal adventure that had led me to this move diminished in comparison with the guilt I felt over leaving my family to fend for themselves.

I shook a couple dozen hands on the way to my new home in room 620. Once inside, I unpacked, read for a while, then climbed into bed and stared at the blue-white ceiling, waiting.

I was waiting to see my family again. Waiting to get started with my new career, waiting for validation that I had done the right thing. I don't know what I was waiting for. After all the hoops I'd jumped through in the past year, it just seemed like the thing to do.

I lay in bed for hours, long after the dorm quieted and midnight passed. I never slept a wink.

New Agent Training began Monday morning in classroom 211 with a formal welcome from the Assistant Director in Charge (ADIC) of the Academy. A tall, imposing man entered with a couple lackeys and folded his hands behind his back in a superiority gesture I'd coached my old boss never to use in public. The ADIC assured us in measured prose that if we did not perform up to Bureau standards, we'd be scouring the want ads in next Sunday's *Post*. For the next thirteen weeks, we were his. No weekends off the grounds for the first month and a half. Midnight curfew on weeknights. Classes until noon on Saturdays. No overnight visitors in the dorms. Oh, and the dress code was written in stone: National Academy officers wore green polo shirts and khaki trousers. DEA recruits wore gray shirts, black BDU fatigues bloused into the tops of their spit-shined combat boots. We wore business suits. Casual wear was acceptable after dinner, but jeans were forbidden at all times. No shorts outside the gym.

I sat along the back row in my alphabetized seating assignment and stared down at the Bureau's catalog model of the perfect agent. This guy never cracked a smile the whole time he talked. His red and blue club tie propped his head forty-five degrees to the cut of his razor sharp Brooks Brothers collar. The plane of his forehead creased slightly whenever he pronounced the letters *F B I*, like a flag dipping at taps. Even the air hung flaccid between sentences, as if waiting to swell on his next provident thought.

The ADIC's number two man stood his post at the side door without ever looking up to engage us. The class counselors stood at parade rest against the back wall among our primary instructors, who introduced themselves with a title of Supervisory Special Agent and a last name.

"Son of a bitch," I mumbled, "these guys are cool."

When the Assistant Director finished and disappeared to attend to more important matters, an equally tall white male descended from the back row, walked up front, and stared at us with an almost venomous glare. The room froze. Apparently, all pleasantries had ended. This guy wore the face of Death I'd read about in Dante's *Inferno*.

"My name is Supervisory Special Agent Ronald C. Dirkson," he said. "For the next thirteen weeks, I will serve as your staff counselor. Those of you who last long enough may call me 'sir.'"

The face of Death paused just a moment, like Mephistopheles at the edge of the great precipice. None of us breathed for fear of wasting his rarefied air. The entire room hung in awe of his presence.

"FBI stands for Fidelity, Bravery, and Integrity." He paused to let the concept rattle around in our heads. "That's your new first, middle, and last name. You're one, now, in Mr. Hoover's private army. Any life you brought with you is gone. Any personal aspirations are now the Bureau's. From this point forward, you are mine, and I . . ."

Something in his eyes started to change, like dawn emerging.

". . . I . . ."

His broad shoulders began to heave beneath his dark blue suit.

". . . I swear to God that guy is wound just a little too tight."

With that, he erupted into a belly laugh so pronounced, he had to turn his face away from us to keep from crying on the front row.

"I'm sorry," he said, "but some of the people around here take this shit just a little too seriously."

With that, we began in earnest our indoctrination into the finer points of life with a gun and shield. Ron and two other class counselors spent day and night with us, trying to make sure we had everything necessary to learn the ropes. Most of those lessons came during long hours in the classroom and on the firearms ranges, but plenty came over beers in the on-campus Boardroom. The Academy staff cared about one thing: turning civilians into agents. Ron served as our guide.

By the end of week two, most of the mystery behind the FBI image had faded into a 7:00 A.M. to 5:00 P.M. regimen of academic instruction, defensive tactics, and firearms matters. Each day began at 7:00 with breakfast, moved to a training area for four hours of instruction, paused for an hour at lunch, then resumed at least until dinner at 5:00. Many days, we worked long into the night, practicing things like low-light shooting, high-risk arrests, and night surveillance.

Somewhere in between, we found time to study for the exams that came with relentless frequency. At least once a week our entire class huddled together, reviewing notes and making sure the less prepared among us would feel ready the next day. As our letters stated, a score of 84 or lower in any course would result in a New Agent Review Board and disciplinary action. If you failed to achieve 85 on a makeup exam or performed similarly on another exam, you were gone.

Though most of us hoped to begin New Agent Training on the firearms range, our instruction began with the fundament of all law enforcement curricula: the Constitution. Our Legal I instructor opened the class with a firm reminder: "Everything you do from the time you graduate to the time you retire will revolve around this document," he said. "It's what this law enforcement thing is all about."

He lectured in great detail about the personal protections and liberties guaranteed by this remarkable document, then backed them up with case law. Though he talked slowly and clearly, with the erudition of a man well suited to the law, humor crept into most of his lectures.

"All the bullets and bravado in the world won't win you a single conviction in a court of law. An FBI agent's job is to investigate potential violations of federal statute, make arrests where necessary, and assist in successful prosecution. All that other stuff about guns and handcuffs and high-speed car chases is just for show."

Each day I learned new words like *misprision, curtilage, voir dire,* and *tort.* Each night I scoured case law, trying to understand why we could chase a bank robber into his sister's house but not search for loot without a warrant. I sat in study groups arguing the merits of Miranda warnings and how, contrary to television lore, we didn't need to use them unless the subject was in custody at the time of interrogation.

I'm not sure I expected this sort of rigor when I signed up, but I began to enjoy it. Three members of the class dropped or failed out by the time we finished Legal I, but everyone else pulled together against the pressure. When our instructor stood at the front of the lecture hall one day and defined the gravity of our work, the challenge made more sense.

"The primary difference between your job and that of the cop on the beat is accountability," he said. He had already told us that FBI agents don't work traditional violent crime such as murder and rape. Federal involvement usually requires an interstate aspect, or some financial loss to a government interest.

"Federal courts hold us to higher standards, from the forty-five-day speedy trial mandate to the way we maintain chain of custody with evidence. You make a single mistake in an investigation and a jury will put Satan himself back on the street because of it."

He handed out 3×5 booklets to illustrate his point. Each of the bright orange FBI classification guides listed all 257 different violations of federal law that the FBI investigated.

"Many of the crimes we work are very complex," he said.

I ran my finger down the list, pausing at standouts like impersonating a 4-H officer, violating the Migratory Bird Act, or transporting an unsafe refrigerator over state lines.

"You have to know the elements of the crime, prove them beyond reasonable doubt, and stand with conviction on the witness stand. A score of eighty-five will get you through this course, but it will not serve you in front of a jury. One hundred percent perfect is your standard in there."

And I understood. Those little orange booklets also included things like foreign counterintelligence, bank robbery, wire fraud, interstate transportation of stolen property, and drugs. From that point on, I paid closer attention when the White Collar Crime instructor tried to bore us to death with details about banking statutes. I fought harder to stay awake during forfeiture lectures when program managers from Headquarters explained how we could take a dope dealer's car without charging him. I even endured fingerprint identification class with renewed vigor, realizing that the difference between a tented arch and a whorl might help me track down a Top Ten fugitive.

The FBI clung to protocol and statute because of its responsibility. It made sense.

❖

Our role in the closeted world of the FBI emerged a little more clearly each day. Communications class taught us that FBI assets are divided across America among fifty-six field offices and 128 satellite offices called resident agencies (RAs). Each field office or division is run by a Special Agent in Charge (pronounced S-A-C) and one or more Assistant Special Agents in Charge (ASACs). Squads are run by supervisors, who oversee the day-to-day activities.

Although each SAC rules his or her domain, most of the really big decisions are made at FBI Headquarters in Washington, where more than a thousand management-level agents keep an eye on virtually everything the Bureau does. The line of command is very well delineated. The Director oversees the Deputy Director, who oversees a handful of Assistant Directors in Charge (ADICs), who oversee section chiefs, who oversee unit chiefs, who oversee supervisors. From there, the managerial pyramid sprawls into bureaucracy of biblical proportions.

Deep beneath all these layers of management lie the street agents who do the majority of the work. They function like private contractors, drumming up business by cultivating informants, answering criminal complaints, and sniffing out malfeasance. Business hours stick pretty much to a 7:00 A.M. to 6:00 P.M. schedule, but business runs the clock, and nights, holidays, and weekends wield no immunity. You work when there's work to do.

On a practical level, an agent's workday revolves around

basic investigations. Each agent is assigned to a squad and given a number of cases, depending on the scope and importance of the violation. One agent might work a single major case for several years, for example, while another might juggle thirty or forty smaller investigations at the same time.

The casework itself can get a little more complicated. A brown and white file jacket is opened for each individual criminal investigation, and listed sequentially by office of origin and classification. If an armed bank robbery occurs in Cleveland, for example, the "rotor" (Bureau slang for squad file clerk) will check his little orange book and tag it with a 91A classification. After that, he adds the office's initials and the next number in the series. In this case, the file jacket will read 91A-CD-21338. Results of all subsequent investigation will be placed inside.

Each file contains stacks of paperwork, including chain-of-custody forms, surveillance logs, electronic surveillance (ELSUR) transcripts, search warrants, affidavits, and a hundred other Bureau forms you'll never hear about until you show up in court.

FBI files contain some of the most famous cases in American history, including the Lindbergh kidnapping, the Kennedy assassination, and the Jimmy Hoffa disappearance. Reports on Hollywood celebrities, skid row bums, and Mafia hit men rest in dust-covered file cabinets with equal anonymity. Virtually everything the FBI has ever done falls into one or more of these files, eternally vulnerable to examination by history, Freedom of Information Act inquiries, and the nation's highest courts.

That perpetual scrutiny, our instructors argued, is why accuracy, thoroughness, and truth are so important in all we do. From the first interview to the last word on a witness stand, every single gesture is recorded in the file, through one FBI document or another. The results of evidentiary interviews are documented on FD-302s. Nonevidentiary information is written on Investigative Inserts. Material evidence is sent to the laboratory under an FD-620. Photo lineups are called FD-427s. Travel vouchers are FD-540s. The list goes on and on and on. Even the document cataloging all the FDs has an FD number.

Paperwork, however, is just paper. Real crime solving takes place on the street, and education in matters of the street came from the Practical Applications Unit (PAU). Early in the third week, they summoned us across Hoover Road to Hogan's Alley, a full-scale town built with all the realism of a Universal Studios back lot. Driving up the access road, you'd never expect that this sleepy rural community could boast the nation's highest crime rate. You'd drive by the Dogwood Inn, the Biograph Theater, the Bank of Hogan, and, of course, the ubiquitous trailer park and think yourself safe. But after a few minutes in town you'd notice nefarious activity everywhere.

The FBI built Hogan's Alley as a sort of High Crimes and Misdemeanors theme park, and we spent plenty of time on all the E-ticket rides. Most of the training there revolved around scenarios crafted by instructors from their real-world experiences. Professional role players acted out crimes, based on elaborate scripts. New agents applied skills they learned in the classroom.

I arrested my first armed subject in the Main Street Pool Hall. I took a .32-caliber paint pill in the leg during a felony car stop that went bad behind the warehouse. I processed a realistic-looking crime scene in a motel room at the Dogwood Inn, and I learned the value of a high-risk weapons search during a mock bank robbery when the suspect reached into his pocket and shot me in the back of the head with a .22 blank gun.

The big difference between Hogan's Alley and a real

town was that I didn't have to die for my mistakes. I learned the value of technique and the importance of caution.

Over the next nine weeks, PAU instructors led us through everything from mobile surveillance to high-risk building entries. We learned to stagger vehicle surveillance with four or five cars, so the "mark" would never get a good enough look at us. Instructors led us for hours at a time through the roads of Northern Virginia as we tried to keep up with them without getting burned. I learned a valuable lesson while following one "subject" into a local bar to watch him play pool. Though he probably wouldn't have noticed me as I sat at the bar, the bartender did.

"Watch out, everybody!" she called out when I ordered a Coke. "I got one of those baby FBI agents drinking soda pop over here."

With more than six hundred new agents rolling through the Academy and the surrounding towns that year, I guess agents weren't the only ones getting schooled.

Some days we practiced room entries and clearance techniques with paint-ball guns.

"Work the angle in small increments, like you're trying to cut pieces of a pie!" an instructor yelled. He edged the corner slowly, trying to show us how to enter unfamiliar space without getting ambushed. "Keep that muzzle pointed down range, not at the ceiling. This ain't Miami fucking Vice."

They scrutinized the way we handcuffed subjects.

"Clear their hands." "Keep 'em off balance." "Always holster up before you move in to make the hookup," they said. We learned most of our technique in a separate Defensive Tactics class, but PAU instructors added a few tricks of the trade that made everything a little simpler. Handcuffs can become a deadly weapon, for example, if you get one on a subject and he breaks free.

"I saw a guy take the hasp right through his jawbone one

time," an instructor told us. "Hooked him like a big damned carp. You never give up control of that thing until both cuffs are on and double locked."

He slapped a set of Peerless cuffs on one wrist and swung the loose end at the wall, to demonstrate his point. The hasp tore through the Sheetrock and lodged in a two-by-four framing stud. I doubt his little demonstration made the maintenance crew happy, but it hammered home a valuable point. In all the arrests I made after that, I never lost control of the loose cuff.

They gave us answers to questions we hadn't even thought of asking.

"What do you do with your gun when you have to use the crapper?" they asked. "You can't hang it off the coat hook. Undo your belt buckle and it falls on the floor, scaring the hell out of the guy in the stall next to you. Worse, it goes off and turns the toilet into a pile of shattered porcelain. Believe me, it's happened."

Hadn't really thought about that. Then again, the basic mechanics of lugging a gun around every waking hour isn't something most people think about, period.

"The pistol goes right in the crotch of your pants where they hang between your knees," he said. "Ladies, you might want to plan your lingerie purchases accordingly."

Other areas of concern ranged from clothing (have a tailor sew an extra layer of lining into your jackets to keep the gun's handle from wearing a hole) to how to carry your credentials in the right breast pocket so you can reach for them with your weak hand and shake with the other. Watch the rearview mirror as you approach a car. You can read a lot from the way someone's eyes move. Carefully pat a subject's pockets before you reach inside. It's no fun jabbing yourself with a needle or an open knife. Never stand in an open door. The backlight frames you as a perfect target.

On and on, the lessons covered just about every aspect of life as a federal agent.

"Don't forget that all the stuff you learn here is just an appetizer," one of the instructors said, cautioning against overconfidence. "You won't know what this job is really all about until you spend six months working fourteen-hour days trying to hunt down some asshole bank robber and your supervisor busts your balls for missing some stupid form.

"You finally get a phone call during your kid's birthday party telling you that this guy's been spotted at his girlfriend's house — the same girlfriend who swore on her mother's eyes that she had no idea where he was — and you go hook him up. Two hours later, he makes bail and is back on the street before you finish your paperwork at the courthouse.

"Then it's a toss-up whether the shitbird's lawyer serves a civil suit on you for violating his rights or the supervisor writes you up a letter of censure for double parking your car during the arrest.

"This job is a ball buster. It's also the best time you'll ever have in your life. Don't fuck it up for the rest of us."

Speeches like that altered my whole attitude about the career change. Nothing I ever could have done in Washington would compare to a three o'clock raid on a dope house, gun drawn, shoulder through the door, legal authority in my pocket to save the world. No speech delivered to a Rotary luncheon or press release announcing some supplemental appropriations bill could give me the satisfaction that I would get in a single felony arrest.

From that point on, I was hooked. No more trepidation. No regrets.

By the end of my first month at the Academy, everything about my world had improved.

Rosie had closed on our house in D.C. and driven to New Hampshire to stay with my parents until graduation. The weekly exams came and went, with my scores far outside the range where I'd need to worry. The daily workouts honed my body into the best shape I'd enjoyed since college. The cafeteria provided all the food I could eat, and I never had to wash any dishes. Maids even cleaned our bathrooms once a week and brought fresh bed linen.

All the misgivings I had felt during my first evening at the Academy hardened into a close-knit jacket of invulnerability. The class hardened as a unit, too, prideful of all its individual and collective accomplishments.

And then came the real treat. One bright sunshiny day, they marched us over to the firearms vault and gave us each a gun, with all the ammunition we could shoot.

Growing up in the country among a family full of hunters had instilled a fundamental respect for firearms, but I'd never really had any formal instruction in how to handle them. That changed just a few minutes into firearms training, when Ron sat us down in a range classroom for our first session with the new revolvers. You could feel the tension as our primary firearms instructor, Danny — a savvy veteran of Philadelphia's bank robbery beat — entered the room.

"Good morning," he said.

At that time, each new agent received a Smith and Wesson Model 13 revolver with a three-inch bull barrel chambered to .357 caliber. Semiautomatics were still considered too unreliable and complicated for day-to-day carry.

Danny reached into his holster and drew a shiny new specimen. Suddenly, the whole room smelled of Hoppes No. 10 cleaning solvent and hardwood from its quarter-checked hickory grips.

"For the next twenty to thirty years, you're going to carry one of these everywhere you go. You carry it on a plane. You carry it when you take the family out to dinner at a nice restaurant. You take it to your kid's third-grade play."

His right hand held the gun up as if it were a permanent fixture in some glass display case.

"This is an awesome responsibility."

The class bristled with emotion, ranging from excitement among people like myself who found the whole idea enthralling to those who were scared shitless.

"I'll tell you what: We can teach you how to shoot it, clean it, wear it properly." He let the concept sink in for a moment. "But what nobody can teach you is how to use it to take another human life."

Things calmed considerably at that point.

"No matter what you learn here," he said, "you're going to walk out into society a couple months from now, armed with the ability to kill someone with the pull of a trigger. That can leave you with some heavy baggage."

Thirty-six sets of eyes locked on the pistol in his unwavering hand.

"I know. I shot a man to death four years ago next month."

Something in my gut hardened. Looking into his eyes, I could see reflections of myself as a small boy who shot his first deer while still in grade school. I remembered what it felt like to make something bigger than myself lie still, to watch the life drain from its eyes. Those were animals, though. He was talking about a person.

"I'll tell you what I'm gonna do right now." Danny stared out into the classroom, animated with pure altruism. "I'm gonna walk down the hall for a cup of coffee. While I'm gone, I want you to think about whether you want to put yourself in a situation where you have to draw your weapon, look another human being in the face . . . and kill him. Because that's what this is all about. We don't want you to leave here with a gun so you can show it off to your buddies. We want you to leave here knowing that this job could cause you to use deadly force in defense of your life, your partner's life, or the life of someone you've never even met.

"Killing someone isn't like shooting holes in a target. It's not all clean and fast like you might think. You make them bleed. Sometimes they scream, or worse — they just cry. The guy I shot didn't die until just before the ambulance arrived. He kept wheezing when he tried to breathe. Gasping. I didn't want to touch him."

You could see the whole scene playing out behind his eyes. This ate at him, even four years after the fact.

"While I'm gone, you need to make a decision. You have to ask yourself if you're ready to take another life. May never happen. Probably won't. But it happened to me."

He collected himself.

"If you have any reservations at all, you need to leave. Causing yourself a little embarrassment now is a whole lot better than costing some innocent person his life a few years from now."

He turned around and left. No one spoke a word. No one got up to go.

Each of us already knew by heart the gravity of deadly force and the rules under which it could be used. "An FBI agent will not use deadly force except where his life or the life of another is in peril of death or grievous bodily harm." They taught us that in Legal I.

They also taught us that warning shots are not allowed. Trick shooting (bouncing bullets around corners, shooting guns out of people's hands) is not allowed. Trying to wing a subject is not allowed.

The rules made sense to me. Trying to shoot someone in

the leg or the arm when he is threatening your life is just about impossible for most people. Adrenaline pumps through your veins, increasing your heart rate and making your front sight hard to track. Your shoulder muscles pinch down on your carotid artery, occluding blood flow to your brain. Your eyes try to focus on the other guy's gun at the expense of your own sights. Your mind flips through the most illogical thoughts, trying to make sense of a situation few people ever dream of confronting. Fine motor skills fade. Vision narrows. Sound disappears.

Eight out of every ten rounds fired in law enforcement gunfights never hit anyone anyway, so the highest probability for success comes with aiming at the largest part of the offending person and pulling the trigger until he goes down or you run out of rounds. You take your chances with all that other stuff later. Maybe that's the point of the trigger pull test.

So much for accuracy. Now, try making a life-or-death decision in the time it takes to finish this sentence. Whoops. Too late, you're dead.

Or worse, the wrong person is dead. You just made a mistake that will haunt you the rest of your life. Civil litigation is a given. Administrative action could cost you a month's salary or more. That's if things go just slightly wrong, like you crank off an accidental discharge into the back tire of a parked car. Should you fall into a "bad shoot," you face jail, public vilification, and emotional trauma you don't want to guess at.

You could go an entire career without drawing your weapon, or you could shoot half a dozen people in one monster mash. Luck of the draw. If you shoot, the review board comes in, looks at a totality of circumstances (including things you should have but may not have known), and renders judgment. If it finds you at fault, you're on your own.

When Danny returned, he looked around the room, noted that no one had heeded his warning, then nodded.

"Okay," he said. "Forewarned is forearmed."

With that, we started a painstakingly detailed course in the finer elements of hand gunning. He and his cadre of line instructors taught us structure. They began with what was called the "modified Weaver" stance, where you move one foot forward as if preparing to box someone. You thrust your strong hand forward, lock your arm straight, and cup your weak hand around everything but your trigger finger. Then you center the front sight between the rear ramp posts and slowly pull on the trigger.

The Bureau forbids the cocking of a double-action weapon, believing it tempts too high a chance of accidental discharge. Adrenaline tends to screw up the best of intentions, and years of experience had proved that the nine-pound pull of a Smith and Wesson K-frame pistol does wonders to prevent warning shots.

We practiced four hours at a time in all kinds of weather, during daylight and at night. Standing, kneeling, prone. We shot from inside cars, behind barricades, over walls, under fences. We fired shotguns: 12-gauge Remington 870 pump guns with sawed-off barrels. Danny opened case after case of buckshot and slugs, filling the five-shot magazines until our shoulders throbbed. Several members of the class forgot to hold the butt into their shoulder from time to time and wore black eyes as signs of their oversight. Shotguns kick.

In the twelfth week, they marched us out to the fifty-yard line for final qualifications.

Of all the tests I studied for and fretted over, this one worried me the most. It wasn't that I thought I'd fail; it was that I wanted to win. Anyone who finished up with a two-round average of 98 or better qualified for a run at the "Possible Club," an elite group of names listed on a wall outside the gun vault. Of the tens of thousands of agents hired since 1908, only a couple hundred have earned that honor. I wanted my name on that wall.

The morning of quals, Danny handed us each sixty rounds of .357 Magnum ammunition and the rules of the course. On the buzzer, we would go prone and fire six rounds strong hand at a target fifty yards distant. After reloading, we'd fire three more rounds kneeling strong hand, and three rounds standing. From there, we'd move in to the twenty-five-yard line and closer. Time limits made rapid fire a necessity.

On the whistle, we blazed away. I squeezed the trigger just as they'd taught me, focusing on the front sight and not the target. My gun barrel rose and fell in recoil as regularly as a metronome.

When it was over, we shot it again. Danny announced our scores in the bleachers.

"Whitcomb: Ninety-nine, one hundred."

I had "thrown" one bullet of the 120 I'd fired. Though not perfect, the score still entitled me to a run at the Possible. The times would be tighter in the record match, but I felt good. All I had to do to get my name on the wall was bring one errant round into the fold.

Three of us earned the chance to try. Only one made it.

Unfortunately, it wasn't me.

Regardless of my missed opportunity at New Agent immortality, I entered the final stages of training feeling as sharp and as capable as any agent in the Bureau.

The only nagging detail that lurked at the back of my well-taxed mind was where I would get to ply my new trade.

My acceptance letter covered the relocation issue with eloquent indifference.

"It is understood you are to proceed on orders to any part of the United States or Puerto Rico where the exigencies of this Bureau may require, and it should be clearly understood that you will continue to be completely available for any assignment whenever and wherever the needs of the Bureau demand. Further, you cannot expect an assignment to an office of your own preference."

That sounded simple enough: Despite family concerns like a spouse's career, inability to sell a house, or anything so selfish as personal preference, agents could rest assured that the only place in America they could not go was where they wanted. My career felt like a pair of smooth red dice before a crapshoot.

The FBI, like God, often works in mysterious ways. Many of its odd customs and habits are holdovers from the Hoover era, when the Director basically did anything he wanted, and in 1987, Hoover hadn't been dead long enough for most people to trust the news. The transfer policy clearly fell within that category. Hoover believed that leaving an agent too long in the same office might lead him into temptation and corruption. So every few years, he stirred up the pot a little by moving New York agents to L.A. and vice versa. Personal concerns such as community ties, family needs, and job satisfaction meant nothing if the Bureau somehow felt it benefited by uprooting you and shipping you off to another part of the country.

One of the obvious flaws in Hoover's logic was that any agent susceptible to corruption on the East Coast would probably face the same weakness on the West Coast. The transfer policy made for a lot of disgruntled agents and prevented very few malcontents from breaking bad.

Regardless, few moments in an FBI agent's career ring clearer than the day when he receives his first set of orders. It is a rite of passage in which a new recruit yields himself up to the whims of some faceless clerk at FBI Headquarters and accepts, with profound surrender, the ways of the Bureau.

I figured that signing on to adventure required a certain belief in destiny, and I didn't want to cloud the Fates with intention. On a Friday afternoon midway through our stay at the Academy, the ADIC held us after class. He propped thirty-six envelopes on the lectern, pulled a letter opener out of his double-breasted suit coat, and outlined the ritual. When called randomly, each of us in turn would walk up to the front of the class, accept a white letterhead envelope, and make a public wish for assignment. As the rest of the class waited with bated breath, we would then open the envelope, look inside, and discover our first billeting.

Somewhere between my seat in the back row and my position next to the ADIC, I decided to wish for New Orleans. I don't know why that struck me as the best place in America to settle my young family, but I didn't get much time to fret over the decision. I opened my letter, unfolded the orders, and promptly read "Kansas City."

The news surprised me so completely, I couldn't for the life of me figure out where the hell it was. I'd lived on both coasts and in London, England, but the Midwest never meant anything more to me than an occasional tornado strike on the evening news.

What the hell, I thought. They must have some crime out there or they wouldn't need to send me after it.

Besides, the Bureau kept a list of big offices called the Top Ten, and time in Kansas City meant a three-to-five-year reprieve from the likes of New York or L.A. That sounded just fine to me. Something about spreading my $24,000 per annum salary over sorghum fields and county fairs seemed a whole lot more palatable than Fifth Avenue.

And so we proceeded, the last week of June, into the Academy Forum for graduation. My entire family joined me on the big day as we, the members of New Agent Class 87-10, marched across the proscenium, gathered up our credentials, our gold shields, and that intangible sense of honor that comes with taking an oath to defend the Constitution against all enemies, foreign and domestic.

I raised my right hand, as my father and mother and wife and son looked on, knowing that nothing I would ever do in any career would carry the gravity of that oath. Nothing I could ever do would instill in me that same sense of commitment.

For one brief, incomprehensibly promising moment, I felt part of all that was good about this country. I felt proud.

3

FNG

I rolled in to Kansas City, fresh out of my three-month FBI Academy training with a suitcase in one hand, a Smith and Wesson wheel gun in the other, and the blue flame of ambition shooting three feet out my ass. A first office agent lies just below gum on the sole of your shoe in most FBI offices, but the Bureau considered my Capitol Hill job to be "former government service" and offered benefits usually reserved for veteran agents. They put us up in the Kansas City Hyatt, a big beautiful hotel overlooking the city, and assigned me to a reactive squad working bank robberies and fugitives. While lots of my 87-10 buddies earned their bones running background investigations in Queens, I got to march in Fourth of July weekend looking forward to the kind of "work" every new agent dreamed about: kicking doors, running down desperadoes, chasing violent criminals.

The Special Agent in Charge of the Kansas City office sought me out at Quantico just before graduation to welcome me into the division. I'd get my own car, he said, and twenty to thirty cases that would keep me busy until I generated more on my own. The probationary period outlined in my acceptance letter would last one year. A training agent would answer questions and show me the ropes. Beyond that I was on my own.

I remember looking out over the city my first night in town, absolutely wired with all the pride and excitement of a new life emerging. Rosie and baby Jake lay on the bed, wondering how in the world they'd ended up in this situation, but I couldn't sit still long enough to try to explain. After twelve months of interviews, tests, background checks, and bureaucratic form letters, thirteen weeks alone at the FBI Academy, and four days driving from Virginia to Kansas City, I stood nine hours away from my first day on the job as a Special Agent of the FBI.

Everything I could quantify, project, and remember about my life distilled down into the mottled horizon as I looked west from my twelfth-story window. For reasons that probably never made sense to anyone, they'd given me Kansas City, a former cow town sporting a little Mob trouble from the Bonano family and a gray Midwestern ennui. I didn't think much about my career or where I would be five years from then. All I knew was that this darkening city waited quietly below me, and that more than anything in the world, I wanted to light it up.

My first day in the office lasted precisely long enough to sign in to the "One Register" (FBI version of a time clock), introduce myself to the squad supervisor — a battle-hardened street sweeper named Tom Devreaux — and grab a cup of coffee.

I met Ray Venable, my training agent, while standing at the urinal.

"Guy comes up to the office the other day, looking for a job," he said, saving his handshake until after I'd finished. "So I ask him if he has any qualifications — you know, like lawyer, CPA, minority status. But the guy shakes his head and says, 'No. In fact, I'm disabled.'"

Ray tucked himself back into his Sansabelt pants and moved to the sink. His hair shone in the tight rows you get with a palmful of Brylcreem and an Ace pocket comb. I had no idea who the hell this guy was or why he was bothering a stranger in the fifth-floor men's room.

"Disabled? What's the problem?" Ray's voice sounded a whole lot like a 747 waiting to take off. He washed his enormous hands while talking into the mirror.

"'Well,' the guy says, 'I got my privates blown off during the war. Doesn't bother me much except that I gotta squat to piss.'" He gritted his teeth and hunched up his shoulders at the thought. Ray stood about 6'4", 260 pounds. He was sporting a three-piece suit, clip-on tie, nicotine-stained teeth, liver spots all over his face.

"'Well, that's actually good,' I tell him. 'You can get bonus points in the application process for being a veteran. You get more points because you have a nondysfunctional disability, and with no testicles and such, you probably get the lawyer exception, too. Tell you what . . . why don't you show up tomorrow morning around nine and we'll get you started.'"

Ray dried his hands and waved for me to hurry up. Unfortunately, I felt so distracted by this unprovoked story, I just stood there with my fly open, wondering what the hell to do.

"'Nine o'clock?' the guy says. 'I thought you feds started at the crack of dawn.'"

Ray tossed his paper towel into the trash can and moved toward me.

" 'Oh, we do,' I tell him, 'but we just sit around drinking coffee, reading the paper and scratching our balls for the first couple hours. And I guess you don't have to worry about that.' "

He reached over the urinal divider for a handshake.

"Ray Venable," he said, by way of introduction. "They give me all the fucking new guys, and you seem to be the project du jour. Now let's go. I've had my coffee and I ain't got time to watch you playing with yourself."

Five minutes later, one of the agents on the squad radioed in to dispatch saying he had located a particularly wanted bank robber in an east side rambler. The agent and his partner had established surveillance from the street, but an informant had told them the guy had his girlfriend and two little girls in the house. They didn't want to make the arrest without putting together some kind of plan and a backup.

Tom Devreaux climbed out from behind a pile of paper and pushed me through his office door, yelling to the rest of the bull pen to grab their radios and vests. Time to go to work.

Day one. Hour one. Armed and dangerous bank robber under surveillance in preparation for arrest. Just what I expected of my new life in the FBI.

An electric charge ran from the tips of those balls Ray warned me about all the way up my spine as the squad room rose to life. Shotguns, handcuffs, handheld radios, body armor, binoculars. The equipment appeared from under the government-surplus desks and behind ancient oak file cabinets. Four months of training swelled up inside me, ready to explode if I didn't get out there and shackle that shitbird myself before he took another breath.

I knew everything an FBI agent needed to know, from

search warrant affidavits and Miranda warnings to shotgun tactics and how to extract a confession. This seemed like the perfect opportunity to prove myself. The blue flame of glory burned so hard I feared I'd better move fast or torch the whole damned building.

We rolled on my first arrest in a gold 1985 Volare with flat vinyl upholstery and an AM radio tuned to Muzak. Tom talked over a familiar melody as he drove, feeding buckshot rounds into a Remington 870 shotgun with one hand and marshaling the troops with a radio mic in the other. He drove with his knee, watched the road with one eye, and studied me in the rearview mirror with the other. With the exception of a Mexican plate spinner on the Ed Sullivan show, I'd never seen a more dextrous manager.

The ASAC rode shotgun. He hung his right arm out the window, letting his hand rise and fall in the eighty-mile-an-hour breeze like a kid playing airplane. I sat in the back seat with my arm stretched across the rear window. Hell, my last job included Republican leadership meetings at the White House and luncheons in the Capitol dining room with visiting heads of state. It made perfect sense that I'd ride with the people calling all the shots.

Tom and the ASAC considered their situation, assessed the threat level, and came up with a plan in the three blocks between the parking lot and I-70. We knew the bad guy was armed and dangerous and that he had as many as three potential hostages inside the house with him. Storming up to the front door would likely get somebody killed, and calling with a surrender demand would lead to a standoff.

"We got to lure him out," Tom decided in a voice that drowned out an elevator version of "Hey Jude." "I say we do a drive-by, then pull everyone in to map this thing."

The ASAC agreed. He knew of a Winn-Dixie just down the street where we could meet without heating up the neighborhood. I nodded, trying to look supportive without calling attention to my fucking new guy (FNG) status. The ASAC's hand bounced up and down in the wind as we jettisoned I-70 at just under 100 miles an hour, with Tom fighting a front-end vibration so bad the radio station skipped a channel.

Roland Darrington and Jeff Millette met us in the parking lot just as Tom had planned. Our drive-by hadn't offered much in the way of intelligence. The neighborhood looked like a million other cookie-cutter subdivisions built in the '70s: single-story ramblers fronted by chain-link fences and astro-turf lawns. A narrow walkway led from the driveway up three concrete stairs to a stagger-windowed front door. Open backyard. No dog. Pretty straightforward, based on what I'd seen at Quantico.

I laid out a plan in my head just in case they asked. Surround the block with the unmarked units, call in the locals for a deep perimeter, and get the SWAT team on standby in case things go bad, I decided. We send two guys to the front door peddling magazines or canvassing for the Playboy Channel or something, and when the shitbird breaks the threshold to see what we're selling, we deck him, hook him up, and go get a barbecue sandwich. They should probably send me in on the ruse because I looked young and hadn't been an agent long enough to look the part.

"All right," Tom said, as we assembled near a pile of empty muscatel bottles, "here's the way I see it. We need to get this guy out on a ruse so we can get him away from those kids. Let's close down the block, call KC metro for a perimeter, get Butch's SWAT boys to stand by, and send two guys up to the front door selling something so we can get a look inside. Maybe we can get him out of the house and take him down right there."

Bingo. Just like I planned it. Maybe I didn't have the experience of a veteran agent, but I had the mojo. Now, who gets the ticket?

"Roland . . . you got some ruse in mind?"

Roland, a 5'8" black guy sporting a Richard Roundtree Afro and fade-to-clear Foster Grants, pointed to Jeff. So much for my idea of going to the door. No matter. If they needed backup I knew I was in better shape than anyone else in the parking lot. I would get there first to help with the arrest.

Tom ironed out the details, assigned positions, and handed out weapons assignments. Two shotguns, three of the new single-action MP-5 submachine guns. The rest of us had to make our stands with service revolvers.

We climbed back into our Bucars and headed back into the quiet suburban neighborhood to get our bank robber. Tom and the ASAC discussed the plan as we drove. Roland and Jeff would park in the driveway, go up to the front door, and knock. If our man came to the door, they'd tell him they were selling raffle tickets for the local Little League team. They actually had in the trunk a new VCR Jeff had picked up for his wife and they'd offer to show it to him in hopes of getting him away from the front door. Then there was the signal. If Roland reached for the bill of his KC Royals cap, the cavalry would roll. They'd throw down on him, press on the cuffs, and call it a day. Sounded like a plan.

Fifteen minutes later, Tom confirmed metro coverage at both ends of the street, checked to make sure all his agents felt ready to go, and gave Roland the nod.

I sat in the backseat, ready for war. My brand-new .357 rested in a crisp leather holster at my hip, but I'd pulled the hem of my suit coat clear and tucked it into my waistband to facilitate a quicker draw. I checked the speed loader just left of my belt buckle and the extra six rounds in my left coat pocket. Eighteen rounds better be enough, I thought, but then again, I'd never been in a firefight. There was no way to guess how long two reloads would last if this got heavy.

The ASAC reached to turn down the Muzak as Tom rested his hand on the gearshift and pushed his Coke-bottle glasses back up his nose. I looked to make sure my door was unlocked and rested my hand on the door handle.

Nothing I'd ever experienced matched this. Adrenaline flowed through my veins like quicksilver, thinning the air in my lungs, brightening the sun. I flashed back to the feeling I got on the first kickoff during football season when the whole game waited on one whistle. My skin prickled where the shirt stuck to it in pools of sweat. My vision cleared in small areas of focus, obscuring everything small and petty. The muscles in my arms and legs locked rigid, waiting for the whistle to blow and the game to begin.

On command, Roland and Jeff wheeled into the driveway, climbed out of their car, and walked up to the front door. I sat in the back of the Volare, trying to keep my heart from beating all the way out of my chest. No one said a word. I watched through Tom's window from about 150 feet down the street.

Roland opened the storm door and knocked three times. Jeff stood just off to his right, trying to look like a Little League coach selling raffle tickets. Unmarked cars full of agents lined the street in both directions.

The next thing I knew, the front door flew open. A black man dressed in Bermuda shorts and a wife-beater T-shirt stepped into the darkly lit frame and drew the biggest, brightest Magnum I had ever seen in my life. He stuck it right in Jeff's face.

"Gun!" I heard Tom yell as he yanked the shotgun up out of his lap and kicked open his door. Roland dove off the porch to the right. Jeff dove to the left. I couldn't tell whether the subject had fired up that big hogleg, but by the sounds of things, it didn't matter. This party was heading south in a hurry and I needed a piece of the action.

"This is the FBI!" someone immediately yelled over a car PA. "Drop the gun!"

I spied Roland through Tom's bouncing door as he scrambled out of a boxwood hedge and took cover around the corner of the house. I couldn't see what happened to Jeff. All I knew was that sitting in the back seat of that Volare seemed a bad idea at that point.

"Get some cover!" the ASAC yelled, bailing out himself. He pulled his service weapon and met me behind the trunk.

Three other Volares full of agents emptied at the same time as the whole world erupted in a cacophony of PA commands, screaming agents, and distant sirens.

Kansas City metro, the FBI SWAT team, news crews, ambulances . . . just about everyone in the east end of the city showed up as we set up for a blazing shoot-out.

Guns came from everywhere: 9mm pistols, .357 revolvers, 12-gauge shotguns, MP-5s. Everybody pointed something at the house.

No fool, I drew mine, too, and took up a position using the car for cover, just like they drilled into our heads at the Academy. I knelt on one knee behind the rear tire, recalling that the rim and rubber would stop any rounds bouncing under the 2,000-pound Plymouth. Unfortunately, all this took a couple seconds too long. I drew the ramped front sight of my revolver on the subject just as he backed into the house and slammed the door shut behind him.

Two hours on the street and I was knee-deep in my first shoot-out, I thought. Damn, what a job.

"Whitcomb!" someone yelled.

I turned an ear toward the voice, anticipating the call to

lead the assault team up to the front door. Two agents in trouble. This is where heroes are born.

"Whitcomb!" My name, again, piercing the raucous din of battle. "Put that fucking thing back in the holster and leave it there!"

What?

"Put it the fuck away!"

I turned to my left, toward the ASAC, who stared a hole right between my eyes. For reasons I never really figured out, he looked a whole lot more concerned with me than with the bad guy.

"Sit your ass behind that tire and don't move until I tell you to."

I looked down the street as agents ran from cover to usher the growing crowd of spectators out of the line of fire. Agents in blue and gold FBI raid jackets leaned into shotguns, talked into radio mics, gestured wildly in the heat of battle. Everyone seemed completely engaged.

You got to be shitting me, I thought. My first day on the streets looks like something out of a Francis Ford Coppola production, and this guy was treating me like some kind of extra.

"Now!"

I did just what he told me. I crouched behind a Goodyear radial, holstered my well-oiled weapon, and tried to blend with the street.

"Hey, Whitcomb!"

That name again. Someone else was yelling at me from up near the house.

"Where's your gun?" Sandy Patten, the squad's only female agent, crouched behind a tree, waving her own pistol like it was some new invention.

I just shrugged my shoulders and tried to look tough, like I didn't need weapons.

"What's going on out here?" Another voice turned my head. It was a little old lady from across the street, walking up behind me with a broom in her hands.

"Get back in your house!" I yelled.

Now I felt better. I was actually participating. But she kept coming, shuffling past the astro-turf walkway in a yellow housecoat and nursing-home slippers. The whole neighborhood followed, spilling out onto their lawns to watch the action.

I yelled in my most authoritative voice, the one they'd taught us at the Academy.

"This is the Federal Bureau of Investigation! Everything is going to be all right!"

People stared at me like I was nuts.

Without thinking, I reached again for my gun. It came out almost as a reflex this time, as if that little old lady and her friends were trying some flanking maneuver. Screw the ASAC, I thought. If I'm going to take a ration of shit over this, I'd rather have it come from him than my family for getting shot.

I don't know if it was the gun or the chorus of authoritative voices or the sudden realization that this was not a game, but something clicked in my head at that moment. I felt connected to things they'd only hinted at back at the Academy. I looked up at faces peering out of the corners of windows all up and down the street, and at the faces of agents trying to keep a violent criminal from hurting more people. I watched my first day at the office turn into a hostage situation with the pristine realization that things had changed forever. No more political games, no coffee breaks, no first, second, and third drafts of a speech for some Kiwanis Club luncheon. This job carried consequence.

"This is the FBI! Come out with your hands up!"

The command sounds kind of cliché now, with so many

television shows and movies trying to re-create the thrill of legal violence. But that July morning in 1987, I felt like those words came straight from God.

❖

Five days later, the SAC transferred me to the Springfield, Missouri, Resident Agency, a six-agent satellite office near the Arkansas border. Though the Gateway to the Ozarks boasted international notoriety as the home of Bass Pro Shops, cashew chicken, and Edna, the world's largest crappie (a fish, they told me), I bristled at the reassignment as a step away from the front lines. But the SAC assured me that despite its reputation as the Buckle of the Bible Belt, Springfield offered some of the best cases in the Bureau, including a veritable treasure trove of bank robberies, fugitives, and informants.

He talked a good game, but I felt disheartened by the whole turn of events. I felt like I'd failed my tryout. It didn't matter that negotiators had talked the bank robber out of the house and led him away to a long prison sentence. My white hat had been stomped in the mud.

It wasn't until Senior Supervisory Resident Agent Eugene Brodie flew all the way up from Springfield to talk to me about the job that I felt vindicated. Maybe my particularly adroit performance behind that car tire had spread to the corners of the division. After all, how many first office agents can make a smooth transition from gunslinger to safety officer in the time it takes to fall out of a car?

Whatever his motivation, Eugene wooed me over a sixteen-ounce cheeseburger at the Black Angus and convinced me that a four-hour shuffle south would amount to an excellent career move. That and the fact that the ASAC had assigned my Bucar to someone else before I even got back to the office helped me make up my mind. Springfield came calling. Springfield it would be.

So that night, Rosie, Jake, and I repacked our suitcases, pointed the Jeep south, and set out for the next big adventure. I reported Monday morning to One Corporate Center, a green-glass-and-concrete office complex that looked more like a home to accounting firms than an outpost on the frontiers of crime.

Ruth, the RA secretary, held me at the bulletproof glass reception area until Eugene emerged with a cup of coffee in one hand and *USA Today* in the other. Apparently, Ray Venable's assessment of the Bureau's morning routine held true no matter where you hung your hat.

Springfield offered little in the way of cultural refinement. Theater boiled down to the Box Car Willie Revue in nearby Branson. Music reached to the borders of both country and Western, with mid-tour stopovers by AM radio stars like Vern Gosdin and the Mandrell Sisters. Fine dining included open pit barbecue, catfish, sorghum, and just about anything I'd ever heard of "country fried." Major sporting events were limited to rodeo, but to see the big names like Donnie Gay or Tuff Hedeman you had to drive four hours west to Tulsa.

And there was fishing. Springfield boasted some of the finest freshwater angling in the nation. The only thing more popular than tobacco chewing seemed to involve jetting a 225-horse Evinrude out to your favorite shoal, sitting back in the 110-degree swelter, and wasting the next eight hours watching a bobber. Despite earnest effort, bass fishing and I never completely engaged.

Culture shock aside, I quickly fell in love with the place. Housing seemed cheaper than anywhere I'd ever lived, it rarely snowed, and traffic wasn't bad. On top of that, people said hello on the street. They offered sweet tea with dinner, referred to each other as "you'ns," and considered "inside the beltway" the place where you tuck your concealable weapon. People carried shotguns in the rear windows of their pickup trucks, sold produce using an honor system at the side of the road, and looked forward to an answer when they asked "How you'ns doin'?"

Something about this place felt sheltered from the fast-paced, impossibly cynical world of Washington politics. Within four months I had gone from navy bean soup in the Capitol dining room to chicken-fried steak at the Silver Saddle restaurant. What the hell, I loved the irony.

Big Al, a grizzled senior agent, pulled me into his office just after I arrived and made a valiant attempt at jetting back the blue flame, which the Kansas City experience had merely fueled.

"We do things a little different out here," he said in a slow, confident drawl. "Three rules you got to abide by if you want to succeed in the Ozarks: Never embarrass the Bureau, decide who you want to believe and trust their advice, and never go near a trailer park in a thunderstorm."

I nodded, trying to cover the fact that I had no idea what the hell he was talking about. It didn't really matter, because the way I was going, I'd probably end up breaking most of the rules anyway.

4

GOOD VIBRATIONS

Accepting FNG status in any FBI office means sitting down behind a stack of cases no one else wants to work, taking the territory no one wants to travel, and covering it all from the driver's seat of the oldest car in the fleet. You order last in the restaurant, take phone duty when everyone else goes to lunch, and watch the back door during search warrant entries. Nothing new. That's the nature of the workplace. Unfortunately, FNG status also means living under a microscope for the time it takes to figure out exactly what the hell you're about.

Big Al didn't believe in wasting time. He gave me a couple of days to find a stapler, adjust my chair, and fill out the administrative paperwork. Then he marched into my cubicle Wednesday morning with a lead in his catcher's-mitt-size hand and announced that he'd run down an 88 out of Tulsa, wanted for armed robbery.

In the FBI's own private lexicon, 88 means Unlawful

Flight to Avoid Prosecution, or UFAP. This is a no-strings-attached kind of arrest where you hook up a fugitive who's escaped across state lines and hand him over to the nearest authorities for extradition. Very little paperwork, lots of excitement — the perfect case. According to Tulsa's inter-office communication, this guy was armed and dangerous and an obvious escape risk. Heaven with cheese.

"Grab your shit," Big Al said. "I got a racquetball game at eleven."

Five minutes later I sat in the front seat of yet another Plymouth Volare, this time silver with burgundy upholstery, listening to a Rachmaninoff concerto as Big Al spat chewing tobacco out his open window. He steered his way through traffic with the first two fingers of his stubby right hand perched on the wheel, with his balding pate brushing against the head liner. He pushed the bench seat all the way forward so his legs would reach the pedals, making my ride uncomfortable to the point of mention.

"Mind if we move this thing back a little?" I said. "I think my legs'll go numb by the time we get there."

His presence filled the car like scent from an evergreen air freshener.

"Sorry, but I got the body of a six-foot-seven man, and I'm only five-eleven," he said in a baritone so rich it sounded like paid narrative. "That means I'm missing about eight inches in the way of legs. Almost didn't qualify for jets because of it."

"Jets" meant F-4s in Vietnam. Though I wouldn't know his full pedigree for years, Big Al carried a remarkable life story into our association. Four years as a Division I offensive guard at Oklahoma, followed by flight school and two tours of Vietnam. A midair collision dropped him behind enemy lines and started a harrowing escape through the jungles of Southeast Asia.

He'd installed wiretaps in Pocono hotel rooms during the famous Abscam case, circled the skies over Manhattan as a surveillance pilot, manned the perimeter during the Leonard Peltier standoff at Wounded Knee, and arrested dozens of felons.

Big Al walked like a Brahma bull, with his short, kneeless legs pumping from the hips in the pulling guard motion he'd practiced at Oklahoma. Shirts never fit him because his arms, like his legs, mismatched the rest of his frame. He sort of rolled around like a well-worn bowling ball, tucking in the tails of his shirt and trying to cinch up his collar, which never made it completely around his neck. A stainless steel Chief's Special five-shot peeked out of his belt, all the firepower he ever needed in this job.

"So what's the plan with this guy?" I asked as we pulled off into a low-rent neighborhood full of two-bedroom ranch houses and dirt driveways. I felt that same slow nausea rising in my throat, just like the previous week in Kansas City. Something was about to happen, but I didn't really know what.

"Plan?" he responded. "Plan is we put this sumbitch in jail in time for me to make my game."

Big Al spoke with confidence. Despite his rambling, terminally chaotic look, he simmered with the patent conviction of a man who had seen enough life and enough death to understand the relationship. He always meant what he said, fundamentally.

"You stay with me and we'll do just fine."

With that, he checked the address on the Tulsa lead, matched it with the numbers on one of the bungalows, and spat a brown, sinewy wad of Levi Garrett out the open window. He braked to the side of the narrow street, slipped the shifter into Park, and dropped the sheet of paper on the seat between us.

"You got a vest?" he asked.

Yup, right in the back seat. I nodded, trying to decide whether he wanted me to put it on. I knew nothing about this fugitive other than his armed-and-dangerous status and the basic idea that he lived in the pea-green HUD shack just off to my right.

"All right, then, let's do it."

Al pushed open his door and started toward the house.

Do what? I thought as I ran to catch up. Granted, I had limited experience in this arrest business, but from pickup football games to career paths, I'd always thought a plan made reasonably good sense.

Al walked faster than most men jog, so giving up the first four or five steps to introspection proved shortsighted. I just barely caught him as he leaped up the two steps leading to the porch and kicked in the front door.

Wait a minute, I thought, following him past the splintered lock set into a dark living room cluttered with Budweiser cans and broken furniture in simulated wood grain. What about knocking and announcing? For all this guy knew, we could have been bookies rolling in to collect a bad debt. He could have taken a whack at us just because he didn't want his legs broken.

"Dear Mrs. Whitcomb, we regret to inform you that your husband was killed by an armed-and-dangerous fugitive who mistook him for a loan shark breaking into his legal residence." I could almost hear Eugene Brodie making the call as I ran.

It's amazing how experience allows the human mind to cycle entire thought processes in the blink of an eye: Big Al assessed the room, spotted our man in an adjacent bedroom, and threw his naked, trembling body to the floor before my eyes had adjusted to the dim light.

While I was still trying to navigate the unique miasma of

stale bongwater, skunked beer, and severe body odor, Big Al
had plowed through a curtain of love beads, spotted his fugitive in a country pine water bed, and grabbed the poor wild-
eyed bastard by his long, skinny neck.

"Don't kill me! Don't kill me! Don't kill me!" the guy
kept yelling.

Big Al knelt his 235-pound torso squarely on the man's
windpipe and wrenched one arm behind his tattooed back. I
heard some pathetic mumbling and the long slow whistle of
breath leaving his lungs.

"FBI. You're under arrest," Al said with all the excitement of a fast food order.

Beautiful, I thought, gazing down at the reason parents tell
their kids to stay away from drugs. This sad, skinny, pathetic
wretch struggled for breath as Big Al ground him into the
shag carpet and cuffed him for another five to seven years.
The moment felt almost poetic.

"FBI. You're under arrest," I muttered to myself, practicing Al's deadpan authority. "You want fries with that order?"

Braced with the experience of a couple bold arrests under
my belt, I arrived at the office the next morning wearing a
new suit and rubber-soled shoes that I hoped would give me
footing in my first hand-to-hand combat. I paraded into the
office, past the rest of the guys reading the morning papers,
dropped my shiny new briefcase on my desk, and stripped
off my jacket. The only bad thing I could find in the day was
that it had just begun.

"What the hell is that?" one of the guys asked me as I
rounded the corner and reached for a cup of coffee.

"What's what?" I asked.

The guys liked to draw chairs together around the secretary's desk first thing in the morning for a review of current

events. I grabbed the sports page from *USA Today* and pulled up a seat.

"What's that thing under your arm?"

Brad Lawrence had exactly three months more experience than I did, but he acted like a crusty veteran. He wore an air of superiority that rose to the point of insult, right down to his Cole Haan broughams, double-breasted blazer, and the Hart Schaffner & Marx pants which he referred to as "slacks." Brad wore his refinement as a bulletproof ego so thick, nothing so base as decency could dent it.

"That's a fucking gun, pretty boy. Break yours out of your desk and you'll know what one looks like" would have been an appropriate reply if not for the rest of the guys looking up at me with the same question perched on their lips.

That "thing" under my arm was a brand new Smith and Wesson Model 686 L-frame revolver, chambered to .357 Magnum, with custom Pachmayr grips, tritium night sights, and a six-inch barrel. It hung elegantly under my left arm from a Safariland breakfront shoulder holster dyed a neutral fawn to match absolutely everything in my GS-10 wardrobe.

Handgun selection is an intensely personal issue in law enforcement. When I started in 1987, the Bureau still forbade the use of semiautomatic pistols except among SWAT teams and some special-duty squads. Though no one ever clearly said why, the average agent's choices in personal protection were limited to Smith and Wesson products in .38 or .357 caliber.

Within those parameters, it seemed, you could judge an agent's ambition and tenure with a glance at his belt line. The grizzled old GS-13 journeymen wore effete-looking five-shots, like Big Al's, usually tucked into ankle holsters. New agents packed the distinctly unglamorous Bureau-issue Model 13. They wanted to fit in, to make their mark without announcing to the world that they were trying.

And then there were those enlightened scions of federal peacekeeping like myself who reached out to the display cases of every gun dealer in town, looking for that unique personal statement of style and authority that could make them the stuff of American folklore. What would Patton be without his pearl-handled 1911 .45s? Who could suggest that Rooster Cogburn trade in his Colt Peacemaker for a two-shot der-ringer? Something about James Bond carrying a Walther PPK just works. And try telling Rambo his movies would have drawn more viewers if he'd opted for a double-barreled skeet gun with engraved hunting scenes and a tooled walnut stock.

"It's a gun," I said.

"Damn, boy, you planning to go to war or make a movie?" Big Al shook his head and shuddered a little under the force of his laugh.

"I know what that is, but what the hell is *that?*" Benny, a soft-spoken Arkansas native working interstate theft cases, pointed to my belt.

"You mean my badge?" I asked, sensing I might have waited a couple more weeks before introducing the newest trends in law enforcement hardware to the guys.

I wore my bright new FBI badge in a leather belt clip that hung just behind the first loop, right of the buckle. My entire New Agent class had ordered them before we left, at the sug-gestion of a Practical Applications Unit instructor. Unfortu-nately, word of this particular accessory hadn't reached the Springfield RA. Most FBI agents carried their badge and creds in their shirt pocket like a government-issue pocket protector.

Eugene let me read my paper before calling me into his office with a few words of advice. Seems I'd violated Big Al's first two rules in the same moment. I'd embarrassed the Bureau, at least the way these guys defined it, and I'd embarrassed him by ignoring his advice on the benefits of fitting in.

"Al's going to take you around town, introduce you to the locals, the U.S. Attorney's office, the marshals," Eugene said. "He's going to make you a good investigator. So go back to your desk and take off all that ridiculous shit before somebody calls us up and accuses you of impersonating a DEA agent."

What the hell was wrong with carrying a full-size gun and wearing the badge where everyone could see it? I'd worked my ass off to get this job and felt enormous pride in what I'd accomplished. Something about the simple act of carrying an FBI credential swelled up inside me every time I pulled it out and ran my finger across its art deco graphics.

"This is to certify that Christopher Whitcomb is a regularly appointed Special Agent of the Federal Bureau of Investigation," my credentials read, "and as such is charged with the duty of investigating violations of the laws of the United States in cases in which the United States is a party of interest."

I sometimes read the verse aloud while sitting in traffic, just to savor the import. I found the words elegant, no doubt written by one of Hoover's felt-fedora-topped lawyer gods in a moment of bureaucratic revelation.

"Geez, Eugene, I didn't think anyone would notice."

So I did as I was told. I began to pay attention to the small things other cops did as a matter of habit. I liked the way Big Al dangled a set of cuffs from the gearshift of his Volare. I noticed how Benny opened conversations with a couple comments about fishing or the weather before he pulled out his creds and casually introduced himself as a federal agent. I studied Bill's paperwork, and Matt's attention to detail, and Eugene's knack for opening doors with a confident smile instead of a size 11 Florsheim.

I put the big hogleg back into my desk, still cased in the beautiful leather shoulder rig, right next to my mint-condition badge, forever enshrined in that dark leather belt clip. They'd told us at the Academy that if the Bureau wants a blue suit, you give them a blue suit. Springfield, Missouri, was a long stroll from Headquarters in Washington, but as far as I was concerned Eugene was the Bureau, and if he wanted me to wear blue J.C. Penney fashions tailored in blended man-made fabrics, that's just what the hell he was going to get.

Due to the FBI's mandate to enforce federal laws throughout the country with a little more than 11,000 agents, resources sometimes get spread a little thin. The Springfield RA covered southwest Missouri from the Arkansas border, west almost to Joplin, east halfway to St. Louis, and north to Jefferson City. My chunk of that real estate included five sparsely populated counties reaching almost 200 miles to the east and south. Since Eugene gave me free rein to allocate my time as I saw fit, that meant lots of time in the car.

One morning early in my first month, I was just setting out to shag a lead when a woman showed up at the front door with a box of papers. Ordinarily I wouldn't have minded talking to her, but I was in a hurry and didn't want to waste time with another nutcase. Big Al had already introduced me to Special Agent Red Ryder 749 I Am Black. He was neither Special Agent nor African American, but he made it his business to visit the office once a month to explain, in lucid detail, the intricacies of a government plot to kidnap the president.

I sat at my desk for more than an hour one day, listening to this idiot while Big Al and the others lounged in his office laughing their asses off at my gullibility. Until then, I had no idea how many poor tortured souls seek solace with the local FBI.

Unfortunately, today everyone else had beaten me out of the office. I was trapped.

I peeked around the corner of my cubicle into the reception area and saw a perfectly normal-looking, relatively attractive woman waiting for assistance.

No big deal, I thought. Maybe this was the opportunity I had been looking for: a big case all wrapped up in a rather pretty package.

I neatened the paperwork on my desk, arranged a chair for an interview, and adjusted my tie. Ask her about the weather, I thought, flashing back to Benny's deft ability to frame conversation. I'd conducted my share of interviews, but not since my newspaper days. Build a little rapport, I thought, harking back to Congressman Conte's knack for animating absolutely any discussion. Make her feel comfortable in the intimidating environs of an FBI office.

I slipped the file I'd been working on into a drawer, arranged the potted plant near the window, and straightened my tie again. This would be one of the first actual FBI interviews I'd conducted, and I wanted to make certain I covered all the bases. Make a favorable impression on introduction, they taught me; establish rapport, ask open-ended questions, affirm responses, monitor nonverbal behaviors, and finish with a summary. I knew the standard format. All I had to do now was make it sing.

"Hello," I said, approaching the woman. She wore a light flower-print sundress and carried a canvas bag over her shoulder.

"I'm Special Agent Whitcomb. How may I help you?"

"Well, I don't want to bother you, but I've got this problem I'd like to talk about." She looked suspiciously at the receptionist who typed away, oblivious to our conversation.

"Sure, why don't we go over to my office."

We walked the five steps to where my desk sat behind a five-foot portable divider. Compared to my last office overlooking the Capitol, this seemed a bit of an embarrassment.

"Please, sit down."

The woman looked terribly uncomfortable, as if she'd endured a long ordeal and needed someone to share her secrets. I gathered a yellow legal pad and a government-issue pen and poised for my big break. Soviet spies, perhaps? Maybe an interstate fraud I could spin into the search warrants and wiretaps and informants that would define me as a rising star in the organization.

She arranged herself in the chair, crossed her legs, and sat back with such a strange look on her face, I imagined she must have hurt her back. Her eyes faded a bit at the edge of consciousness and then gathered again in the moment.

"Are you all right?" I asked. "Would you like a cup of coffee or a glass of water?"

There was no telling what trauma or malady had brought her here, and I wanted to make sure she understood that she could trust me with her most intimate insecurities. I was the FBI, after all, and the sound of the Assistant Director administering my sworn oath rang in my ears as she gathered her thoughts. "All enemies foreign and domestic."

"No, that's all right," she said with a long sigh through pursed lips.

Something in her eyes grabbed me. I'd seen the look before, but I couldn't exactly remember where. She stared through me more than at me with a strange melange of pain and fear.

"Why don't we start with your name, ma'am," I said, turning away from her face. The cubicle seemed impossibly close now, as if the desk had swelled around us. "I'll need it for my records."

"My name . . . my name is Karen. You want to know where I live?"

That and her Social Security number and her date of birth. Standard information I needed to gather before moving into the really good stuff. I could sense something eating at her, some brash imperative tearing at her soul, reaching out for help.

"That's great, thanks. Now what can I do for you?"

"I just can't stand it anymore," she said, starting to tremble in her chair. The purse slipped off her shoulder as she stared at me. Her upper lip started to quiver as if she were about to cry. I could see the muscles tighten in the tops of her thighs as she pressed her hips deeper into the chair. Her knuckles curled around the armrests so hard I thought her long, delicate fingers might snap.

"It happened about . . . two months ago . . ." The experience filled her, rose up in her face.

I gripped my pen, waiting on the edge of my seat for her to spill this unspeakable crime so I could run out of the office and take these shameless assholes off the street. She showed such penetrating emotion, I worried that I might have to console her before she'd tell me the whole story.

". . . they came after me in the middle of the night."

Wait a minute. Middle of the night? This didn't sound good. Rapists and burglars are about the only people who come in the middle of the night, and they're not federal beefs. I started to slouch.

"They came in the middle of the night and took me away with them."

Kidnapping? *That's* a violation of federal law. Now we were getting somewhere.

"They took you? Where? Who took you?"

I knew the federal statutes governing kidnapping offenses: forcible entry, transportation across state lines, malicious intent. If I were going to open this case, I'd have to show certain elements of the crime.

"You know . . ." She leaned close enough that I could smell clove cigarettes on her breath. A small diamond solitaire dangled from a gold chain into the V of her slightly open blouse. ". . . the Martians."

Aw, shit.

"They took me outside to their ship . . ."

Dammit! She looked so normal when she came through the door.

". . . and I followed them inside this big, lit-up room . . ."

The look of desperation grew on her face as she arched her back and closed her eyes.

". . . and they laid me down on this big table . . ."

"Ruth?" I summoned the receptionist. Suddenly I knew just where I'd seen that look in her eyes, and I no longer wanted to share it alone. "Ruth, could you come over here please?"

Karen rolled her head around on her shoulders, just slightly, breathing more and more heavily.

". . . and they pulled up my dress . . ."

"Ruth!" I didn't like the looks of this at all.

". . . and pulled down my panties . . ."

She opened her eyes and stared right at me with a look of desperation so pitiful, I almost reached out to hold her.

". . . and they inserted a vaginal fibrillator inside me . . ."

Oh shit. Red Ryder 749 was a complete lunatic, but at least he kept his clothes on.

Her hips started to move back and forth in the chair, rhythmically. Her chin fell down toward her chest. Ruth emerged from around the corner.

". . . and induced a continual state of . . . oh yeah . . . uh, uh, oh yes . . . oh my God . . . *orgasm!*"

Ruth recoiled like she'd been hit with a cattle prod.

"... and I just ... can't ... make ... it stop ..."

With that, her words turned unintelligible and she started whimpering with the overwhelming exhaustion that I imagined would accompany two months of continual climax. I tried to remain professional, but nothing on the orange criminal classification booklet in my desk included psychotic women trapped in a perpetual state of carnal rapture. Nothing in my extensive training prepared me to handle the unique mental and physical demands of a woman lost on a trip-hammer chill. Not even Eugene's expert supervisory oversight or Big Al's broad experience or my years of romantic expedition had prepared me for the unique demands of this first big interview.

Who cares, I thought, as Ruth searched for words and Karen shuddered uncontrollably. My job was to keep the public safe and happy. At least this client was still smiling.

5

SWEET TEA
AND DOBERMANS

As it turned out, the Ozarks proved to be a good place for a man of my lust and ambition to learn the value of pace. Law enforcement can be an unforgiving trade, and the guys in the office taught me how to temper enthusiasm with common sense and perspective. Four years of writing on deadline had left me with an acquired taste for pressure. When I couldn't find it around me, I sometimes tried to create it. That would not fly in this new line of work, they assured me. It would get me killed.

Eugene Brodie assigned me enough tired old cases to keep my blue flame from singeing any eyebrows. I thumbed through the stacks of brown and white file jackets sitting on my government-issue desk, learning the investigative process. My caseload included unsolved bank robberies, interstate thefts, bank frauds, and a few "old dog" fugitive cases that stood out from the pile like giant chunks of tenderloin in a rich summer stew.

The case files read like how-to manuals, detailing with painstaking chronology the steps an FBI agent should take along the path to conviction. Poring over the files gave me a sense of the organization the way old newspapers had taught me the journalism business. From search warrant affidavits to chain-of-custody forms, the old files offered me a blueprint I could use to build new cases and construct my own investigations.

Big Al and Benny spent more than enough time answering my questions and recounting war stories about their own mistakes and successes along the way.

"Most of the people in your counties have never seen an FBI agent," Benny reminded me more than once. "Ask them questions the right way and they'll tell you anything you want. Act like a damned New Yorker and you'll spend the rest of your time here running background checks on federal judges."

They punctuated their advice with local stories, including that of the Buffalo, Missouri, farmer who killed fourteen members of his family, then inflicted a superficial wound on himself and stuck the gun in his nephew's hand to make it look like the kid had gone mad. He probably would have gotten away with it, but a cagey highway patrol investigator named Tom Martin figured out the kid was left-handed. He never would have shot all those people with his weak hand, Tom reasoned. That hunch and some good old-fashioned police work led to a death penalty conviction and a little justice.

I listened to their warnings about the hazards inherent in working vast stretches of open road without backup. In my first month, I attended three funerals for law enforcement officers killed in the line of duty. At one of them, I joined hundreds of fellow officers in laying to rest a Missouri highway patrolman who took sixteen slugs from a MAC-10 before collapsing near his patrol car on a rural farm road. At another, I bowed my head and walked past the casket of a local sheriff who had been killed with a booby-trapped rifle as he attempted to serve a simple custody warrant on a trailer house. The murderer had aimed the rifle at the side of the door, knowing law enforcement officers try to avoid the "vertical coffin." When the sheriff tried the doorknob from the side, he tripped a drag wire and took a .30-06 round right under the collarbone.

Slowly but surely, I began to gain through experience and research the skills that would define me as an FBI agent. I spent long days on the road visiting the outlying counties, introducing myself to rural sheriffs and chiefs of two-man departments. Most of the officers wore blue jeans and T-shirts, with nothing but a tin badge and a sidearm to distinguish them from a combine operator. Missouri state law required more training for certification as a hair stylist than as a law enforcement officer. Many of the locals I worked with got a code bar (emergency lights) and a badge when they joined the force. As for a squad car, a gun, and a uniform, they had to fend for themselves. And when it came to ammunition for training, they paid their own way, too.

Big Al helped me there, stacking two cases of Bureau-issue .38 ammo in the trunk of my Grand Prix and explaining the virtue in charity. Handing out a box here and there to demonstrate good will would go a long way, he said, and demonstrate that the FBI could occasionally be relied on for something more than aggravation. Besides, fostering trust with local and state colleagues could pay off in terms of a backup some cold, dark night. Each of us worked twelve-hour days just trying to keep up with our own caseloads. Taking a full day to run down a lead in some outpost like Zanoni with another agent meant making the time up on a weekend or late at night.

The better option seemed to rely on local officers or the highway patrol. They knew the territory and they knew the job. Most cops make more arrests in a week than an agent does in an entire year, anyway. Getting someone with that kind of experience to take you under his wing can make the learning curve a whole lot flatter.

It took time to win their trust, particularly with my New England accent, but perseverance paid off. I began to pull in stats — statistical accomplishments — which the Bureau keeps on all agents and their offices. Arrests, search warrants, economic losses prevented, recoveries, and other successes become a pedigree, distinguishing one investigator from another. Lots of supervisors spout party line that stats don't really matter, but I realized quickly that the better your numbers, the better your performance evaluations and the better your reputation. That adds up to things like incentive awards, newer cars, and better cases.

Stats also add up to job satisfaction, because the harder I worked, the more fun I had. The more fun I had, the better my stats got. Eugene Brodie never played down the correlation. He forgave the shoulder holster incident pretty quickly and left me to run my investigations without much supervision.

I dove into the old-dog fugitive cases, treating them like personal challenges. I analyzed them to try and figure out where the previous case agents had gone wrong, what they had missed, where they had overlooked some piece of evidence that could have led to a solution. I studied their 302s, searching for questions they hadn't asked or techniques that had failed. And I made things up on my own, like the ruses I'd seen in Kansas City or bullshit stories for family members who lied to me about people I needed to find.

I caught one unsuspecting runner, for example, by making a special trip out to see his parents with a letter I dummied up on Bureau stationery.

"Due to pressing concerns in other investigative areas and the Missouri statute of limitations, you are no longer considered a criminal suspect," it read.

I delivered it to his parents myself, with the caveat that he had to sign my waiver form restoring his due rights as an American citizen. The Bureau letterhead came off a form used to requisition office supplies, but it looked official to the unsuspecting eye. When he met me at a local Git-n-Go to sign off on his newfound freedom, I spread him on the hood of my brand-new Caprice and slapped on the cuffs.

"You can't lie to me like that! It's entrapment!" he yelled.

Like hell it is. All's fair in love, war, and UFAP investigations.

One time I rolled in to a small rural town, looking for an escaped murderer from Colorado named Terrence. My paperwork noted that he'd shot a man in the face with a 30-30 hunting rifle during a drunken brawl, and cautioned that he'd probably try the same thing with anyone who attempted to put him back in jail. I'd used a 30-30 myself to shoot animals. I remembered the wounds. Caution seemed appropriate.

Cases like this beg for creativity. Nearly anyone can stay hidden in this big country if he really wants to, but fugitives are human, and humans make mistakes. When Mother's Day comes around, or a child's birthday threatens to pass without a call, they get soft. Eventually, just about everyone surfaces long enough to reestablish ties. They think we'll forget, but we don't.

This guy fit the profile: six-year-old daughter, estranged wife living with his parents in a 1970s-model double-wide. I knew his family wouldn't tell me jack about how to find him, so I zeroed in on the chink in his armor: the daughter. No matter how hard the felon, they always find a way to contact their kids.

Hoping for a lead, I surveilled his wife long enough to watch her walking their little girl to kindergarten one morning. That's when I knew I had him. I simply followed them to school, waited for Mom to leave, and went in to see the teacher. After I showed the woman a copy of Daddy's criminal report card, she agreed to help. All I needed her to do was gather the kids in a circle and play "Where's My Daddy?"

The little girl stood up and told the class that her daddy had been gone for a long time, but had just come home. As a matter of fact, he was sitting at home on the couch at that very moment, watching TV.

Thank you. Three hours later, the mother returned to pick up her daughter and walked right into a tall man in a dark suit sitting on the schoolhouse steps.

When I politely introduced myself and asked about her estranged husband, she swore to God that he hadn't contacted her since his escape. God must have one hell of a sense of humor, because the common denominator I found in every liar was a shameless willingness to swear to his or her Maker. This woman proved no exception.

After she'd run out the lie, I told her how much her daughter liked having Daddy home on the living room couch. She cursed me for involving her little girl, but still denied any knowledge of her husband's whereabouts. That's when I played my trump. Harboring a federal fugitive is a federal crime, which means federal jail. Mothers in federal jail can't walk their six-year-old daughters to kindergarten every day. In fact, a mother facing federal jail couldn't even walk her six-year-old daughter home that day. If this Mom didn't help put her old man back in the joint, the kid was coming with me.

The choice sounded simple. I was leaving that sad little town with one of her relatives in my car: either her daughter going to social services or her husband going back to jail.

Forty-five minutes and a mason jar full of tears later, I ratcheted my Peerless cuffs around the guy's wrists and buckled him into the back of my car. No shots fired, no hostage standoff, no sweat. I actually felt a little shame about using the girl against her mother in the ploy until the guy opened his mouth halfway back to town.

"You ain't got no fucking niggers in that jail you taking me to, do ya?" he asked.

I paused to make sure I'd heard what he said.

"You can haul my ass back to the penitentiary, but you ain't going to make me spend one fucking minute in no backwoods country jail with no fucking niggers. You tell them that when we get there."

At that moment, any feelings of regret escaped out into the passing breeze. Sometimes reading about a man's past, even if it's marked by crimes like murder, won't paint an accurate portrait. People make mistakes. We're human. We err. But listening to this man spill out the hatred that defined his violent, wasted life, I shook off any sense of misgiving. I made sure I honored his request when I booked him into the Greene County jail and told the deputy just what he'd said. Prison saves its own particular courtesies for guys like that.

The little girl was better off without him on her couch, anyway.

My new life seemed impenetrably wonderful midway through my second year in the Ozarks. Rosie and I had parlayed our gain in the D.C. housing boom into a spacious home south of town on an acre of lawn. Our second child, a son named Mickey, was just learning to walk. His older brother, Jake, dragged me fishing at every opportunity, instilling a sense of calm I'd never known. I even built a tree house in the backyard, more for myself than the kids. We slept out there in the summer, enjoying the smells of honeysuckle and starshine.

FNG probation had ended several months earlier, allowing me the security of anticipating a long, rewarding career as an agent. My stats now boasted a string of meat-and-potatoes successes. I'd worked everything from violent bank robberies to foreign counterintelligence surveillances to a murder case under the Crimes on a Government Reservation statute. I'd helped Assistant U.S. Attorneys present cases in federal court, testified in front of grand juries, sworn out search warrant affidavits, worked all-night stakeouts, sat on wiretaps, and learned the FBI's paperwork jungle.

All the best experiences I'd hoped for in this career played out just like the brochure promised. Some of the cases seemed asinine, like the time I raced up to Fort Leonard Wood to investigate a cryptic call from an Army Intelligence officer who had just opened a jacket on a potential espionage matter. By the time I shook the thing out, I discovered that a seventy-two-year-old retired highway worker had visited the post stables looking for some horse manure to spread on his roses. He made the mistake of trying to generate a little small talk about how the fort had grown over the years, while he forked horseshit into his old pickup. By the time I got there, a weasly little warrant officer had blown the thing into a matter of national security, claiming the guy was probing troop strength and plotting military infrastructure.

"Right," I said. "If the Russians rely on moles like this, they're a lot worse off than we imagine."

Some of the cases surprised me, like the time a Taney County farmer drained a contaminated cattle pond only to find a cache of U.S. Army computer tapes marked TOP SECRET. Never did figure that one out.

There was the man who called up at the start of the Gulf War to tell me he had blueprints to Saddam Hussein's secret bunker. As it turned out, the guy had worked as construction supervisor for the company that built it. He still had the blueprints locked up in his basement, until we shipped them back to the CIA.

And there was the man who called up to tell me he'd been a nuclear physicist working on classified government projects at Los Alamos national labs until a group of radical Mormons chased him through Mexico, trying to murder him. I almost threw the report of his phone call into the Red Ryder 749 file, until a little research proved him right.

There was the self-proclaimed Ambassador from the State of Israel who got busted for driving around with homemade license plates and claiming diplomatic immunity from the sovereignty of his 200-acre farm. He filed a civil rights beef because the Laclede County jail required him to wear a bright orange jumpsuit. His religious convictions prevented him from wearing polyester, and he wanted the FBI to investigate. Good thing I showed up instead of the guys in leisure suits from my entrance exam.

I learned every investigative trick, technique, and device anyone would show me, gathering the tools like a magician stocking his trick bag. Benny even taught me the power of prayer, which I used on one occasion to lure a bank embezzler to redemption. We brought out the whole family and sat in a circle holding hands and singing hymns until the recalcitrant sinner confessed and joined me in my Bucar for a little pilgrimage to the federal penitentiary.

I developed informants from all walks of life: skid row

bums, business leaders, long haul truckers, former felons, and upstanding members of the community. Anyone who could provide information of value to my investigations seemed like fair game.

Some of them helped out for a few extra bucks. Some helped out because they loved the intrigue of wearing a wire or playing secret agent. Some helped out because they felt it was the right thing to do. Whatever their reasoning, I thanked them for their assistance and tucked their intelligence into file jackets, spawning cases, arrests, and convictions.

All this work brought a gut-deep confidence in my own abilities. Whether executing a high-risk dope raid at three in the morning or introducing myself to a victim teller in a bank robbery, I felt self-assured in ways I'd never imagined. Part of this comfort came from carrying a gun. Part came with the considerable power of an FBI badge. But most of it sprang directly from a fundamental trust in the organization.

I believed in the FBI and its righteousness the way some people cling to religion. If Title 18, U.S. Code, said it was bad, I knew it was bad. If the FBI Manual of Investigative and Operational Guidelines said it was right, I knew it was right. The FBI stood for certainty, from evidence collection to rules on use of government vehicles. I felt part of some directed, uncompromisable good. That made me strong by association.

FBI agents work two basic types of investigations: cases opened inside the office, and "leads," which are basically just requests for assistance from other offices. Most agents consider leads a nuisance, because they seldom amount to more than a dead-end interview or a records check. On top of that, they take time away from your own cases.

I had just returned from the U.S. Attorney's Office one afternoon when a lead of a whole new color came down from the Kansas City office. Just a couple days earlier, a Kansas City IRS agent, his wife, and one of their daughters had been killed. The daughter had been raped, then savagely beaten to death with a homemade mace. The parents were killed when they came home from work.

Because of the extreme violence of the crime and the IRS involvement, every media outlet in the city had turned out in force, making this one of the highest-profile crimes in recent history. Kansas City metro had quickly narrowed its suspects to the family's adopted daughter and her unemployed boyfriend, an Olathe County doper named Bobby Matthews. They swore out warrants and arrested the daughter, but Matthews had disappeared. Assuming he'd fled interstate, they requested assistance from the FBI, which dedicated a large task force of agents to finding him. Early investigation determined that his ex-wife lived in one of my counties, and they wanted me to see what I could find out.

I tracked Bobby's ex, a soft-spoken young woman, to her parents' house in Buffalo, Missouri. She hadn't seen him in some time, she said, but he had called the previous day and told her he had screwed up. He wanted to talk in person.

Whatever relationship they'd shared had cooled considerably, but she consented because of the tone in his voice. She knew this was serious.

I never got comfortable trusting wives, girlfriends, ex–love interests, or mothers with information about suspects, but Matthews's ex-wife seemed genuinely willing to help. Her parents insisted that they wanted nothing to do with him. Everyone seemed afraid of this guy, and no one seemed surprised about the allegations. She and her family agreed to lure him to their house later that night on the condition that we intercept him before he entered. Eugene Brodie agreed, dedicating the whole office to the job of setting up a surveillance, protecting the family, and planning Matthews's arrest.

Just after dark, seven of us arrived in two of the least official-looking cars in the fleet. Eugene sat with the family inside their house while the rest of us established a perimeter, cleared fields of fire, and positioned one of the cars to block his escape once he turned into the driveway. I slipped a thirty-round magazine into a semiautomatic MP-5 submachine gun, pulled a level-three bulletproof vest over a hooded sweatshirt, and crawled into an outer layer of black clothing. Brad, Al, and I found hiding spots around the house in case he tried to sneak in. Benny hunkered down in the blocking vehicle in case we needed wheels in a hurry.

And we waited. That's the scourge of law enforcement work. The waiting. Bad guys don't follow schedules. Whenever an informant set up a ten o'clock meeting, he'd get to it around midnight. Set up on a midnight truck hijacking and the thieves would show up at three if they ever showed up at all. I began to swear by Benny's one-in-ten rule that postulated a 10 percent chance of anything ever happening the way it was supposed to.

Matthews's 9:00 P.M. appointment came and went without so much as a barking dog. An hour passed as we sat out under the flat Missouri skies, then another and another. No phone call, no headlights, no surprise knock on the door. By 2:00 A.M., we invoked the one-in-ten rule and called it a night.

Perhaps the most difficult thing for me to learn about casework was that FBI investigations often take a long, long time. When I graduated from the Academy, I fully anticipated wrapping up every crime by the end of the day so I wouldn't have to lose sleep worrying about loose ends. I just assumed that once we got wind of a felony, we'd dedicate our lives to the investigation, working nonstop until we hooked the bad guys up and put them in jail. Wrong.

By and large, FBI investigations take months or even years to complete. Local cops can produce a search warrant with a phone call, but federal affidavits rarely turn into warrants in less than a twelve-hour day. Metro police departments can arrest someone because they don't like the color of his hair. Bureau agents have to obsess over every detail, elevating their evidence to the higher standard of a federal grand jury. This doesn't imply that local and state investigations produce questionable convictions; federal cases simply require investigators to jump through a much longer course of hoops.

I suspected pretty quickly that the Bobby Matthews investigation wouldn't fall into the quick-wrap category. Eugene assigned me the case and told me to put everything else on hold until I developed some decent leads. That sounded like music to my ears, because nothing in my life excited me as much as an armed-and-dangerous fugitive hanging just out of reach. Searching for buried treasure would have carried no greater thrill. Catching this son of a bitch became my personal mission in life.

Early the next morning, I picked up the ex at her parents' house and drove twenty miles out into the country to visit the old in-laws. We talked on the way about Matthews's past, his hobbies and aspirations and interests. Other than an occasional bottle of Jack Daniel's, his goals seemed limited to whatever household chemical he could inhale to get high. Qualities like shiftless, drunk, worthless, and scary popped up quite a bit in our conversation. When I asked about how she got involved with him, I got the familiar shoulder shrug and "No idea."

"What about his family?" I asked.

I'd already given the issue considerable thought, but wanted to run it by her just the same. Confronting the family usually ends up a last-ditch effort to scare a fugitive out of hiding, but in this dramatically violent murder case, I felt comfortable appealing to their sense of dignity.

If that failed, I'd fall back on the "please have him surrender to us before the locals kill him" appeal. Moms don't want to turn out their sons, but they don't want them lying dead at the edge of some farm road, either.

"His family's worse than he is," she lamented. "White trash." She shook her head again, embarrassed that she'd ever gotten involved with any of them.

"Will they talk to me?" I asked.

"They'll talk to you, but they won't tell you where he's at."

"What about his brother?"

Kansas City authorities had already tracked his only sibling to a trailer right next to the parents' place.

"He might, but he's strange," she said.

"Strange? What do you mean, strange?"

She started to smile.

"What do you mean?" I asked again. "Strange" in this occupation could mean a lot of things from a personality quirk to a proclivity for serial murder.

"He's just kind of different." She started to giggle now. I'd barely seen a smile on her face since we met, yet something about her former brother-in-law struck her funny.

"Look, I've got to talk this guy into helping me find his murdering, raping, fugitive brother," I explained. "Strange could get me killed. If you know something that might help, I'd sure appreciate you telling me. Is he dangerous?"

"Might be if you was a dog." The giggle became a laugh.

"A dog?"

"Yeah, he likes dogs . . . you know, in a sexual way."

Oh, that kind of strange.

I met his girlfriend, a seventy-five-pound Doberman bitch chained to a stake in the front yard of his trailer. Derek leaned into the engine compartment of a '67 El Camino sporting racing mags and a factory 427. The Bondo and primer finish complemented his tattered coveralls.

Cindy introduced me as the FBI and Derek never missed a beat. Though not long on basic intelligence, he understood my intentions. He nodded at me and returned to his attempt at prying a four-barrel carburetor from the massive V-8.

"Ain't seen him" was all he'd say.

"Ma home?" she asked. Derek sort of shrugged toward the trailer.

I don't want to poke fun at those less fortunate than myself, but I had to shake my head and smile at the scene around me. From Derek's four-legged love interest to the half-dozen General Motors products jacked up on blocks around the yard to the dilapidated mobile home, the Matthews estate lived up to all the worst Ozarks stereotypes. Garbage lay strewn about the yard, spilling out of black Hefty bags, with egg cartons, coffee filters, Budweiser cans, and aluminum TV dinner trays glistening in the morning sun. The place smelled of dogshit, crankcase fluid, and despair.

Cindy knocked on the torn screen door. I waited off to the side, suspecting my suit and tie might scare anyone who came to answer.

"Morning, ma'am," she said, betraying more than a little distance. "I got the FBI with me here. They want to find Bobby before the sheriff kills him."

I winced a bit at the introduction. Opening with that sort

of consequence leaves little room for leverage down the line. It also tends to escalate any sense of misgiving a parent might feel toward law enforcement. Murdering rapist or not, Bobby still entered this world through great pain and effort from this woman. She wouldn't give him up lightly.

Surprisingly, she invited us inside and offered a glass of sweet tea. I stood near the door, partly because of my last experience looking for an armed-and-dangerous fugitive in a trailer house, and partly because of the stench. The only reason garbage littered the front yard was because there was no more room for it inside. If not for the brand-new thirty-six-inch television blaring the Phil Donahue show, I would have sworn we'd taken a wrong turn into the county landfill.

The door opened into a single large space that seemed to quiver with ill-defined life. I counted five cats, two sleeping dogs, and a vaguely human figure reclining in a tattered La-Z-Boy. So many flies filled the air, they sounded like the static you get from bad reception. Discarded clothing, food scraps, beer cans, and the detritus of rotting lives gave the place an aura that almost made me gag.

"Sit down," the woman said, pointing to what once might have been a settee off to my right. The fabric had stiffened with years of spilled food and sweat.

She handed me the tea in a Tupperware glass and crossed in front of me to a couch on the other side of the room. I started to take a drink until I noticed that someone had chewed all around the edges of the cup like the stopper end of a Bic pen. At that moment, I felt like I'd entered the scene in *Papillon* where Steve McQueen takes the cigar from the leper.

Oh, well. I did what I had to do, and drank from the chewed cup. Then I moved toward the couch and tried to focus on the matter at hand. Visions of Derek entertaining his canine date on the couch invaded my thought process as I pushed aside a purple velvet pillow embroidered with a map of North Vietnam on one side and "Death don't scare me, I've already done my time in Hell: Da Nang, 1968" on the other. What the heck, I thought, I'd risked worse than skin infections for the opportunity to make an arrest.

"Watch your step," she warned. I looked down at a two-foot hole dropping through the tobacco-colored shag right down to the good old Missouri clay.

"That's good tea, Mrs. Matthews," I said, trying not to think about what the glass had been through. I sat on the edge of the couch, trying to save a dry cleaning bill. "Now about Bobby. We've got to get this thing straightened out before it gets any worse."

Three hours later, after enduring the family photo album, stories about her oldest boy's few redeeming qualities, and an overwhelming need for a shower, I stood up to leave. Bobby's mom knew approximately where her son had run off to, but she wouldn't tell me until she'd had a chance to talk with him. She swore up and down, like any mother would, that he'd done nothing wrong, but she knew what waited for him if he didn't surrender, and the thought of reading about his violent death in the *Springfield News Leader* left her visibly shaken. The three of us set up a plan to try and convince Bobby to call me and talk over his options. I agreed not to trace the call and promised a safe arrest if he turned himself in to the FBI. Mrs. Matthews promised that Bobby would call later that night.

"I raised that boy up right," she said. "It was them drugs that fucked him all up."

"I'm sure you did the best you could, ma'am," I agreed.

Bobby called me at my home late the next day. We talked on the phone three different times, covering just about every aspect of his sad life. I'd heard stories like his a hundred times. The details change, but the net result is always the same. People who commit heinous crimes can't really admit to what they did, so they rationalize their actions, project blame on others, and minimize their involvement. At first Bobby claimed he didn't remember, but then admitted that his girlfriend hated her adoptive parents and the stepsister who taunted her with good looks, the right friends, and a biological connection to the two people they both called Mom and Dad. Bobby didn't know the stepsister, but realized he could never have someone with her social connections.

Shortly after his girlfriend concocted a plan, he converted his distaste for bloody murder to a lusty appreciation for rape. He stopped by Home Depot on the way to the house and bought a two-by-four and a pound of six-penny nails. He drove the nails through the plank, waited for the sixteen-year-old sister to get home from school, and spent the afternoon high in a cloud of cheap vodka, pot, and violent sex. When he'd had enough, he beat the girl to death with the homemade mace.

None of the skills or lessons I'd learned at the Academy helped reel him in. I just listened. Like Benny said, people will tell you anything if you give them the chance.

Bobby surrendered two days later, outside a 7-Eleven in Tucson, Arizona. He emerged around the corner looking like everyone else in the busy strip mall, squinting against the sun.

Agents from the Tucson office jumped out of several cars, guns drawn, and splayed him out on the pavement. One of my classmates from the Academy ratcheted on the cuffs as I sat back and watched.

That's how I learned the hard way that agents from one FBI division do not fly into another division to make an arrest. Regardless of Bobby's stipulation that he surrender only to the man he'd come to trust with his life, I'd violated Tucson's sovereignty. I could ride along, but Bobby was their collar.

After they'd cuffed him, I walked over to him and introduced myself.

"Hello, Bobby. I'm Chris Whitcomb."

"Thought you promised to do this yourself, you asshole."

There at my feet lay a bona fide, world-class, cold-blooded killer. A vicious rapist. Scum.

I wanted him to spring to his feet and try to run away so I could stop him myself, kick his teeth down his smartass throat for ruining the lives of everyone he'd ever rubbed up against. I wanted to inflict some of the torment he'd visited on that family, watch him beg for mercy, his life ebbing with each delirious blow as I showed him what it feels like to die an empty, powerless, meaningless death. I wanted to watch his eyes filling up with the horrifying realization that nothing he could do would stop the pain. I wanted him to suffer. I wanted him to pay.

But in that same moment of rising bile, I realized what gave me the right to carry a gun and a badge. I was not like this guy. Hate infects — good people, bad people. It turns soccer moms into road-raging maniacs. It takes a man coming out of church with a fresh perspective on the week and makes him swear at someone for singing with a bad voice.

Authority means more than carrying a loaded gun everywhere you go. It means learning restraint, understanding the primal urges that prompt some men to kill.

Most of all, it means respecting the difference between right and wrong that brought you here to begin with. I knew hate as well as anyone, but I could also draw the line and not step over to where it owned me.

"Sorry, Bobby," I said. "It's time to go to jail." For life, as it turned out.

He was still wearing the Dunham hiking boots he'd used to kick in the girl's skull. Blood had stained the suede a darker brown.

6

CODE THREE

Every first office agent dreams of stumbling into his first "big case," that soul-tapping test of ability that adds a couple character lines to your face and defines a career. A few come over the transom in the form of legitimate complaints. Others come from informants who sober up between cash payments, strap on a wire, and dance in among their cohort of thieves. Once in a while the big cases grow out of those small, seemingly insignificant complaints like alleys off a dimly lit street.

Springfield didn't really have that sort of thing. What it did offer was an opportunity to try on just about every hat in the FBI wardrobe. Though my Academy classmates sometimes got stuck in dark rooms listening to wires, or pigeonholed on long national security surveillances, I got a run at just about anything I wanted to try. After a few months, I decided that my future lay in violent-crime investigations: bank robberies, kidnappings, fugitives. Eugene rewarded my enthusiasm by making me bank robbery coordinator and shoveling most of the bigger cases onto my plate.

Reactive work thrilled me. Since childhood I had always loved puzzles, being presented with a set of circumstances and the assumption that someone else thought himself more clever than me. I loved crosswords, acrostics, word games, brain twisters, anything I could find that piqued my problem-solving ability. Bank robberies and fugitive investigations seemed like a grand challenge, offering a closed set of circumstances and unfettered access to all the clues.

Fortunately, bank robbers aren't the brightest stars in the criminal firmament. I have often wondered why someone would risk ten years in prison to walk into a building full of cameras and witnesses, grab a bag full of marked bills and a dye pack, then tempt the investigative will of the world's most sophisticated law enforcement agency. It made a whole lot more sense to stand on the street corner holding a "Will work for food" placard.

Maybe that's why I felt a visceral rush every time a bank robbery call passed from Ruth's lips through my Bucar's encrypted radio speaker and into my ears. I knew I could catch them.

The adrenaline that came with a blue-light-and-siren response meant nothing compared to the sense of anticipation I savored for the investigation. Every time some moron risked his life to steal a couple thousand dollars, I took it as a personal attack on the integrity of the FBI.

So when Ruth fielded a bank alarm one June morning from the Dallas County, Missouri, sheriff's office, I jumped in my car and headed north. Information usually comes only sporadically during the early moments after a bank robbery. Witnesses need time to decompress. The locals need time to secure the crime scene. In this case, the FBI needed time to get there.

Traffic seemed light that morning as I sped north on Route 65, flipping through local frequencies trying to pick up radio traffic on possible getaway vehicles. I peered into every car that passed me, looking at the driver and passengers for telltale signs of a blown dye pack or mussed hair, indicating a mask. This proved pretty tough running eighty miles an hour, loading rounds into my Remington shotgun with one hand, talking on the radio with the other, and steering with my knee. Tom Devreaux had made it look much easier than it actually was.

By the time I rolled in to the First National Bank of Buffalo forty-five minutes later, three marked sheriff's units had already secured the scene and started dusting for prints. That's usually the way we worked. Due to our lack of manpower, the locals typically processed and collected evidence, then handed it and the witness interviews over to us. Armed robbery is a local offense, of course, but federally insured banks suffer a federal loss, and that makes the recovery an FBI issue. Besides, bank robbers are often serial criminals who move from one town or state to another, trying to outrun the law. Lots of local agencies simply don't have jurisdiction or resources to chase felons outside their city or county limits.

I gathered the basic facts pretty quickly: two white males wearing camouflage hunting masks had walked up to the front door, blown it away with a load of 12-gauge buckshot, then terrorized two female tellers before making off with about $3,700 in cash. Unfortunately, the bank's video camera was down for service and the robbers came in so violently and quickly, the tellers hadn't had the opportunity to hand out exploding dye packs.

So far we had no prints, fibers, or eyewitness details on a

getaway route. Other than the two 12-gauge hulls lying in a pile of shattered glass, and a missing bank deposit bag, we had almost nothing to chase. The bank sat just off the main road, but I saw no homes or businesses within a mile to the north or south. If I were a bank robber, I would have licked my chops over a place like this.

I had just finished interviewing a badly shaken teller when the phone rang. One of the neighbors, nearly a mile east, had just found a man lying on her front lawn, the caller said. He looked beaten, confused, and perilously close to heatstroke. They'd called an ambulance, but he wanted to talk to the FBI; something about being kidnapped early that morning outside the Bank of Buffalo.

By the time I got there, an ambulance crew had hung an IV bag and moved him into the shade. The man refused transfer to the hospital until he talked to someone in law enforcement and I happened to be the first badge on-scene. He told me his name and that he was all right, speaking in short, halting breaths. His enormous gut rose and fell as he lay there, a massive, sweat-stained hulk of a man, prostrate beneath the wrinkling heat of a southwest Missouri summer.

"Two men," he wheezed. "Said they was going to kill me."

Tears welled up in his porcine eyes.

"Where?" I asked. "Where'd they attack you?"

That mattered for a couple of reasons. One: Kidnapping in commission of another felony could as much as double the sentence on conviction. Two: We might have a separate crime scene that could yield evidence such as footprints and tire markings.

"Outside the bank. I was just setting there . . ." He paused to catch his breath and fight back memories of the awful experience.

I let him collect himself. Witnesses often need time to process information that gets pushed to the sides of their consciousness due to a "trauma spike." They recall everything back to a certain point but have to work hard to pierce the cloud of adrenaline, fear, and disorientation that comes with having your morning interrupted by a shotgun muzzle in your face.

". . . They stuck me in the trunk and drove me out into the woods. There's no room in my trunk. I kept praying they wouldn't leave me to die. I got three kids."

He started to sob, quietly, embarrassed that I was watching.

"I could hear them talking about killing me. I could hear them standing outside, arguing over whether or not to blow my head off."

"Would you recognize their voices?" I asked.

"Maybe . . . yeah, I guess. They sounded like everybody."

❖

From there, the investigation went like most other bank jobs in the early stages — nowhere. Unless you find something right off the bat, things slow down to the point of frustration within a few days. The most intriguing crime scene can turn into just another note in your file if you don't stay after it. With thirty or forty cases tugging at your attention, a dead end can just fade away.

Because of the violence, though, I worked this case a little harder than most. I spent the first week running through the checklist of interviews and drive-bys. My informants had heard nothing on the street. Neighbors saw nothing unusual the morning of the crime. Newspaper stories generated nothing of interest. Our national bank robbery index showed no other crimes with similar M.O. Nobody called the office looking for a reward in return for information.

With no promising leads left, I turned to my buddies at the Springfield Police Department. No matter what credit the FBI takes for its triumphs, almost all successful agents have someone in local law enforcement to thank. Beat cops, task force members, homicide investigators, and detectives work the underworld a whole lot more than most agents do, and they know where to look for the day in, day out criminals who cloud civilization.

"Got to be the Jenks boys," a Springfield police detective named Steve Davis told me over a plate of cashew chicken at lunch one day. "Billy and James. I got everything you want to know about 'em back in the office."

Billy and James Jenks are living proof that not all of humanity is descended from a common ancestor. From rap sheet to reputation, they showed lineage directly to the rodent genus. People like these brothers drift at the edges of society, confounding sociologists and bleeding-heart liberals who want so badly to believe that criminals are all basically good people.

Bullshit. James and Billy would lie when the truth suited them better. They had done time for the kidnapping and rape of a woman they pulled off the street in broad daylight. At trial, James testified that he never actually raped the woman; Billy had done all the raping. James was just sitting in the car getting high. When Billy got a little too rough, though, James pulled him off and beat the piss out of him for his trouble. The woman was so grateful to James, he said, she took him off into the bushes and had sex with him voluntarily. He actually testified to that in front of a jury.

James looked handsome enough that he could have had all the women he wanted without resorting to violent abduction. Though only about 5'8", he carried broad shoulders on an athletic body and wore a rugged confidence, like a prize-fighter. One tragically beautiful eighteen-year-old girlfriend of his told me about how she used to go into bars with James and pick up middle-aged men. She'd take them to some dark parking lot and start blowing them as James crept up with a lead sap in his hand. James got to beat the hell out of the "dates" while she watched, then they'd take the money, buy some meth, rent a room, and party. She spoke of their evenings together with fondness.

"James is hard to understand for most people," she told me. "He's a little bit scary, you know? Like death."

Armed robbery, assault, rape, even allegations of murder followed the Jenks boys around like a bad scent. It was simply a matter of time before James and Billy killed someone, and I knew I couldn't let that happen.

Finding your first positive lead in a case is a wonderful moment. It's like playing I Spy when you're a kid and getting that big clue. A hunch from a local cop is a lukewarm place to start, but it's a start just the same. Where you take it from that point on is what makes you worth your paycheck.

I started with the basics: phone book for numbers and addresses, public utilities records to find out who paid the bills and how often, Department of Motor Vehicles printouts for driver's license data and registration records, NCIC (National Crime Information Center) indices for arrest warrants, rap sheets for prior convictions. Both men had prior convictions and jail time for violent crime, but no outstanding warrants.

After tracking down virtually every detail on public record, I decided to make the customary drive-by. James and his wife, Becky, lived with their three kids in a run-down duplex ten miles west of Springfield. Billy lived in a two-room rambler in the West End. Neither neighborhood provided decent prospects for long-term surveillance.

Next, I looked at the family for weak links. Sometimes a criminal stands out from his kin as an anomaly. Some families actually cooperate with authorities, hoping it will get their son or brother or husband the help he needs.

Not the Jenks tribe. What I found in their family tree looked more like *missing* links than weak links. James and Billy were violent, brutal men raised by a mother who kept their alcoholic father in a shed behind the house. Eldridge, her oldest son, tried to beat a rape sentence by killing his dad's drinking buddy, then burning his body and using it to fake his own death. He might have gotten away with it except that the stand-in was too skinny to burn well.

Armed robbery, murder, kidnapping, rape — these guys read like pulp fiction.

Unfortunately, I wasn't the first to hear about their taste for mayhem. It seemed like every snitch in town knew about the Jenks brothers, and no one would talk about them. When I finally convinced one of my least credible sources that he needed to help me more than he needed to go back to jail, he pointed to a possible chink in James's armor. His wife.

Becky and James shared a fairy tale romance, from the way he showered her with crystal meth to the way she helped him steal. I could see how he must have attracted her, once upon a time, the way he attracted other women, with his bad boy arrogance. The fact that she came from a decent family didn't matter. Her parents had done everything they could to save her, but it hadn't worked. Once she started hacking paint (inhaling the fumes), it was downhill all the way.

I followed her to the Chestnut Expressway one morning. I had already asked more questions in close circles than I could expect to get away with. She and James didn't know much about me, but they had to know I was after them.

So, when morning traffic lightened up, I decided to pull her over in a public place to give her an out. If anyone she knew happened by, she could tell them I was just a cop in an unmarked unit writing her up for speeding.

Once I hit my siren and bubble light, she pulled off immediately. I parked behind her, checked for tails, and climbed out into the August sun.

My heart pounded. I'd been waiting more than a month for this moment. Sometimes an entire case comes down to the way you make an introduction, and I wanted so badly not to blow this one.

"Treat 'em all like human beings," I could hear Big Al telling me. "You start talking strong with these people and you're going to bleed a lot."

That advice seemed strange coming from the man who taught me how to kick down doors and make open-field tackles. Then again, that advice had already saved my life at least once. Just a couple weeks earlier Big Al and I had tracked an old-dog fugitive named Johnny Billieau to a rural trailer in Taney County. An informant told us that Johnny had contacted his family after several years on the run, but no one knew whether or not he'd actually returned for a reunion. We decided to try his estranged wife and found her entertaining six or eight other family members in her living room. Big Al covered the rear door just in case, while I went inside for a little chat.

"Hi, I'm Chris Whitcomb with the FBI," I said. "You probably know why we're here."

The answer looked obvious in all their faces, but true to form, they denied any knowledge of Johnny. I looked down the hallway for signs of life, but we had no search warrant and couldn't legally take the thing past conversation.

We finally caught Johnny later in the day and threw him into the back of Al's car for the long trip home. Since UFAP warrants involve no investigation, other than turning the fugitive back over to local authorities, we never questioned him. For whatever reason, though, he started talking as we drove, recounting some of the very words I had used on his family in his wife's living room.

"How the hell did you know that?" I asked. Somebody in his family must have had a damned good memory.

"I knew because I was standing on the other side of the wall with a pump shotgun in my hand, waiting to blow your fucking head off," he said, flashing a four-tooth smile.

"Why didn't you?" I asked, trying to cover my surprise.

"'Cause you din't talk me down in front of my kids," he said. "I din't want 'em to see me shoot you when you gave me no cause."

That taught me plenty about basic decency. To a very large extent, working the Missouri Breaks involved more bullshitting than gunfighting. If necessary, we could yank out the shotguns and the MP-5s and call in the SWAT boys from Kansas City. But when it came to chasing down leads, weaseling confessions, and solving cases, a little conversation went a long, long way.

"Hi, Becky," I said when she rolled down her window and held out her hand for the expired-license ticket. "I'm Chris Whitcomb. I think it's time we talked."

Becky Jenks stared at me the length of time it took her dope-rotted mind to recognize my name, then she broke down in tears. As tough as she had become, Becky didn't want to spend the next ten years in a federal penitentiary. I don't think she would have missed her kids, but meth would be a lot harder to come by.

Looking into her swollen, bloodshot eyes, I realized my timing couldn't have been much better. James had obviously just beaten the living hell out of her. He and his brothers were violent, brutal men. Even the local cops spoke of James with respect.

"Fair fight . . ." one of them told me, explaining an ill-conceived test of manhood during a drunk-driving arrest one night. "The bastard kicked my ass. Better watch him. He's stout."

What I saw in Becky's purple face did little to impress me with James's fighting skills. As I heard it, James had come home in a drunken rage the night before after learning that Becky had screwed one of his pool buddies for a couple lines of coke. To teach her a lesson, he knocked her down, dragged her into the bathroom, and beat her like a mongrel dog. Just to make sure the lesson wouldn't be lost on future generations, he dragged his three kids in to watch.

Judging from what I saw in front of me, he must have spent some time on the lesson. Becky's nose looked broken, her face all lumpy.

"Where you want to do this?" she asked. Tears stuck in her throat as she tried to pronounce the words. Her lower lip cracked open and began to bleed.

"Follow me," I said. "We don't want James to cause you any more trouble."

Over the next two months, Becky worked just about as faithfully as any other snitch. When James treated her nicely and bought her drugs, she helped him. When he beat her or the kids, she came to me. Ultimately, it was the kids who made her give him up. It's always the kids who suffer most; always the kids who end up lost in the process of courts and family services and long nights fending for themselves, alone.

I'll never forget the time I arrested a bank robber in his house with his wife and their three boys. We swarmed the place with a dozen local, state, and federal officers, but I was the one who actually had to throw Daddy over the La-Z-Boy and wrestle on the cuffs. I got him to his feet while Big Al dealt with the screaming wife and the other guys searched for guns, money, and evidence of the crime. Typical deal, until we started toward the door with our subject. Suddenly his five-year-old leaped at me like a pit bull, grabbed hold of my leg, and started screaming.

"Leave my daddy alone!" he cried. "Don't you hurt my daddy!"

I had to peel a five-year-old child off my leg. Little-boy tears poured out of his eyes as he stared at me with a hatred deep as any full-grown man's. I remembered what it felt like all those years earlier when three agents came to talk to my own dad. What would my boys think if it were me being pushed through the door at gunpoint?

Kids never understand. They just lose.

Becky must have thought about that herself, because her kids eventually saved her. The final straw fell during the last week of December, when I met her and the kids with a couple gifts. Everyone in the family knew me at that point. The two who could talk called me by my first name, like an old family friend.

"So did you kids have a nice Christmas?" I asked them. Jared, the oldest of the three, shook his head back and forth, exaggerating the gesture.

"Nah. That Grammy Jenks just had to go and ruin Christmas again this year," he said. He spoke like the head of the family. He was seven. "Tried to waste Mom with Toad's twelve-gauge."

Nothing surprised me at that point, except the calm in his voice. He was used to this sort of thing.

It turned out that Grammy Jenks did, in fact, spoil Christmas. She almost spoiled Becky, too, along with the floor, and the rest of the trailer. The family had gathered to open presents at the home of James's sister — a woman they called Toad. Becky somehow pissed off her mother-in-law as the kids sat around the Christmas tree opening presents. So the old woman stomped back to her bedroom, grabbed a pump shotgun, and proceeded to blow holes in the place, trying to waste the kids' mom under the mistletoe. So much for Yuletide spirit.

According to Becky, the old woman got three rounds off before James convinced her to drop the gun. Christmas at my house seemed a little boring by comparison.

"Becky, this has got to end," I argued. Even a paint hacker ought to be able to see the light of reason after dodging 12-gauge slugs around the Christmas tree.

"I know," she said. It was difficult to tell whether she was referring to her marriage or the robberies. I didn't really care, because James was coming off the street either way.

"If he finds out about this, he'll kill me," she said.

Her look cut deep. Despite our cooperation to this point, she didn't trust me any more than she trusted him. Probably a lot less. Becky was a junkie, and James gave her dope. My only leverage was that I usually visited on days when the welts on her face hurt a little more than the craving in her arm.

"Look, Becky," I said, trying to drive home a point with logic, "he's hit three banks in the last month. It's a miracle that nobody's been killed."

For some reason that made her smile.

"He is a crazy motherfucker, ain't he," she said.

Why so many women found that endearing I'll never know.

❖

The next week, while I was back at Quantico for some in-service training, James and Billy hit a bank in Christian

County. I never found out for sure if Becky told them I was gone, but the timing struck me as a little odd. Regardless, they attacked a small bank out in the country with their trademark shotgun blast through the front door. They so badly traumatized the sixty-seven-year-old teller, she couldn't respond to investigators' questions.

Nobody found anything surprising about the operation. James and Billy stuck to what they knew and wasted little time on creativity.

Solely because the breaks eventually had to roll our way, Big Al happened to be just a mile east when the robbery occurred. Within half an hour, he and a couple local cops had tracked down the getaway car and recovered enough evidence to bring the whole thing crashing down. By the time I rushed back from Quantico, they had obtained arrest warrants, followed James to his brother's house, and pulled a felony car stop worthy of any action movie. Ma Jenks was in the car with James when they took him down.

Our guys found a .32-caliber automatic in Ma's purse, cocked and locked, but she never made a move for it. James gave up without a fight.

As soon as my plane touched down in a slow Missouri drizzle, I raced over to the U.S. Attorney's Office to begin setting up the prosecution. Though Al had gathered enough evidence to make an excellent case, we still had a lot of work left to do. Witnesses had to be interviewed and shown photo lineups for solid identification. Laboratory reports had to be compiled, exhibits prepared, documents turned over to the public defender's office. I'd been to trial almost a dozen times already, and knew the next month would bring lots of very long nights. Solving the crime is just the beginning. Taking the case to court is a whole separate process.

Fortunately, Becky handed up details on where they stashed the money, how they stole getaway vehicles, and when they planned out the jobs. She refused to testify in court, but that didn't really matter. We stacked up enough evidence to make the U.S. Attorney's Office dance in circles. After almost a year of chasing Southwest Missouri's most prolific bank robbers, we had them by the short hairs.

A week later, I had just finished Xeroxing my final prosecutive report when the Greene County sheriff's office called to throw us a curve. James had escaped. It happened during a morning exercise session, when he somehow scaled the yard wall, crawled through triple-thickness concertina wire, and jumped twenty feet to the ground outside. Guards held their fire, fearing they might hit a nearby office building. By the time they raced outside, he was gone.

Here we go again, I thought. Billy was still a fugitive at that point. It made sense that he'd help arrange an escape. They were probably already halfway to Wichita.

Most of our office showed up within minutes. Deputies found a blood trail reaching from the car James had landed on to a grassy lawn across the street. If Billy had picked him up, we reasoned, it wasn't near the jail.

Dozens of law enforcement personnel joined the manhunt. Local media broadcast bulletins, warning nearby residents to lock their doors. James and Billy Jenks had become desperadoes of considerable import by then, and no one underestimated the potential for further bloodshed.

The Missouri Highway Patrol brought in K-9s to follow the blood trail. Didn't work.

The Springfield Police Department scrambled its fledgling SWAT team. Uniformed officers locked down twenty square blocks around the jail.

I reached into my trunk for an MP-5, a bulletproof vest,

and a raid jacket. Screw Eugene's distaste for firepower, I thought. James had proven himself violent enough to merit precaution.

Four hours later, amid the largest manhunt anyone could remember, a small boy hurried into his house to tell his baby-sitter there was a man hiding in an old refrigerator box out in the garage. The man was bleeding and he wanted a glass of milk.

Greene County deputies sent dogs into the garage after him, and helped James consider the efficacy of escape in a whole new light. By dinnertime, they had transported him to the Springfield Medical Center for Federal Prisoners, a maximum security correctional institution just three miles away. He'd sustained serious cuts going through the wire and a badly broken leg in the fall, but he had still managed to run half a mile and evade arrest for several hours. Nobody ever figured out how the hell he made it up and over the exercise yard wall.

The trial went fairly smoothly. A tall, meticulous Assistant U.S. Attorney (AUSA) named Mike Johnson prepared the government's case with the care usually reserved for mobsters and serial killers. He dotted every "i" and crossed every "t," knowing full well that conviction in a case this high-profile was the only option.

It barely fazed Mike when the judge moved the case an hour west to Joplin, Missouri, acknowledging the defense team's argument that publicity made a fair trial in Springfield unlikely. Our case seemed strong, from physical evidence to circumstantial. The jury looked reasonable, with the exception of a heavyset woman in rose-colored glasses who passed James salacious looks all day. By the end of the first full session, the jury actually seemed disgusted with the whole sordid story.

James's lawyers did their best, considering what they

had to work with. They came up with a last-minute alibi, but we shot it down quickly. It seemed that Toad had never heard of perjury. As soon as she realized that we had her trapped in the lie, she changed her mind and magically disappeared from the defense's witness list. Ma testified, but she made such a complete fool of herself, you could see several people on the jury actually shaking their heads in disgust.

Against his lawyers' advice, but to no one's surprise, James insisted on taking the stand. Testifying on one's own behalf can have its advantages, of course. Jurors really want to hear someone take a sworn oath and say "I didn't do it." But testifying also carries a downside, in that it allows prosecutors the opportunity to introduce things they'd never get in otherwise — important factors like criminal history, motive, and even some evidence are inadmissible unless brought up with the defendant on the stand.

In James's case, testifying seemed like a grave miscalculation. As soon as he took the stand, the AUSA leveled him with questions about previous arrests, including the abduction/rape and other violent offenses. Throughout, James talked with the same bad boy arrogance that made him popular with ill-bred women.

This time it didn't work. When he testified that he couldn't have robbed the bank because he was somewhere in Kansas passed out in the trunk of his car after an all-night bender, two jurors laughed out loud. When he offered up his lame story about intervening in Billy's rape party, one of James's attorneys actually started to cry. I had to clench my teeth to keep from cheering him on. Though our case seemed strong, we couldn't have presented anything as damning as James's own words.

I testified myself, for what seemed like forever. The defense tried to attack virtually every step I'd taken during the entire investigation. I simply told the jury in plain language what I had done and how I had done it. Four years of testifying in criminal trials had taught me an important lesson: Nothing a defense attorney can use to trip up a witness will change the truth. James Jenks was guilty and all I had to do was point to the evidence.

Al testified. Benny testified. Brad testified. We brought in experts from the laboratory in Washington to match glass found in James's car with glass from the scene. Eyewitnesses, fingerprint experts, ballistics experts, other investigators. The case felt seamless.

Then, when all the talking had ended, the case went to the jury. An hour went by. Then two. No problem, we figured. It takes a while just to read the judge's instructions. Another hour of deliberations. Two more. Dinner. Recess for the night.

What the hell is this all about? I wondered. James had no legitimate defense.

Wait a minute. What about the girl in the rose-colored glasses? Had James gotten through to her? Wouldn't be the first time. Many court cases are won or lost before the first witness takes the stand, simply with jury selection. You never know what a jury is going to do. Sometimes you throw them an airtight case and they toss it right back in your face. Sometimes you float a real loser and they bite. You just don't know. All it takes to hang up a verdict is one sympathetic juror. Maybe that was our problem, we speculated. Maybe James had won her over with all his attention from the defense table. Maybe we were in trouble after all.

I shied from thinking about the consequences of a not-guilty verdict. If James got out and hooked back up with Billy, their next job would be vicious. Becky was good as dead. I'd have to watch my back, too. James hated me for turning his family against him.

The next day, deliberations resumed at 9:00. An hour passed. Two more.

We were just leaving for lunch when the bailiff called in with a verdict.

The AUSA and I walked back into the courtroom and took our seats. James and his attorneys found theirs just across the room. James stared at me with a smirk on his face. I tried not to offer him anything more than professionalism, though it was difficult not to laugh at how he'd kept the tailor's tag on the sleeve of his cheap suit. I supposed his family planned to return it as soon as he was done.

My heart began to pound. Of all the things I had experienced in my life as an FBI agent, the one I hated most of all was the suspense before a verdict.

"I can indict a ham sandwich in front of a grand jury," one of the prosecutors once told me, "but proving a case in federal court can be a sonofabitch."

I thought back to my first trial, where a mother had scalded her child to death in a tub of boiling water. Guilty. I relived the second trial, where we put a small-time thief in jail for stealing surplus from a Fort Leonard Wood bombing range. Guilty.

Then there was the bank robbery case we couldn't lose. We had everything but a confession. Not guilty. Jurors told us afterward that we had too much circumstantial evidence. It seemed that one of them had seen on television that circumstantial evidence didn't count. No one on our prosecution team thought to counter that kind of nonsense with truth. I guess we should have thought to offer guidance on the merits of *L.A. Law*.

"Will the defendant please rise." The bailiff prepped the

room for the verdict. James stood, still smirking. He stared at the woman in the pink glasses.

My vision narrowed. All the long nights I'd missed with my family came flashing back. I had two kids under the age of five and could actually count the times I'd tucked them in during the past two months. My wife worked a full-time job and went to graduate school at night. We were virtual strangers.

I thought about the victims James and his brother had traumatized. The man on the lawn, gasping for air, and the tellers working for minimum wage who had to deal with lifetimes of nightmares because he was too fucking lazy to work for a living like the rest of us. I saw his kids — sweet kids who beamed at the simplest kindness. The thought almost made me sick, because I knew they'd grow up just like him. Poor little bastards never had a chance.

"Have you reached a verdict?" the judge asked.

"We have, your honor."

I stared blankly at the wall. There's no place to look at a time like this. The jury doesn't dare look at the defendant. The defendant doesn't dare look at the judge. The prosecution doesn't dare look anything but confident. Everyone is shaking beneath their facade of confidence. There's so much consequence, so much to lose for everyone.

"We find the defendant James Jenks . . ."

Someone always has to lose.

"Guilty."

That day, it wasn't society.

Under federal sentencing guidelines, judges have to assign prison terms within fairly narrow parameters. James's prior offenses and the particularly violent nature of his trade turned the judge against him. Ninety-four months was the sentence; almost eight years of quiet time in Leavenworth Federal Penitentiary. The maximum.

Maybe I should have felt some sort of satisfaction in sending James away, but I didn't. His brother Billy remained a fugitive, and my caseload pulled me right into another frenzy. After four years in the Ozarks, the crime and punishment business had become just that, a business. I felt no glee in putting a man in prison, just an overwhelming familiarity with the loss and sadness he left behind.

Though my colleagues would argue that four years is barely enough time to learn the basics as an FBI agent, I felt hungry for a new challenge. I'd arrested dozens of men and women (including a personal-best three fugitives in one day). I'd sat on Title III wires, laughing at the crazy things people say to each other when they think no one else is listening. Surveillance, search warrants, manhunts, drug raids, file reviews, quarterly firearms qualifications, road trips, cases, cases, cases. My day-to-day life as an investigator still presented the possibility of thrill and challenge, but my mind wandered to the next step, something a little more . . . something different.

I had joined the FBI out of a naive, Norman Rockwell–style sense of righteousness. From my moment of epiphany at the State of the Union speech, I'd wanted to go to bed at night with a sense that I'd played a direct role in making the world a little bit better for my kids and the kids down the street. Instead, I woke up every morning and kissed my wife and kids good-bye, only to spend the day mired in tragedy from the Laclede County line all the way south to the Arkansas border.

I still loved casework, which I saw as the foundation of FBI life, but the sense of accomplishment that I needed in my job had faded away. No matter how hard I worked to make society safe, all I saw at the end of the day was more crime. Every time I put some violent thug in jail, another three would leap out of some locust grove and stand in their stead. The criminal justice system seemed like a revolving door of appeals and loopholes and scumbag defense attorneys sugarcoating what I saw with my own eyes to be human garbage.

I needed more.

As luck would have it, the FBI felt the same way. Just a couple weeks after James Jenks's trial ended, word filtered down from Kansas City that my time in the Springfield RA was running short. Just as my acceptance letter had outlined, the day would come when "due to the needs of the Bureau," some paper pusher in Washington would arbitrarily move me and the family to another city. The SAC's secretary told me my name had risen to the top of the transfer list. Brad and Matt had just received orders to Los Angeles and Newark respectively, and I was next in line.

Fine, I thought to myself, but if I'm going to move, I'm going to move on my own terms. I'd just seen an airtel advertising the annual two-week selection process for a special branch of the FBI known as the Hostage Rescue Team. It was time to make the leap.

HRT represented something almost mythically grand at that point in my life. Though little known in the outside world, this small group of men was spoken of in hushed tones of awe within law enforcement circles. Virtually every agency bigger than dogcatcher fielded a SWAT team, but no one outside the military had anything like HRT. As the nation's primary civilian counterterrorism asset, they enjoyed benefits outside the purview of all other FBI offices. They trained or deployed to missions for a living. No cases, no informants, no trials, no administrative ligature, no appeals, no loopholes. Just missions.

Every time something big happened in the United States,

HRT flew in, strapped on black Nomex flight suits and submachine guns, and straightened it out. This is it, I thought. This is what I envisioned the day I decided to pin a badge on my chest and play guardian angel.

The timing felt right. I had tried my hand at casework and accomplished just about everything I'd set out to do in the field. I was ready for a new challenge.

If I made the Team, I could expect a transfer to Quantico in September. If not? Well, "if not" never really entered my mind.

Rosie and I talked it over and decided to set our sights on Quantico. The next day, on my thirty-second birthday, I began training for selection. Whether I made it or not, our days in paradise were numbered.

BOOK TWO

We are the pilgrims, Master,
We will always go a little farther . . .

BRITISH 22ND SPECIAL AIR SERVICE MOTTO

BOOK
TWO

7

SELECTION

Two months later, I found myself standing among a pack of thirty-six men, naked except for pride and ambition. The clock on the wall read 3:55 A.M. Fluorescent lights stammered and hummed above our heads. The air stood stiff with musky locker room smells and silence. There was an occasional nervous cough or the crack and pop of a joint being stretched, but no words. Conversation was not allowed.

The men around me bristled with nervous tension, the way horses snort and twitch before a big race. Lean muscle jacketed their chiseled frames. Close-cropped hair shimmered in the flat white light. All of them had trained for this two-week Hostage Rescue Team selection. They'd spent months honing their bodies and minds for fourteen days of physical and emotional hell.

The youngest was a twenty-seven-year-old former Marine, now working foreign counterintelligence in New York. He looked more like a linebacker free on waivers from the

Jets than a G-man. A hand, stiff as a meat hook, ran slowly over his scalp as he caught me sizing up his chances. His eyes darted off to another corner, then lapsed back into a look of dazed concentration.

There was no emotion in the room, but the air absolutely stank with anticipation. HRT operators in their gold T-shirts and black shorts milled about, breathing through their noses, trying to sniff out fear.

One can learn a lot about a man by watching him prepare for battle. I knew that some of the candidates would destroy themselves before they even got to the field. Some of us would feed on the pressure and use it to our advantage. Those who reached deep would stand a chance of making the team. The others would merely survive. That is never enough.

They'd come from FBI field offices all over the country. Some had been through this before and knew what lay ahead. Others, like myself, had only heard the stories. HRT selection was veiled in secrecy then, but we were all experienced investigators and had done our homework. There were phone calls to friends and bar calls with former squadmates who had failed in their own attempts to make the Team. War stories flow pretty easily from a beer bottle, especially among men who gave everything they had and lost.

Everyone I asked told me the same thing. HRT selection varies from year to year, but the process remains constant. There was only one constant that I could count on. Pain. That part never changes.

The men ahead of me formed a single-file line and shuffled through a gauntlet of operators. We moved slowly toward a scale, where two of the more intimidating specimens measured our height and weight. I knew this formality was just a way to increase the stress level before the physical fitness test, which is the first actual training evolution of the two-week process. I understood that this naked procession was nothing more than theater, a way for HRT to demonstrate exactly who stood in charge. Unfortunately, it didn't really matter what I knew. Selection was going to suck, no matter how much I tried to intellectualize the process.

All engines idled at half throttle, but even in this cold locker room, many of the men around me started to sweat. I could almost hear their hearts pounding and their muscles filling up with adrenaline and blood. We knew what was coming.

I tried to keep my mind in the room and focus on things I could control, but I couldn't help looking for signs of weakness. Scars. Knees, shoulders. Torsos and heads. I guessed at which joints would hold up and which would fail. The tall guy with the long pink smile inside his left thigh: anterior cruciate ligament. He'd never survive the long runs. The goofy-looking Headquarters type with the stiff shoulder: rotator cuff problem — he'd wash out in the upper-body grinder. I hoarded the information like ammunition that might help me in the days ahead.

One of the men in front of me, a flattopped former cop from Omaha, looked ragged, with more surgery marks than I'd ever seen on one body. He was lean enough that I could count his heart rate by watching the veins on his forehead. His ears flattened against his skull like a fighting dog's. His mouth hung at the corners, and his nostrils flared as he slowly rolled his head and shoulders like a boxer and tested his fists. Even his unconscious sneer looked like some kind of emotional wound that never healed. He was used to this. Pain meant nothing to this man. He'd make it.

"Whitcomb," someone said. The word sounded hollow and distant in the thick air.

I stepped forward onto a scale as an HRT operator measured and weighed me.

"Six foot, four inches. Two hundred and three pounds."

Two hundred and three pounds? They must be talking about some other Whitcomb. I felt bigger than that, stronger than a tall man could be at 200 pounds. I'd spent the last five years lifting weights and eating like a bull shoat just to get big enough to shake being called "Slim." They must have mistaken me for someone else in line.

But then I stepped down from the scales and caught a glimpse of myself in a wall mirror. The old bulk I remembered had been replaced with a different mass. The muscles in my chest wrinkled as I moved my arms. I could count the ridges in my stomach. My face looked long and thin like a distance runner's.

I'd lost twenty-five pounds during the previous ten weeks, and it showed. I'd ditched power lifting for push-ups. Raw eggs and yogurt shakes were replaced by organic fruit and lean chicken. I had been warned that the HRT selection course is a grueling endurance test that places more emphasis on running than bench-press and deadlift totals, and I had cut four years of hard-earned muscle in a couple of months to prepare myself for it.

The gamble seemed ill-advised as I hurried back to my shorts and sneakers. I was thirty-two years old, about average among the candidates in terms of age. Dropping weight had cost me upper-body strength and I knew that. I couldn't do the 150 push-ups or 30-plus pull-ups that some of the other guys could. Fortunately, years of ski training in the White Mountains of New Hampshire had given me deep lungs and strong legs. I could run six-minute miles all day and lug a heavy pack as far as they wanted to push me. I'd given up one strength to bolster another. I'd know soon enough if this was an effective strategy.

The line of men stretched behind me, back into the shadows, nearly to the rear wall. Some of the candidates looked like they couldn't wait to start. Others probably shouldn't have gotten out of bed at all that morning. Their eyes looked wide and watery. You could see the lumps in their throats bobbing up and down as they shuffled quietly along and pretended no one else noticed. They'd made a bad mistake, and they regretted it already.

The men around me came from SWAT teams in the FBI's biggest offices: L.A., New York, Chicago, Miami. They were former Marines and Green Berets and Navy Seals and Division I athletes. Fewer than half would make it through the two-week trial. HRT would select no more than a handful from the survivors. I was out of my element there, and I knew it.

My own confidence started to wane. Self-doubt rose in my throat like a bad meal. I felt too heavy. I felt too light. I'd trained too hard. I hadn't trained hard enough. Doubt infected me. Selection hadn't even started yet and I was psyching myself out, letting stress erode my resolve. All the preparation, the long hours of working out, the afternoons on the shooting range seemed woefully inadequate now.

Even my résumé seemed unimpressive. I'd spent the last four years chasing bank robbers and fugitives in a small Ozarks outpost. I'd never worked the big cases these guys had. Most of them had cut their teeth on high-risk dope raids and felony SWAT arrests. The Springfield Resident Agency didn't even have a SWAT team. I had never served in the armed forces or been a police officer. Hell, I'd never even been a crossing guard.

I was a writer, a former journalist who had come into the FBI from a U.S. congressman's office, where I'd composed speeches and handled the press. The closest I'd ever been to combat was a reelection campaign, and that had been mild even by local standards. I knew more about Shakespeare and Ibsen and Faulkner than I did about rules of engagement and close-quarter battle. My credentials seemed pathetically weak for a man about to try out for one of the world's premier counterterrorism teams.

These were pros. I'd never played for money.

One Monday morning each year, in a quiet gymnasium at the FBI Academy in Quantico, Virginia, three dozen of the FBI's bravest souls gather for two weeks of trauma. HRT selection is not just a test of physical ability, shooting skills, and brains, it is a carefully crafted evaluation that culls out those rare humans who will pick their friends up when they have no strength left for themselves. HRT wants individuals who work well as a team, type-A achievers who thrive on challenge. It wants people who are clear thinkers under the greatest stress. And it wants warriors who prize the value of peace.

HRT members take pride in their heritage, and it is very difficult ever to count yourself among them. I knew that when I filled out the application. It's why I came.

My tryout began promptly at 4:00 A.M. with a fight-style weigh-in and a lengthy physical fitness test. HRT did not decide on an early wake-up because they like beautiful sunrises. They knew that each of us has a defense mechanism that helps us deal with day-to-day stresses — kind of like an emotional immune system — and that this mechanism is prone to failure. The human psyche is designed for regeneration during sleep, and the system doesn't work well when its fragile equilibrium gets altered. It's why cops and military units plan raids for dawn. It's also why HRT starts the week early. They don't want to see what you can do on your best day. They want to see what you can do on your worst.

Hostage rescue, at its essence, is a game for thinkers. Operators have to feel comfortable riding a 180-decibel flash-bang grenade into a room full of terrorists and screaming hostages, differentiating between the good guys and the bad, fingering the trigger on their submachine gun, taking aim and *not* shooting. That's right — not shooting. HRT instructors can teach a monkey to blow holes in a bull's-eye target; what they want is a mind strong enough to know when to back off. Operators are not soldiers facing a generic enemy, they are law enforcement professionals who will have to account for every bullet they send downrange. Every time they pull that trigger, someone is going to die, and in America, state-sponsored death has become very expensive.

Finding people capable of that sort of split-second judgment can be difficult business. Some of us are better suited to armed conflict than others, but no man is born a warrior. We all carry inherent flaws, fears, and shortcomings that affect the way we perform under stress. Being able to run marathons or shoot tight groups on paper targets does not mean you will feel comfortable excising a bad guy's head from his body while he's holding a pregnant woman in his arms. That type of sangfroid requires a fairly complex thought process, refined motor skills, and the kind of confidence that can be misconstrued as arrogance. HRT is a national asset, the last line of defense in civilian law enforcement. If they fail, there is no one else to bat cleanup. Selecting the right people is crucial.

Any FBI agent can apply as long as he or she has three or more years of field experience and a superior performance appraisal. HRT doesn't care about sex or skin color or religious background or the size of your feet. The only way it discriminates is by ability. If you can cut it, you make the Team. If you can't, they fully expect you to find a rewarding career elsewhere in the Bureau. Political correctness has no place at the tall end of a ninety-foot fast rope when you've got sixty-five pounds of ammo, breaching gear, and weapons on your back. If you can't carry the weight, you will fall to your death. And if you die, you will jeopardize the mission. That is the ultimate sin.

All current HRT operators participate in each year's selection. They clean up after the candidates go to bed and they stand there waiting for them when they wake up two or three hours later. They wallow in the same mud, negotiate the same obstacle courses, and shed the same sweat all the candidates do. Year after year. Every year. They will never offer a word of encouragement or smile or frown to betray their impressions. They will simply jot notes on little white cards and formulate opinions. Quiet professionalism.

The HRT selection process is designed to make you fail. It puts you in impossible situations and then tests how well you overcome your own inadequacies. It is a painfully fair process, but it is also merciless. If you screw up during this two-week gut check, they can send you home without so much as a handshake.

I knew nothing about defense mechanisms, sleep cycles, or quiet professionalism as I stood in the line of men that morning in March 1991. All I knew was that very few of the thirty-six men in that cold locker room would become members of the Hostage Rescue Team and that I wanted to be one of them more than I'd ever wanted anything in my life. That was good, because what I was about to do would take all the resolve and desire I could summon. And then some.

◆

The first day passed pretty painlessly. I cruised the fitness test with reasonable numbers. Push-ups, pull-ups, sit-ups, a 110-yard shuttle run, a two-mile run, a rope climb, and a 200-yard swim. The minimums are not difficult (twelve pull-ups, fifty-five push-ups, and so on), but protocol is strict and stress seems to sap energy. In order to stay competitive, you have to double or triple the minimum standards. Some inevitably stumble. We lost three guys before breakfast.

The psychological testing that followed caught me off guard. The Minnesota Multiphasic Personality Inventory had questions like "Have you ever read *Alice in Wonderland*?" and "Would you rather write poetry or work on a car?" That seemed somewhat confusing. Yes, I'd read *Alice*. So what? I liked to write poetry as much as I liked to work on cars. I didn't get it.

Then came questions like "Does evil consume you?" "Do you ever think about committing suicide?" "Do you ever get so angry you want to hit something?" I began to figure out that this test was designed to weed out wacks, people not to be entrusted with guns. Most of the answers came naturally. The others I faked.

After lunch, they issued us old .38-caliber Smith and Wesson revolvers and lined us up on one of the Academy ranges. Half the front sight of my gun had been broken off, but no one seemed to care. The barrel looked straight and I didn't want to whine.

We shot the FBI's standard sixty-round qualification course: twelve shots from the fifty-yard line, eighteen from the twenty-five, the rest from up close. There was a shotgun course and another handgun trial. I knew the routine and had practiced in Missouri, but I ended up throwing a round anyway. It didn't matter. All you needed to stay and compete in the real selection was a score of 80 in each course, and Helen Keller could have shot that using a mirror.

By the end of the first day, fourteen hours after standing naked in that cold locker room, I felt my first sense of belonging. Several of those stone faces had already vanished, but I was still there. The pass/fail events were over. The only way they could get rid of me now would be to break my legs. This wasn't so bad after all. A good meal and an early night would put me in great shape for the next day. I started to relax. That was my first mistake.

Four days later, I found myself staring absently at a blackboard with nothing on it. I'd slept just seven hours in the past three days, and most of that had been fitful. Food was scarce, and we had little time to eat what we got. The day's ration had consisted of a box lunch containing a scrawny chicken wing, a roll, an apple, and one oatmeal cookie. One of the HRT operators, a wry, deliberate former Marine called Spuds, cracked the side door and tossed in eight box lunches.

Most of us would have considered the meal a smorgasbord except for the fact that there were only eight dinners for sixteen men. The other twenty members of our selection cohort had either "dropped on request" or had suffered debilitating injuries that forced them to leave. They'd whittled us down by more than half in less than four days.

Dinner was served in the "classroom," a table-and-chair-littered cavity deep within the Team's fenced-in compound where we waited between events. There were no windows. A paper terrorist target stood at the front of the classroom, taped to a plywood bullet trap. He wore an evil grin and two 9mm bullet holes between his beady eyes.

Things worked differently here. There just aren't many FBI offices where agents can hone their handgun skills around the coffee machine.

I stared at the target as I sucked the marrow out of my daily bread. This food wasn't intended as nourishment. Like everything else in the selection process, it was just part of the challenge. Another hardship. They wanted to see how we'd react to hunger, how we'd divide the food among ourselves. Everything they did elicited some kind of nefarious response, lured out greed or anger or resentment or some other character flaw. They searched for signs that we were faltering and noted every sarcastic smile, every frustration on those 3×5 cards they always carried.

Only sixteen men remained. Thank God, I thought. I'd hate to have to share with anybody else.

Sitting there, listening to my stomach growl, I started to understand things about myself I'd never thought to ask. I'd never gotten to a point like this where my entire sense of identity hung by a tiny sinew of ambition. Most people find a comfort zone, which they sometimes stretch but never exceed. They live in there, thinking they know themselves. Some define that sense of identity in terms of what they can do. Others define it in terms of what they won't do. All I could think about, right then, was that I would never do this again.

HRT selection shoves people off familiar ground, into terrain most of us never plumb. While stumbling around, we demonstrate the true "self" behind the social facade. Operators know that, so they carry small note cards in their pockets, outlining the characteristics they want to see in potential teammates. When candidates meet these expectations, operators give them a check. When they fail, operators give them a stroke.

All candidates wear a uniform designed to strip individuality. The uniform consists of a numbered pinny over a blue T-shirt, a wristband to show rank, and blue shorts or camouflage pants, depending on the event. Team leaders (rotated daily) wear a gold band. Everyone else wears blue. I was Charlie 7. It's what they called me, the generic persona that I became.

Selection coordinators allowed no jewelry, no watches, no clothing other than the uniform issued. They didn't care what I looked like on the outside, they wanted to know what I looked like on the inside. The only way to tell me from the others was by my pinny number and where I placed in the standings.

Our five-man team proved itself a fast group. Once attrition slowed, we settled into familiarity: a forty-one-year-old Japanese American nicknamed Yoda; a former Golden Gloves boxer with more than two hundred fights under his belt; a track and field star/lawyer from Minnesota; a complete lunatic from New York whom I'll call Beckett; and myself. We'd won every team event to date, and all of us except Yoda had finished among the top five or six in each of the running events. After four days, it looked like we all stood a decent chance of making the cut.

Thursday seemed particularly challenging. By itself, the 4:00 A.M. wake-up surprised no one. Most of us were used to early reveille. But sleep deprivation had scraped off whatever veneer I'd brought into this contest and left me feeling red and edgy, like a day-old wound. The fatigue and the prolonged physical suffering were taking their toll.

Only one person could finish first in each event, and every contest demanded reckless self-sacrifice. The winner gained the satisfaction of knowing he'd won. Everyone else looked ahead to the next event in hopes of doing better.

Each event began in the same nausea-inspiring manner. One of the HRT operators stood in front of us with a note card in his hand and read a "warning order." The directions always sounded the same. The words echoed like the grating trill of tree frogs on a summer's night.

"This is an individual event of indeterminate length," an operator read. "You are expected to give a maximum effort throughout the event. You will be evaluated on your performance."

Spuds recited the warning order particularly well.

Thursday's first individual event required us to run seven and a half miles, beginning on a wooded hill course called the Yellow Brick Road. It's a Marine Corps obstacle course highlighted by a fifteen-foot rope cargo ladder, several sheer rock cliffs, barbed wire "bear pits," and a dozen other opportunities to break your ankle or dislocate your shoulder. You race as fast as you can go while wearing a military flak jacket, two canteens of water, and an M-16 rifle. Since you don't know how far the course stretches until you're done, you run it as if it were a forty-yard dash, over and over and over again. Each forty-yard dash gets slower and longer and more difficult. There are no strategies or tactics. You simply go as fast as you can for as long as you can.

Strange things happen in the mind during times of suffering. First you come up with a mantra you can chant against the pain. When that no longer works, you set small goals, promising yourself that you'll lighten up if you can just get up one more hill or across one more obstacle. If the body insists on tearing itself up further, the mind starts playing tricks on itself, trying to stop the torment.

I remember running up to one of the obstacles, thinking how easy it would be to bang my head against it and knock myself out. One brief misstep and I could disassociate myself from all the agonies. No one would know. My family might even feel sympathy. Nah. Rosie would see right through it. I just kept running.

When we finished, they regrouped us according to team, issued each man a backpack filled with thirty-five pounds of sand, and demanded that we stuff another ten pounds of personal gear on top. Finally, they handed each team a canvas duffel filled with medicine balls and sent us on our way. The only rule stipulated that the forty-pound bag could not touch the ground at any time and that the fastest team won the event.

The course covered fifteen miles of uneven terrain, including "challenges" such as the U.S. Marine Corps's high obstacle course, which we negotiated like a parking lot speed bump. This was a team race. You worked together, hoping personal weakness wouldn't jeopardize the chances of the rest of the group. I ran and climbed and crawled until the straps from my pack rubbed my shoulders raw, each breath cut deeper into my lungs than any breath before it, and a voice in my head called "reason" pleaded with me to stop. Then I ran some more.

We traded the bag among ourselves every half mile or so until Yoda peeked his head out of a huge suffering and came up with the idea of using a tree limb to distribute the load. Things picked up considerably after that. I'm sure some operator noted Yoda's inventiveness on one of those little white cards.

The last of the four teams dragged their butts back to the HRT building just before 6:00 P.M. We'd raced twenty-two and a half miles, with gear, since daybreak. Every joint in my body ached, and it wasn't even dark.

Fortunately, the weather was cool and dehydration hadn't become a serious problem. In other years, large numbers of candidates have fallen by the wayside or worse. One year, thirteen men lay in a grassy clearing far from medical facilities with intravenous bottles hanging out of their arms, trying to regain their senses. They were luckier than one of their fellow candidates, who fell face first into the dirt and lapsed into convulsions. After a week-long coma in the hospital, which included a prognosis of certain death and last rites from a Catholic priest, he awoke, looked around, and asked, "Did I make the Team?"

Right.

Just before 7:00 P.M., Spuds walked into the classroom. I had just finished an apple (my share of the box lunch) when he began to read the next operations order. We had been chasing an imaginary fugitive named Jim Frazier since Monday night and had gone through an exhaustive series of arrest scenarios without success. Spuds told us Frazier had hooked up with a criminal associate and taken refuge in a local trailer park. Each team had to come up with an arrest plan and apprehend him before he left the trailer. We had ten minutes.

Go.

I wore the gold wristband on Thursday, so it was my turn to formulate a plan and muster the troops. Operators in white polo shirts flooded the room and hovered around us as we worked. I leaned over to Beckett, who had his head in his hands, and asked him if he was all right.

"Leave me alone," he mumbled. "I've got killing on my mind."

Beckett didn't make the cut.

Fourteen agents survived the two-week tryout in 1991. We made it through the Quigley, a grueling obstacle course punctuated by a swim through a frigid, stagnant sewer, and the claustrophobia test, where they give you a blacked-out gas mask and make you crawl blindly through heating ducts deep beneath the FBI Academy. We made it over the Stairway to Heaven, a fifty-foot log ladder straight up in the air that would give a circus acrobat second thoughts. We shinnied and scraped our way to the top of the Heartbreak Hotel, a rickety four-story tower, dangled our toes over the edge, lifted our arms out to the side, and called out our pinny numbers. Fall and you're history. It would have ended the suffering.

Fourteen of us made it through the water events. In one test you have to hold your breath and walk seventy-five feet underwater with thirty pounds of weight in your hands. HRT has a dive team and a maritime mission. They want to be sure all operators can either swim or hold their breath long enough to walk to shore.

There was the helicopter ride, where you sit on the deck with your feet on the skids, wearing blacked-out goggles. Beckett was the star of that show also. We sat shoulder to shoulder with two other teammates as we flew along, 500 feet over the Quantico reserve. I rested, grateful for time off my feet, until an air pocket lifted my ass off the deck and my stomach up into my throat. All of a sudden, Beckett declared, "That's it! I've had enough of this shit. I'm gonna jump. Just to fuck with you assholes, I'm gonna jump!"

I believed him, but he either changed his mind or one of the operators got a handful of his belt before he launched. When the bird landed, Beckett landed with it.

Two weeks and a thousand miles after that first morning in the gym, fourteen men emerged from the most physically, psychologically, and emotionally demanding experience of their lives. HRT never announced how many slots they planned to fill, but I felt pretty good about my chances.

On Friday afternoon of the second week, I called my wife to tell her I'd survived. Then I packed my small bag of filthy clothes, caught a cab to the airport, and collapsed into my seat. A broad smile broke out across my face as the pilot fire-walled the throttles and headed to Missouri. No matter how things turned out, I had succeeded where most others had failed. In just a few hours, I would get to hug my wife and kids, knowing I'd given my absolute best. No excuses. No second guesses.

The best thing the FBI ever gave me was an opportunity to prove myself. That day, I could barely muster the strength to open my complimentary bag of roasted peanuts, but when I fell asleep, I did it with my head held high.

8

NEW OPERATOR
TRAINING SCHOOL

Monday morning after returning from Quantico, I dove right back into my cases as if nothing had happened at all. No matter where you work, two weeks on the road means two weeks behind when you get home, so there was no point in malingering. My desk looked like a Midwestern twister had swept across it. Billy Jenks still hadn't been found, one of my informants had gotten himself arrested, two more banks had fallen to gunmen, and my handgun qualification had lapsed.

Seeking consolation at home proved no more rewarding. Rosie notified me that I hadn't been the only Whitcomb suffering from sleep deprivation in the last week. Mickey had come down with the flu and Jakie had pulled a dresser down on his head, requiring three stitches above the eye. Our dog, Maggie, had lost a pissing match with a skunk, and the county had just served notice of a sewage treatment consolidation with the city, which meant a $2,100 plumbing bill.

I saw no point in looking anywhere for sympathy. My complaints would have fallen on deaf ears.

By the end of April, though, things had slowed considerably. Kansas City still hadn't called with orders. HRT still hadn't issued word on the year's selections. Maggie only smelled bad when it rained.

Benny invited me to a law enforcement golf tournament, thinking I could use the diversion, and I jumped at the chance. I brought nothing to the match except a high handicap, but the thought of spending four hours away from my day-to-day grind sounded like early parole. Maybe the added stress would help me hit the long ball.

I was sizing up a three-foot putt for the lead when my pager sounded. I reached down to turn it off, recognized the number, and froze. The only people I knew in the 703 area code worked for the Hostage Rescue Team, so I dropped the putter where I stood and started running toward the clubhouse. Benny called after me, yelling something about screwing him out of a door prize, but he was just kidding. Everyone in my office knew that HRT telephoned only those who made it. The other guys got a letter.

Spuds answered with a distant hello when I finally ran down a pay phone. I stood at the waiting end of the line with my heart in my throat.

"Yeah, Chris," he said, "we've got a New Operator class coming up in September and we were hoping you could make it."

All I could think about was that day in my Capitol Hill office when Wayne called to offer me a New Agents class. My mind raced. My heart pounded. You just don't invest yourself that deeply in self-examination without praying for validation. This was it. Spuds sounded a whole lot more involved than Wayne had, but his pitch must have come from the same FBI manual.

"Thank you, sir," I said, after we had talked logistics. "I'll do my best. I'll make you proud."

Make you proud? I shook my head as I hung up the phone. The last time I said something that stupid was when they offered me a dishwashing gig at the Dutch Treat restaurant. When I was thirteen.

Of the fourteen men who completed the HRT selection process in 1991, seven were offered slots: a former Marine pilot, a cop, an Army Ranger, a Navy explosive ordnance disposal expert, a nationally ranked competitive shooter, and a lawyer. And me. No one ever told me what promise they saw in a former speechwriter, but I didn't really care. Seven men were slated to become the eighth generation of HRT operators, and I was one of them.

Rose, the silent partner in this whole endeavor, took the news with the same sense of adventure I did. She just laughed when I showed up with a flattop haircut like those I'd seen most guys wearing at Quantico. Not a word passed her lips when the guys in the office kept me out late celebrating with way too much tequila. She never complained when we packed two kids, a dog, and a cross-country trek's worth of gear into our Isuzu Trooper for the ride east. Even the kids cooperated. They were still too young to understand what "moving" meant, but they seemed to like motel pools.

On Labor Day weekend, after a week's vacation at my parents' house in New Hampshire, we rolled in to the Dunning Mills Inn, south of Fredericksburg, Virginia. We'd found a decent house just outside the back gate to Quantico, but closing was still a month away. Everyone, including the dog, piled into a one-room efficiency and settled in for the long haul. Transition from normal agent duty to life on HRT wouldn't be easy on anyone. I knew that.

What I didn't really understand, until the following Tuesday, was how much of a transition we were in for. New Operator Training School, or NOTS, is a cross between Outward Bound and a slave galley, a five-month indoctrination into a whole different world.

Each day begins early and demands new expressions of commitment. Our NOTS coordinator, a rigid former Marine called Masher, beat out a rhythm as we passed through the 5:00 A.M. agility drills, the 8:00 A.M. close-quarter-battle lessons, the 11:00 A.M. fitness grinders and distance runs, the afternoon shooting sessions, and the evening lectures. He watched as they pushed us to sprint faster, jump higher, and take more preposterous chances than we'd ever dreamed we could. He challenged us from the time we got up until the time we dragged our tired, broken asses back to bed.

"The only easy day was yesterday."

"Pain is weakness leaving the body."

"There's a fine line between hard and stupid."

He spouted a million hokey clichés, but the point was always the same. Suck it up. Do what you have to do. You volunteered for this job. You can quit any time you like.

What I soon discovered in NOTS was an elegantly refined rite of passage that takes you from knot-tying classes to explosives breaching with rhythm and sense. One day you learn the intricacies of rapid fire shotgunning. The next you work your way through a five-mile land navigation problem. There is rappelling and fast roping and helicopter operations. They teach you dignitary protection and climbing and patrolling and high-speed evasive driving. It is hundreds of hours of the finest instruction of its kind in the world.

It is not all pleasant. Veteran operators never let you forget that you are not part of the Team until you graduate NOTS. They make every effort to pretend you are not even there. They will not acknowledge your presence, let alone talk to you. Your existence means nothing more than inconvenience, less coffee in the pot, another class to teach. They expect total sacrifice every day but pretend they aren't even watching. They want everything from you. All of you. They couldn't care less about your mundane personal concerns. The Team is what really matters.

I remember standing at a urinal one day, next to one operator I'd seen nearly every day for three months. The bathroom is a pretty personal space, and I knew no one else was around, so the natural thing to do was nod and say "How're you doing?"

He looked straight ahead, sniffed like I had fouled the air, and pretended I wasn't even there. He wasn't trying to play the party line or impress some of his buddies. He believed in this. I represented something less than him. I wasn't worth responding to. Another month and we might end up on the same team. We'd probably be friends one day. But at that time I was just a NOThead, and even in the privacy of the toilet, we were distant as two strangers on a crowded street.

Though I didn't like it, I understood the process. There are more than 270 million people in America, a couple hundred thousand cops, and 11,000 FBI agents. Fewer than 200 men have ever served on HRT. The Team members cherish their heritage and protect it with every calculated stare, every cautious hello.

NOTS hasn't changed much since its 1983 debut. Each generation begins with a two-week crash course in the basics of combat handgunning. Right after orientation, the equipment clerk issues each new operator two custom-made, high-capacity pistols as part of his tactical kit.

HRT operators don't look at weapons as a nuisance that you keep in a briefcase or the trunk of your Bureau car. The weapon is a lifeline, an invaluable tool of the trade which may at any time become the dividing line between life and death. Weapons are what you clean at the end of a sixteen-hour shift, before you clean yourself and go to sleep. They're what you spend five days a week trying to master. They're your bread and butter, the way you pay the rent.

"Gunfighting is the ultimate confrontation," the instructors growl.

You hear those words over and over. Life or death. Success or failure. When you burst through a door and start working your way through a wall of terrorists toward their captives, you accept a solemn responsibility to the hostages and to the teammates working around you. This isn't the kind of job where a mistake will get you counseled. It's the kind of job where a mistake will get you killed.

"This ain't no ballroom dancing! Lean into that thing!"

A voice thunders across the range as Homey, a 250-pound former NFL linebacker and twin to your worst nightmare, walks the line. He stops to make a point, drawing his own pistol and cranking off a couple of rounds. The .45-caliber chunk of blue steel looks like a derringer in his bear paw as he shoots. The barrel barely flinches. Both shots print as one ragged hole.

"What the hell are you waiting for? You gonna stand there and die or you gonna fight?"

Everybody jumps back into their shooting stance. Shoulders forward, arms slightly bent, feet shoulder-width apart.

The instructions flicker through your mind as his voice gets closer and the rounds stray further and further apart.

"Sight alignment! Trigger pull!" He recounts the fundamentals of marksmanship. "Concentrate!"

It all sounds easy, but it's not. HRT operators draw from the holster differently from most other FBI agents, they present the weapon toward the target differently, and they perform combat reloads differently. It is a bastardized shooting style born of techniques that are taught by some of the nation's finest competitive shooters and private instructors.

"Watch that front sight through recoil." T.J., the other primary instructor, stands so close you can feel his breath on your neck.

"Squeeze that trigger, Whitcomb, don't slap it!"

T.J. scrutinizes my target a moment, barks out a few more words of advice, and moves on. He's one of those extraordinary instructors you want to learn from. You want to show him that all he's investing in you is going to pay off. He strives to make you a better shooter because he knows he's going to depend on you some day, and you work to prove you're worth the effort.

Besides the instructors, a dozen or so operators mill about behind you each day, checking to make sure they didn't vote for the wrong guy. That's how each of us got to HRT and we know it. Votes. After the two-week audition ends, the Team gets together in the classroom with stacks of paper and a slide projector. Each candidate's face flashes up on the screen and the selection coordinators start listing test scores, fitness standings, peer evaluations, phobia test results, and a dozen other rankings.

Operators take notes, rank the names of those they want to call teammate, and cross out the names of those they don't. Some focus on fitness scores, while others look at leadership skills and firearms standings. Each operator knows that he could have to depend on the person he votes for to save his life. He might also have to spend a week in a tent with him during an operation. In some ways, compatibility is just as important as capability.

But selection felt like ancient history as I stood on the range and fought for control of my abilities. Nothing seemed to be working. My old habits died hard and ruined a lot of targets along the way.

"Smooth is fast!" T.J. chanted, knowing our brains would eventually accept the mantra.

It worked. By the end of the second week, all seven of us were shooting better than we'd ever thought possible. On the buzzer, we could draw, fire two rounds, reload, and fire two more within three seconds. We could shoot a six-inch head-plate from the holster at ten yards in less than a second. Running, turning, lying, kneeling, weak hand — it didn't matter. We were becoming gunfighters. Technicians. Part of the breed.

❖

Confidence grew one accomplishment at a time as NOTS progressed through the first month. We moved up the capability scale from first aid training through mechanical breaching, dignitary protection, and land navigation to tactical helicopter operations.

Along the way, they tested us informally with events like the James River jump. It's an old HRT tradition, one of the informal rites of passage each new operator has to endure. While all your teammates watch, you climb up onto the gunwalc of a ship, high above the water, check to make sure your helmet is buckled, and launch. It's like bungee jumping without the cord.

They tell you it's totally optional, but everyone knows it is not. Climbing all the way back down the caving ladder is a disgrace no one wants to suffer, especially since word of the failure will certainly beat you back to the HRT compound. No one wants to face the embarrassment of balking at one of the Team's oldest tests of manhood.

I remember standing there when it came my turn. I could see ten miles to the south, out into the mouth of the James

River toward where it spills into the Chesapeake Bay. The Virginia coastal plains rolled away from me in brilliant autumn foliage. Vagrant gulls hung on open wings among the thermals and sea breezes, crying out in their childish voices, mocking me and my predicament.

"Concentrate on the horizon, hold your hands at your sides, and keep your feet together," Masher said. "If you look down, you'll fall forward and crush your face. We don't need any medical problems out here."

That's when the view changed. I turned my focus from the horizon to the water forty feet below. It was a long ways down. I'd checked a couple of times just to make sure.

Two Zodiacs full of Navy Seals, working a separate training trip, motored around the bow of the *Penacolen*, the '30s-vintage freighter we were using while it waited in wet dock for the next war. Tiny black helmets floated in the murky waters below me. I couldn't make out their faces but I knew they were gloating. This had to be fun to watch.

"Wait until Walt gets out of the way," Masher cautioned with all the charm of a chain gang guard. "I'll tell you when to jump."

He looked over the edge to check on the first of my classmates to take the plunge. I hoped to see him coming up for air any second.

The jump Masher referred to threatened to take me from my perch on the rusting steel gunwale of the *Penacolen* into the river below in just over a second. A handful of HRT divers stared up at me like I was some suicidal bridge jumper waiting for inspiration. A flicker of sea breeze, colored with the unique scent of municipal sewage, sobered me for a moment. I shook my head, as if given smelling salts, then looked around for reference.

"You ready?" Masher asked. It sounded more like a taunt than concern.

I nodded and looked down again, past the anchor chains and steel climbing ladders just to make sure Walt was not on his way to the river bottom. The sound of his body hitting the water echoed off ships moored around us, as if the sheer stupidity of this jump needed repeating.

Suddenly a black Pro-tec kayaker's helmet bobbed up like a cork. A loud whoop rose out of the water. The HRT divers yelled their delight, calling out scores. Walt posted eights and nines, mostly, because he was looking down when he landed and made one hell of a splash. He patted his head and waved, a sign that everything was all right.

No blood. Okay. He jumped and survived. No reason I couldn't too.

This is nothing, I told myself. You've been much higher.

Yeah, but I'd never jumped.

I should have been used to working at heights. I practically grew up on a rappel rope. My dad led a mountain rescue team in the White Mountains and taught me to climb the steep, exposed rock of Franconia Notch before he taught me to ride a bike. I remember long, relentless vertical afternoons on the Cannon cliffs and magical views from Artist's Bluff, overlooking the deep, ragged notch. While other kids watched television, my friends and I scrambled up rocky crags high above the tourists. We would jam and smear and edge our way into the sky, fighting to untie the knots in our stomachs and bear down on each handhold as if it were some intricate chess move.

I remembered the view, then, from those cliffs. It had been twenty years, but the awe rushed back with the precision and detail of insight. It was the elation of elevation I savored; that intangible closeness to life you get when the only thing between you and death is a single strand of 10mm rope. It was one of the few, pristine places in the world where you could almost hear the hinges creaking on the

Pearly Gates, that proximity to the other side that makes all the trivial, mundane moments bearable.

Luckily, altitude plays a large role in NOTS training. Instructors rely on it as a metaphor for risk. By building scenarios in precarious situations, they offered us a sense of consequence. You had to trust in their advice or give in to the insecurity we all brought, in one form or another, to this process.

Just the week before, I had stood on the skid strut of a dark blue UH-1 Huey, ninety feet above the ground. The bass drum cadence of rotors spinning above my head lent a strange rhythm to my predicament. The pilots held a steady hover as we checked the ropes that secured us to the fuselage and took in the view below.

The vast forests of the Quantico Marine Corps Base stretched out beneath us for miles in every direction. The FBI Academy looked small and distant below my feet. Hawks circled above Lunga Reservoir, inured to our fun and games. Yoda and Ricketts stood in the doorway opposite me, silhouetted against a cerulean sky. They showed no expression. Walt stood to my left, rigid as spite.

"Get ready!" Pete Anderson, the rappel master, yelled over the rotor wash, jet exhaust, and blood throbbing through my head.

He squatted just to my right as I stood there in the open door with my left hand on a nylon tether and my right hand on the business end of a 150-foot rappel rope. Rotor wash tugged at the rope bag carabinered to my gun belt. The big awkward chopper dipped left, then right as the pilot adjusted for a sudden crosswind.

Treetops drifted in a gentle breeze fifty feet below me: verdant tufts of red oak and cedar and poplar. They looked like a vast mattress waiting to catch us if we fell.

I held the belay line like life itself. It's not the height or the knowledge that any of a dozen links in the safety chain could snap that holds your attention. It's the belief that for those few fleeting moments, you alone are the master of your own destiny. All the training and the experience in the world are just guidelines. What it really comes down to is you. If you function properly, you'll live. If you falter, let your mind wander at the wrong time, or allow the moment to consume you, you'll die. It was that allegiance to fate, not adrenaline, that thrilled me.

The week's training ran through my mind as I adjusted the slack on my rope and squinted the wind out of my eyes. I adjusted my feet on the helicopter skids as the pilot found his hover. The rappel master hung his upper body out the door, scouring the trees below for a suitable drop zone. I felt my dad's hand on my back as if we'd just summitted a long climb and he was sending me down ahead of him.

Pete looked back at us and crossed his arms in front of his chest as if warding off demons. Then he flung his hands down to his sides and yelled.

"Go!"

Down. Free fall.

Miss the brake zone and you get a forty-foot oak up your ass. Brake too soon and you will pendulum into the guy across from you, like Eddie, who ended up with a boot through his chin. He was lucky to settle for twenty stitches. Most people would have blacked out and hurtled to their death.

Down I go, lightly fingering the rope as it passes through my gloved palm, finessing the brake just before I hit the top of the trees.

I descend through the trees, kicking the branches out of the way as I go, trying to get to the ground as quickly as possible. The rappel master can't see you once you disappear into the trees, and the pilots don't want to get caught up in the foliage. They give you a ten count to get down, but after that everything is a crapshoot. So you fight your way through the trees, hoping you have enough rope in the bag at your side to make it all the way. And then you're on the ground and off the rope and ready to fight the next battle, the real battle, the reason you came.

"Go."

Masher's tone imparted no particular immediacy, but it snapped me out of my recollection. Rappelling was last week. Today's business was falling.

"Go!"

I knew at that point in NOTS that I could do anything they told me to do. Anything. HRT is not about building individuals. It's about building a stronger link in the chain and welding the whole thing together through commitment. The mission.

The fifty feet to the water would pass very quickly, but this step in the process would last forever. They have instilled confidence where there used to be doubt and fear. The shooting and rappelling and defensive tactics just take practice. This came down to trust: trust in your teammates and trust in yourself. To the dismay of voices screaming in my head, I pushed one foot out in front of me and leaned into the void.

That is where I traded my old life in for theirs.

After all the foundation principles have been laid comes the final and most critical aspect of New Operator Training: close-quarter-battle training. CQB is the cornerstone of hostage rescue, a choreographed ballet of rolling thunder. This highly demanding and extremely violent confrontation requires each shooter to adhere to defined fields of fire while working in a 360-degree shooting environment. He must trust his teammates enough to work within inches of their bullets. He must move fluidly from one room to another, immune to the concussion of explosive breaches and flash-bang diversion grenades. He must feel comfortable shooting on the move as hostages reach out for him, and he must never mistake furtive gestures for weapons.

"Key on the hands," the instructors told us. "They can't shoot you with their eyes."

We started in the FBI Academy gym at 5:00 A.M. each day, working with plastic weapon simulators and blocking dummies. Movement, position, and concentration comprised the early lessons as our instructors taught us how to enter a room and dominate a sector. We practiced weaving between obstacles with our weapons always at the ready, head down, arms extended, knees bent to absorb the impact of each step without throwing off our aim.

"Speed, surprise, and violence of action," they chanted over and over and over again. Another mantra.

After two weeks of dry runs with plastic guns, we stacked our thirty-round MP-5 magazines with 10mm ammunition, slammed our bolts forward, and flipped the fire selector to three-round burst. The drills started simply at first, with two-man entries into a single room. Fundamentals. The instructors followed every move, honing each step and making sure we understood the importance of each shot before we took it.

"Misses mean failure. Ignore distractions. Concentrate on fields of fire. Key on weapons. Know your assignment. Excel." The instructions came as commandments.

Time after time after time, we ran our routes, moving up to four-man entries and then into two-, three-, and four-room sequences. Flash-bang grenades, multiple targets, moving targets, lunging hostages, smoke. The runs got harder and harder until we began to work as a team. It can take years to become truly proficient at this form of assault, but we didn't have that much time. We had five months. After that, we were on our own.

Whatever challenge I found in jumping, rappelling, and indoor shoot-outs, nothing seized my attention quite as much as fire training. HRT works with explosives, from small-caliber bullets to diversionary grenades and monstrous breaching charges. Explosives can cause fires, and fires can make hostage rescue an even more threatening enterprise. In order to work and survive in a hot environment, new operators need a little time in the fire itself.

That comes during the seventh week, in a space made for devils.

The Prince William County Fire Academy maintains a three-story concrete tower called "the hot house." Its walls are charred from years of abuse. Steel shutters over the windows are welded shut. A mesh floor lets the smoke rise freely to the top, where it rolls over and billows back down again, creating a vertical wind tunnel that seethes and roils, sucking out all the air and filling the place with misery.

We all knew we might have to fight in an environment like this one day, running from room to room behind our submachine guns, searching for hostages and ferreting out the threats. So we had to train in it too. No one ever feels comfortable in a place like this, but we'd have to be familiar with it in order to be effective. There's no point going into a crisis site unless you're confident you can get out.

After a brief orientation and a demonstration, the instructors lit a fire of wet straw and pallet scraps in the basement. As thick, acrid smoke wafted up to the third floor and circled back down, they led us to a fire escape platform just beneath the roof. We stood in line with simple instructions.

"Find your way down to the first floor and get out without falling or passing out."

Sounded simple enough.

The instructor pulled open the door and pushed me inside.

"Motherfucker!" I yelled, wasting most of my air. The room hit me like a body punch.

No one answered. Nothing changed. It felt like a nightmare, hugging me, trying to crawl inside me, sucking the life out of my body. I held my breath as long as I could, but that couldn't have been more than a minute. My heart throbbed like a trip-hammer.

I felt along the walls with the back of my hand, like they taught us.

There has to be a door in here, a stairwell leading down, I thought.

The space around me felt alive, crowded, black, hell hot. I tasted no air. I saw no light. There seemed to be no escape. The heat seared my lungs. My nose closed involuntarily, dismissing my craving for oxygen in order to keep from becoming cauterized. Tears poured out of my eyes as my body fought to compensate for the caustic smoke.

Suddenly, I felt consumed with an almost primal need to survive. Prior to NOTS, I might have mistaken the feeling for panic. But panic is an irrational response to challenge. Panic will not save your life. It has to be ignored like the smoke and the heat and the darkness.

Survival became my objective. *Fight, you fucker,* I screamed at myself. What else can you do?

I started to the right, stumbling over furniture I couldn't see, moving from the slits of light in one boarded-up window to another. I moved methodically, like they taught us in

CQB training, concentrating on the tools that still functioned: touch, instinct.

"Discard what doesn't work. Focus on what does. Calm yourself," I whispered on the exhale. "Conserve energy. Fight the adrenaline. Slow the heartbeat."

I started sucking air in short, measured breaths, trying to let my lungs farm the precious little oxygen from each mouthful of black sap.

Bang. I hit a railing about waist level. Had to be the top of the stairwell.

Down.

I followed the hot steel lifeline down the stairs, squinting even though there was no light to see. My eyes burned. Snot flowed out of my nose, mixing with the tears and the spittle, choking me, reminding me that my body did not like this shit.

My feet bottomed out on the second-floor landing, and I started the search all over again. I smacked into a table, then a couch, falling, crawling, down on my hands and knees to the next stairwell.

Down, again, to the first floor and finally the exit.

Out.

I knew the sun was shining brightly as I emerged into clear air, but I couldn't see much. My eyes were swollen and black with soot.

"Over here," one of the fire academy instructors yelled. He held a garden hose to wash away the pain. I heard the rest of my NOTS class spilling out of the burning building behind me. They coughed and wheezed just as badly as I did.

"Hurry up," the instructor prodded as I stumbled toward him. "You've got to make your second run before the fire dies down."

Second run?

Ten minutes later, we did it all over again with a 150-pound dummy over one shoulder.

I didn't really mind the second time. I knew the route and I had survived once already. I survived just like I survived the jump off the ship and the rappel out of the helicopter and the shooting-house runs where my teammates pumped 10mm and .45-caliber rounds within inches of my face.

I had survived selection and relocation and living as a NOThead, an outcast among the Team members. I had survived so many things — from inconvenience to threat — just to get here. I didn't care that I still had to jump off a forty-foot tower into an air bag or that it would knock the wind out of me when I landed wrong. I had learned that I could accomplish anything I wanted if I just believed it possible, kept my head, and trusted in myself.

People spend entire lives and huge amounts of money searching for the self-realization that I was given in twenty weeks.

It is not enough to fail, the instructors taught us. It is not all right to give up.

❖

On graduation day, five months after we arrived at Quantico, all seven members of my NOTS class filed into the HRT classroom for final ceremonies. The sparsely furnished room looked no different than on any other day. I saw no diplomas. None of us had prepared a valedictory address.

Ray, a hulking cruiser-weight with the presence of a stage actor, walked to a lectern at the front and cleared his throat. The entire Team looked on as we stood along the far wall.

Unlike most graduation ceremonies, HRT commencement turns on action, not words. Our wives and children weren't invited to see us march. There would be no Phi Beta Kappa keys or magna cum laude designations. If we wanted the yellow T-shirt that served as the HRT diploma, we'd have to earn it in one last comprehensive final.

Terrorists had taken hostages in a Washington, D.C., embassy, Ray said. Generation Eight new operators were being deployed to effect their release. Intelligence indicated at least five hostage takers. All five were heavily armed. They had threatened to kill everyone within an hour if their demands were not met. Negotiators were just about ready to sign off on the assault.

Ray read from his operations order in a voice that carried no emotion or urgency. His gravelly baritone rumbled through the room as we shuffled against the wall and took notes.

Team assignments reflected the CQB tactics we'd been running all month. I stood fifth in the line of march, behind Ricketts and just in front of Dale. Curtis, our former explosive ordnance disposal technician, would breach the front door. Snipers had the perimeter and would take shots of opportunity once the command element began the assault countdown. Everything was planned. Every detail was clarified. There were no questions.

Gear up and be ready by 13:30 hours, Ray told us. One-thirty. Less than half an hour.

We left our last position of cover at 13:22 precisely. Walt took point. Yoda covered the rear. The rest of us fanned our weapons out to cover 360 degrees against possible threats. We moved toward the shooting house, using cover and concealment wherever possible. We stepped carefully, toes first, then heels, like stalkers creeping up on spooked prey. A gas mask covered my face, limiting my perspective to a broad tunnel of black rubber and clear plastic.

Earplugs closed out all noise but the occasional squelch of radio haze and the hiss of breath escaping from my mask's filter. A black balaclava flowed out from beneath my Pro-tec helmet to shield my neck from the explosive door breach. Everything I wore was black except the small American flag sewn to my left sleeve. So what if the bad guys could see it in the dark? It's why we were there.

Veteran HRT operators ringed the high walls of the shooting house and the observation tower, waiting for us, watching to see if we'd perform up to their expectations. We moved deliberately toward the door, poised for battle. There was no exposed skin, no vulnerability, no appearance of humanity.

Walt stopped just short of the front door and trained his MP-5 at head level. Anyone steps out and they're dead. Eddie, the team leader, motioned with his hand, and Curtis hurried to the door with his two-by-four-foot explosive breach.

I waited in line, mentally running through an equipment checklist and my tactical assignments: MP-5 submachine gun, safety off, flash-bang grenade cupped loosely in my left hand — check the door handle, then toss it into the room.

"You have 2.7 seconds, once the spoon pops, before the blast," I reminded myself. "Finger off the trigger until it's time to kill. Look all the way into the danger zones for threats before turning into the room. Key on weapons, not movement. Maintain fields of fire. Don't fuck up. Don't fuck up. Don't fuck up . . ."

I glanced down at my primary .45 in a low-slung tactical holster just below my hip. The hammer rested quietly cocked and locked. A second .45 waited in a cross-draw shoulder rig fastened to the ceramic trauma plate on the front of my body armor. It carried a light, in case the one on my primary weapon failed.

Pistol magazines hung precariously from my gun belt. MP-5 magazines rode in a thigh pad designed to offer quick access. Ten or twelve flash-bang grenades rattled around in a bag hanging off my left hip. Three strip charges (explosive door breaches) tapped against my calf in the lower leg pocket of my Nomex flight suit.

The load of body armor and weaponry weighed more than sixty pounds, but I felt lighter than the air around me. Adrenaline coursed through my veins, but in perfect doses, just enough to tune the thinking and clear the vision.

I sucked a deep breath and ignored the hiss as I leaned forward over the back of the man in front of me. Curtis set his charge and crept back from the heavy wooden door at the front of the crisis site. He removed the mechanical safeties from the trigger mechanism and visually checked a line of detonator cord that snaked up to the 400-grain flex-linear breaching charge. The explosion would cut a hole in the door and clear a path for the assault. It would also take your head with it if you jumped the command or got too close. These rude, violent charges are so powerful, the over-pressure and spalling can knock you down even when everything goes right.

Curtis took a knee eight feet from the door, turned his back, and nodded to Eddie. Time.

"Bravo One to TOC," Eddie whispered into a tiny mic near the corner of his mouth. "We're at green." That means go.

There was a brief pause, then a confident voice. Ray read down the count.

"Stand by, I have control. Five, four . . ."

I turned my eyes from the door so the blast wouldn't blind me.

". . . three, two . . ."

Snap. Snap. Snap. Snipers engaged targets of opportunity from 100 yards away. Their bullets zipped just over our heads with a loud, supersonic report.

". . . one . . ."

Boom!!

Curtis shot the charge. The shock wave rattled through the line as we leaned into the violence and stormed the room. Huge explosions rocked the building as we lobbed flash-bangs ahead of us and executed terrorists (three-dimensional mannequins) where we met them. We charged along rote patterns, dominating rooms as we went. Head shots. Door breaches. Flash-bangs. The hiss of breath through the gas masks and the monotone *thunk, thunk, thunk* of raging hearts.

"Key on weapons, shoot surgically, think four steps ahead."

I subconsciously chanted the creed as we blitzed to the hot spot, a room at the back of the building where intelligence reports placed the hostages. I ended up second in line on the door as we worked our system of touch commands. We staggered our charge for the split second it took me to lob a grenade into the room.

Door's locked. Shit. "Breacher up!"

Curtis stepped in front of me with a sawed-off 12-gauge shotgun and chipped out the dead bolt with two specially designed Hatton rounds. In went the bang.

Booom!!!

I cleared the door, third in line, half a step behind Ricketts, and turned right. Fifteen feet across the room, an HRT operator sat with his hands cuffed in his lap as two terrorist mannequins held guns to his head. Curtis, still moving forward, dropped the bad guy on the left with a three-round burst of 10mm fire to the forehead. Ricketts took out the bad guy on the right. I lowered the muzzle of my weapon and moved between the streams of bullets toward the hostage. With no more than a foot of clearance on either side of my head, I reached down for his shoulders, pulled him under my arm, and launched for the door. Ricketts and Curtis cleared the rest of the room behind me, and we were gone.

The hot spot entry took no more than three seconds. All the bad guys were dead. All hostages alive.

We passed.

❖

NOTS is designed to extend one's abilities to the point where individuals can function best as a team. It is designed to imbue each new operator with the basic skills and confidence that will allow him to contribute to the overall mission. No one can really predict how a warrior will fare in true combat, but centuries of training have demonstrated that people perform as they train. Those who practice most usually win. HRT practices a lot.

The military has known about this process for hundreds of years. It's the psychology of regeneration — the phoenix principle. You take a capable, earnest spirit, then break it down, strip away any trace of ego, dig a crater of insecurity and need. Then you fill it back up with dogma and ability and trust. The talent you started with becomes harder, forged of a different metal and tempered in another image. It's an old process, perhaps ageless, but it works.

When you begin NOTS, you are like anybody else, part of the world. When you graduate, you are different, better, harder. Capable. You are enough.

9

DISCIPLINE

Shortly after NOTS graduation, team leaders from HRT's six individual cells met to divvy up the new bodies. HRT was broken into two sections at that time, Blue and Gold, with two seven-man assault teams and one eight-man sniper team in each section. Each team got to pick from the incoming NOTS class based on staffing needs and a rotation schedule that worked a lot like the NFL draft.

New operators didn't have much say in the process. The front office asked us to write down whether we wanted to become snipers or assaulters, but this turned out to be nothing more than a courtesy. They had already decided they needed snipers more than assaulters in 1991, but only two of the guys volunteered. I was not one of them.

Sniping, at least within the HRT environment, was a thankless and distinctly unglamorous job in 1991. Assaulters got to ride the fireball into the room and whisk away all the hostages. Snipers had to lie out in the weeds for days at a time, enduring subzero temperatures or sweltering jungle heat, hoping for an occasional glimpse of the bad guys. There was no question in our minds that when they published the HRT calendar, assaulters would get the cover.

My decision seemed simple enough. Since my first tour of the HRT building way back in New Agent Training, I'd dreamed of swooping down in a black helicopter, fast roping into a burning building, and going hands on with the world's most deranged terrorists. That's the primetime commercial. That's how they get people to try out. Nobody ever talked about the chance that I might have to spend the next few years playing tick bait in some rat-infested bayou.

Guess what I got.

Friday afternoon at 5:00, the front office assembled us in the classroom to announce our assignments. Three guys went to the assault side. Four to the sniper teams.

I felt sick to my stomach as they read off the names.

Walt, Charlie team. Ricketts and Eddie, Echo team. Whitcomb, Gold snipers.

All the pain I'd suffered while training for selection seemed like a colossal waste. Two weeks of hell. Five months of NOTS. All of it seemed like a monstrous fucking mistake.

I tried to look pleased with the assignment, but acting is not my strong suit. My first cogent thought was how long a commute I'd have to make if I refused the assignment and took a transfer to casework at the Washington Field Office. That was the only choice, of course. Accepting orders to HRT meant accepting orders, period. Personal preference was limited to cream in your coffee.

Fortunately, my new team leader took me aside with a congratulatory handshake so sincere, I felt like I'd won the lottery. The team gathered around me with encouragement and a couple cold beers. I knew the faces: Boat, Raz, Metz, Spuds, Masher. They looked content.

What the hell, I thought. Maybe there was something to this sniper business after all.

Two months later, as spring moved toward summer, I found myself crawling face down through a muddy swale, covered in long ribbons of burlap, mosquito netting, and deer ticks. A thick Virginia swelter hung over me like a sodden wool blanket. Sweat dripped off the tip of my nose and tapped out a slow rhythm on the scope of my sniper rifle. I had just pissed my pants for the second time since dawn, and I was kind of worried about the fact that it was the best feeling I'd had all day.

"Snake."

The word rose anonymously out of the field around me, somewhere off to the right. It sounded like an observation, nothing more.

Bushes ruffled behind me. I heard another man's voice.

"Don't move," he said. "I'll take care of it."

The sharp Appalachian twang filtered through the saw grass as heavy footsteps grew closer. It was Staff Sergeant Carl Morton, United States Marine Corps, and he sounded serious. I was glad not to be that poor snake.

"Snake!"

This time, the word carried a little concern. I couldn't identify the voice, but there was no mistaking the urgency behind it.

"Stand by. You stay right the fuck still until I . . ."

"Snake!" Another voice. This time it sounded closer. Maybe fifteen feet off to my right.

I lifted my head just high enough to clear the dirt with my

chin and look right. Something scaly was slithering my way, and I didn't feel like serving as a speed bump. This is his chunk of Virginia clay, I thought. If he wanted it, he could have it.

"I see you, sniper. Hold still." Morton was closer, now, but I couldn't see much from where I lay.

"Snake." A fourth voice. This time it was no more than a body length off to my right. I couldn't see the man through the grass, but I could hear him breathing, the way an animal breathes through its vocal cords when it's trapped in a corner.

"Snake!" Urgent.

Morton bounded through the grass from my left, a walking stick in one hand and a big Motorola radio in the other.

"Ahhhhh!!!"

A ghillie-clad Marine sniper leaped off the ground, so close he almost landed on my rifle barrel. He was trying to get the word *fuck* out of his mouth at high volume, but the four-foot copperhead hanging from his upper lip made enunciation difficult.

All I could see of the poor bastard was a thrashing pile of muddy burlap and two flailing hands as a long brown reptile in attack mode tried like hell to bite holes in his face.

I rolled over to my left to avoid the man's recklessly stomping combat boots as the snake loosened its grip to launch another strike. Unfortunately for the snake, his tail was still a foot off the ground and he had no base to strike from. The beast thrashed like a bullwhip in midair, yanked its fangs out of the man's lip, then fell to the ground and disappeared into the field. Staff Sergeant Morton arrived just in time to take a Mickey Mantle swing with his walking stick, but he missed.

I stared up at this bizarre Kabuki as Morton threshed the

grass, yelling at the Marine to "calm the fuck down" and inadvertently booting the hell out of my ribs.

"Snake," someone else observed as the serpent slithered off in a panic of its own.

The stricken sniper grabbed at his face with both hands and muttered something brave but unintelligible. Morton dropped his stick and pulled the man's hands clear long enough for me to make out his identity. Two bloody holes appeared just below his nose.

Shit, it's Boland, I thought. His face was starting to swell already.

Morton sat Boland down and radioed to another instructor for first aid.

"You need some help?" I asked. My fifty-hour NOTS first aid course seemed like a viable tool at that point.

"As you were, sniper," Morton barked. "You're still under observation, so get the fuck back to work."

I rolled back onto my stomach, pressed my head into the mud, and lay perfectly still as a pine slug worked its way up the bridge of my nose. "Still under observation" meant the snake attack offered no respite from the job at hand. I still had to find my target and kill him before he killed me.

"This is a training exercise, for godsakes," I whispered into the loam. It seemed like these guys were taking this stuff just a little too seriously.

Just then, two other instructors bolted out of the saw grass, hovered over the bitten Marine for a couple minutes, then guided him away. Morton looked left, then right, and called out in a voice loud enough for everyone to hear.

"There's snakes out here," he said, standing on understatement. "Big fucking surprise. There's snakes in the jungle, too. So deal with it. You see one, call out. Until then, get back to work. You got forty-five minutes left."

Not one of the thirty snipers in the field uttered a word. I fought the urge to breathe.

The radio in Morton's hand cackled out a command.

"Hawk to Walker One. I need you to move right twenty meters, southeast. Hurry up. I got a sniper and he's moving on me!"

The earth rumbled slightly beneath me as Morton leaped right and disappeared into the brush like a spooked buck. Suddenly my lungs filled with air and my heart began to beat, but I didn't dare move. The hawkers, or spotters, used this ploy sometimes, just to trick snipers into giving away their position. They knew we could hear them over the radios and they knew we would try to move when they weren't looking our way.

I'd made that mistake before and learned from it. At this point I thought it more sensible just to lie there and sun myself with the copperheads.

"Suck it up," I whispered.

I am not a patient man, but I can be disciplined.

The U.S. Marine Corps Scout/Sniper School occupies a tiny sprig of land in a remote corner of the Quantico base, near the rifle training battalion's machine shop. There are no ivy-covered libraries at this academy. In fact, there is no campus at all, just a nondescript cinder block building with blacked-out windows and a single classroom. Nothing about the sniper school stands out from the rest of the military base. That's just fine. Snipers like to blend with their environment. It's their way.

Despite its austere facilities, this school is widely recognized as the finest training ground of its kind in the world. It has produced some of the most capable killers in the history of warfare, including celebrity marksmen like Carlos Hathcock, a legendary exterminator of North Vietnamese. The sniper school admits very few students, and graduates only the handful that pass all courses of instruction. It is a grueling two-month indoctrination into the finer points of long-distance rifle marksmanship, field craft, observation techniques, camouflage, and stalking.

The curriculum is straightforward and uncomplicated: how to kill people from considerable distances without getting caught.

Until recently, HRT received three or four of the coveted billets each year. When I joined the Team, HRT spent plenty of time prepping each sniper for the course by offering intensive seminars in the art of the kill. Part of the reason was to get us ready for the Marine Corps school, and part of the reason was to help us re-jet after NOTS. Sniping is a painstaking discipline, and senior team members recognized the importance of slowing us down from balls-to-the-wall CQB runs through the shooting house. Snipers earn their living by moving at a snail's pace, whether sneaking up on an unsuspecting target or preparing for the shot. Speed is a bad thing.

We started with a trip to the Academy gun vault to pick up our rifles. Each of us received a carefully crafted weapon certified to shoot a quarter minute of angle at 200 yards. This meant that under perfect conditions, our rifles could print three consecutive rounds in the same hole. Our ten-power Unertl scopes carried bullet drop compensators, which tamed distances up to 1,000 yards with a simple twist of the fingers. All the sniper had to do was estimate distance and turn a dial to the appropriate number. Hold the crosshairs on the target and pull the trigger.

Once we got used to shooting from a prone position, each of us built a ghillie suit, considered haute couture in the trade. Developed by Scottish game wardens in the 1600s, the

ghillie suit became a popular means of woodland camouflage during World War II. There is no standard ghillie. Each
is hand built to reflect the personality of its owner and the
environment it will be used in.

Crafting this garment to individual tastes can be a long
and arduous process. It is a deeply personal business, too.
Other than your rifle, this is the only tool of the trade that
distinguishes you from everyone else. I spent days weaving
mine together from burlap strips, cargo netting, unbraided
hemp, and tree-bark-colored Cordura. When it was done, I
dragged it behind a truck through the mud, rubbed deer shit
all over it, and draped it reverently over the Marine Corps
sniper god, a darkly painted Styrofoam wigmaker's head,
which hid quietly in the forest behind the classroom building.

Crawling into a suit like this means crawling into a space
outside day-to-day society. It is a hard, unforgiving world
bordered only by cunning, discipline, and endurance. Marine Corps snipers often spend days stalking into position
just for the chance to take one shot at half a mile. My ghillie
smelled like roadkill and felt like a hair shirt soaked in mar-
malade, but it blended well with the local flora. I didn't care
about the way it made my stomach lurch, I just wanted to fit
in.

Full-time sniper training at the Marine Corps school began
for me in April 1992 with marksmanship instruction at the
1,000-inch (25-yard) range. National shooting champion
Gunnery Sergeant John Wayne "J.W." Patterson stepped into
the classroom Monday morning and introduced himself with
a ship captain's smile.

"I don't know where you men come from, and I don't
really care," he said. "My job is to turn you into the finest

marksmen in the world. I've got four weeks to do it, so I'll require your complete attention. Do you understand?"

Several men nodded.

"I'll ask you again. Do you understand?" He spoke in a conversational tone, with a nod of his head.

"Yes, Gunny!" The response came in unison, save four FBI voices just slightly off cadence. Military life came as a bit of a surprise to me at that point, but I tried to coalesce.

"In this business, you get one shot to make your point. One cold bore shot, based on a bullet strike differentiation of zero. That's your cold zero. You pull out your rifle, lie down behind it, and do what you were trained to do. If your cold zero is good, you win. If your cold zero is off, you lose. It's as simple as that. We ain't in the losing business."

After a brief lecture on physiology and bullet trajectory, each of us selected a .22-caliber rifle from a rack of weapons and headed out to get horizontal. HRT furnished shooting mats, beanbag supports, spotting scopes, and every other imaginable piece of gear, but none of this luxury seemed necessary that day. I could have shot the ear off a hummingbird left-handed with a snub-nosed pistol at 25 yards. I wondered why we were wasting our time on a Boy Scout plinker's range. We were ready for the big stuff.

Wrong again. There was nothing simple about the course or about what they wanted us to do. The scope on each rifle was just 2×, one-fifth the magnification of our regular scopes. Shooting the small-caliber round with the myopic scope closely simulated a much longer .308 shot, minus recoil. Like every other aspect of the school, this was a carefully planned building block designed to give each of us the foundation we would need to drop a man at considerably greater distance. Each and every meticulously organized instructional period offered one of the skills essential to becoming an effective sniper. Each and every skill contributed to an ability to kill without being killed. This was just the first step.

Gunny Patterson explained the rules of the first competition, Snipers' Poker. Each rifleman got five bullets and a target showing fifty-two overlapping playing cards. The object of the game was to build the best possible poker hand by marking the cards of your choice. The problem was that only a tiny margin along the edge of each card peeked out from between the others. If we touched one of the other cards, our shot did not count. The margin for error seemed impossibly small.

Dilemma: Do you go for four of a kind, knowing that one miss might still result in a good hand, or do you go for a straight or a flush to secure the win? Do you play it safe, counting on at least one miss, or do you go for the win, knowing it's all or nothing? It was just a game, but there was already a strong rivalry between HRT operators and the Marines. Every one of us wanted bragging rights to the first show.

To me, the strategy seemed simple. I took aim and went to work.

Twenty minutes later, we lined up with our targets in our hands for inspection. One of the Marine sniper candidates, a likeable young staff sergeant from Camp Lejeune, strutted like a gamecock among the group, flaunting four aces.

"It's the winning hand, boys," he said. He smiled out loud, boiling over with leatherneck pride. "Looks like Gunny Patterson's war dogs just kicked some FBI butt!"

He nudged my arm, looking to prove that he'd beat me, too. "What you got, Hoss?"

I held up a royal flush. Clean.

HRT had no battle howl, so I nodded and moved off to stow my gear.

On the first day of qualifications, in which we started at the 300-yard line and moved back to the 700, all four HRT snipers made the grade with flying colors. A considerable number of the Marines did not. Some failed the makeup as well and disappeared from the rolls. This success gave us credibility among the Marines and slowly transformed initial suspicion into a tight bond of mutual respect.

Land navigation came next. NOTS had already offered us considerable training with maps and compasses, so this two-week block of instruction passed like a nature walk. Methods of observation went well, as did range estimation, hide construction, and field craft. The four of us held our own while the rest of the class was whittled away in large numbers. Each day, another two or three of Gunny Patterson's war dogs packed up their cammo, collected their bus tickets, and skulked off. We grew stronger and more confident.

Then came stalking.

When Staff Sergeant Morton took the reins from Gunny Johnson and closed the classroom door the day of the first stalking lecture, I knew this would be a whole new kind of experience. Morton was a rigid tuning fork of a man who slept at parade rest and dreamed in Marine Corps red and gold. He wore tattoos of skulls and crossbones and the grim reaper (most of which he'd drawn and colored himself) from wrist to shoulder and ankle to thigh. His hair looked like a perpetual five o'clock shadow, so high and tight he could barely close his piercing blue eyes. His mouth opened grudgingly when he spoke, and he used conversational English only sporadically to accent an otherwise steady string of obscenities.

Morton was a hard man the way combat is hard. Though I found him certifiably mad, I immediately liked and respected this man who confided to me later, after graduation when we'd become close friends, that the Marine Corps had gotten too soft for him. He wanted to leave and join the French Foreign Legion.

Staff Sergeant Morton taught us the rudiments of stalking, then took us out to a clear-cut swath of land, hitched his hands to his hips, and told us this was where we would make or break ourselves as snipers. All the marksmanship in the world wouldn't do us a damn bit of good, he said, if we never got close enough to take the shot. Stalking our prey would require discipline, guile, and a mastery of all the field craft we had been taught.

The goal of Morton's little game sounded simple enough. Each of us would have four hours to move 300 yards to a position where we could see and shoot a spotter or "hawker." The spotter would be looking for us, too, with binoculars and a 40× spotting scope. Unfortunately, he would know approximately where we were. We would have to find him ourselves. And we'd have to get inside 100 yards to take our shot. Fire from anywhere farther away and the shot would not count.

Scoring sounded a little complicated. Each of us would receive a score between 0 and 10, depending on where in the process we were caught. Moving into a suitable forward firing position and taking a single shot before being spotted would get you 5 points. If you were successful, a "walker" would move to within five feet of you and command a second shot. The spotter would watch the area around his walker as you shot, looking for muzzle flash or other telltale signs.

Then it got tricky. If you got the shot off without giving away your position with muzzle flash, smoke, or "blowback" of surrounding vegetation, you got 7 points. In order to get 8, you had to identify the spotter and verify that you could actually see him and weren't just cranking off a round into the ground.

In order to get 9 points, you would have to remain invisible while the walker stood within arm's distance, reached out, and touched the top of your head. How do you earn the tenth point? You have to get away undetected.

Detection, for any reason, prior to the first shot resulted in a score of zero. Snakes, biological functions, and bad judgment changed nothing.

"Right," I said to myself. How in the hell were we supposed to find a camouflaged, highly trained spotter without getting seen first, then shoot him while he was staring at us with high-powered optics? Even if we did make it that far, how could anyone hide himself so well he couldn't be seen with someone touching the top of his head?

"You'll do it," they said, "and accumulate at least seventy points during ten stalks or you're gone." There would be three warm-ups for practice.

What the hell, I wanted to be an assaulter anyway.

Twenty minutes before noon our last day stalking, I crawled into a root pocket beneath a large deadfall and caught my breath. I felt protected in there, a refuge of cover and concealment the Marines call defilade. It felt like the perfect place to regroup and come up with a plan for the remainder of the day's four-hour suck. I'd been low-crawling since dawn, through a quagmire of mud, tick nests, and animal shit, and I still had no idea where the spotter was hiding. Several of the other snipers had taken shots, but I couldn't tell what they were aiming at. Things were starting to look bleak.

I pulled out my compass for bearings and decided, based on what I'd heard and seen, that the "hawk" had to lie within a five-degree sector just off my right shoulder. Plenty of time still, I thought. Hell, maybe I could see him from where I lay. So I added a new layer of camouflage greasepaint to my face, adjusted my tattered ghillie veil like they taught me, and pulled out some tiny binoculars. I inched my way up through the dense wall of roots and branches and dead leaves until I found enough of a hole to scan the huge field ahead of me. The tree line rose no more than 100 yards dead ahead. But there was no one there.

Then I saw it. Just to the left, at 287 degrees magnetic, sunlight flickered off something shiny. The morning dew had long since dried up. Whatever the sun was catching had to be man-made. It had to be him.

I trained my binoculars on the flicker, trying to crawl down the lens tube to get closer. Adrenaline started to course through my dehydrated veins, taunting me with excitement, trying to get me to do something quick and stupid, trying to make me human. But I ignored it, channeling the energy into discipline. I clamped my muscles down among the roots as tightly as vise grips, using the roots' structure and rigidity like a skeleton to compensate for my weak flesh.

Discipline. Calm the fuck down and search, I screamed at myself.

And then I saw him, at the base of a huge bifurcated oak. The flicker that had caught my eye was noon sun gleaming off the riser of his spotting scope tripod. There he sat, bigger than life, a staff sergeant instructor named Metcalf. He was scanning the field with a 40× spotting scope, looking for students to bust, snipers to kill.

Got you, you prick.

I choked down the adrenaline that rose in my throat at the thought of putting crosshairs on a human being and blowing his flattopped skull into the underbrush. Slowly, carefully, I lowered myself back down into the root cavity to prepare myself for the kill.

I checked my watch. Ten minutes before noon. That isn't enough time to load a round at the pace I was moving. This disciplined lethargy I'd forced myself to adopt had begun to work against me.

Then I realized he couldn't see me there in my hole. He couldn't have spotted me if I'd stripped naked and screamed out "Bang bang, you're dead!"

But taunts wouldn't get me a "kill" today. Attention to detail would. That's what they taught us. *Focus. Think like the snake that got Boland,* I told myself. *Work for it.*

I pulled my rifle out of its drag bag and loaded two brass blanks. The first round goes directly into the breech, so there is no question about whether it seats or not. The second goes in the four-round magazine, and the bolt slides forward, over the top.

The sniper rifle is a simple, elegant instrument. It has an on/off switch and a cheek pad. The trigger breaks precisely with the same pressure every time you touch it, and the barrel directs the bullet where you aim it. There is no judgment or jealousy or spite. It is pure utility. If not for its weight and aquiline profile, it would seem virtually benign.

I adjusted the ghillie veil over my head, rubbed mud into the greasepaint on my face, and ground some bark into my gloves. I checked the flash suppressor attached to the objective lens of my Unertl 10× scope, and started up again. This would be a blind movement until I got into position and lined up the scope. With any luck, the hawk would still be searching some other part of the field and miss my mistakes.

"Five minutes!"

Morton and the other walkers started yelling to us from

all over the field. Five minutes. Five minutes and today was over. So far my score was still zero.

"There you are, you rotten son of a bitch," I whispered, condemning him through the deep tube of my sniper scope. I was sick of this nonsense. He was a dead man breathing. "I got you now."

I guided the forestock of my rifle down the length of a dead root and shielded my face behind the stump. The rest of my body lay comfortably perched on a slope of soft wet Virginia clay.

Suddenly, I felt all the power of a 6'4" pit viper with a 100-yard neck. This Marine was about to die a violent death, like an unsuspecting rodent.

I looked left and right to make sure nothing would give away my position: no blade of grass that muzzle flash might sway, no stray roots touching the barrel, jeopardizing accuracy. I checked behind me to make sure I had a vegetal backdrop to keep the sun from profiling me and betraying my lair. I pulled the ghillie veil over the scope like an old-fashioned photographer, disguising any profile.

Killing like this is a mechanical process, an anonymous task.

I eased the rifle stock into my shoulder and lined up the shot. It was a gimme: 100 yards over flat terrain. I felt no real wind to speak of, no angle of incidence, no boiling mirage that hot plains could create that time of year.

My rifle felt every bit as steady as the resolve in my heart.

Staff Sergeant Metcalf's face looked almost life-size through the 10× scope. He was young; a handsome, stoic man whom I had talked to only once or twice. He wore Oakley sunglasses and a big wad of Levi Garrett in his right cheek.

I fingered the trigger and adjusted my own cheek on the leather stock pad with slow, monotonous precision. He would not see me in this hide unless I gave myself away with movement.

The morning wind settled into a fawn's breath, and the field lay still around me. Any movement at all would strike his trained eye as evidence of an intruder. Move too quickly and this stalk would be over: four hours of crawling and bleeding and swimming in pools of my own sweat and piss wasted. Six weeks of rivalry would dissolve into catcalls of "Busted!" as I carried my tired, defeated, sorry ass back to the bus to wait for the men who had already made it.

Fuck that.

I quartered Metcalf's face.

The secret of killing from a hide is knowing when to breathe, I reminded myself. *Don't you fuck up.*

Gunny Patterson's shooting instructions echoed in my ears.

"Take the muscle out of the equation," he said. "Rest bone on bone. Gather your sight picture, breathe out, and squeeze."

I tried to will my heart rate down, to make it beat with the rhythm of the lightly swaying grasses.

"Take out the brain stem."

I settled the crosshairs on the tip of Metcalf's nose, imagining how the 168-grain boattail hollow-point bullet would enter his skin at twice the speed of sound. It would pierce his skull with the force of a locomotive, bisect the cerebral cortex, and sever the spine from the brain. The temporary wound cavity created by the bullet's passage would liquefy all that was life, all the memories of childhood, all the love and hate and pride and envy that had defined him. It would snuff out a life that had barely begun, bleed all the promise and hope of noble intention out through his suntanned ears. My bullet would blow a hole the size of an angry fist right through the back of his head and land in the ground as benignly as a small stone. And it would all happen in less than the time it took my eye to record it.

Boooom!

The report echoed across the field and absolutely leaped in my heart. Got you, you rotten bastard.

I cycled the bolt quickly, without ever taking my scoped eye off him. Metcalf swung his own optics toward me like primitive radar, scouring the field for my position, looking for the brazen intruder he'd allowed to crawl up close.

"Who fired?" a voice called out behind me, maybe twenty or thirty yards.

"Who fired?"

He moved closer, trying to track the shot.

I waited until he walked within hissing distance before speaking up.

"Whitcomb."

The name sounded funny rolling past my tinder-dry lips. I fought the urge to move even my jaw muscles for fear of giving the hawker something to spot.

Staff Sergeant Morton vectored in on my muffled voice and lifted a handheld radio to his mouth.

"I got a shooter at your seven o'clock, hawk," he said, with overtones of resentment. He looked left and right for reference, then nodded his head. "He's inside the window. What do you see?"

I watched Metcalf through my rifle scope as he steered his own optics toward me and scoured the pregnant ground around Morton. There was a sniper within arm's reach of his spotter and he knew where to look. He'd sit there silently for several minutes, dissecting patches of earth, looking for anything less than natural. He'd look for mismatched color, displaced vegetation, unusual reflection, exposed skin. He wouldn't find any of that. I'd hidden myself just like they taught me.

Metcalf and I stared at each other through our respective scopes. He was searching. I was engaged, waiting for the kill. I could have taken out his wisdom teeth with another press of my trigger. All that separated me from him was 2.5 pounds of pressure and a vapor trail.

"Turn right," he barked through the radio. "Two steps."

Morton turned back toward me and did as he was told.

"Shit! What's he see?" I gasped. "I'm buried under a damned tree, for godsakes."

Morton stopped just off to my left and stood there. Walkers are not allowed to help the spotter. They merely respond to the spotter's commands.

"One step right."

Morton moved right and stopped in front of me. The barrel of my rifle scratched his back just above his middle belt loop.

"One more step right."

Morton moved past me, and I realized what Metcalf was doing. He couldn't see me after all, so he was guessing, "bracketing," hoping his walker would step over me or move in an odd manner that would give me up. He was cheating. They all did it.

"Sniper at your feet," Metcalf said.

Morton looked down at his muddy jungle boots.

"Nothing here," he lamented. My heart began to beat again.

"Who is it?"

"Whitcomb."

"Are you within five feet?"

"Yep."

"Ask him what I'm doing."

Metcalf lifted his cover and waved it up and down slightly.

"Moving his hat," I whispered through my nose, without even moving my tongue.

"He's got you," Morton radioed back.

We waited what seemed like an eternity, and then the spotter issued the 7-point command. "Tell him to take his second shot."

Now I was feeling my oats. I had put this guy on the ropes, just like they'd taught me. It was a tremendous feeling of accomplishment, seasoned with the awesome power of knowing I could stare this man down, right through the telescope that stuck out of his face, and whack him without consequence. I felt a chill running from the back of my neck all the way down my spine and into my balls. It felt like that stomach flutter you get cresting a hill too fast in a car. Weightless, toe-curling, mind-freeing thrill.

"It ain't over yet," Morton mumbled, looking straight ahead. He wanted to signal his buddy, but he couldn't. There are rules in this sniper game and honor forbade him to break them.

"Ain't but three guys made it so far. Metcalf's good."

The words eased the tension in my trigger finger, and I relaxed a moment, gathering the lessons they had given me. I had sixty seconds to take the second shot. No need to hurry.

"Always seize the advantage," Staff Sergeant Morton told us. "Give your enemy nothing."

So I waited, knowing that the victim's eyes were more tired than mine. He'd been working that scope all day, searing the ground with experience, trying to smoke me out. But he was human, too, and right then I held all the cards. He'd have to blink sooner or later.

That's when I'd do him.

I counted the seconds off in my head, trying not to let adrenaline speed up the sequence.

. . . fifty-two, fifty-three, fifty-four . . . He blinks.

BOOOOM!

My second shot hit him at the bridge of the nose, right above the scope lens. I could see the cherry and black blemish in my mind's eye. I allowed a brief fantasy in which Metcalf crumpled to the ground and poured out into the earth.

Elation, pure unadulterated thrill, shuddered through my body. My mind clouded in afterglow, just a little too much like sex.

I wandered away from that dark, wet, stagnant place to one like it, a long time ago. I faded back to a clearing in the woods outside Bethlehem, New Hampshire, one cold November day in 1968. My Uncle Mike led me toward something I didn't dare look at but couldn't wait to see. We'd been sitting in a sniper's lair of our own for most of the day, waiting for prey, holding the silence between us, sharing an occasional shiver and a wink. It was a dugout covered with fallen trees and moss and leaves, as natural as our instinct to hunt.

My ears still ring from the sound of his rifle. He took just one shot. It struck with little violence, no more than thirty feet away. There was a flinch and a tiny puff of fur.

I followed behind my uncle, plodding through ankle-high grass as the rain turned to sleet and stuck in balls to my red wool jacket. The ground was icing over, leaving everything around us glazed in a gray-white brilliance. The sun, nothing more than a suggestion, started to sink below the hill behind us, darkening the stormy air.

Uncle Mike, my personal hero, said nothing as we walked. This wasn't a place for words. It was a different moment than any I've lived. I felt the weight in my legs as we got closer and in my heart as he bent down and pulled out his gutting knife.

It was dead. A big buck, an animal twice as large as me, lying steaming in the snow, blood staining the ground bright red. The deer's left eye stared up at me without condemnation. Steam rose off his wet fur. He smelled like my jacket, only with a musky wildness I'd never known before. I couldn't see the hole where the bullet entered, but blood seeped down his coat like a decorative stripe.

"Big bastard, huh?" my uncle bragged, sniffling.

The voice registered, but his words bounced off my brain. This thing was dead. I'd seen him walking moments earlier, stepping carefully past our hide, moving through the crab apple orchard, searching for an evening meal. Majestic. I'd seen the breath rising from his nostrils. I'd seen his eyes searching for food and predators. I'd watched him move nobly beneath the rack of antlers. I'd felt his presence and his grace.

My uncle tucked the blade of his knife under the deer's heavy leg. He pushed it in and pulled up, laying open the shallow white fur of his underbelly, all the way to his breastbone. And then he reached in and pulled out the steaming red and blue and white guts, out onto the snow, cutting and yanking and tearing with the skill of a man who'd done this all his life. I looked on as if a thousand miles away, watching through a giant tube. Uncle Mike sniffled again with the storm. He cleared his throat, but said nothing.

"What's he doing?"

My uncle rolled the deer over, away from the gut pile.

"What's he doing?"

He handed me his rifle and tied a rope to the deer's hind hoofs.

"Whitcomb, can you see him? What the hell's he doing?"

Morton's voice called me back to a different kill. Uncle Mike faded as quickly as he'd come.

"He's giving me the finger," I answered.

I couldn't blame him. Nobody likes to lose.

"Indicate." Metcalf adjusted the focus ring on his scope as if the clarity weren't already perfect.

I knew what that meant. Morton had to "indicate" my position by placing his hand on the highest part of my body. In my case that happened to be the top of my head. This was nut-cutting time, the difference between 8 points (a good day) and that region of endless endeavor: a perfect 10.

Morton moved backward two steps, lifted his hand high over his head, and with great showmanship slowly lowered a finger right onto the top of my ghillie-covered pate.

A pause. I didn't even breathe.

"I got nothing," the radio barked. Metcalf sounded defeated. He knew he was dead.

I fought the urge to smile. Discipline. No point in gloating yet; I still had to get away.

Metcalf broke the silence.

"Tell him to exfil, we've got to get . . ." *BOOOOM!*

Another shot echoed across the field. It sounded close, probably no more than thirty feet away. Someone else had Metcalf on the ropes.

Without a word of congratulations, Morton bounded off toward the report, yelling "Who fired?" just like he did with me.

I waited until I saw the spotter shift his attention before slinking back down into the hole and granting myself the smile.

Ten. Fucking 10! I had just beaten a professional at his own game using his rules, which were stacked overwhelmingly in his favor. I had proven to myself that I could hide in plain sight and kill without consequence.

A light breeze pushed ghillie against my face as I sucked in a deep breath, full of pride and distance from where I'd started. Killing changes a man. Even when it's just in fun.

10

THE BIG ONE

I knew little about the Hostage Rescue Team when I reported for NOTS that Labor Day weekend in 1991. Despite their involvement in most of the previous decade's biggest cases, HRT remained a poorly understood organization even within the FBI. I'd heard stories since I joined the Bureau, about how the Team cloistered itself at Quantico, pumping iron and wasting ammunition until called in to take the glory jobs. Several friends in Kansas City had warned me not to try out, pointing to one reason after another why the job would ruin my career. No one ever really backed up his advice with credible reasoning — they all just *knew* that HRT operators were a bunch of arrogant knuckle draggers.

Part of this rationale dated back to the origins of the Special Agent job itself. Whether working forensic examinations at the lab, teaching paperwork at the Academy, or knocking down doors as a SWAT team breacher in Miami, agents consider themselves equal. They flash the same credentials, talk the same language, share the same identity. Each considers himself completely interchangeable within the organization — a human cog in the larger mechanism.

When Headquarters culled fifty agents out of the investigator population in 1983 and gave them their own compound and a license to play warrior, eleven thousand others went ballistic. Most considered counterterrorism the work of military units like the Army's Delta Force and the Navy's Seal Team Six. On top of that, each FBI office and nearly every law enforcement agency in the country, from small sheriff's departments to the U.S. Postal Inspectors, already had a SWAT team.

"Why should the FBI get even more deeply involved?" people asked.

The answer is pretty simple. Local, state, and federal SWAT teams train to handle limited situations with a relatively low threat level. With the exception of large metropolitan police departments like those of New York and Los Angeles, most agencies don't have the explosive breaching capability, air assets, or sheer numbers to handle a terrorist attack. It's not a question of individual ability. These departments boast extraordinarily capable SWAT officers. The primary problem is resources. The FBI can put fifty fully equipped operators in virtually any American city within six hours and back them with everything from helicopters to the investigative support of the world's most sophisticated cop shop.

Also, SWAT and hostage rescue are two different animals. SWAT tactics focus on slow, deliberate entry, using mirrors and body bunkers. This works well when executing high-risk dope raids and felony arrests, but can fall short when lives hang in the balance. While some big city departments have moved toward hostage rescue techniques, most of them realize it's a business they just can't afford.

I reported to the Gold snipers in the summer of 1992, with five months of NOTS training and two months of sniper school under my belt but no real sense of how we fit into the FBI's whole crisis response scenario. The only real orientation anyone ever gave us was a beer hall lecture on the Commandments of Public Behavior.

"Four things you never do during your time on the Team," Spuds warned. "No gold chains. No Speedos. No tennis on road trips. And *never* ask a woman to dance."

That sort of advice helped us select our wardrobe, but didn't give us much sense of the Team's provenance. All I had to guide me were the long rows of framed photos hanging in the HRT building's central hallway.

I had to ask before anyone told me about the Fawaz Younis arrest off the coast of Lebanon in 1987, which resulted in the longest flight from an aircraft carrier in U.S. history. I had to read an article in *Time* magazine to learn how Younis, one of several hijackers indicted for the piracy of a Jordanian flight, gave up religious martyrdom for drug dealing when the bottom fell out of the terrorism market. Federal agents used money and bikini-clad operatives to lure him into international waters, then brought HRT in to scoop him right off the deck of a private yacht. It was one of the boldest, most complicated arrests in the annals of American law enforcement, yet no one talked about it.

I had to ask about some of the other photos, too, including a sequence showing a man, a woman, and a child walking across a field outside Sperryville, Virginia. That, I learned, was the site of one of the most remarkable "open air assaults" since Lee Harvey Oswald shot JFK and Governor Connally with the same bullet. I eventually learned how an FBI SWAT team from the Richmond division had cornered a man wanted for the abduction of his estranged girlfriend and her son. When they found him holed up in an abandoned farmhouse just outside of town, their SAC called HRT.

After lengthy discussions, negotiators decided the man posed an imminent threat to the woman and her child, so they complied with his demand for a helicopter. HRT snipers secreted themselves in the woods around a large clearing and waited for him to emerge. Unfortunately, he came out with the woman at gunpoint, and the three-year-old boy strapped to his back.

Snipers sizing up their shot had to consider shooting a fast-moving target, just inches from a terrified little boy. Shots like that involve a very risky series of assumptions and calculations. If the sniper pulled the shot too early, he would miss just in front of the kidnapper, alerting him to the assault and prompting him to kill the woman. If he pulled a millisecond too late, he could kill a little boy. The margin of error is minuscule.

HRT commanders had already decreed that no one was getting on that chopper. The pilots had orders to lift off as soon as the bad guy got within fifty feet, no matter what. That left snipers with a narrow time frame in which to execute the most difficult assignment anyone could ever face. Once he showed himself, they had to shoot. No more stalling. No more options.

The man walked closer and closer, until everyone ran out of real estate. On command, an HRT assaulter lobbed a flash-bang grenade into the field. The chopper lifted off. The kidnapper turned toward the diversion, shielded his face from the prop wash, and in the blink of an eye, exposed the side of his head to an HRT sniper.

Boom. One shot.

The man and the boy fell to the ground. The woman turned and ran. Men in black flight suits raced across the field. They had no idea who was hit until they got to him and found a grisly sight. The little boy was fine, but the man's head lay in fragments all over the field. The hostage taker had died before he hit the ground. End of situation.

The wall inside the HRT building is lined with photos depicting missions like that, dating back to the Team's inception in January 1983. Top Ten fugitive arrests, prison riots, a white supremacist camp in the Ozarks, a murder standoff in Utah — an honor roll of outstanding successes.

Though operators seldom discuss old jobs, they all know which generation was responsible for each mission. HRT superstition states that New Operator classes are measured by the number and seriousness of the missions they bring to the Team. Generation Eight reported to Quantico on August 30, 1991, the day HRT assaulted a maximum security federal penitentiary in Talladega, Alabama, for example. Fifty operators blew their way in, using a monstrous door breach, stormed through the burned-out, riot-torn cellblocks toward a previously identified hot zone, and freed nine hostages in thirty-eight seconds.

No shots fired. No serious injuries on either side. Big success.

Bringing that sort of luck to the Team immediately put us in good standing with the rest of the operators. Generation Eight was seen as a good omen for the future. Positive karma. Healthy mojo. By any definition, we piped on with the promise of a bright future.

My own first taste of mission came midway through sniper school, in response to the Rodney King riots in Los Angeles. I was rebuilding an old Linkert motorcycle carburetor in the garage behind our new house when the 888 message scrolled across my beeper window. Three eights meant work, our code to assemble at the HRT building, pack our gear, and caravan north to Andrews Air Force Base for military airlift. I had waited impatiently for several months, hoping to see that message on my pager. I checked it from time to time just to make sure I hadn't missed the three simple numbers that would send me off to a place I'd never visited for a dose of that adrenaline chill.

888.

I took the time to wipe the grime off my hands, then grabbed my Browning Hi-Power off the workbench and tucked it into my belt. My kids were still too young to understand the concept of going away on a mission, but they knew very well that "putting the lump under my shirt" meant it was time to leave for work.

They ran into the house, screaming "It's the big one, Mom! It's the big one!"

I laughed to myself as Rosie helped me find an overnight kit among the still unpacked moving boxes. I had joked out loud, every time my pager sounded, that the tone would one day signal "the big one." That's what the job was all about, after all — that mission no one else in the world could handle. When my pager finally went off for real, the boys jumped up and down like the X-Men had landed.

The mount-out process still seemed a bit mysterious as I raced toward Quantico. We'd airlifted a training mission to Camp Lejeune just after NOTS, but that lacked the electric ingredient of consequence. It's the difference between riding around in a fire truck and actually getting to turn on the siren. Once someone officially says "Go!" a magical animation fills the air. Your legs just feel like pumping.

I didn't have to wait long to get a taste of the effort and coordination necessary to move fifty men and their equipment cross country on short notice. The place was already rocking when I pulled in to the compound and headed for the Gold sniper equipment cage. The front office was dealing with Headquarters, trying to reconstruct details of the situation. Our intelligence cell was identifying known threats. The logistics unit was lining up resources. One of the supervisors was drafting an operations order. Operators were loading the gear.

The Team is almost wholly self-sufficient, so gear includes virtually every imaginable bolt, gizmo, and article of clothing necessary to maintain seventy-five operators and support staff for at least five days. HRT carries its own vehicles, tents, weapons, food, ammunition, medical supplies, communications equipment, generators, climate-appropriate clothing, logistical equipment, and a thousand things that don't fit in any particular category. The trick is to move it all from the Quantico compound to virtually any spot on earth in time to resolve the crisis.

When I first joined the Team, we had to fit everything in a single Air Force C-141. Despite the plane's impressive size, the fuselage limited our payload to a couple of utility trucks, three pallets of gear, and a helicopter or two. Operators had to pare their personal kit to a tactical bag, which held things like body armor, flash-bang grenades, flashlights, and assault boots. They carried an MP-5 subgun and spare magazines in a black Cordura case, and a backpack full of personal effects. Snipers got the added "luxury" of their primary .308 rifle, a CAR-16 or M-14 patrolling weapon, and an expedition pack filled with the specialized clothing they'd need to spend time in the weeds.

"Sixty-five pounds of high-speed, lightweight gear," guys said, referring to the standard duty load. "When are we going to stop trying to fit ten pounds of shit in a five-pound bag?"

Every man on the Team carried additional mission-specific equipment, depending on his specialty. Golf team swimmers saw to the mountains of dive gear. Climbers packed everything from ropes and caving ladders to friction boots and face bolts. The EMTs replenished drugs, IV bags, splints, trauma dressings, intubation tubes, and suture kits on the ambulance.

The load masters configured the tons of equipment to meet military weight regulations, the team leaders briefed their men on the mission, and the communications technicians set about trying to ensure that everyone could talk to each other once we hit the ground.

In one well-oiled, conversation-free push, the Team packed up its toolbox, drove fifty miles to the airport, and strapped it into a plane. Flight time aside, we felt capable of responding to any crisis within the contiguous United States before the bad guys' barrels cooled down.

I remember how anticipation gurgled in my stomach as we rolled down the runway into Edwards Air Force Base outside Ontario, California, en route to the L.A. riots. Though the L.A.P.D. surely could have handled the situation by themselves (and in fact did), the politicians had put out a national 911 — a Mayday of historic proportions — and HRT responded. It had been twenty-five years since a major American city went up in flames, and everyone with a gun and a badge rolled into town looking to join the fight.

We didn't touch down until mid-afternoon of the day after, when the serious violence had already passed. But it still felt urgent. As soon as the cargo doors opened, we jumped off the plane, shuffled our battle gear into box trucks, and climbed aboard a big yellow school bus headed for South Central. The FBI crisis response juggernaut gathers steam quickly, and this was no exception. SWAT teams from Salt Lake City, Chicago, Phoenix, and other cities touched down all around us in a steady stream of incoming flights. Negotiators, communications technicians, crisis response teams, everyone with an angle had their hook in this one.

The bus fell quiet leaving Ontario on I-10, as I sat back in my seat and glowed with pride at being part of some huge altruism, of reaching out to save Americans in peril. I remember looking out at the L.A. skyline as thick black smoke drifted in giant plumes over Watts. This was no skirmish. This was anarchy in the City of Angels. Civic dissolution.

I felt part of it — part of the cure. My dad had been chief of Franconia's volunteer fire department when I was a kid, and I remembered watching him race out of the driveway every time the big whistle sounded. I felt pride in his authority, if just by lineage.

I sat in the back of that bus sucking slowly on a wad of broadleaf chewing tobacco, knowing that I had become everything HRT taught me to be. Invincible. All I needed was the opportunity to prove it.

But as is so often the case in America today, the response was too big and too late. We stumbled over ourselves, looking for bad guys who had already fallen back into average, everyday lives. We filled the parking lot outside Dodger Stadium that night with what had to be the largest assembly of police blue and SWAT black in American history. L.A.P.D., L.A. County Sheriff's Department, California Highway Patrol, FBI, Marshals Service. Thousands of them: SWAT teams and crisis response groups, all clad in tactical Nomex and Velcro. Guns and riot gear. Salvation. The righteousness in that vast parking lot was so thick you could feel yourself pumping up just wading through it.

We took to the streets that night in Chevy Suburbans, staring out the windows from behind assault rifles and body armor, showing a "presence." A few people waved and smiled, but most looked at us with that visceral contempt for authority that pervades youth and ghettos. A vehement hatred seethed behind the torn curtains and piles of burning yard furniture as we passed.

I remember the look on one little boy's face. No wonder or respect glistened in his eyes. No dad had ever taught him that the police were there to serve and protect. No brother or cousin or friend had ever joined the police force. The cops just came to beat up his brother or harass his uncle or accuse him of dealing drugs. The police came to take his people away. We were the bad guys, the men in blue suits who made his mother cry. He didn't want our help in making his life better. He wanted us gone the way he wanted a fever gone.

What I saw in his eyes was a reflection not of a rider on a white horse galloping in to fight back the rioting hordes but the devil himself, tearing apart everything he knew to be safe and familiar and true. These people did not need us. They didn't want to be saved. We were the enemy.

By nightfall on the second day, South Central had settled back into boredom. Its residents had no use for a thousand white cops in end-of-the-world gear. The initial furor, or "civic rage" as some of the news reports called it, blew off like a random storm and passed the way it always does, on to some other place, in a distant rumble.

Shortly after the riots, I got word of another kind of mission. The Border Patrol's elite BORTAC unit had geared up for a three-week drug interdiction effort along the Mexican border and offered HRT two slots on the team. Hooch, the Blue sniper team leader, asked for volunteers, and I jumped at the opportunity. A couple weeks later, we packed our gear for a little fun and sun along the Rio Grande.

Explaining this to the boys took a little longer than the L.A. trip. Their interpretation of "the big one" now boiled down to lots of days between games of tag and fishing trips with Dad. Rosie made sense of my ten days in L.A. by showing them where I was on the evening news each night, but there would be no news reports about the Mexico jaunt. My two-week absence during HRT selection had set a personal record for child neglect, so trying to give them a sense that I was ever coming back at all took a little creativity.

After a few waves of little-boy tears, I joined Hooch aboard the Bureau's Saber Liner and set out for a little adventure. Four hours later, we landed into a Southwest sunset and spent the next three weeks patrolling the well-worn trade routes north of Nogales to abandoned airstrips and tank roads in the Coronado National Forest.

Some days we saddled trail horses and rode into remote bivouacs for three-day interdiction ambushes. Other days we fired up a stable of dirt bikes and rode the thin wire fence that marks the southern edge of prosperity. BORTAC called the process "cutting track," where you search for evidence of caravans ferrying dope north to Tucson. Once you "cut" human tracks, you simply follow them right to the source. Dopers move slowly through the night and hunker down in crudely built shelters during the day. That gave us time to catch up.

We worked at night, mostly, plying the darkness with image-enhancing optics and ears trained to distinguish human sounds from lesser nature. I learned to pack my gear meticulously so I'd know the touch of every fabric and the utility of every device. I learned the danger of noises that didn't belong. I learned to repack my MREs by food group so I'd know where to find simple carbohydrates at 3:00 A.M. when the shaking became uncontrollable and the cold made concentration a consuming effort. I figured out how to piss in a bottle without moving enough to give away my position. I built a routine of duty that allowed me to segment the night into manageable shifts complete with distraction and stupor. The whole process became as natural as any day at the office.

We were playing basketball at a Tucson motel one afternoon when word came down from Border Patrol headquarters that intelligence experts had intercepted plans for a mule train carrying several hundred pounds of Peruvian flake to a weigh station just inside the American border. The operation commander in El Paso wanted a fire team of eight men to pack light for a one-night movement.

Doug Bob, our rugby-playing team leader, called out seven names, including mine. Traveling light meant one MRE, two quarts of water, a poncho liner, a medical trauma pack, and whatever ammunition we wanted to lug. The plan called for us to fly in to a remote landing strip, then land-navigate five miles to an overwatch above the station.

Just before midnight, eight of us climbed aboard a U.S. Customs Service King Air turboprop which had been seized from a Colombian drug cartel. We flew a nine-minute hop to a remote airstrip on a barren valley floor. The pilots slowed the plane just long enough for us to pile out and then fire-walled the engines in a stop-and-go turnaround designed to look like a dope drop. I found it odd, as we hurried across the tarmac into a waiting cattle hauler, that in some parts of America it makes better sense to act like a criminal than the law.

Once aboard the trailer, no one said a word. My feet slipped in the cow shit on the floorboards as the trailer hopped along the potted gravel road. I slammed the bolt forward on my CAR-16 and activated the three-power Litton nightscope. I wore cammies, jungle boots, face paint in a tiger-stripe pattern, a boonie hat, and thin polypropylene underwear. The 40-degree air cut right through the material, but I knew I'd heat up once we started walking.

"Travel light, freeze at night," my dad used to tell me on camping trips. I never really figured out whether that was a strategy or a warning, but that night, I opted for less.

The dual exhaust of the big Chevy truck covered the hushed tones of Doug Bob's last-minute briefing: We'd ride three miles down an isolated stretch of farm road to the mouth of a narrow mountain pass, then patrol southwest in two-man teams. The truck would slow down enough for us to jump out, but not enough to alert possible sentries. Doug Bob cinched up the shoulder straps of his ruck, suggesting the landing might feel a little stiff.

We performed a final equipment check. I carried standard-issue Marine Corps deuce gear, my CAR-16, my Hi-Power, a half-dozen flash-bang grenades, and a trusty poncho liner, which served as bedroll, parka, and lightweight sniper hide. A laminated topographical map rested in the right side pocket of my cargo pants, along with a red lens penlight and a trauma dressing.

A compass hung from my neck with a knotting cord that would allow me to maintain a pace count and calculate linkup points by distance traveled. Working several hundred square miles of desert with just a threat of moon makes navigation difficult. There are no road signs, no mile markers. The tiny rock outcropping we'd designated as our linkup point was just another elevation line on a very large map. That compass felt very important.

I checked and rechecked my gear, then jumped up and down just to ensure that it didn't make any noise. It's never the things that go right that hurt you, it's the things that go wrong. The only way to stack the odds in your favor is to obsess about the details.

My BORTAC partner, a short, soft-spoken biker type named Subee, and I jumped last. I rolled into the bar ditch, crawled through a barbed wire fence, and hunkered down behind a knee-high prickly pear cactus. We waited until the truck disappeared over a hump in the road, leaving us alone in the vast desert valley. Subee stood up first and took point with the map and compass. I kept the pace count — 65 steps per 100 meters — and covered our movement through my rifle's nightscope.

With or without night vision goggles, everything looked the same: threatening. Fifteen-foot saguaros rose out of the rocks and underbrush like a thousand sentries. Mountains towered above us, to the left and right, channeling us south, but the horizon disappeared into the landscape beneath the star-crusted sky. If I'd been sitting in a hot tub at some dude ranch I would have considered this one of the most beautiful scenes of my life, but with every other step leading to a few more cactus spines in my shins, the scenery offered little comfort.

Just before 2:00 A.M., Subee held a fist above his head, signaling stop. Three hours of steady walking had warmed me to the point where I wasn't shivering, but the night stung just the same. My pace count put us within 50 meters of the rally site, so I pressed my eye against my scope bellows and scanned the area looking for friendlies. Doug Bob's operations order called for all team members to activate "fireflies" when they got into position. These matchbox-size infrared glow plugs blink every two seconds in a light spectrum visible only through night optics. Fireflies allowed us to spot each other without giving up our position to the bad guys.

"Evening, boys," Doug Bob whispered. His bush hat blinked a warm white glow about eight feet from my trigger finger.

I counted three other signatures and focused on their faces: Doug Bob's partner, Gary, and Team 2: Fish and Matt. Looks like we actually beat one of the other teams into position.

"Grab yourself a seat. It looks pretty quiet."

Doug Bob pointed west about 250 yards to what, in this light, looked like just another rock outcropping on the dark side of the moon. I peered through my scope and realized it was actually an old ranch with the remnants of a corral and three small outbuildings.

"Where's the trail?" I asked, taking a knee and picking a few cactus quills out of my leg. The dopers supposedly used the house as a supply post to catch a bite before moving north.

"You're standing in it," he said.

I stepped off into a swale beside Doug Bob and the others.

"We sit here until they make the house, then we set up for the hit."

The hit, according to the arrest plan, would look a whole lot like a standard military "L" ambush. Doug Bob and Gary would straddle the trailhead to prevent their escape. The rest of us would line the trail, waiting for them to pass. Once the dope train fell into the elbow, we'd announce our authority in Spanish, then move in for the hookup.

Border Patrol agents don't work much with arrest or search warrants. They rely on probable cause, and as Doug Bob repeated on several occasions, "Wandering around in the middle of the desert with a bunch of dope makes it probable cause enough for us to arrest them." Unlike the carefully scripted, anal retentive operations orders I'd grown used to in my outfit, the Border Patrol did things the old-fashioned way: by feel.

By the time I checked my watch two hours and ten minutes later, the cold had come for us in earnest. The shaking had gotten so bad I didn't think I'd make it through the night. The lightweight polypro and woefully thin poncho liner felt useless. I had already used up all my mind games, trying to fantasize about warmer times, doing isometric exercise to heat up the muscles, and shaming myself into not acting like a pussy. But this had become serious.

Hypothermia dulls your fine motor skills and dims rational thought. At first you start to cool from the walk, as your body settles back into its rest metabolism. After a while, you pull the poncho liner loosely over your shoulders to stop the radiant heat loss. When that no longer works, you pull it tightly around you, tucking in the edges to conserve body heat. Next you pull it over your head, cutting down on what you can hear, but preserving your cognitive abilities.

When that no longer works, you reach into your ruck for the food you've carefully packed for energy. The entree acts like a big log that will smolder for a long time, and the dessert acts like kindling, sparking the fuel in your stomach to restore heat through your limbs and feeling in your fingers and toes. Finally, when the meal wears off and nothing seems to work anymore, you just shake, realizing that the cliché about packing light and freezing at night is God's honest truth. You curse yourself for getting into a position like this to begin with, and vow to carry everything but a Coleman stove next time out.

I had long since reached the thin line between hard and stupid when Doug Bob called out an end to the suffering.

"Saddle up, boys; I got movement."

His Texas accent sounded familiar even at a whisper.

I moved my frozen right hand slowly around the pistol grip of my rifle and lifted the scope to my eye. The night sky turned jade green, and I could see them in outline just outside the corral, moving toward us — three, four, five mules. It was still too early to count bodies.

"Nobody twitches until I call the shot," Doug Bob said.

I knew the drill from here on in, but despite my several months of HRT experience, this still qualified as my "first time." Most of these guys ran raids like this a couple of times a month or more, working the vast no-man's-land between Southern California and El Paso. I'd run down my share of bad guys, but none of them ever walked a mule train through open desert with high-powered weapons. Suddenly the cold seemed to disappear.

No one spoke.

I busied myself with gear considerations. I hung a flash-bang off the little finger of my right hand so I could work the trigger in a firefight and still yank the pin with my left hand. I adjusted my scope's focus on the back of Fish's head to anticipate close contact. I arranged the spare magazines, making sure the bullets faced forward for quick reloads. I pulled the poncho back over me, breaking up any human outline and blending myself into the rugged terrain.

The mule train moved closer and closer until I could hear the unshod hoofs in the loose gravel.

Five mules. Four men.

They moved slowly without conversation, like upright shadows.

A final shiver ran up my spine as I touched the safety with my thumb and laid my finger along the trigger guard. The other seven guys squatted to my right and left. No noise.

The first man walked past me, close enough that I could smell him. Then a mule, a second man, another mule. Even in the dark I could see the boredom and loneliness on their faces. One of them carried a walking stick. I saw no weapons.

"Freeze! Federales!" Doug Bob's Tex Mex Spanish sounded foolish in the gravity of the moment. I almost smiled at two weeks' worth of bar memories and war stories, but then the whole place just fucking exploded.

Everyone else in the ambush erupted in a chorus of Spanish. "Freeze. Put your hands up. Hit the ground. Police."

"Don't you fucking move!" I screamed the line I'd found

success with during my Missouri years. So what if it was English. They'd need a little in the penitentiary.

The trail boss jumped three feet straight up in the air and hit the ground running. No talk, no "What the hell is that," no excuses. He just disappeared.

The mules started to buck, knocking one of the runners to the ground long enough for Fish to jump him and pin him beneath the stampeding hoofs.

BOOOOM!!
BOOOOM!!

Somebody tossed a couple sting balls into the mix, spewing steel shot in all directions and pissing off the mules even more than all the yelling had.

Two of the animals booked, their loads strapped down so well we never found a single errant brick. Subee grabbed one of the beasts by its halter, and the fourth spun in circles, lost in the melee of Border Patrol agents and bad guys.

I leaped out from under my poncho just as the third man in line tried to exit toward Mexico and caught him right in the knees with a cross-body block. I made it to my feet before he did, jammed the muzzle of my rifle close enough for him to understand American directions, and tried to make sense of the roiling confusion. The only way I could tell us from them was by the volume of their voices and the darker color of our clothes.

"Stop! Stop, you asshole," Fish yelled as someone disappeared over a rocky shelf into the brush. He started after the man, then pulled up. We had most of the dope and two of the runners. Chasing the others through this kind of turf could create a lot more trouble than we needed.

"That's enough!" Doug Bob yelled out.

Everything quieted.

I sucked in great lungfuls of crisp, dry air, panting. The

mules twitched on their tethers, backing and turning like some low-rent rodeo.

"That's enough, dammit. This is the Border Patrol. You're under arrest."

Border Patrol? I thought. After all my time in the field, NOTS, sniper school, and a couple of missions, my first real action came in a remote desert pass with seven men from an agency I'd hardly even heard of.

"Border Patrol. Shit," one of the Mexicans said in passable English. He sounded like he'd been there before.

After a while, it seemed like all our missions ended up like that one, freezing our asses off against some tree in the middle of a godforsaken wilderness. Most nights, we sat out in the woods, fighting to stay awake, desperately trying to keep from lapsing into complacence. That seemed one of the toughest parts of the job. The CQB and the shooting and the land navigation and the other skills we could learn and practice. It was out there in the night that I struggled to maintain focus twelve hours at a time, concentrating on every sound, every scent, culling out that one stand-alone sensation that might accomplish the mission. I accepted the cold, knowing that the one moment I got to prove myself might come and go so fast I wouldn't even recognize it.

My third mission began with the same midnight shivers. Headquarters had just deployed us to an isolated chunk of wilderness bordering the eastern rim of the Grand Canyon. A convicted murderer named Danny Ray Horning had escaped from a maximum security prison, navigated ramparts of concertina wire, and crossed a stretch of desolation so barren, most state officials originally believed him dead. To prove them wrong, Horning kidnapped a family of tourists and shot a local deputy sheriff who tried to rescue them. Park rangers narrowed the chase to a 7,000-foot-high isthmus of underbrush and evergreen before realizing they possessed neither the manpower nor the resources to run him down.

That's when they called us.

"Hey, Whitcomb."

Eight hours into our first shift, my partner, Spuds, and I found ourselves guarding opposite sides of a pine tree. He and I had been paired up since I'd graduated from sniper school, but this was our first actual mission together. He struck me as a quiet, intense former Marine who walked board straight with his lips pursed like a smoker without the cigarette. I'd worked with people like him before, but always at a distance. His face suggested torment, like faces on strangers you push your children away from.

Spuds was old-school HRT, trained by the first- and second-generation guys who'd earned their bones in the jungles of Vietnam. He was hard, like punishment; the kind of soldier you can push out to the edge — the real edge.

"What?" I spoke the word as quietly as possible, merely lending it to the predawn air.

"You awake?"

Awake? Of course I was awake. I had mentally field-stripped all fourteen weapons assigned me by the team, recited from memory the title, plot, and approximate production dates of all thirty-six of William Shakespeare's plays, debriefed my Border Patrol and Los Angeles missions, reclimbed a particularly scenic 5.10 crack route up the Cannon cliffs, and come damned close to reconciling quantum mechanics within my unification theory of the universe. I'd spent the last eight hours too miserably to consider the possibility of where and when I might next get to part company with consciousness.

Why would the man who inspired a reasonably well educated English major from a good family to spend a virtual lifetime leaning up against a fucking pine tree for absolutely no reason at all want to know if I was awake?

I turned to say something clever, but Spuds beat me to the punch.

"I just relived every erotic experience of my entire life," he said.

Law enforcement is built on partners. From *Dragnet* to *The X-Files,* America has based its sense of crime-fighting culture on pairings. HRT was no different. Snipers work best in teams of two, with one man watching through a scope while the other rests. Sometimes one man covers a target with his rifle while the other works the radio. Partnership works well in these situations.

Unfortunately, partners do not always share the same perspective on the world. Sometimes they don't even come from the same world.

"Oh," I said.

It was the only response I could think of. I didn't know him well enough to inquire about details. My early experiences in the Springfield RA had taught me the consequences of stepping out early. I was still one of the FNGs, and my job was to listen.

HRT is like a fraternity in many ways, with carefully circumscribed rules of behavior and a clearly delineated pecking order. When the top dog buys Oakley sunglasses, everyone else buys Oakley sunglasses. If one of the dominant personalities decides the team is going to a particular bar after training one night, everyone goes with him.

It's part of the integration process, part of proving yourself worthy, every single day, of the trust others place in you. When Gold snipers held a team meeting, I sat at the edges, waiting for a safe opportunity to try and sound connected. In the full-Team meetings, which are held every day at 8:00 A.M., I tried to run clear of the smartass wit and ribald humor that could turn quickly on all but the most intrepid Team veterans. Fifty well-educated, extremely capable alpha males tend to grate on one another from time to time, and I just wanted to lie low long enough to figure out the rules.

My relationship with Spuds went pretty much the same way. I would spend the remainder of the week trying to impress him, measuring every step, calculating each comment in hopes of gaining his trust. I would sneak through the woods like my Uncle Mike had taught me, as we searched land grids for Danny Ray. I would lie perfectly still for hours at a time during the night surveillances, hoping Arizona's desperado of the week would slither by so we could throw him back in jail.

I even sat patiently as we waited for the assault teams to parade him past us at three o'clock in the morning once the dogs ran him to ground. I could have done a dozen things to make myself more comfortable during my shifts with Spuds, but I didn't because I wanted to create a favorable impression. The HRT way.

Partners are partners, right? What would James West be without Artemus Gordon? How would Woodrow Call get by without Augustus McCrae?

Other tandems whiled away the time in small talk. Not Spuds and I. Those were the only words we spoke all night.

11

EARLY MIDNIGHT

One of the most important lessons HRT taught me in my first year was how closely training and reality ski the same fall line. The only way to prepare for war, after all, is to inject a little violence into everyday life. Snake charmers sip a little cobra venom to trick their bodies into developing immunities. Sword swallowers grow calluses to shield against the blade. Even athletes tear down their muscles so they'll grow stronger for competition.

That's the idea behind HRT's day-to-day training schedule. Combat requires extraordinary personal commitment. When the bell goes off for real, you never know what lies around the next corner. Just as in tryouts, you don't know if the race of your life is going to last forty yards or ten miles, so you run as hard as you can as long as you can, knowing that you have done everything humanly possible to prepare for the finish.

Sometimes everything goes well. Sometimes it doesn't.

The only way to stack the odds is to run it as close to real as possible. Over and over again.

To do this, HRT concentrates a significant amount of time on "core skills training." Firearms and CQB are the primary tools of tactical resolution, so much of the daily schedule revolves around these fundamental competencies. Two weeks at a time, half the Team stands in duty status, ready for crisis response. The other half concentrates on the basics.

Workdays run pretty much the same for everyone. Monday through Friday, the day starts with an 8:00 A.M. meeting in HRT's classroom. Everyone attends. All operators sit and listen attentively as the front office provides updates on pending missions, world news, training schedules, special events. The informal meetings are one of the Team's oldest traditions and a central proving ground for pecking order. Lots of times the wit and banter in that room would bring a professional stand-up comic to tears.

After the meeting, operators break to the equipment cages to prepare for the morning's activities. Three days a week, operators ingest a heavy diet of small-caliber ammunition, high explosives, and violence. Assaulters practice CQB on Tuesdays and Thursdays. Snipers head to the rifle deck or one of the Marine Corps ranges to work on technique. On Wednesdays, the assaulters focus on handgun and MP-5 drills while sniper teams take over the shooting house for their own CQB drills.

HRT operators get two hours each day for physical fitness training, and usually one session of defensive tactics. They can pursue martial arts training on the side if they want, but the job is not about fist fighting. Team members focus on a very limited number of hand and foot strikes designed to destabilize people they can't shoot. Hysterical hostages running at an operator, for example, can get in the way of a vital shot. Taking them to the ground with a simple kick might not look good on the evening news, but it might save their lives and the lives of other hostages.

Monday is set aside for specialty training, such as medical refreshers, fast rope descents, breaching, climbing, photography — a dozen or more perishable skills. Fridays are usually P&P, or projects and planning, days. Each operator is assigned some sort of research and development project. This gives them a chance to catch up on everything from unstable shooting platforms to new sighting devices.

Due to the nature of the business, HRT stresses realism everywhere possible. Training for combat carries a risk in its own right, but operators need to understand the ordered chaos that spins through violent confrontation. They have to know that every time they pick up a gun, they face life-or-death consequences. Lapses in judgment can kill, even in training. The Team lost a man in 1986 when he fell from a helicopter and died during a fast roping scenario. Our military counterparts have lost people in training exercises to everything from gunshot wounds to drowning. It's part of the deal.

To counter this sense of consequence, HRT trains in the most realistic situations possible. That's why the FBI buys each operator more than ten thousand bullets a year. Some people might consider this kind of target practice a waste of taxpayer dollars, but they don't understand that firearms training is not just about maintaining accuracy. Turning a corner into the maw of a blazing .45 doesn't seem so intimidating if you've done it a thousand times in rehearsal. Every bullet you shoot adds a layer of familiarity with the trade. The sound of every shot fired conditions the ear to accept the rage of combat. Every twitch of recoil teaches the hand how to hold the weapon true. Every bullet whizzing past your face braces the adrenal glands in trust of your teammate's ability.

Some instructors talk about the "muscle memory" this

kind of repetition ensures. But muscle has no memory. Only the mind has memory, and conditioning it through the pulse of close personal combat is essential to hostage rescue. When someone rages into a dark basement at four o'clock in the morning to save you from some terrorist (don't think it can't happen), you want him to know in his heart and in his soul that he is better prepared, better equipped, and better suited to victory than anyone else.

"How do you deal with that kind of stuff every day?" a friend asked near the end of my first year. We smoked cigars and worked on motorcycles in my garage most Friday nights. "It's got to be stressful."

"Stressful?" I said. "Never thought about it like that."

I really hadn't. Running CQB routes day after day conditions you to confrontation. I knew, when I made the Team, that my new job presented a very high likelihood of mortal confrontation, but I thought about it the way you think about dying of a heart attack. You know it might hit someday, just not this day.

Ninety percent of winning is knowing you can. That's why every member of the Hostage Rescue Team treats training scenarios as if they were actual missions. We responded to many in my first year on the Team, but one stood out particularly well.

"Hang on once we clear the jetty, boys; this thing will slap you around!"

Big Jack engaged the transmission and settled the boat's twin Chrysler V-8s into a throaty rumble. I sat second in line on the right gunwale behind my team leader. Five other Gold snipers straddled the bench seat behind me, one hand on their MP-5 and one hand on the pommel loop. Blue snipers lined up beside me on the other gunwale. Big Jack drove standing up, beside a Seal Team Six navigator.

No one talked.

The ass end of the boat settled into the water and we pulled forward, past a row of seagulls who had absolutely no idea what to make of sixteen men clad in black Nomex and machine guns, motoring their way into the predawn Atlantic. The gray profile of our rigid-hull inflatable boat, or RIB, blended with the water, almost invisible in the moonless sky. The dim amber light was enough for Big Jack and his coxswain to read their navigation instruments but not enough to give away our position.

"This is going to feel like a thirty-minute train wreck," Jack told us in the pre-op briefing. The twenty-eight-foot craft looked like a cross between a Boston whaler and a Zodiac, but could almost stand on end when the pilot slapped on some power. "Don't try to fight it, just go with the seat and let me worry about the driving."

No problem, I thought. We had ridden on helicopter skids running at 100 knots so low the treetops stained our boots green. We'd fast roped onto ships under way in the dead of night with seas pumping so hard we had to time the swells or risk breaking our legs on the lurching deck. What could be so tough about a boat ride?

I looked around just to make sure everyone else shared my optimism. Beef sat directly across from me, so big his body armor slapped against the man behind him. He would have been a good bellwether to watch during the ride, except that he didn't function like most normal people. I read one time that Reggie Williams, the great Dartmouth linebacker and Cincinnati Bengals defensive captain, attributed his success to "speed, agility and the inability to recognize pain immediately." That was Beef, except for the speed and agility part.

As soon as we hit the breakwater, the big V-8s let out a high-pitched scream and proceeded to hand us a beating that made my days boxing at Finley's Gym in D.C. look like a shadow match. Over and over again, the prow rose high out of the water, hung a second longer than death, and slammed down, knocking the hell out of everyone but Jack and the Seal. They stood up front, casually leaning into the sixty-mile-an-hour breeze, somehow immune to this organized ass kicking.

"Motherfucker!" I yelled out loud, less at the ride than their lack of interest in it.

Thirty minutes later, I flipped the night vision goggles (NVGs) down like a visor and prepared to disembark. Every inch of my body felt like it had been tuned with a ball peen hammer.

For now, however, I had to focus on the mission ahead. This scenario focused on five members of Earth Forever, some obscure environmental group that had taken thirty to forty people hostage in an oceanfront resort near Nags Head, North Carolina. According to negotiators, their original plan included nothing more serious than a pipe bomb on an old scow used for dinner cruises. Things went to hell when the bomb detonated prematurely, killing three people and injuring a dozen more. They sent two pregnant women out once negotiators arrived, but threatened to kill everyone inside unless they were guaranteed free passage to Chile.

Our operations order called for a tactical assault just before dawn. It never said anything about paper targets and shooting-house walls. All we knew was that our weapons were loaded with real bullets and that all breaches would go explosive.

"Wait until he calls to un-ass the boat," I heard myself say as Big Jack throttled back to idle. The moonless sky offered almost no light, no noise except for the low rumble of V-8s and water slapping against the hull. The boat crept closer to the sand dunes. Tiki lamps from a restaurant dangled beneath the stars about a half mile to my left.

"Go."

Jack issued the command just loud enough to hear through my radio earpiece.

Over the side.

I climbed off the motorcycle-style seat, bounced a foot over the rubber gunwale, and disappeared underwater. Down, over my head, down until my feet hit the soft bottom, running.

I sucked about a half breath between the time I realized Big Jack's miscalculation and the time water shortened my horizons. Sixty pounds of kit weighs a lot more when you try to swim it. All I could do was push myself toward shore, along the bottom, flashing back to the ammo-can carry in the pool during selection.

My lungs burned for air as I finally broke the surface. Every piece of war gear on my person poured out seawater. I tried my NVGs. History. I cycled a round out of my MP, only to watch water running out the bottoms of my double-stacked magazines. Do flash-bangs work when they're wet? I wondered. How about our breaching charges?

I still didn't know the answers when we hunkered down behind our last position of cover about fifty yards from the restaurant. Gold snipers huddled behind a dumpster shed to assess and wait for the Blue snipers to link up with their assault component at the front of the building.

The HRT commander had augmented the assault teams with Blue and Gold snipers to compensate for the number of hostages and size of the building. Even though we earned our living through a scope, all snipers begin life as assaulters and stand ready to play a dual role if called.

I looked up at the two-story building in front of us. The

breach point looked humble. A simple slap shot would pop it quicker than any key.

"We up?" the team leader asked.

Six thumbs. No talk.

I had fought like hell to keep sand out of my weapons, but the darkness made it all but impossible to make sure they'd function. I assumed that the light on the end of my MP had fried just like the electronic brains of my night vision optics. The Aimpoint sight had probably also died.

"Gold snipers to TOC. We're at yellow. Request compromise authority and permission to move to green."

At least my radio still worked.

"Copy, Gold snipers, stand by."

Yellow means last position of cover and concealment. Green is the no-man's-land between yellow and the breach. If everything went right, we'd move up to the door, set our breaching charges, and launch a coordinated attack. But sometimes things go ~~wrong~~. Sometimes you hang your ass out in the no-man's-land between safe and fucked, and the bad guys see you. All you can do is fight on. That's compromise authority.

"TOC to all units. I have all teams at yellow. You have compromise authority and permission to move to green."

Boat moved off in front of me, ten feet between us, just like we'd planned. He crouched down, pointing his weapon at the building, searching for something snipers on the perimeter might miss. I watched the second level, anticipating a sentry on the porch. Shadows provided our only cover, and they felt a little thin.

Boat gained the building quickly, and I crouched down behind him with a tap on the shoulder to let him know I was up. Everything goes by hand signals when you get close. The slightest noise can ruin the whole operation.

We waited what seemed like a half hour for the other

teams to crawl into position. I strained my ears, listening for the sounds of the Little Birds. I knew they were bringing Charlie and Echo teams to fast rope down to the roof. Our job was to fight our way up. Their mission was to fight their way down. Hopefully, we'd meet up at the rear staircase, with a houseful of free diners and dead shitheads.

Metz stepped out of line and fastened a slap shot between the dead bolt and the frame. The door looked too flimsy to bother with explosives, but hey, who wants to carry a ram? He fed the translucent detonator cord back away from the door and fastened a shock tube initiator. One pull of this explosive trigger and we were going to war.

"TOC to all units. Stand by, I have control."

I heard them, the Little Birds rolling in, low off the maritime horizon, darker than the surrounding air. They whine like those little Cox-engine planes I flew when I was a kid.

"Five . . . four . . . three . . . two . . ." *BOOM!*

The only time you ever hear the order to execute is if your door charge fails to function as designed. Bad sound. Fortunately, I didn't have to worry about that. When I charged in on Boat's heels, the door was already gone.

We moved inside three steps, then right, down the hallway, past a utility room and a storage closet, just like in practice earlier in the day. Our intelligence officer had tracked down the blueprints from the builder, so we knew every crack, turn, and stair.

BOOM! BOOM!

Door breaches and flash-bangs rocked other parts of the building as we moved, weapons trained ahead in case someone tried to escape toward us.

The line halted at the end of the short hallway. Boat tried the door. Locked.

"Breacher up!"

Metz hustled up and blew the lock with a single Hatton

round from his Remington 870 12-gauge. The pistol-gripped weapon looked no longer than his forearm.

I reached out to Boat's vest and pulled a flash-bang from the stretch Cordura holder.

Pull the pin, lob, three, two . . . *BOOM!*

Entry. The blueprints showed a first-floor conference room, but the plans had changed. I had no NVGs and my light didn't work, but in the dim red glow of the emergency exit sign, I could see partitions, tables, boxes, furniture — some kind of office space.

"FBI! Get down, get down, get down!" Everybody was yelling. Familiar voices.

Move, my mind yelled out, forcing me into position: four-man entry, move left off Boat's zig toward my corner and right, down the wall.

POP, POP, POP.

Gunfire behind me. I suppose I flinched for just a moment, searching for what I thought a gunshot might feel like through all the adrenaline and the concentration.

POP, POP, POP.

A white guy with a crew cut jumped up in front of me, a pistol in his hand, rising up toward me like a wave from a passing neighbor. I couldn't see the bullets strike in the dark, but he fell in the corner at the edge of a light-colored partition. Had to be dead.

"Banging!" I yanked another flash-bang, pulled the pin, and tossed it into the next room as I continued ahead.

BOOM! A hundred and eighty decibels of distraction.

I closed my eyes the instant it took to save my night vision from the million-candlepower flash. I cut the corner, stormed the room, and stared down my muzzle into a vacant closet.

"Clear!"

BOOM! BOOM! BOOM!

The sounds of all-out war echoed through the rest of the building.

Flash-bang powder burned in my nose, but I sucked in breaths, just the same, big breaths, trying to clear my vision.

"I got one here, Boat!" My voice.

The lights flashed on, humming fluorescent exposure overhead.

"I got one!"

"Hold what you got!" he yelled back.

"Gold snipers to TOC. We have two dead subjects." Boat sounded calm in my earpiece. He was used to this.

I realized I was sweating. Everything stopped. Quiet.

This is where the pause comes; where you gather yourself. I could hear the other teams in my earpiece, calling in with stats. Three, four, all five bad guys dead. All operators safe.

Metz showed up beside me and pushed my boot off the bad guy's throat.

"Nice group," he said, referring to where my double tap had dotted the dead man's forehead. Small holes. 10mm blemishes never heal.

"Okay, let's cut it," Boat called out. "It's getting late. Let's wrap this thing up."

Raz stepped over a toppled chair and walked toward me.

"Hey, Whit. How'd you like that fucking boat ride, huh?" He shook his head and checked my target. "Think we'll make last call downtown?" he asked. "This shit makes me thirsty."

Fortunately for America, terrorism has not yet invaded our borders the way many experts predicted it would. HRT continued to prepare for that eventuality during my first year, but it also branched out into other areas where a highly trained tactical team is the only solution. Things like high-risk prisoner transport, dignitary protection, sophisticated surveillance, and maritime operations also pop up from time to time. HRT stays busy with these sorts of missions, working around busy training schedules and high-profile deployments.

By the end of my first year, I had ingested enough mount-out-style operations to gain a sense of the tactical world. We had just returned from a little trigger time on the rifle range one afternoon when word came down from the front office that we could soon expect a visitor. His code name was Tom Clark, and he was the primary witness against the Blind Sheik in the World Trade Center bombings. Several credible sources had warned of threats on his life by known terrorist groups. The New York office needed somebody to keep him alive until trial, so they turned to us.

Two days later, I found myself working another night shift at a Northern Virginia safe house. This time I wasn't hiding in some deep dark forest. I had a nicely painted roof over my head, heat, light. In fact, the only discomfort I could complain about was having to stay awake while Clark laughed his way through reruns of *Three's Company*.

"HR-78 to HR-28."

Finally, I thought, a little break.

"HR-28, go ahead."

"I got the Suburban in the basement. You want to bring him down?"

Clark heard the transmission and stood up from the couch. He knew the drill.

Every morning at 5:00, we brought one of our blacked-out Chevy Suburbans around to the basement and waited near the secure elevator. One of the two duty agents — in this case myself — would roust Clark off the couch and haul him downstairs for a ride out to his morning constitutional.

"Ten-four," I said. "We'll be right down."

Clark, a six-foot, 275-pound Egyptian with a temper like Mount Vesuvius, had convinced the Bureau that hiding in an FBI safe house was hell on his physical health. He needed some kind of workout every day.

Actually, "convinced" sounds rather lame. He had terrorized the Bureau into allowing a daily outing, overruling protests from the guys on the protection detail. Ultimately, all the decisions affecting this guy came out of New York. He was their witness, after all. We were just a bunch of well-armed baby-sitters.

I flipped the television off and stood up to walk Clark downstairs. I'd been sitting in that chair so long the blood rushed out of my head, making me a little dizzy. Maybe it was the fluorescent lights, which made the windowless room look the same day or night.

"Hey, Metz." I tapped on the door to alert my new partner. Spuds had just transferred over to Golf team, earning a slot as a full-time diver. After three years lying in the weeds, no one could argue that he didn't deserve it.

"You ready?" he said, emerging from a quick nap in the side room. Metz talked with a Chicago accent despite living since high school in New Jersey.

Clark emerged from the kitchen with a bottle of water. He looked well rested and ready for exercise, considering he hadn't slept all night. He wore a sky-blue Adidas warm-up suit and shiny white Nikes. A gold chain the width of my watchband dangled around his fire hydrant of a neck, weaving out of sight in the jungle of black hair that climbed out of his T-shirt. He had that Franco Harris body suit, with a clean line just below the Adam's apple, where the shaving stopped.

Clark said nothing as we led him to the elevator. That was just fine with me. Two days earlier he'd almost ended our careers by making us shoot him. Tom had suddenly decided, at 3:00 A.M., that he'd had enough of the FBI and wanted out.

That presented two problems. One: This guy was in protective custody, not under arrest, so we couldn't legally hold him against his will.

Two: Our orders stated that he wasn't going anywhere. The mission was to protect him against everything from international hit men to hangnails. New York needed him at trial in three weeks and they expected us to deliver him with all his fingers and toes.

In one of his unpredictable eruptions, Clark jumped up from *Three's Company,* threw his arms in the air, and started screaming that he wanted to leave.

"I want fucking out of thees place!" he hollered in his thick Middle Eastern accent. "You can't keep me here no more!"

I pointed the channel changer at John Ritter and punched up the volume.

Raz, who had been taking his turn at a couple of z's in another room, jumped up and came running out as if terrorists had broken down the door in a frontal assault. Metz just glanced over at me and shook his head. This guy threw temper tantrums like a spoiled child. Most passed within minutes.

Raz, who'd just rocketed out of a sound sleep, found no humor in Tom's histrionics.

"Sit the fuck down and watch TV, man," he said. Raz had lost a few pounds since his defensive-tackle days at Baylor University, but he didn't have to ask most people twice.

"Motharefoocker. Peess. Sheet. Foock." Tom liked to run the gamut of Anglo-Saxon invective during his tantrums, but his Queen's English pronunciation crumbled in direct correlation to his blood pressure. At that point, his head looked like it was about to pop. "Coont. You foock. Sheet," he screamed.

The walls shook. Watching television lost all its charm. Metz stood up from the couch. What the hell, I thought, this thing was screwing itself into the ceiling real fast. I might as well get up too.

Sensing the direction of things, Tom turned and headed out the door. He had only two options at that point: to turn right toward the security doors leading out to the stairs, or to turn left toward the elevator. Either way, he was gone.

Raz pulled his hand across his throat as we followed Tom toward the elevators. This guy wasn't going anywhere. Raz coordinated all protection details for the Team and had run successful operations all over the world. This should have been a bed tuck and kiss goodnight operation. Unfortunately, all our contingency plans concentrated on making sure no one got in. Nobody thought of how to deal with him if he tried to get out.

"Tom," Metz said, "calm down a minute here." Metz spoke in a down-to-earth, Midwestern tone that put most people at ease. Tom hailed from the Middle East. He didn't get the nuance.

"Look, buddy," I said, harking back to Big Al's theory that talking it out beat shooting it out most days, "it's a long walk back to New York. You've got no money, no identification, and a shitload of people want you dead. Let me make a phone call and we'll see if we can't get you out of here for a little fresh air."

Whether he heard me or not, the next few seconds skipped a beat, the way time changes during a car wreck.

Raz jumped into the elevator ahead of him. Metz and I moved into a standard defensive tactics triangle, surrounding him, yet clearing fields of fire. Tom, who claimed to be a former Egyptian special forces colonel, national judo champion, and general badass, leaped into a fighting stance. All I saw was 275 pounds of fury working himself into a bar brawl tizzy. One move and this thing was going to get ugly.

Tom's eyes started to bug out of his head when he realized what was about to happen. I'd put on about twenty pounds since joining the Team. Raz and Metz carried less weight, but they knew contact. In fact, the last time Metz found himself in a standoff like this, the other guy ended up dead.

Humans show two reflexes when cornered: fight or flight. The FBI usually tries to avoid cornering subjects for just that reason. Fights always end up with someone getting hurt, and there's almost no way to tell who will run and who will rumble.

Tom snapped his head left toward me, then right toward Metz, and then back at Raz, who stood his ground in the elevator. Metz and I knew something Tom didn't. One of us would have to back off, draw down, and whack him if things got out of hand. All three of us carried our Brownings in belt holsters. Things happen quickly in a fight. If Tom got hold of one of our guns, we'd have no choice but to shoot him.

I stared at this asshole, wondering how in hell I'd erased all my options. If we backed down, he'd walk away, causing embarrassment at the least and a complete debacle at worst. I could hear the prime-time teaser: "*NBC Dateline* has the exclusive story of how a star FBI witness escaped from a Hostage Rescue Team protection detail and walked right into the path of an oncoming Peterbilt."

If we stood our ground, it was going to go violent. That teaser would read "FBI Special Agent shoots unarmed witness in protective custody." Neither ending would look too good in my personnel file.

Eyes narrowing. Sweat beading on foreheads. Fists knotting. Knuckles turning white.

I'd waged more than my share of fistfights, and this was going to be one I'd talk about for a while. You get to that point just before the blood starts spurting when there's no turning back.

"Motharefooka!" Tom yelled.

He dove into the elevator, shouldered Raz out of the way, and started beating the living shit out of himself against the stainless steel wall. Metz and I filled the door while Tom vented weeks of pent-up rage on his own swarthy face. He pounded his head and fists against the wall, fighting like a caged animal against his own temper.

When he was finished, he hung his head, turned around as if nothing had happened, and pushed through us, back to the TV set. The elevator still wears the scars of his rage, but the cuts and bruises on his face healed pretty quickly.

Memories of that incident swirled in my head as Metz and I waited with Tom at the elevator to take him for his morning stroll. Just forty-eight hours had passed, but he seemed quiet as a mosque mouse.

"You ready?" I asked.

He nodded his head and followed Metz toward the elevator. We'd shared little conversation since his meltdown.

Raz met us in a basement holding area, carrying an MP-5 and a radio. I jumped into the front passenger seat. Metz climbed in the back with Tom.

No one said a word. Our previous conversations had included endless stories about Tom's accomplishments, his ability to kick the world's ass, and his moneymaking prowess. Somehow, the elevator episode had awakened him to the realization that he was an overweight, middle-aged informant hiding out from the Islamic world in a tiny apartment. Even the million-dollar reward he stood to collect for his cooperation was slipping away. One of the New York agents told us Tom's ex-wife was sharpening her talons in preparation for a settlement.

"We're in; let's go," Metz said.

We drove quickly through the predawn darkness to a heavily wooded area several miles from the nearest house. Raz found a place to pull off the gravel road, killed the lights, and shut down the engine.

"Wait here," I said. Tom sat there uncharacteristically quiet.

Raz and I checked the area to make certain we were alone, then I opened Tom's door and motioned for him to follow. He stepped out into the warm, humid air and rubbed sleep out of his eyes. He seemed beaten, almost meek.

"This way."

I led Tom into the woods, down a logging road. Three guys from Echo team had scouted our route and cleared it of potential threats, so I walked quickly, trying to give Tom the exercise he bitched so loudly about.

We'd walked about ten minutes when Tom stopped and shook his head.

I turned to see what had happened. We'd scheduled thirty-five minutes for his exercise session.

"This is far enough," he said. "You do it here."

"Do it here?" I asked. "Do what?"

I looked to Raz and Metz, hoping for some insight, but they just shook their heads.

"I go no farther. Do it here."

I sniffed the air and tried to focus on Metz's face.

"I know why you bring me to this place," Tom said. "Kill me here. I walk no more."

No fear, no resentment. This man was ready to die. He came from a world where strolls like this ended with a bullet to the head. I imagined he'd pulled the trigger himself a couple times.

I started to laugh but caught myself. Suddenly I understood his taciturn behavior. From the time this guy failed in his escape attempt, he believed we planned to kill him. Maybe he thought it settlement for the embarrassment. Maybe he thought we just didn't like him. Whatever the reason, he had quietly made his peace, climbed into the truck, and walked out into the dark, dark woods with three guys carrying guns.

That took balls.

I learned a lot about resolve and the Middle Eastern character that morning. You can read about terrorism all day long, but until you come face to face with the type of man who's willing to die without grumbling, it really doesn't make sense. I thanked God that Tom Clark stood on our side that morning. Too bad there are lots of others just like him who don't.

BOOK THREE

I travel'd thro' a Land of Men
A Land of Men and Women too
And heard and saw such dreadful things
As cold Earth wanderers never knew

WILLIAM BLAKE

12

MOUNT-OUT

One year almost to the day after moving to Virginia, my perspective on the sniper trade changed forever. I was eating pizza and drinking beer in the HRT classroom during a teammate's going-away party when Raz pulled a chair up next to me, palmed a slice of pepperoni, and leaned close.

"I was just up front," he said in a voice soft enough to capture my attention. "I think we got a job."

Job. The word evoked an immediate sense of excitement. Though the Los Angeles riots and the Danny Ray Horning manhunt had tempered my enthusiasm a bit, *job* still meant opportunity, another taste of that rare cocktail of anticipation, adrenaline, and thrill.

He whispered, "I hear we're going to Idaho."

It's hard to explain the anticipation endemic to this line of work. You train for trouble, plan for every contingency, and spend most waking moments preparing for disaster. But preparation seldom hastens need. You spend the vast majority of your time enduring peace, hoping in the back of your mind for trouble. Firemen know the feeling. And prizefighters. Gunfighters. It's the business of misery that nobody wants to admit he enjoys.

There was no mission alarm or fire whistle in the HRT station house. Occasionally we'd get the 888 call-out code, but more often than not, talk of a mission would begin with an overhear, just a rumor. It was like an attitude, really, that descended upon everyone without notice, almost as a sixth sense. Guys would start looking at each other with flared nostrils and a nod. You could smell tension in the air, among the common odors of gun-cleaning solvent and sweaty flight suits. It was like fifty identical twins sensing their brothers' emotion at the same time.

"Something about some U.S. marshals getting shot up," Raz said. His voice gave away little emotion.

I forced a swallow of pizza down and mumbled a few questions. Who? How? Why?

Everybody else in the room seemed to hear the rumor at the same time. Questions floated around in hushed tones, as if the answer might be too precious to expose out loud. Guys started disappearing to pack or prepare their gear on the chance that something might actually come of the speculation.

Minutes later, the team leaders got called up front to a closed-door meeting, and the guys headed out back to make preparations in earnest. Team leader meetings like this almost always meant the same thing. Work.

Idaho. Word spread quickly as the send-off broke up and everyone headed for the equipment cages. There was no general announcement, but the rumor wailed louder than any whistle.

I was already rearranging my tactical bag when the rest of my team arrived in the Gold sniper cage. Each sniper section has a room-size storage area where its members keep weapons, tactical gear, and other tools of the trade. It's a locker room of sorts, usually filled with laughter and taunts and camaraderie. We spent a lot of time there cleaning weapons, maintaining our gear, and shooting the bull. On August 21, 1992, the cage was all business.

Early word indicated that at least one deputy U.S. marshal had been killed on a remote mountain ridge by a pack of radical white separatists. It had been a bloody firefight, during which several marshals had been pinned down by heavy fire. The weather up there would be cold this time of year, one of the guys said, and we might be there a while. Better pack warm.

I dug into a duffel full of cold weather clothing, Gore-Tex rain gear, and polypropylene underwear. Years of winter camping in northern New England had taught me the value of proper clothing, and HRT had furnished us all with the best money could buy. I sorted what I thought I might need and stuffed it into an expedition-size backpack.

Next, I pulled out my rifle and checked to make sure I had restocked a numbered lot of match grade ammo. I torqued the trigger assembly, cleaned the scope, inspected the barrel, and made certain my logbook was up to date. Every round I'd ever fed through its twenty-four-inch barrel was recorded in that log, a shot-by-shot guide to the effects of heat, cold, humidity, and altitude on accuracy. Since sniper school, I'd run more than 3,000 rounds downrange at distances up to 1,000 yards. I'd shot from tall buildings at high angles of incidence, in sere desert air, during subzero January winter, and in heat so intense the boiling mirage rendered the scope unusable. Every shot earned its place in the research library I'd built for myself to document variability. No one ever asks how you made a shot, but they always ask why you missed.

From the way I loaded the first round to the rhythm I breathed when calculating movers, everything about long-range precision shooting made sense to me then. The craft of marksmanship seduced me. Every shot proved challenging because of the almost infinite variability. Simply holding the crosshairs on a target and pulling the trigger means nothing. Knowing how to read the wind, lead movers, and predict the effects of weather all play into the mix. Something as trivial as the way sunlight enters the objective lens of your scope can change the bullet strike an inch or more at 200 yards. That's not much when you're tossing a baseball over the plate, but it could mean untimely death to a hostage.

Bold white letters on my rifle case labeled it "The Truth" because that is what it represented to me. I handled The Truth with the respect one affords a family heirloom. It was the primary tool of my trade, and it possessed an awesome power that I knew I might have to rely on someday to save my own life or someone else's. That rifle always came first when I prepared for mount-outs. If push came to shove, it would make the difference.

But there were other weapons in my quiver and I had to see to them as well. I inspected and packed my CAR-16, a fully automatic assault rifle in .223 caliber that I used for patrolling. It was light and small and very accurate at distances up to 200 yards. The Truth would serve me once I set up and established a sniper position, but the CAR would make sure I got into position to begin with.

Finally, I detailed my M-14, a semiautomatic relic of the Vietnam era that maintained relevance by offering the accuracy and devastating power of the .308-caliber round in a package light enough to carry over long humps. Several of the HRT snipers still relied on the M-14 as a patrolling weapon, but I kept it solely as an unstable-platform weapon for shooting out of helicopters or off ships.

"Where the hell is Idaho?" Raz asked, slamming his own gear into a black assault bag. He was a native Texan who had done a brief first office tour in Mobile, Alabama, but still believed nothing worthwhile ever happened north of the Brazos.

"What difference does it make?" Boat answered. "You aren't gonna have time for any sightseeing."

Raz smiled as he stuffed a 40× spotting scope into his tactical bag. His first HRT mission had been to restore law and order on St. Croix after Hurricane Hugo decimated the island in 1989. Hugo had stripped away the lush vegetation, flattened the houses, and turned the island into a huge garbage dump. Criminals freed from local jails to prevent them from drowning in the storm repaid the favor by taking over the streets and looting whatever hadn't blown away. The FBI deployed HRT at the president's request to restore order. They stayed in mud-floored military field tents and worked double shifts patrolling the streets and rounding up the itinerant thugs. There hadn't been much opportunity for sightseeing on that mission either.

We had just organized the last of our gear when a voice over the intercom confirmed the rumors.

"All operators report to the classroom."

Time to go to work.

HRT designs its deployments around what military units refer to as a five-paragraph order. This tactical operations plan, or "op order," outlines every imaginable aspect of the crisis response. A less detailed "warning order" usually serves as an initial briefing until the HRT staff can put the larger document together. The warning order includes a synopsis of the crime or crisis, a general plan of movement, and information of immediate concern, like weather conditions and special threats.

Supervisory Special Agent Steven "Mac" McTavish, second-in-charge of HRT, waited until we'd assembled, then stepped into the classroom, closed the door, and cleared his throat.

HRT has always had its share of remarkable and accomplished men, but Mac stood out. He wore a thick jacket of muscle over broad shoulders and had short dark hair and eyes like a gargoyle's. In a room of a hundred people, he would be the first person you'd sense but the last person you'd see. He moved with quiet deliberation and spoke in soft, reserved tones until something required authority. Then he became authority.

Steven McTavish wore a rare aura of confidence that shone over the men who worked for him. He could drink beer and tell stories with you Wednesday night and chew your ass Thursday morning without batting an eye. He could outrun, outbench, and outshoot most of the guys on the Team, and he knew it. No one ever wanted to challenge him because he would rather die than lose.

Mac's pedigree included service in the Marine Corps, years as a police officer, and a stint with an intelligence agency. He had worked his way up to the rank of FBI supervisor by being an outstanding operator, a revered team leader, and HRT's staff training officer. No one on the Team knew more about tactics or the way HRT worked than Mac did, and everyone turned to him when shit hit the fan. He was a heroic, larger-than-life character imbued with that intangible quality that allows some men to lead others through the front doors of hell. When nut-cutting time came around, a calm descended upon him and his face darkened. When he spoke, people listened.

"We just got a call from uptown," he said, referring to FBI Headquarters in Washington. "A team of deputy U.S. marshals was engaged in a shoot-out this morning on an isolated mountain near Bonners Ferry, Idaho. We still don't have a lot of information, but at least one of the deputies was killed and they have been pinned down. We've got a bird gassing up at Andrews and we're looking to go wheels up by twenty-one hundred."

Fifty sets of eyes fixed on Mac's stoic face.

Cop killers.

Shoot-out on a remote mountaintop.

Armed-and-dangerous subjects.

You could almost hear the gears turning in people's heads, see the emotion rising in their faces. We were all professionals, but someone had murdered a federal officer, and that touched a raw nerve. FBI agent or deputy U.S. marshal, we all wore the same badge. He'd carried a gun just like we did and had sworn himself to defend the same America we'd pledged our lives to. One of our own had been gunned down in Idaho, and the assault seemed personal.

We loaded a stake-bed truck with two odd-looking yet sophisticated field shelters called DRASH tents ("deployable rapidly assembled shelters"); two Army field tents; a couple dozen cases of MREs; electric generators, lanterns, and a panoply of other equipment. The EMTs loaded our ambulance, a specially configured Chevrolet Suburban, with trauma and life support packages. The helicopter pilots readied the MD-530 Little Bird and gathered all its collateral accessories. Our intelligence officer checked and loaded a remote control robot into its van. The tech staff crammed a couple thousand pounds of electronic gear into a specially designed box truck.

Snipers stacked their rifle cases full of day guns and night guns, the suppressed .308s and the Barrett .50-cals and the CAR-16s and the M-14s. They packed their field camouflage and their land navigation gear and their night vision goggles and extra ammo. Assaulters lugged out their breaching gear, their tactical bags, and their body armor.

Everything progressed with well-oiled familiarity. Some of the gear hadn't even been unpacked from the most recent mission, hunting escaped murderer Danny Ray Horning in the Grand Canyon. In terms of the nuts-and-bolts mechanism of deployment, this mission went just like all the others: perfectly.

Just after 9:00 P.M., a fully loaded C-141 transport, operated by the Air National Guard's 459th Mobile Air Detachment, lumbered down a dark runway at Andrews Air Force base near Upper Marlboro, Maryland, and lifted off into a murky night sky. The four-engine jet transport sagged under the weight of HRT and its support staff, their gear, a four-wheel-drive van containing a remote control robot, the Chevy Suburban ambulance, a four-wheel-drive box truck, and the MD-530 helicopter. Inside, the Hostage Rescue Team sat quietly reading, or contemplating the night ahead, or trying futilely to grab a few hours' sleep.

A C-141 carries no first-class section. Coach in this plane resembles a windowless warehouse that vibrates like an old washing machine and roars at 110 decibels. The cargo bay is loaded front to rear with kit bags, vehicles, boxes of electronic equipment, rifle cases, and the helicopter.

Passengers sit on canvas bench seats that run the length of the fuselage. You fly sideways with your knees up against the vehicle in front of you and wear foam plugs in your ears to keep from going deaf. You can't see out of the windowless fuselage, you can't hear a thing over the four jet turbines, and after an hour or two hunched up like a monkey screwing a football, you can't feel much either. Other than the sound of flaps extending and retracting, there is no way to tell whether you are landing, taking off, or flying at 35,000 feet. So you sit and vibrate and think about what you'll have to do when you get there.

We didn't talk about the mission on the way out. We couldn't. We could barely hear ourselves think.

The flight took more than five hours and was particularly rough. Commercial airliners typically get the smoothest altitudes and military flights have to take the choppy air no one else wants. I remember sitting in my cramped insomnia that night, trying to hold down the pizza in my stomach while watching the ambulance bounce up and down in front of me like a tethered mule. The only thing commercial travelers have to worry about is keeping their drinks out of their laps when the air gets rough. That night we were concerned about keeping seven tons of four-wheel-drive truck from landing in ours.

We touched down at Fairchild Air Force Base outside Spokane, Washington, just after 2:00 A.M. local time in a gentle, steady rain. I remember the rear cargo ramp opening at the back of the plane and feeling the wave of cold wind billowing through the fuselage. Mist rose from my mouth with each breath. Virginia is hot in August. We sure as hell weren't in Virginia anymore.

The helicopter came off first, then the trucks. The men shuffled off the plane, into the darkness, and formed conga lines to shuttle the tons of tactical and communications gear into three U-Haul trucks. Some of us helped bolt the rotor blades onto the Little Bird, while others unchained the trucks and drove them off the plane. We clapped our hands together and jumped up and down on the tarmac, trying to stay warm in the frigid rain. I looked at my watch and thought it ominous that we had already been up nearly twenty-four hours and weren't even in Idaho yet.

Once we off-loaded the plane, several of us walked a short distance to a terminal building, where a line of rental vehicles rested patiently. I climbed into a small Chevy sedan and stared out into the thick night as we pulled away from the airport and headed west down I-90 toward a town I'd never heard of before.

Taillights stretched out in front of us. Headlights followed in close formation. All I could think about was the marshals, waiting out there in the rain, shaking with the cold and bleeding into the sodden ground.

Four hours later, twelve rental cars, three Ryder box trucks, a white Suburban, a red Chevy box truck, and a tan van parted a low fog and pulled in to a small National Guard armory outside Bonners Ferry, Idaho. A chalky mist rose from my mouth as I climbed out of the car and rubbed fatigue out of my eyes. It was nine o'clock in the morning. The excitement of deploying on a new mission had long since worn off. The only anticipation I felt was for something to eat and a warm bed. Like most of the guys on the team, I was spent, and the day hadn't even started yet.

We climbed out of the cars and moved inside the armory, which was smaller than I'd expected. We talked among ourselves about the trip out and what lay ahead. The concrete-and-cinder-block building smelled of motor oil and musty canvas and coffee. An American flag covered most of one wall. Large glass windows looking into side offices covered the other. Lots of people I'd never seen before milled about inside with a vague sense of importance.

Faces change from crisis to crisis, but the roles are always the same. Investigative agents chase leads and work timelines and intelligence logs. The technicians string phone lines, throw up radio repeaters, encrypt communications equipment, and make sure everyone can talk to everyone else. The Tactical Operations Center (TOC) personnel make sure the command staff has everything it needs to make informed decisions. The negotiators talk endlessly, plotting and scripting all the while. The Special Agents in Charge storm around, demonstrating their resolve, and their minions storm around after them, trying to demonstrate their resolve, too.

There are always a few high-ranking representatives of the agency we're inheriting the problem from, usually traumatized and edgy. And there are always a few poor mopes, like ourselves, who've just had their asses handed to them — the guys freshly out of the trenches who need a little help but don't know exactly how to ask.

We operators were there to offer a tactical option. Assault. At ten o'clock that morning I felt like a warrior preparing for battle. But that's the irony. HRT, the biggest, strongest knuckle draggers at the ball, always had to wait for some suit-clad manager to start the music. The negotiators had to negotiate, the psychologists had to psychoanalyze, and all those invisible bureaucrats back in Washington had to bore with the sounds of their own sanctimonious voices before HRT took the stage. From what I had seen up till then, the process of crisis resolution always seemed to follow the same plotline, tedious as a run-on sentence. HRT invariably became the terminal punctuation, but not until all the talking was through.

Standing in the armory that morning, I realized the process had just begun. We'd been given precious little information about the battle we were about to enter, but I suspected, as did many of the others, that it would outlast our collective patience. We knew all too well how to jump through hoops only to sit around for hours or days and then jump through hoops again for the real thing. I knew that riding this roller coaster of emotions would wear me down if I let it, so I found myself a clean spot on the concrete floor, stretched out, and closed my eyes.

Whether I dreamed or not, the rest didn't last. Someone

leaned out of a side conference room and announced that the briefing would soon begin. The briefing. Finally.

There is always a time and information lag once you hit the ground, but we'd been here five hours already and knew very little about what lay ahead. Modern communications make it possible to talk from a C-141 to the ground, but the sheer roar of the jet turbines makes phone conversation a stern challenge. If anyone in this building knew what we were getting into, it wasn't me.

I climbed to my feet and inserted myself into the sea of camouflage as it flowed into a briefing room at the back of the armory. Someone had tacked up poster-size photos of a wooded area to show topography and ground cover. These are important details to a sniper, so I craned my neck trying to examine them as the HRT commander moved to a lectern.

Dick Roberts seemed a distant and complex man to me during my first years on HRT. Officially, he was the Team's commander, an ASAC (Assistant Special Agent in Charge) assigned to the Washington Field Office. Being an ASAC is not a huge responsibility in the FBI. It is the second rung on the career ladder and usually carries an administrative role in a field office. ASACs do a great deal of the dirty work in an office until they prove themselves capable of a command of their own.

Roberts was different. Although officially subordinate to the SAC of the Washington Field Office, he answered only to the highest levels of FBI Headquarters. He was head of an isolated unit outside the mainstream bureaucracy that few understood or took the time to question. His men worked no investigations, oversaw no informants, and never had to worry about sticky career snags like Title III wiretaps or high-profile counterintelligence matters. HRT operators came to work in shorts and T-shirts. They trained two hours a day in the gym. They fired thousands and thousands of bullets each year without filling out a single form. That is not the way FBI agents work in the field.

Roberts had become a sort of hero in the wake of the Talladega prison rescue. He had elevated the Team to a new level of confidence. Everyone in law enforcement from Attorney General William Barr on down held Roberts in high esteem. The victory, after all, did not belong to the grunts who risked their lives and performed flawlessly, it belonged to the commander who masterminded it, grew the balls to push for it, and counted down the biggest door breach ever used in an American law enforcement operation.

Dick Roberts was intelligent, charismatic, and articulate. He was going places, and he knew it.

In August 1992, Roberts wore a bullet-proof coat of ego that gave him a sort of star quality. You could see it in the way he walked and the way he talked to operators on the Team. He ruled like an emperor who had little time for pedantry such as the names of his operators or any of their concerns.

One time, I grew sideburns a little longer than normal. Roberts pulled Mac aside and asked who I was.

"You mean Chris?" he asked.

"Yeah, what's his last name?"

"Whitcomb," Mac reminded him. "Chris Whitcomb."

Roberts started to turn red with anger. He could go from calm to ballistic in the time it took for your butt to pucker.

"Yeah, well, tell Elvis those sideburns went out twenty years ago," he growled. "I want them gone."

I shaved that afternoon.

Roberts is a tall man, perhaps 6'3", and thin. In good moods he could appeal with that transcendental charm politicians use to win support from the masses. When provoked, he would fly into bouts of temper so violent that to witness one was tantamount to standing at the foot of a great waterfall, drowning in the crushing torrent. His anger filled the room with a thunderous roar, frothing and swirling about you as you started to drown. First, something in the air stilled, the way air stills before a tornado. Then his thin lips tightened like piano wires. His eyes bulged slightly beneath translucent brows, and vitriol rushed to his face, throbbing at his temples and turning his ruddy complexion bright crimson. His razor-sharp features began to cut and mince, shredding lesser men like paper.

His outbursts became legend at Quantico. On more than one occasion, he called what he considered obstreperous operators into his office and turned them into Jell-O.

"I'll cut your balls off and send you back to Washington Field Office!" he would bellow. Banishment became his hippocket threat. We all felt that getting kicked off the Team would be worse than death, and he knew it. Exile became a riding crop he could use to straighten out the troops if they "dropped their packs."

Dick Roberts ruled HRT like a blowtorch, dormant and nonthreatening when he wanted to be, but white hot and searing with any spark. Like everyone else on the Team, he took a nickname: Big Red 1, in reference to his coloring and his position at the top. We called him BR-1 for short.

That morning in Idaho, BR-1 absolutely filled the room. He looked magnificent through filters of fatigue and anticipation. I think he felt truly invincible on August 22, 1992. He believed in his heart that this would be over within a day or two. This was his element.

The HRT commander spoke clearly and concisely from a small lectern in the Bonners Ferry National Guard armory. The local marshals' office held federal arrest warrants for two men: Randall Weaver and Kevin Harris. They were friends who had lived for more than a year in a mountaintop cabin with Weaver's wife, Vicki, and the couple's four children. Early the previous day, Weaver and Harris had opened fire on a team of deputy U.S. marshals at a trail crossroads not far from the cabin. Deputy Marshal William Degan, an experienced federal officer, was shot and killed during the firefight. It had been a bloody and unsolicited attack on law enforcement officers legally performing their sworn duties. Weaver and Harris were believed to have returned to the cabin.

Our job would be to establish a perimeter around the cabin, secure the area, and eventually effect the arrest of Weaver and Harris. A small potato field just below the ridge would serve as base camp until the job was done. That's where we'd head next.

Those of us in the room passed around fuzzy, blown-up driver's license photos of Harris and Weaver as Roberts talked. They were heavily armed, he repeated, adding that Weaver was a former Army Green Beret and expert survivalist. They had demonstrated a propensity for violence and were subjects of standing arrest warrants. Though the investigation had started with the Bureau of Alcohol, Tobacco and Firearms, it had turned into a Marshals Service case once Weaver failed to show for a court appearance. Now that federal agents had been assaulted in the line of duty, it was an FBI investigation.

The briefing took less than ten minutes. Roberts told us we'd caravan a short distance to a field just below Ruby Ridge and set up a command post. We would deploy snipers to encircle the Weaver cabin, establishing a perimeter and getting "eyes on" what had been described as Weaver's stronghold. I was surprised to learn that no one had been watching the cabin since the shoot-out the day before. For all we knew, Harris, Weaver, and his family could have packed up and moved out. They were survivalists, capable of living off the land. They had been self-sufficient in their mountain exile for quite some time. I felt there was a pretty good chance that they had just packed up and headed into the hills.

Roberts directed our attention to aerial photographs of the cabin and surrounding terrain. The large color photos offered our first glimpse of the crisis site, but they afforded little idea of what the place actually looked like. Two-dimensional photographs poorly indicate topography, and these gave no suggestion that the cabin lay atop a geographically protected ridge accessible only by foot.

No one said a word during the meeting. No one made a sound.

When Roberts finished, we filed out of the room and back into the rental cars to start the trip out to the cabin. I remember thinking as we left the National Guard armory in the cold rain and the clouded reality of sleep deprivation that this might be a little more than Roberts bargained for.

13

JOCKING UP

Ruby Ridge is the local name for a small rocky thumb that juts out over the Kootenai River valley, in an isolated Idaho wilderness called the Panhandle National Forest. Route 95 runs north past Bonners Ferry, through Boundary County, forty miles to Kingsgate, British Columbia. Tall, imposing mountains rise along an ascending range to Smith Peak at 7,650 feet and provide the thousands of acres of timber that sustain a large percentage of the population. Fifty-foot larch and pine and birch grow out of rocky slopes that climb steeply from lush mountain fields. Hawks soar on heaven's air. Trophy bucks and black bear and cougars roam the wilderness. It is a stark, rugged place marked with the simple beauty God saved for adventurers. This was no place for war.

But as we rolled full force across a feeble log bridge and into a lonely potato field August 22, none of this beauty showed itself. A low cloud cover obscured the mountains above us. Rain turned the road and the field into an infuriating quagmire and made setting up camp a wet, miserable plod.

We had just started erecting the tents, around 11:00, when word came from sniper coordinator Lester Hazelton that Blue snipers should gear up for immediate deployment to the ridge above the Weaver cabin. Echo team would prepare for an emergency assault, as was typical of all operations. The Hostage Rescue Team always kept at least one tactical element ready for the unforeseen problems that define crises. According to our maps, Weaver's cabin rested atop the rocky knoll overlooking our camp. For all we knew, he may have heard us coming and set up a sniper position of his own. Echo team would serve as a greeting committee should the need for a response arise.

That left Gold snipers and the remaining three assault teams to break down the gear and set up the tents. The work went quickly. Physical effort took our minds off the fatigue and warmed us against the seeping cold. Tactical gear stayed in the box trucks. Personal kit such as sleeping bags and clothing went into the tents. Communications hardware, medical supplies, command staff equipment, and logistical materials found their way into the DRASH tents.

DRASH tents — state of the art at the time — look like light brown igloos. They come with generators and heating units that create a living space vastly superior to the old general purpose medium tents (GPMs) that military men and women have suffered in for decades. Unfortunately, they also cost as much as suites at the Waldorf Astoria.

Once set up, these odd-looking shelters turned the potato field into a mysterious-looking outpost, as if we'd stormed in from another planet. Tall radio antennas sprang up all around us. Assaulters in camouflage fatigues and body armor filled electric generators with diesel fuel and fired up the chugging, clanking machines to power lights and computers and encrypted satellite phones. Machinery of war poured out of the trucks and into the tents. Operators checked their weapons and their ammunition.

The command element, which included Roberts, Mc-Tavish, supervisor Bill Mazzone, and sniper coordinator Lester Hazelton, hunkered down in the Tactical Operations Center to work out the game plan. They had to prepare logistics, draw up manpower assignments, establish communications with FBI Headquarters, and incorporate other local and state agencies into this growing crisis. They had to do all of this while trying to tend to the real business at hand, which at that time centered on locating and arresting the murderers of United States Deputy Marshal William Degan.

To complicate matters further, the HRT command element had none of the modern conveniences they'd rely on in an urban setting. Landline phones, computers, fax machines, and a coffeemaker would arrive before nightfall, but during the early hours after our arrival, it was just maps, lanterns, and whatever the tech guys could jury-rig together. Roberts and his command staff might as well have been working in the Stone Age.

By midday, the idyllic mountain field had become a thriving community with all the charm and aesthetic appeal of a trench latrine. This isolated Idaho potato field was turning into a small city of canvas and steel the way mining towns and gold rush camps once exploded out of reluctant wilderness.

Boat returned from a team leaders meeting, as we worked, to report that BR-1 had changed his mind and wanted to send all snipers up on the ridge as soon as possible. We dropped the tent pegs and tore into our packs for the polypro underwear, rain gear, ghillie suits, and field equipment we'd need to work the shift. Boat told us to pack light because we wouldn't have to spend the night.

HRT carried just thirteen snipers at the time and two of them hadn't arrived. That left eleven men to encircle the cabin, set up observation posts, and maintain a leak-proof perimeter. As with any crisis, we'd try to cover all four sides of the cabin, or "crisis site," and furnish intelligence to the command staff based on our observations. Roberts wanted two of us to establish an overwatch position across the ravine to cover our movement up on the mountain. Raz and Yoda drew the short straws and the overwatch, a losing hand by all estimates. The command element wanted us on-line as soon as possible. That meant now.

Unfortunately, "now" almost always meant "Get ready now so you can wait around for several hours until someone figures out what the hell it is they actually want you to do." The language of crisis resolution sometimes rivaled Mandarin Chinese in terms of complexity.

I packed my drag bag with two quarts of water, an MRE, a radio with an extra battery, a spotting scope, and a poncho. I visually inspected The Truth, and slipped it muzzle first into the drag bag along with a box of .308 ammunition and some camouflage face paint. I hung a compass around my neck, slapped a thirty-round magazine into my CAR-16, and grabbed a Browning just in case. That was it: no more than forty pounds — a light load that I could carry quickly up the mountain and rely on until dark.

On the way out of the box truck, I reached for my ghillie bag and found that it somehow hadn't made the trip. Fortunately, Metz's had arrived without him. I reached into his bag for a veil and hurried to catch up with the others.

As anticipated, Boat's imperative turned into another false alarm. We stood around in the steady rain for nearly an hour until Les Hazelton stepped out of the TOC and gave us the news. Revised plans called for four-wheel-drive vehicles to transport us up a logging road to a trailhead above the cabin. It would save us a significant amount of time and offer better security should Weaver and Harris have decided on an ambush. Stand by, Lester said, and the vehicles would be here soon.

Two hours later, word leaked out of the TOC that plans had changed again. We would now have to climb up to the ridge along a small trail that led northeast along steep, rocky terrain. Had we started on schedule, we'd have been halfway there already.

"Gear up and be ready to go in five minutes," Boat said. So we scrambled again to check and adjust our equipment.

Another false alarm.

Two more hours lapsed before Lester passed word that Headquarters had signed off on new rules of engagement and that Roberts wanted us up on the mountain as soon as possible.

It was now almost 3:00 P.M. We'd been standing around, waiting, in full gear for nearly five hours. We still had no perimeter around the cabin, and no one could say with any certainty that Harris, Weaver, or the rest of the family were even still in Idaho. It was now more than twenty-four hours since the shoot-out that killed Degan and no one had even contained the crime scene.

Lester met us outside the TOC in the middle of the access road five minutes later. He was accompanied by a quiet, stern-looking man whom I'd never seen before. The rain seemed to let up for a few minutes as he began to talk.

"This is Mike Reynolds with the Marshals Service," Lester said. "He's been up to the cabin before and he's going to show you the way."

We looked him over, wondering why we needed a tour guide. There were no handshakes or nods. No smiles or high fives. This was business, a brutal and costly business, and he was not looking to make friends.

As Lester spoke, Reynolds nodded and listened without words. He was a large and imposing figure with a lantern jaw and the kind of countenance that comes with time in battle. The men who had come under fire during the past twenty-four hours were his friends. Now the FBI, who had flown in to town with all the grace and tact of an air raid siren, stood poised to end what Reynolds's men had started. That had to be a tough pill to swallow. Despite their ability and their loss, the Marshals Service had relinquished control of a personal and emotional tragedy. Mike was about the only dog they had left in the fight.

Les pulled a spiral notebook out from underneath his camouflage parka and rubbed fatigue off his game face. The rain started again, as if to spite him, soaking the paper in his hands and leaking into our earnest resolve.

Mist rose from our mouths as we breathed.

"All right, listen up," Les said, sniffling against the cold. "Headquarters just signed off on the new rules of engagement."

He stared into his wheel book at something he had written in a scratchy cursive. We all knew Roberts had asked for modified rules of deadly force and that Headquarters had stalled our move up the mountain to look them over. If Weaver and Harris were really as bad as everyone said, this could be one of the most hostile situations law enforcement officers could face. They were heavily armed, well trained, and ready for war. Roberts's new rules would simply even the playing field.

"These are your rules of engagement: If any adult in the compound is observed with a weapon after the surrender announcement is made, deadly force can and should be employed to neutralize the individual. If any adult male is observed with a weapon prior to the announcement, deadly force can and should be employed. If compromised by any dog, that dog can be taken out. Any subjects presenting a threat of death or grievous bodily harm, FBI rules of deadly force apply."

I remember staring at him for a long moment as he read from his handwritten notes. The words surprised me.

Lester Hazelton was a natural leader of men, a warrior — the kind of boss you never question. Like McTavish and Billy Mazzone, he was former military with many years of experience on HRT. He had worked his way up through the ranks, serving as an operator, a team leader, and then as sniper coordinator. He spoke quietly and with certainty from behind a thick mustache and an ever present wad of Beech-Nut chewing tobacco. He walked in a slow, deliberate shuffle as if carrying the weight of the world upon his shoulders, and he rarely smiled. When he did, it was just to accommodate a loud, infectious laugh that sounded like no one else's. Everything was business or pleasure for Les. One or the other. The two never mixed.

Though we snipers looked up to Les Hazelton with a thinly veiled reverence, Dick Roberts did not assign him the same kind of stature. Roberts never much cared for snipers, and though Les constantly fought for our interests, Roberts usually treated him like spare baggage. At the time, Les didn't have supervisor authority and he didn't want it. He enjoyed his reputation as an outsider, like the rest of his men, and never kissed Roberts's or anyone else's ass. The respect Lester inspired in his HRT snipers came from his experience, skill, and good judgment, not from any political clout.

Our loyalty sometimes carried a price. Les demanded a great deal from all of us and would often issue long, brutal assignments just because no one else wanted to do the job. Anyone who ever argued that we were FBI agents, not Marine Corps privates, eventually paid for his irreverence. Les did not suffer fools or pussies gladly.

Les expected his snipers to work longer hours than the assaulters. He openly told us to get used to freezing, sweating, and starving our asses off while the assaulters waited in comfortable warehouses for the bell to ring. We could count on working twelve-hour shifts, then jump into our blacks and take part in the assault too.

"It comes with the turf," he said, "so I don't ever want to hear you bitch. You want out, you can get the fuck out right now."

That's all Les ever had to say. Though I didn't always agree with him, I always respected him.

So we listened as he read the new rules of engagement. The older guys stared straight ahead as if this were nothing unusual. The new rules were good enough for them, and I wasn't about to question their judgment. That's the way the Team worked. Everything was based on seniority. The older guys got the best cars, the best trips, the best assignments. They made the decisions and handed wisdom down to the rookies. We were a civilian law enforcement organization, but everything we did, from five-paragraph orders to flight suits, had a military pedigree of unmistakable clarity. New guys shut up and did what they were told.

"I'll read the orders again," Lester said. And he did.

Deadly force "could and should" be used.

I heard no emotion in his voice, no sense of urgency or direction. He simply read the rules of engagement as if updating us on the weather.

Lester worked efficiently, and he believed deeply in the nobility and honor of the FBI and the Hostage Rescue Team. If there was any skepticism in his mind about these rules of engagement or what they meant, nothing in his voice betrayed it.

I looked around without turning my head, canvassing the faces of my fellow snipers for impressions. Nothing. Their eyes lurked behind sheaths of torn burlap, face nets, and camouflage face paint. Their thoughts hung deep in the shadows, as quiet as the gray mist that was falling slowly upon us. If they shared my surprise, nothing in the way they held themselves gave it away.

Curtis, the former Navy explosive ordnance disposal diver, sniffled at the rain and adjusted the drag bag on his shoulders. Dale, a former Marine Corps helicopter pilot, pulled his ghillie veil over his shoulders and squinted. Yoda, who was a former Army Ranger, a judo master, and a bishop in the Mormon church, stood stiff as a granite pillar, like always, relentless in his mind-over-matter discipline.

They were my NOTS mates, as new to this as I was. But they were also veterans of similar deployments, military men familiar with rules of engagement and orders from commanding officers. I watched them like a kid trying to learn proper manners. I searched for clues about what exactly this all meant. New Operator Training School never addressed this sort of situation. That initial orientation taught us how to do everything a sniper needed to do except how to walk up a mountain in the middle of nowhere, quarter a human being with the crosshairs of our rifle scopes, and kill him.

Can and should use deadly force.

I looked to the other snipers, the veterans: Mark and Luke, who had served as Marine Corps infantry officers; Hooch, a West Point graduate, former Army Ranger, paratrooper, and line officer; Beef, a Naval Academy offensive tackle; Boat, a former Marine grunt. Only Raz, Warren, and I had no military training. They said nothing. Maybe this was par for the course. I didn't know; I'd never been to a party quite like this before.

I suddenly felt confident, the way a dog feels confident in a pack. I knew why we were there. Dick Roberts's new rules of engagement were just guidelines drawn up to address the gravity of this particular situation. Standard FBI rules of engagement defined any struggle: "Deadly force may not be used unless there is an imminent threat of death or grievous bodily harm to yourself or someone else" always superseded crisis-specific variations.

I didn't wonder, at the time, whether the new rules of engagement were a shoot-to-kill order. If I was going to kill someone, it was going to be because I thought he needed killing, not because some bureaucratic empty suit 2,000 miles away wanted him dead. They hired me for my judgment, and that was just what they were going to get.

What I remember thinking then was that we were about to walk up an isolated mountain into the jaws of a violence that had already taken at least one federal agent's life. I knew the people we would likely face had big guns, were willing to use them, and had home field advantage. I never really weighed differences in the rules of engagement. I fully expected to defend myself if ambushed or attacked and didn't need Les, BR-1, or anyone else to delineate circumstance or doctrine.

"Any questions?" Lester asked.

Mike Reynolds stood silently beside him as Les looked us each in the eye and waited for a response. None came. So he moved closer, entered the hulking, ragged space between us.

"We'll move south into the wood line," Reynolds said, "then back to the north and east, up to the ridge. Once we break out of the tall trees, you're on your own. Keep moving higher on the mountain overlooking the cabin until you find positions."

Les waited until Reynolds finished.

"Call in when you move into your positions," he said. "And watch your asses."

He turned and left.

Reynolds took point, and started away from us along the muddy road that led either toward the Weaver cabin or back to Bonners Ferry, depending on your volition. We fell in behind him, according to preassigned sniper positions, slipped the safeties off our rifles, and moved into the wood line.

I swallowed hard on a stomach filled with nothing but acid and adrenaline. My eyes itched with camouflage paint and fatigue. The only clothing I carried had already stuck to my skin with sweat.

Once we left the road, the terrain went from potato field to mountain within the space of a few steps. I carried a bare bones load that would sustain me for no more than a few hours. The first team always goes in light for a short shift. The "down" team finishes making camp and prepares for a longer stay in position once the perimeter has been established. Based on BR-1's initial briefing, I figured we'd be back by dark.

Reynolds led a single-file column quietly up the mountain. We followed the trail for a time but eventually broke from it into the uncut forest of larch and pine and blazed back and forth across the slope. It was a tortuous terrain marked with sheer cliffs of open rock and talus. The rain had turned the moss- and leaf-covered ground into a slick obstacle course. I slipped several times and felt the polypropylene underwear squish like a sponge soaked with sweat and rainwater. Steam rose off my chest as I opened the layers to let the cold air cool me.

The terrain looked so much like the New Hampshire mountains of my youth, I sometimes flashed back as if a few friends and I had just set out for a weekend sojourn. But then the long dirty strands of ghillie would fall into my eyes and the top of my rifle would bang off the back of my head. This was no casual hike.

We moved quickly, scanning left and right in alternating order for possible ambush. The Grand Canyon mission had taught me the value of proper patrolling techniques, and I took my assignment seriously. None of us expected anything during the first half-hour or so, but after a time, there was no mistaking the fact that this was Weaver's turf. He lived in these woods year round, without the comforts that soften ordinary people. He had no television. He had no electricity. He killed most of what he ate and grew the rest. As vast and wild as these woods seemed, they were his backyard. If he wanted to find us, we likely would have been easy enough to find.

After more than two hours of hiking, Reynolds stopped. He crouched at the base of an enormous boulder and signaled that we had arrived. All around us, huge rocks stood like resolute sentinels at the top of a fortress wall. I looked back out the way we had just come and saw nothing but forest and fog. The trail we had just blazed faded below us into a creeping mist and that incessant, chattering rain.

Word came back down the line in whispered fragments. This was the end of the trail for Reynolds. The Weaver cabin was less than 200 yards to our left, beyond the boulders and across a deep ravine. I craned my neck, trying to maintain cover, looking to prove what I had been told. Once Reynolds left, we would move up above the cabin, along a stubbly ridge, dropping two-man sniper/observer teams as we went. Hooch and Dale would be first. Curtis and Beef second. Luke and Warren would be third. Mark, Boat, and I would occupy the final position, highest on the hillside.

Reynolds moved quietly away from us, back into the mist,

with little fanfare. There was no talk of strategy or any planning session. We all knew our jobs and realized without question that we were now close enough to Weaver for him to take us with a well-aimed shot. He was a former Special Forces soldier and an experienced hunter. He had hunting rifles and long-range optics. If we exposed ourselves, it might cost us dearly.

I could see the Weaver cabin almost constantly as we moved from rock to rock toward our position high above Ruby Ridge. The plywood-and-tar-paper shack off to our left looked much smaller and cruder than I had expected. Maybe it was the gravity of the situation or the sense that any evil great enough to kill a federal officer must come from some grand edifice, but whatever my expectations, this reality came as anticlimax.

Weaver's twenty-by-thirty-foot cabin looked more like an abandoned shanty. A lone stovepipe jutted out of the pitched roof, and thin porches looked forward and back. A single window opened out the east wall, but the distance and the rainy mist made it impossible to see inside. Everything seemed eerily still and foreboding. I remember a feeling of resentment, the same resentment I felt rolling into L.A. after the riots. This crisis seemed once again to have come and gone ahead of us, leaving the empty hush of regret that always follows violence.

We moved away from Hooch and Dale and climbed for a long time. Slowly, quietly, carefully. Curtis and Beef left us first. Luke and Warren left us last. Boat moved higher without noticing their absence until the forest thinned out ahead of us into rough scrub and crumbling rock. He selected a rocky ledge 200 feet above and 300 yards from the cabin as our FFP, then signaled with a raised hand that this would be home.

The FFP, or forward firing position, is a military designation we'd adopted from the Marines during sniper training. It simply referred to the position of cover we would use to observe the crisis site and take a shot if necessary. The ideal FFP provides a clear view of the objective without giving away the observer and should mask the muzzle flash and smoke of the rifle if he takes a shot. The FFP that Boat selected relied on a small evergreen shrub and two television-size boulders for cover. There was precious little else to hide behind.

Because of the precipitous drop-offs and rough terrain, the three of us had to move farther apart than we normally would have. I hunkered down fifteen feet to the left of Mark and Boat on a small granite shelf. The rocky outcrop dropped off behind me into defilade and offered a place to eat, change clothing, or go to the bathroom. It seemed like a suitable, if inhospitable, den, and I quickly set about converting it to a sniper's hide.

First, I pulled my rifle out of the drag bag and rested it on the attached Burris bipod. I pulled my poncho over my head and shoulders, creating a tented shroud, but it did little to help. Rain poured off the front edge, creating a miniature waterfall. The mist from each breath acted like steam on a cold window, leaving a streaky film. The only way I could use my spotting and rifle scopes was to wipe them constantly with lens paper and blow each breath slowly out through my nose.

The first order of business was to call our positions in to the TOC. Mark took care of that. He used back azimuths and distances to the cabin as identifiers, and Les marked us on a map in the command post. We had no laser range finder, but we estimated our distance to the cabin at 290 yards.

After Boat called our position in to the TOC, he and Mark moved back into defilade to work on setting up their gear. I put eyes on the target and concentrated on the ritual of wiping the lens of my rifle scope and trying to glean information about the scene below us. The rain had begun to fall in earnest and the cloud cover had descended just above our heads. The temperature had dropped into the high thirties and steam poured off my sweaty, overheated body. Each breath drifted up between my eye and the scope lens, then into the immeasurable sea of mist descending upon us.

I began to search the scene below for intelligence data. All I could see of the front side of the cabin was the top of the porch roof and two windows above it. We were so high above the building, I could not see the front door, but I could make out a railing and what appeared to be a washing machine. A single window offered a view from the eastern side.

Having endured two decades of harsh New England winters, I wondered how anyone could live here year round in such a flimsy shelter. This was northern Idaho, after all. We were just forty miles from the Canadian border. It was still only August and the temperature was hovering near freezing. The next five months would be cruel and challenging for anyone trying to live in this flimsy shack.

Because of the ridge's topography, it was virtually impossible to establish a classic perimeter. The cabin sat on a rocky knob that jutted out into a ravine. The ravine dropped steeply from three sides. The only road up to the cabin was a narrow, twisting dirt path that passed through a natural earthen gate. Weaver and Harris had established a well-fortified defensive position in a horseshoe-shaped rocky outcrop that rose thirty or forty feet above this road. Anyone attempting to drive up to the cabin would be heard long before he arrived. That would give Harris and Weaver ample time to grab their weapons and run to their redoubts.

From my position, designated Sierra One, I could see the road, the rocky fortress, several vehicles, a woodpile, a small shed, and the kind of yard trash I expected to see in rural squalor. Two dogs paced nervously back and forth at the end of short chains tethered outside a makeshift doghouse. They lived at the crest of the driveway where the road passed up through the rocky overlook. The mangy, desperate creatures looked more like a neglected security system than pets.

I called it all in to the TOC. The other sniper pairs provided details that I could not see. High-powered optics are great magnifiers but provide poor depth perception. Things that may have looked close from my position were better approximated from the three other positions.

A short time, maybe five minutes, after beginning my surveillance, I saw a white male walk out onto the back porch of the house. A sleeping bag hung from a clothesline near the southeast corner of the building, obscuring my view. I watched as he peered out toward the ridge and then disappeared back inside the cabin.

It happened quickly enough that I did not get a look at his face, but it served as a wake-up call that this was not an exercise in futility. It was the first proof we had that adult males were in fact inside the cabin. I remember feeling a familiar but irrational vulnerability. There is a strange sense during any surveillance that the people you are watching can see you. I felt it for the first time as a new agent in Missouri watching a bank robbery suspect. You feel a seedy cheapness in sneaking around to catch a felon. Maybe it's a sort of guilt over acting the voyeur when you feel like standing up and announcing your lawful authority.

I knew Weaver and Harris were waiting for us, for somebody, and that standing up and announcing our authority would not be a good idea. The last person who tried that ended up with a bullet in his throat. Weaver and Harris had run to the cabin from the authority of an ordered society to begin with. They disdained tax collectors and lawmakers as infidels. They had sworn off a workaday world in which their unique and often bizarre views brought them ridicule. Now they had entered pitched battle and had to fully expect the wrath of a Zionist Occupational Government, as they called the federal government. What they started in that mountain clearing the day before wasn't going to end there and they knew it. Someone would come. Men with badges and authority would show up to end their self-imposed exile.

I shook my feet inside the sodden boots that were quickly turning my toes numb with cold. Icy water trickled down my neck, over my shoulders, and into my armpits. My bare fingers looked like shriveled sausages as the shudders crept up my arms and down my back. I just lay there, the exertion of the trip fading with the daylight. I felt as if all the cold, ragged emptiness in that rocky mountain were reaching up to pull me into it, down among the crevices and dull shadows.

I stared through the scope at the cabin. The dogs barked occasionally from the ends of their chains but there was no other activity. I reached out from under my poncho with a piece of lens paper, cleaned the scope, then settled back behind it for another look.

And then it began.

14

THE SHOT

They came out from under the front porch roof with shoulder weapons held at port arms. Two men and a woman. They wore dark coats with hoods that obscured their features in deep shadows, but the shadows faded as they ran, and I caught their intention in my crosshairs. Whatever drew them out of that cabin had stirred a sense of urgency in their movement. This was an immediate-action drill just like HRT and military special operations units practiced for wartime. This didn't look like a casual stroll to feed the chickens. These three looked like they wanted a chunk of somebody's ass.

I held my crosshairs on the lead runner as he ran almost directly at me, toward the rocky outcropping I recognized from surveillance photos. Between us lay almost 300 yards of rocks and trees and the sort of junk I was used to seeing around rural Missouri trailer houses. They looked closer, through the lens of my ten-power rifle scope; bigger.

I tracked the three runners with my crosshairs, thinking

all the while that they were coming right at me, that they somehow had seen us from the cabin. This was their land, their terrain, and I was the enemy. If they made it into the tree line, our advantage would fade considerably.

I remembered the endless battles my friends and I had fought when we were boys playing in the thick New Hampshire forests. Sometimes I'd run after them or away, depending on the day. There was always the adrenaline and that visceral excitement of the hunt. Buck fever. Flush a partridge through a stand of birch. Lie in wait along a deer trail for a trophy stag. Chase a schoolmate around the playground with closed fists and a heart full of aggression. The war games . . . the gut ache before the state football championship . . . the first arrest . . . every mount-out.

My heart raced.

I laid my finger lightly on the trigger. The safety was already off. I never used it.

A faraway-sounding *pop* echoed across the mountain. Then another and another. Gunfire.

A large-caliber rifle makes one hell of a bang. I had heard them all: everything from the .22-caliber plinker my father gave me as a kid to the .50-caliber doomsday device HRT reserved for the most impenetrable targets. I shot a .308 for a living — thousands of rounds a year. I knew their voices. But these shots sounded different, like handgun rounds or a starter's pistol, anemic and hollow. They came in rapid succession. *Pop, pop, pop . . .*

Sons of bitches are shooting at us, I thought.

I tracked them as they darted across the yard, weapons poised for a fight. They ran right at us . . . shooting.

How the hell do they know we're out here? I wondered. Maybe they saw Hooch and Dale moving around down below. I knew Sierra Four was close to the cabin, but I didn't know exactly where, and I couldn't see them from my position.

My mind flipped through months of sniper training in the time it took my finger to add a pound and a half of pressure to the trigger. Just a breath more, the weight of commitment, and it would cough out a 168-grain death pill capable of blowing one of their heads half off.

I did everything just as I'd practiced. I pulled the stock into my shoulder, welded my cheek to the stock, set the proper eye relief. I clenched the butt pad with my left hand to steady the rifle on its bipod.

I sucked air slowly into my lungs and eased it out. It all happened instantly, effortlessly.

And I set my aim.

There are two ways to shoot moving targets, or "movers," as we called them: tracking and ambush. Trackers move their rifle barrel with the target, bisecting its form with the crosshairs, squeezing slowly on the trigger until the round cooks off, then following through the recoil like a skeet shooter. The problem with this technique is that a moving rifle barrel flies in the face of every rule of precision marksmanship. A stationary platform is the best platform from which to shoot. Any movement at all can throw off the fragile trajectory. It is a pointlessly difficult technique that is used by a very small number of snipers.

The ambush technique allows the shooter to take his shot from a perfectly still position by waiting for the target to cross into a predetermined killing zone. The shooter finds an open area, plants his crosshairs just ahead of the mover, counts the mil-dots in his reticle to calculate distance and speed, judges wind, elevation, and humidity, then waits for the target to cross his field of view.

Looking through a ten-power scope at 200 yards, the shooter has less than a second to assess the environment, align his target, and make the commitment to kill: to kill a human being. To shoot a walking, talking, breathing human being with eyes and a mouth and a face. And that is precisely where you aim to shoot him. Right in the face. Into his eyes. You want to shoot him in a part of the skull that will cause irrevocable, instantaneous death.

The margin for error is infinitesimally small. Less than a tenth of a second too late and he runs past your shot. Calculate the same interval too soon and you give him something to flinch at.

You get less than a second to pull off one of the most complex, demanding, and unforgiving feats a human being could ever be called upon to perform.

Make the right decision and you save the day. Make the wrong decision and you spend the rest of your life fighting administrative, civil, and possibly criminal charges, tangling with people who have no idea in the world what this is like. Less than a tenth of a second either way and it's all over. Less than a tenth of a second window of error to kill a human being; to watch him drop to the ground like a bag of flesh and turn into a murky red puddle. There are no second chances. No chance to say "I'm sorry," no "Oh shits."

I ambush. That is my technique.

I knew the distance to target to be about 290 yards, the angle of incidence to be approximately 28 degrees, the humidity to be 100 percent, and the wind to be zero-to-three miles per hour from my left at 45 degrees — a quarter-value crosscurrent. Considering these factors and the foot speed of the runners, I calculated a two-mil-dot lead and pushed my crosshairs out in front of them to set up the shot.

I felt completely confident in my ability to take them out, considering the variables. I never gave that a thought. But I also knew that I'd have very little time to do it. Things were happening almost instantaneously, the way things run together during a long fall. I remember that perfect consciousness, the sense that despite the wretched weather conditions and the abruptness of it all, I knew what I was doing was right.

I didn't feel the cold or the rain or the exhaustion. I didn't feel hungry or nervous or alone. I just felt certain that I had to shoot.

I remember squeezing on the trigger the way they trained me. Our triggers were set to two and a half pounds of resistance depending on the weapon and personal preference. My rifle's jeweled trigger broke slightly heavier than most at just a couple ounces less than three pounds.

I remember pulling all but the last ounce, trying to set up a shot and losing it to a tree or a rock or the shed or the woodpile. I moved the crosshairs, counted the mil-dots, steadied my aim, and lost them behind an obstacle.

Again.

Again.

The first shots, just seconds earlier, echoed in my head. I knew I had to shoot before they reached the wood line. They were running straight at me.

Shoot, shoot, shoot, you fuck! a voice surged through my mind.

But the bullets didn't go.

Pull the trigger! Pull!

And then they were gone. The three runners turned back toward the cabin, and I lost them under the porch roof as they scrambled helter-skelter out of my view.

The whole thing lasted seconds.

"Sierra One to TOC, we've got shots fired."

It was my voice, but I barely recognized it.

I squeezed the transmit button on my handheld radio and spoke into the black face. "Multiple shots. Two volleys."

I released the button, realizing for the first time that I did not know who had fired the shots or if anyone had been hit. Despite a sense of calm, I could feel my heart pounding within my chest, against the cold rock platform beneath me, lifting me ever so slightly away from the granite ballast. The rain clattered against the poncho that lay over my head. Mist rose from my mouth in quick breaths. A strange warmth coursed through my aching limbs. My vision cleared and my hearing became pristine.

And then I saw it. All of it. The whole scene again, in my mind's eye, running by me like some sort of internal instant replay.

I saw them emerge from the cabin just as I set my eye to the scope: three people in dark, hooded coats, rifles held out in front of them like soldiers running into battle. I counted them: one, two men . . . one woman. Randy Weaver, Kevin Harris, Vicki Weaver, I assumed. I didn't really know their faces any better than they knew mine.

They ran out of the cabin like it was on fire, toward what we'd been told was a fortified fighting position, the soon-to-be-infamous "rocky outcropping." After a few steps, they turned toward us and disappeared behind one of dozens of obstacles that grew or lay or rose up like speed bumps in an out-of-sync movie.

Gunshots. Weak, strange-sounding shots, too thin to have come from a rifle. They turned and ran together back toward the cabin. There were no voices. There was no shouting. More shots. Just as they ran up onto the front porch and disappeared from my view. Those same strange-sounding *pop, pop, pop* sounds that I couldn't reconcile with the weapons I saw.

And then I heard it.

The scream.

It started low in the base of my skull like a high-pitched

siren, rising higher and louder as if some apparition had flown out of the ravine below and filled the sky.

"Ayyyyeeeeeeaaaahhhh!!!"

No words can describe the frantic abandon or immense horror of that scream. It was a banshee wail filled with death and rage and anguish. It seemed endless, eternal, punctuated by swells of panic and valleys of grief. It seemed to last for hours, though I knew it consumed just one agonizing breath.

Had I missed it the first time? No, I decided. This was just recollection. It was experience catching up to sensation, the way a surge of pain follows trauma. The mind holds it back at first, as if giving itself time to order its defenses.

"My God," I whispered. "What the hell was that?"

The scream hung in the low clouds, wild and tortured and stark. Echoing. Rising. A woman's voice. A shrill, penetrating gurgle of horror.

"How many shots?" the radio squawked. "Anyone hit? Who fired? Any operators injured?"

The questions came one after the other and I shook my head, realizing I had none of the answers. Fortunately, Sierra Four called in with details. Two shots fired. No HRT operators hit. Unknown casualties down below.

Two shots fired? I'd heard at least six. Two shots fired from Sierra Four. That was Hooch and Dale. Who got the shots off?

I'd waged enough athletic contests to know that perception is often skewed by adrenaline and the confusion of a violent encounter, but I felt certain there had to have been more than two shots.

I looked off to my left, 100 yards down the mountain, to try and guess where Sierra Four had set up their FFP. They were much closer to the cabin and at least 100 feet lower than we were. They would have had a far better perspective on what had just happened. I saw nothing but scraggly larch and the relentless rain.

Then, as if shaken with the chill, I began to doubt, for the first time since I'd joined HRT, my own abilities. Why had I not been able to get off a shot when I felt certain that FBI agents, my own teammates, were in peril? Why had I relayed inaccurate information to the TOC based on what I thought I heard during an agent-involved shooting? Why had I heard six shots when Sierra Four, the men closest to and involved in the shooting, had reported just two?

Suddenly, very little made sense. I reran the course of events through my mind for a third time, searching for details. I stared down at the empty compound but saw the whole thing again with great clarity. Three of them — two men and a woman — came out of the cabin at a run. They looked urgent, directed, as if they knew where they were going and had done the same thing many times before. They crossed the rock- and refuse-strewn yard from left to right through my rifle scope, holding shoulder weapons at port arms like well-trained soldiers.

The weapons. One of them looked like a Ruger Mini-14, an assault rifle designed to fire .223 ammunition from thirty-round magazines just like our CAR-16s. They came in semi-automatic and full auto versions and were formidable weapons. One of the other guns looked like a deer rifle of some kind. I couldn't make out the third.

Then the shots came, one . . . two . . . three. *Pop, pop, pop.*

More movement. *Pop, pop, pop* again. And then they were gone. Boulder, tree, shed, woodpile, boulder, tree, porch. I watched them move together at first and then apart as they seemed to scatter and then dash back to cover inside the cabin.

I tried to time the shots to their positions. I tried to visualize the position of their weapons, tried to recall if they could have fired. But there was too much information to process in those few moments. Everything happened so quickly. My eyes had identified two adult males, my ears heard shots, my finger prepped the trigger, my heart told me to shoot, my mind told me to wait for the perfect shot. It never came.

Trepidation never crossed my mind during the whole event. I never felt the immense weight of consequence I remember feeling the first time I held a deer in my rifle sights. I had done precisely what HRT and the U.S. Marine Corps had trained me to do. Cogent thought had little if anything to do with it.

I lay there as the rain fell uninterrupted by all this, and I swept the crosshairs of my rifle scope through the yard, looking for additional threats. For all I knew, they could still be on the porch, lining up their shots for a return volley.

My radio earpiece began to buzz in my head.

"How many shots fired?" someone asked again.

The voice sounded calm and controlled, but it was also full of immediacy and import.

"Sierra Four to TOC, two shots fired from this location."

"Anyone hit?"

"Sierra Four to TOC, unknown injuries at this time."

The voice on the other end belonged to supervisor Billy Mazzone. I knew he must have felt extremely frustrated down below. He had a clear understanding of how things were supposed to go, but surely none of this was in anyone's playbook. The original plan called for snipers to observe the crisis site and feed information back down to the command element while the assaulters waited in an emergency capacity should they be needed.

Meanwhile the command element would compose a surrender ultimatum, deliver it over a loudspeaker, and sit back to wait things out. It was a well-established practice: crisis resolution. The negotiators always get the first run at things.

Well, now things very clearly had changed.

I waited for the emergency assault to rise out of the long shadows. It had been part of the plan. But no one came. The dogs continued to bark and the rain continued to fall and the mist rising from my mouth continued to clog my scope as I searched for anything noteworthy.

Nothing.

"What the hell was that helicopter doing up here?" Boat asked. He and Mark were waiting well off to my right and slightly above me, but I could still hear them, even in their subdued tones.

Helicopter? What helicopter? I asked them what they meant.

"You didn't hear that? Flew right over the cabin. Maybe that's what brought them out."

I shook my head. I never heard any helicopter.

And then I realized what had happened. Looking around me, the answers suddenly seemed obvious. I'd grown up in mountains like these and knew the tricks they can play with sound. One time as a boy, I'd become separated in dense fog from two friends. We were on an exposed shoulder between two mountains called the Kinsmans. I called out to them and heard voices that seemed very close, but when the fog parted enough for me to see, I realized they were nearly a half-mile away.

Mountains echo and they swallow sound. Voices and trees creaking and stones falling and rifle shots and helicopters get lost in the crags and branches. The first volley of three shots I remembered had been one shot with an echo. Same with the second. That would also explain the crescendo wail that filled the valley and the helicopter I hadn't heard. My eyes hadn't lied, but my ears had.

The radios fell silent after that. Nothing at all happened for what seemed like a very long time. I knew that we snipers had suddenly become very distant and unimportant to the command element down below, but I had no idea what to expect. What had started as a surveillance had suddenly escalated into another shooting, a new crisis.

A law enforcement shooting is difficult even under the best of circumstances, relatively speaking, and this was certainly not the best of circumstances. HRT, at this point, was still pretty much on its own. Dick Roberts had committed all eleven of his snipers to a day shift along the crest of an isolated mountain ridge. No one down below had laid eyes on the crisis site, and the road to and from the cabin had not been properly cleared for passage. The command element had no lines of communication to the cabin. They had no idea who, if anyone, had been hurt, and they had no immediate course of action.

On top of that, the nearest medical facilities were a half-hour away by helicopter. Flying in these weather conditions seemed doubtful at best. It was now nearly 8:00 P.M. It would be dark soon, and none of the snipers carried night vision goggles or low-light rifle scopes. We had little food, limited water, and no warm clothing to withstand weather that was deteriorating by the minute.

We had been up for nearly forty hours under considerable stress and exertion. Many of us had become borderline hypothermic. Leaving us in position would be dangerous. Unfortunately, bringing us back would be dangerous, too; there would be no one left to maintain our perimeter.

As a boy, my friends and I camped out frequently in midwinter and did it with equipment that seemed primitive compared to what HRT issued its personnel. We slept in cotton Sears Roebuck sleeping bags on top of pine boughs and wore wool jackets over cotton union suits. I had once camped out with my Boy Scout troop in air that dropped to twenty-two degrees below zero. We hadn't even heard of wind chill factors then. Twenty below was what the thermometer on our scoutmaster's tent pole read. I had lots of experience surviving in the cold.

This day, however, I knew that hypothermia had become a more realistic threat than gunfire. Nothing I did would stop the bone-racking shivers that tormented me. The dank, steamy cold came in through my sleeves and the cuffs of my pants and the collar of my shirt. It came in waves at first and then settled into a dense, incessant throb. I shook so badly, after a time, that I could barely see through my scope. I found it difficult to talk. Performing simple chores such as changing my radio battery or pulling lens paper out of my pocket became exercises in futility. We would not last into the night.

"TOC to Sierra units."

I remember the words clearly.

"HR-1 wants to know if you can hold your positions until morning."

Who the hell could ask such a question? Surely the same rain had been falling at the TOC for the past eight hours. Surely the temperature hovered just above freezing down where they sat in their tent. All they had to do was walk outside to see that a mallard duck would be freezing his waterproof ass off by now.

That was the way BR-1 worked. It was the type of thing he expected from snipers. The Hostage Rescue Team, to him, meant gallant door knockers in black Nomex flight suits and balaclavas swooping down from helicopters on fast ropes to blow doors away and free terrorized hostages. That was the image he fostered and the persona he projected. He looked at snipers as a necessary evil and conveniently forgot that we went through all the training assaulters did before being sent on to sniper school for eight weeks.

Anger welled up inside me like a hot fever. I think, now, that he blamed us in many ways for his predicament. Had we established our perimeter and furnished information as he'd planned, we could have rotated half the men down, resupplied, and settled into regular shifts. The assaulters could have rolled up in one of the National Guard's Bradley Fighting Vehicles, delivered their ultimatum, and settled into protracted negotiation. That, no doubt, is what he had in mind.

That is not what happened. What he probably did not admit then was that his flight up to the cabin in an HRT helicopter may have drawn Weaver and Harris out. I still believe it was his impatience that precipitated the shooting and sent his plan headlong into the muddy ditch.

"Negative," Boat said in a tone that sounded like a cross between amazement and Rambo's "I'm coming for you" line. Boat had fared no better than the rest of us in this frightful weather, and he knew we would not survive an overnight surveillance.

After a lengthy pause, Lester told us to return to base via the same route we had followed up. That came as welcome news, but we now had other problems. It had grown dark and we had no guide, no maps, and no night vision equipment. The trip up had taken almost three hours during the day when we were much more alert. The trip down would be very difficult.

We packed and started back within five minutes. My little perch stood atop a long, sloped boulder which I had to slide down on my butt. My feet had become completely numb to the point where I couldn't tell when I was standing on rock or thin air. I held on to trees and took slow, careful steps to keep from falling and breaking my leg or worse.

The idea was to work our way back down the way we had

come and pick up the other snipers as we moved down the ridge. Unfortunately, we did not know precisely where the other sniper positions were. The skies had become so dark that you had to stay literally within arm's reach of the man in front of you or you would be completely lost.

We moved in a slow and awkward line down the ragged slope until, using our radios, we located two of the three other sniper pairs. Sierra Four gave up on us and started down by themselves, thinking we had already passed them by.

Mark, a seasoned outdoorsman and rock climber, blazed our trail. Despite his abilities, however, he made slow and poor progress. By the time we climbed down the ridge, to the shoulder of the actual mountain, the skies had turned to sludge. At almost every step, someone took a bad fall and landed in a pile of frustration. No one complained or argued. They picked themselves up and started again, arm's length from the man in front of them, one step at a time, knowing that one misplaced boot might take them over the precipice of a 100-foot cliff. Mark missed two lethal falls by sheer luck. To this day, I think it is an absolute miracle that none of us fell to our death during that hike out.

Four hours and several miles later, nine of us marched up the bog of a road that led to the camp. I remember glimpsing the light of the TOC's small lantern in the distance and thinking it was one of the most beautiful sights I had ever seen in my life. It was nearly two in the morning and I was running on pure will. I had now been awake and running for forty-four hours, during which time I had worked a full day at Quantico, flown 2,500 miles, driven five hours, hiked a ragged mountain in abysmal conditions, set up a sniper hide and participated in the shooting of at least two human beings. That's at least four adrenaline cycles.

The only thing I wanted in the entire world was a warm sleeping bag and a few hours of sleep.

Lester was waiting for us when we trudged back into camp. He told us to square away our gear and meet him for a debriefing, then left us in a long tubular tent illuminated by a single flashlight. We stripped off our soaked clothes and hung them on parachute cord lines tied to the ceiling. The ghillie and Gore-Tex and polypro underwear — all camouflage — hung in dripping, steaming rows and looked for all the world like some tropical jungle. Steam rose off our bodies as we hurried into dry gear and shook our heads trying to coax out a few more minutes of comprehension.

Once we had reassembled, Lester handed out paper and told us to write up 302s detailing our last twelve hours. We had just participated in a shooting, so we knew that what we wrote down could one day be very important, but we were in no mental condition to draft cogent prose. I wrote the broad strokes as I remembered them.

When we finished, Lester excused us and we crawled into our bags. I remember lying there for just a moment and looking up into that hanging jungle of wet, rancid clothing.

What in the hell am I doing here? I wondered. Someone reached up to turn out the light.

The answer never came.

15

RESOLUTION

Ruby Ridge, Idaho, went from isolated pine forest to internationally known symbol of government oppression in the time it took Vicki Weaver's scream to fade into the overcast sky. Within twenty-four hours of Hooch's two rifle shots, everyone from the governor of Idaho and the American Red Cross to a bunch of tear-ass white supremacists clogged the roads leading out to one of the most controversial crime scenes in recent history.

I hadn't really processed the impact of what had happened when I awoke the next morning, to the droning clatter of a gas generator. I gathered consciousness slowly, as if I'd been knocked out and left for dead. A gray-black blur hung about me as I squinted my eyes, trying to focus. My body felt like it had grown down into the lumpy ground, setting roots and becoming part of the whole earth.

"Let's go, Whitcomb," a voice prodded from someplace a thousand miles away. "Time for work."

I thought it was all just an irritating dream at first, some cruel trick my mind wanted to play on my exhausted body. But a leather boot to my side shattered any hope of more rest. Raz stepped over me, pulling a wool sweater over his head.

"They got breakfast outside if you hurry."

I rolled over in my sleeping bag, wiped camouflage paint out of my eyes, and looked down the gray-black tunnel of a tent. Yoda and Mark were stuffing gear into their day packs. Everyone else had already gone.

My watch read 6:50 A.M.

"What's going on?" I asked. The tent smelled of mildewed burlap and bad intestines.

Mark stood up and wrestled a military Alice pack onto his shoulder.

"They want us to close the perimeter," he mumbled. "Boat's in a team leaders meeting. We're supposed to meet him in fifteen minutes. Better hurry up."

Fifteen minutes?

What the hell, I consoled myself as I scrambled to find some dry clothes and a canteen of water. Sleep came grudgingly to this place, and I was out of practice anyway.

I crawled out of my sleeping bag, pulled on some dry pants, and shoved a day shift's worth of gear into my camouflaged ruck. My boots were still soaked, but I managed to chip the mud off the laces enough to pull them onto my feet. I barely noticed how the cold wetness crept back between my toes. My stomach needed attention more than my feet, and I had ten minutes to stuff a ration down my throat before Boat led us back up that mountain. I gathered up my CAR-16 and slapped in a full magazine. By the time I dragged my pack through the tent flap and into the TOC, my mind was just beginning to respond.

"Man, you look like shit." A woman's voice. I stepped out

of the way as Cindy, our logistics technician, steered an armful of Xerox paper into the TOC. Billy Mazzone sat behind the radio base station, off to my left, typing something into a laptop. Sometime since the previous day, we'd acquired a telephone, a couple of electric lamps, and a Mr. Coffee, which, I noticed, had just begun to drip.

"Where'd everybody go?" I asked. The question seemed obvious enough, but no one answered. I asked again.

"Outside," Billy droned. "Better get your ass out there if you want a ride."

Everybody liked Billy. He spoke with a thick New Jersey accent and two very busy hands in a combination sign language/slang that could seem dizzying. He was a first-generation operator — one of the Team's plank holders — and had left just long enough to take a stroll down the career-development path. Now he was back as one of the two assault supervisors, where he belonged.

"How's Hooch?" I asked. The events of the previous night were slowly filtering back into my head the way details return after a hard drunk. Sleep deprivation had the same effect on me. We were now well into day two of the mission, and I'd had less than four hours of sleep to help me with my reasoning. I might as well have been chugging peppermint schnapps.

"Haven't seen him," Billy said, struggling with the laptop.

I stepped outside into a different world than what I remembered. The cold gray rain had passed off to the north, leaving a clear cerulean sky. A brilliant sun exposed treetops and mountain ridges I hadn't even imagined the previous day. If not for the machine gun in my hand and the camouflage paint clinging to my skin like boot polish, I might have forgotten the gravity of the scene and reveled in its beauty.

The camp around me had changed dramatically just in the

few hours I had slept. Our burgeoning tent compound sat in the middle of a forty-acre potato field, astraddle a muddy gravel path that resembled a road. The assaulters had pitched a GP medium field tent to augment the two DRASH shelters. Three U-Haul box trucks painted in the colorful regional murals sat side by side just behind us. The Red Cross had towed in a mobile kitchen. They had already geared up production and begun serving food to the assembled law enforcement contingents. There were long, haggard faces everywhere, faces I had never seen before: marshals, local and state police, emergency medical people. Word had it that the press had descended in earnest, but they were still too far away to bother with.

Weaver's mile-long driveway meandered off a paved two-lane road, across a crude log bridge, and up through a narrow valley bordered by the Deep River. The cabin sat quietly on a ridge, high above our camp. There was only one way in, and we now owned it.

Weaver's only neighbors, a family named Rau, lived in a modest house a couple hundred yards from our little village at the edge of a vast forest. They'd enjoyed virtual isolation to this point in an idyllic existence most of us dream of on Sunday afternoons in May when the thought of traffic jams, smog-infected heat waves, and irrational bosses overwhelms us. I wondered, walking through broad mud puddles and trampled grass, how this all could come to their back door — this violence and hatred and death.

I stepped out into the road just as an olive drab Humvee chugged past, its diesel exhaust rattling blue smoke into the crisp morning air. Something about the moment chipped loose the same vague sense of dread I'd taken to sleep with me a few hours earlier. I wondered where Hooch was and how he felt.

"Gold snipers up!" Boat called from the other side of the TOC.

"Grab your shit," Mark said, "or you're gonna miss the car pool."

❖

I never did get to talk with Hooch about the shots. From that point on, Blue and Gold snipers split the day, working twelve-hour shifts, six to six. Mark and I got the white/green corner, overlooking the cabin from a deep trench, twenty-five yards to the northwest. A monstrous boulder covered our position to the right. The whole Kootenai ridge fell off behind us, lending the scene drama far beyond the burgeoning standoff.

We settled in there, closer to the cabin. I lay in defilade, so close to the building I could gather more information with my naked eye than with my rifle scope. It didn't really matter what I could see, though, because Headquarters had handed the reins to a quiet, slightly lethargic negotiator named Frank Spearman. He came and went like some slow-moving storm.

"Randy, this is Frank," he said, with all the flair of a grade school kid reading lines off an eye chart. "Randy, we need to talk this out." He actually wrote his monologues down on 3×5 cards before bellowing them at the cabin through the tinny PA system.

"Frank," I would have said if I were in that cabin, "why . . . don't . . . you . . . kiss . . . my . . . skinny . . . white . . . ass."

HRT sat back to wait it out. Gold snipers hunkered down all night, doing absolutely nothing. Weaver and Harris had blocked all the windows with cardboard and fabric, making it impossible to see in during the day. At night, they lit candles inside and painted themselves in profile like slow-moving ghosts in the low-spectrum light of our night vision goggles.

The days passed fruitlessly. Nobody inside uttered a word. Nothing changed. The only useful information we could come up with was migration patterns on some Canada geese. So we radioed small talk back to the TOC and fought to stay awake.

That changed on day four, when BR-1 decided to bolster our intelligence-gathering ability by inserting special "spike" mics under the cabin floor. Lester approached Mark and me with the news and told us we'd need to scout an approach right up to the western wall.

A "wagon wheel patrol," he called it. That seemed patently absurd for two reasons. One: We could see the routes quite clearly in daylight. There was no reason to walk them in the dead of night. Two: Weaver and Harris might frown on having a couple of well-armed men sneaking up in the middle of the night. If they saw us, and they surely kept round-the-clock sentry, we'd probably end up dead. This all seemed like a pointless risk.

Four hours later, in the 5 percent illumination caused by an incoming cold front, Mark and I inspected our gear in preparation of movement.

"You ready?" he asked. He sounded empty, almost hollow in the still night air.

"Yeah. I think this is the most fucked up thing I've ever heard of in my entire life," I said, "but I'm ready."

I slapped the bolt forward on my CAR-16. The heavy metallic clank rang out through the valley, odd and foreign among the other night sounds. Everything that flew, slithered, or burrowed suddenly stopped, trying to place the simple voice of a .223 round sliding into battery.

"How's your vision?"

I adjusted the focal ring of my NVGs. The cabin revealed itself through the trees in Day-Glo green.

"Five by."

I reached just beneath the flash suppressor of my CAR-16 and flicked on an infrared laser. The low-light beam is invisible to the naked eye, but it looks like a forty-foot light saber through NVGs. Mine danced through the thick foliage.

"I'll give you ten minutes to get into position. We'll start together. You ready?" Mark adjusted his camouflage smock. The baggy cotton trench coat hung off him like a dark serape, dipping just below his knees.

"Yeah," I said.

No need to linger. I had my weapon, my NVGs, my partner, and eight friendly .308 barrels pointed at that ugly plywood shack. That was the good news. The bad news was that all Weaver and Harris had to do was stick a gun barrel out any number of windows, doors, or hidden firing ports and blow us away. This had been a fairly violent week already, and I saw no reason to believe the killing was over.

"We move counterclockwise, five degrees at a time," Mark reminded me. "That means seven steps on radius."

Thanks for the math lesson, Mark, I thought.

He motioned with his head that I should leave, and I stepped carefully up over the ridge, onto the flat where Weaver had built his shack. I could hear Lester and the snipers trading information about our movement. Knowing they were out there made things a lot easier. Each of them lay behind a night gun — a standard .308 topped with a three-to-ten variable-power image-enhancing scope. Though night optics significantly reduce effective range, they perform just fine at distances inside 100 yards.

I lipped the west ridge to where the tree line broke to the utility shed, and stepped out into Weaver's yard. Pine needles and soft, dusty loam covered the ground. Nothing moved. The cabin leaned out into space like a Hollywood Hills stilt house, offering plenty of room for half a dozen men to sit right under Randy Weaver and listen to everything he said.

I started toward the cabin, pausing every three or four steps to check for movement. It's easier to hear at night than to see, and NVGs provide no depth perception. I knew the other guys would warn me if they saw anything.

"Sierra Two to TOC. I've got movement in blue alpha two."

I froze. What the hell? Could he hear me thinking?

Blue alpha two meant the second window on the right side of the building. Mark was walking straight toward it with very little cover. Anyone looking out that window would have seen him in a heartbeat.

I turned my head right and immediately saw what they were talking about. A vague image of a man in candle-lit profile moved across the window. No particular threat. They were probably just getting something to eat.

I waited until Mark decided the same thing, pulled his CAR off target, and resumed his approach. The air felt cool against my skin, but small streams of sweat trickled down my sides, sticking the radio hardness against my skin. The camouflage greasepaint on my face felt like a cold, wet mask, breaking up my appearance of humanity but driving me nuts with discomfort. I usually wore a cloth mask instead, but it cut down on visibility and I wanted all my faculties.

I stepped out onto the gravel driveway leading up to Randy Weaver's front door. This was the same ground they'd traveled after the firefight with the marshals. I wondered what they were thinking as they ran past this very spot, with the blood of a federal officer on their hands. They must have known we'd come for them eventually. Maybe that was just what they wanted. I'd read *The Turner Diaries* and all that militia garbage, which conceived the Bible as a battle plan for the end of the world. We were not some Zionist Occupational Government, coming in to strip all Americans of their constitutional right to bear arms. We were just doing our jobs.

Why anyone would assume I wanted to march in and take away their guns and their rights to anything absolutely baffled me. I grew up in the same woods with the same guns reading the same Bible all these guys did. No minister ever told me I needed to keep the female members of my family in a separate building during their menstrual cycle. No one told me I could walk away from a valid arrest warrant because I didn't consider myself legally bound by federal law. Nobody ever told me I could stop paying taxes because I don't like abortion, that I could write federal judges threatening letters, or that I could shoot law officers when they came to do the same job they perform a thousand times a day in other parts of the world.

Go ahead and drop out of society, build yourself a shack in the woods, and believe anything you want, I thought. Who the hell cares? Just stay away from all the other people who want the same peace. Don't blame your paranoia on the people who dedicate their lives to protecting you.

Fuck them, I thought. I used the anger to propel me toward the cabin. Fuck them.

I stopped in the middle of the clearing to listen. The road fell steeply off to my left, past the rocky outcropping that provided a fortified defensive rampart. They built this place strategically. A steep canyon protected their east wall. The back porch stretched out to the south, overlooking the Kootenai valley, a million-dollar view and an excellent killing field. The only ways into this place are by air or through the weeds with a ghillie suit.

Calm down and concentrate on the mission, I told myself.

I walked up to the front porch — the very spot where I'd last seen Weaver and Harris and the woman. Things looked different up close. Everything felt much smaller. What they called the birthing shed looked no bigger than the place I stored my lawn mower. Even the trees and boulders hunkered together, explaining why I'd had such trouble lining up a shot that first day. At 300 yards and a high angle of incidence, Weaver and the others couldn't have exposed themselves more than a split second at any given time. How the hell Hooch got two rounds off amazed me.

I was making my way back to cover, feeling a little more confident, when the night erupted.

CRAAAAASH!

I spun right, just off the southeast corner of the cabin toward a hellacious racket. It sounded like the whole Weaver tribe had dashed out the back door ready for the mother of all battles.

CRAAAAASH!

"Shit," I hissed. They'd busted us.

I crouched down to a squatting position, just in front of the porch, gathered up my forestock, and trained the infrared laser on the noise. I swung the muzzle just ahead of my NVGs, ready for an immediate-action drill, prepping the trigger for a two-round burst.

My eyes sorted potential targets: trees, limbs, rocks, Mark.

Mark?

I lowered the red laser dot from his forehead and watched him through my NVGs as he fought to regain control of some overwhelming malfunction. My eyes settled through the grainy viewfinder on a sight I really couldn't believe. Somehow, in the flat, two-dimensional twilight zone of night vision optics, he'd missed the stack of garbage cans and walked as boldly into them as Big Al chasing a UFAP into a pool hall.

Though the scene looked like something right out of the Keystone Cops, I could barely breathe. From inside that shack, Mark's misstep had to sound like the whole Zionist Occupational Government marching its way up for a full frontal assault. If Weaver still had a taste for war, he would indulge it now.

I painted the door and every window I could see with my laser, waiting for someone to come running out with his head down and weapon up. Every hair on my body stood on end as I squatted there, twenty feet from the porch, and waited for this whole thing to end in a blaze of automatic weapons fire. I was totally exposed and close enough to spit on from the cabin.

Mark stood there in the open, right below a large window, with nothing to hide behind but his rifle. Snipers covering our movement would take any threats that they could see, but we had no idea what access the Weavers had to the space beneath the cabin. For all we knew, they could pop out from behind one of the pillars and whack us before we could re-act.

Fortunately, Weaver either didn't have a trapdoor to the crawl space, or he had lost interest in making death. The only noise anyone heard was the adrenaline squirting through my veins and the trip-hammer thunk of two ready-for-war hearts. I just sat there, waiting for what seemed like hours. Finally, I saw Mark move ever so slightly, then begin to back out.

"That must have sounded pretty bad, huh?" he said after we made it back to our FFP.

"Yeah," I said. "Pretty bad."

❖

The FBI is a big and sometimes cumbersome organization, and like most government bureaucracies, it tries to swat flies with frying pans. By the end of the third day, the Ruby Ridge shootings had matured into a crisis of national significance. The Special Agent in Charge of the Salt Lake City division had arrived with a covey of field agents to assume overall command. The local sheriff and head of the state police had arrived in their respective RVs. The National Guard had rolled in with portable water tanks and other logistical supplies. Paramedics in orange jumpsuits, pilots, photographers, communications technicians, typists, clerks, chaplains, health officials, soldiers, lawyers, cops, press. The list went on and on. Everyone came.

HRT's original three-tent camp grew like a fledgling metropolis to the point where some prospective mayor staked a sign at the entrance proclaiming "Federal Way — Idaho's third biggest city." Canvas in gray, brown, and olive drab covered the field. Box trucks and emergency vehicles of every description stacked like cordwood, awaiting every possible development.

FBI Headquarters flew in SWAT teams and specialists trained in all aspects of crisis management from several Northwest offices. The U.S. Attorney's Office sent prosecutors. The Justice Department sent more suits. With them came fax machines, copiers, a field hospital, hot meals, powerful generators, electric lights, a portable darkroom for the photographers, even television. Weaver's dogs, which we'd freed on the second day, paraded through the boom town, acting like happy mascots. It looked like a SWAT Woodstock.

The Marshals Service's Special Operations Group, of which Deputy Degan had been a member, did all they could to assist, but must have felt a good deal of frustration over the fact that the FBI had declined their services. They milled about camp and helped where they could, but they had no direct role in the standoff. HRT snipers controlled the perimeter. An FBI negotiator talked to the cabin. FBI pilots flew the sorties. FBI managers made all tactical and administrative decisions. The marshals had to sit back and watch while our juggernaut rolled on.

After the fourth or fifth night, we knew no one inside the cabin was coming out on his own, so frustration became our biggest battle. A retired Army Special Forces colonel named Bo Gritz showed up on day three with a homemade arrest warrant for the governor, the director of the FBI, and all the marshals on-scene. Two hours later, instead of getting a set of cuffs for obstructing justice, Gritz was given the lead negotiator slot and an armed escort to the cabin. HRT operators shook their heads, wondering how anyone could one moment be inciting a riot among the already livid protesters and end up, an hour later, bidding for the FBI. Like so much about the standoff, this particular chain of events seemed almost surreal.

BR-1 seemed very much at home in that environment. Of course, he lived a little differently than we did. Gold snipers spent the first three days growing rashes we'd never heard of and farming blackheads the size of pennies, because we had no warm water to wash with. BR-1, on the other hand, sent one of his logistics guys into town every day to pick up his uniforms from the cleaners. While the rest of us made do with a toothbrush and a canteenful of murky water, he managed a clean shave and that country-fresh smell.

I will carry to my grave a classic image of BR-1 in full command posture. We had just established a forward TOC in a small clearing just below the rocky outcropping. Someone had found an old beat-up Franklin woodburning stove in Weaver's makeshift dump and pulled it out into the middle of the clearing. BR-1 asked them to fire it up against the cold, but every time they lit a fire, the smoke would swirl around and sting his eyes. Some enterprising agent found two sections of stovepipe and built a six-foot stack. Unfortunately, the smoke simply rose six feet higher than before, then drifted right back down into his eyes.

While one work crew concentrated on the fire issue, another shuttled cases of Dr. Pepper up from the base camp. BR-1 loved Dr. Pepper and demanded plenty on hand at all times, so they stacked cases around him in red and white aluminum walls.

I came across him one afternoon as the light fell low on the horizon, painting his little clearing in long red hues. BR-1 stood in front of an armored personnel carrier with his left foot propped up on a canvas tricorn chair, his clothing perfectly pressed. He held a fax from Headquarters in one hand and a cold Dr. Pepper in the other as the battalions of soda cases rose around him in silence. Smoke from a green fire rose up the smokestack of his Franklin stove, then swirled down, wrapping him in the black pall that seemed to suit him well.

Hey, what the hell, I thought. Rank carries privilege.

Despite BR-1's humorous interludes, life on the mountain became an endurance exercise.

Milestones came grudgingly. Kevin Harris gave up on day nine, emerging from the cabin like a POW to his mother and her husband. No one ever said for certain whether he surrendered to avoid death or Weaver's homeopathic remedies. Weaver had requested cayenne pepper and gelatin capsules for suppositories, and the FBI delivered.

Man! I thought to myself as we delivered the goods, a septic gunshot wound has to hurt, but it takes a real man to tuck a couple hits of cayenne up his ass. Talk about the cure being worse than the disease!

Golf team carried Harris down on a stretcher for the docs

to examine in the field hospital, before medevacking him to real care. The whole camp crowded around him, half consumed with hatred for this cop killer and half embarrassed that it took an outsider, like Bo, to pry him loose. The scene reminded me of the Danny Ray Horning manhunt, when the dog handlers paraded the skinny, beaten wretch past their hounds to reinforce the instinct to hunt. I felt the same way as Harris bounced past me on his Army stretcher. He was why we'd come, the reason we'd sat up here night after night staring at the stars. I almost wanted to reach out and touch him just to make sure he was real.

Vicki's body came and went with similar pomp. She emerged from the cabin in a black plastic body bag with Big Bo leading HRT's stretcher crew down the driveway, through the rocky outcropping and the forward TOC. They carried her in a quiet procession past BR-1's stacks of Dr. Pepper and his Franklin stove, down into the base camp. They laid the bag out at the side of the road and opened it for a preliminary examination.

The forensics guys smoked cigars against the smell as they unzipped the airtight shroud, laying her open for those of us bent on checking her wounds. As Team photographer, I poked my camera toward her lifeless corpse, wondering how hatred had once simmered in those eyes. Vicki's decaying body offered no clue of her accomplishments or her failures, her fears and dreams. I imagined her holding her children or telling Randy she loved him or reading her Bible. I tried to reconcile that tenderness with a willingness to send her kids into armed battle. But every image I conjured of a loving mother quickly faded. What mother would give her fourteen-year-old son an assault rifle and send him out with his father to fight in the woods? What kind of mother would allow her sixteen-year-old daughter to run around the cabin, armed to the teeth and ready to die? How was that possible?

Black holes marked her face where the bullet had entered just behind her jaw and come out through her throat. She looked like winter on black and white television, all shadows and snow.

I'd seen death before. Just days earlier, we had brought her son, Sammy, out of the birthing shed where his parents laid him following the shootout with marshals. One bullet hole appeared below his left nipple. Another tore a ragged, ugly wound where his elbow should have been. His body looked small and pale. No hair or marks suggested he'd ever grown past innocence. Just white, empty flesh bitten twice by death. Irrevocably still.

He was fourteen when he died, the same age I first watched the life force leave. My Uncle Mike, a firefighter/ paramedic, took me with him on an ambulance run. "Monster mash," he called it when we arrived: three cars, six dead at the scene. The first face I saw belonged to a sixteen-year-old girl lying across the floor in the back seat. She looked asleep, quietly resting in the shattered glass, with no cuts or bruises save the broken drive shaft up under her rib cage. Some of the bodies lay in pools of blood. The sweet, pungent smell of alcohol hung over the wreckage.

I remembered how my Uncle Mike pulled me into the back of the ambulance with a survivor, a boy just about my age, but lighter and shorter than myself. The windshield had torn his face off, leaving a seeping red mush and a chin bone jutting out through the hole. My uncle tried to seal the AMB-U bag for a clean transfer of air but his thumb disappeared to the second joint in the boy's throat. Hard as he pressed, the seal would not hold. Small bubbles frothed around the edges every time he squeezed the soft plastic bulb. He'd pull the bag away from time to time and suction blood out of the boy's trachea and lungs, trying desperately to feed him life until we reached the hospital.

I just sat there, helpless, holding the boy's wrist in my hands, counting his pulse, measuring every beat of his heart as his skin began to cool. The beats grew softer and slower as we rode, his body lying against my arm as I tried to pray and will the fleeing life back into his broken limbs.

"What we got?" Uncle Mike asked as the suction filled a clear glass bottle with gore.

"I don't feel anything anymore," I said after a time. I moved my fingers around on the boy's wrist like he showed me, but the pulse had eased, run off someplace. I had no clue how to recover it. He died. I felt him go.

Vicki Weaver's flesh had turned dark, long past the point when it should have been buried. I wondered about the soul that had given her life, a soul nurtured in a religion of violence and paranoia. The God I worshiped talked about love and forgiveness. Hers told her to answer visitors with high-powered weapons. The Bible I read recounted miracles of compassion and faith, saving the war at the end of the world for the devil. Her whole life seemed wrapped around Armageddon, a willful pursuit of the afterlife. Well, she'd found it.

"Good luck," I whispered.

I snapped photos, recording the wounds, her clothing, the marks life had left on her corpse. Wounds. Scars. Death. I'd seen so much of it in my life.

I remembered a lonely house in the woods of Missouri several years earlier. I'd driven there to conduct a pardon investigation for a Korean War veteran convicted of smuggling a machine gun home in the 1950s. He and his wife lived in a house by themselves, miles down a dirt road in isolation not unlike the Weavers'.

I found him sitting in a La-Z-Boy near a fan with his shirt off, watching television. A hot red scar stretched from his throat to his navel, still healing.

I introduced myself, as usual, and we talked about his request for clemency. Only the president can grant pardons, but the FBI gathers facts to support various requests. I tried to concentrate on his face as we talked, but the puckered, graying scars all over his chest and arms kept drawing my gaze.

"Machine gun," he said, reading my wonder. "I been shot more times than most people been hugged." He sucked breath in slow rasps, stretching his eyes for focus and adjusting the oxygen tube in his nose.

I noticed the medals in a box on the TV as he talked. Three Purple Hearts, Silver Star, several others I didn't recognize.

"I feel embarrassed being here," I said. "You're a war hero, for godsakes. I'm sorry this ever happened."

He started to cry. Slow tears welling up in his eyes, as he relived a good life marred by one mistake. Memories dripped down his sallow cheeks. He pointed a finger toward the fan and his wife turned the air on him.

"You all right, hon?" she asked.

He nodded his head, then he died. His eyes simply rolled back in their sockets, tired of this world and ready for prettier views. No violence, no shooting, no car wreck, just passing.

I pulled his body onto the floor as his wife started to scream hysterically, then ran to the kitchen to call an ambulance. I knelt over him trying to remember the CPR procedures — five compressions and one breath? Fifteen compressions and three breaths? The fourteen-year-old boy in the ambulance stared up at me as his pulse faded away, whispering not to bother, that death comes hard and that no one should have to endure it twice. I linked my fingers and pressed down on the open-heart-surgery scar, fully expecting the wound to break open, spilling my hands into his lifeless heart. The skin felt lumpy where the bone had tried to heal.

One and two and three . . .

His lungs pumped fluid out onto the shag carpet with every compression.

. . . and four and five . . .

His wife returned and leaned forward to breathe for him. She stopped with a kiss and I knew he wasn't coming back. We could wait twenty minutes for the ambulance to get there or we could pump him dry, but he had left us and there was nothing on this earth we could do to bring him back.

It's strange how a single sight or smell can trigger a whole lifetime of recollection. I just stood there, staring at Vicki's empty corpse, wondering about the frailty of life, where it wanders.

❖

Finally, on the tenth day, BR-1 decided he'd heard enough from Weaver, from Gritz, from Frank the Negotiator, and from the press. U.S. Deputy Marshal William A. Degan was dead. Vicki and Sammy Weaver were dead. Kevin Harris had surrendered at the edge of death. Randy Weaver sounded badly hurt himself. This operation that had started with a figurative and literal bang had festered and died like everything else on that awful ridge. The FBI possessed a legal arrest warrant for Randall Weaver of Bonners Ferry, Idaho, and the time had come to serve it.

BR-1 issued a final ultimatum through his chief negotiator, Colonel Bo: Come out or we're coming in. I never did learn what inspired that rationale. Randy still had his three daughters inside the cabin. Based on overhears, we knew his oldest daughter, Sara, wanted to fight to the end. In fact, at one point she had told her father that she planned to run out of the cabin blazing so we'd have to shoot her and prove ourselves child killers.

"Simple herb farmers," I laughed to myself as I geared up for the final resolution. That's what their supporters called them, what the national press reported. Paul Harvey offered to pay their legal fees. National publications were wrapping them up in the Constitution as martyrs, defenders of the rights all Americans hold dear. Commentators labeled us as jackbooted thugs for marching up with a virtual army to smoke out a family of castaways who just wanted to live the good life, alone with their beliefs.

Horseshit. I grew up in the biggest hippie enclave on the East Coast, surrounded by communes full of herb-farming, freethinking dropouts. Not one of them ever showed me a gun. Not one of them ever shot a U.S. marshal. Not a single damn one of them ever ended up on the front page of *USA Today* as the poster child for America's fight against the New World Order.

"Sierra Four in position," I radioed to the TOC on the final morning.

Through simple luck, I had drawn the best sniper position on the whole mountain. I lay prone at the base of a utility shed, thirty-eight yards from the stairs leading up the back porch. The sun rose behind me, offering a crystal clear sight picture through my carefully cleaned Unertl scope. The air felt warm for the first shift since we'd arrived. Assaulters planned to enter through the front and side, forcing any escape through the back door. If they came out shooting, I had unfettered access to the end.

Bo Gritz sat inside the cabin talking face to face with Randy and his daughter Sara. Ironically, she was the one who negotiated with Bo as we listened over the radio. Randy realized it was all over, but Sara refused to surrender. She was sixteen years old, and she was telling this supposed Green Beret killer what to do. I couldn't believe my ears.

I shook my head, lying there in the bright mountain air, at how dramatically things had changed in ten days. The FBI had come into this crisis with its Hostage Rescue Team, looking to free a handful of marshals under fire from a group of radical white supremacists. Eleven of us had hiked up a mountain and engaged in a shooting that no one really had a handle on even ten days after it happened. Midway through the standoff, the FBI had relinquished negotiations to a retired Green Beret colonel and presidential candidate who showed up with a homemade arrest warrant for half the federal government. Now we sat idly by as Gritz and the remaining Weavers thumbed their noses at the whole damned process. This sort of thing seemed impossible from the organization that had trained me in the fundamentals of criminal procedure.

Just before 11:00 A.M., everyone within earshot of a radio heard Sara tell Bo the only way she would leave was in a blaze of glory. "I'll never give up," she said, over and over, shaming her father into holding out. And then, before anyone could blink, Bo called to tell us they'd had enough. Randy and his daughters followed Bo out onto the back porch as abruptly as if they'd decided to go for an afternoon stroll. The whole thing ended as oddly as it began. Baffling.

Two hours later, I sat on a stump in a poplar thicket answering questions from a Headquarters supervisor conducting a review of the August 22 shootings. Normally, these inquiries begin within hours of an incident. Investigators put agents involved on administrative leave, take their weapons, and swear out a statement. In this case, Headquarters had had to wait because there was no one else to do our job.

"Right, I understand," I said as the supervisor advised me of my obligation to provide truthful information in his administrative inquiry. Unless advised of Miranda rights, FBI agents have no choice but to talk candidly in any Office of Professional Responsibility or other administrative inquiry. No lawyer, no counsel, no partner. Everything you say can and will be discoverable to civil litigators should the incident result in a lawsuit. Everything you say can and will be used against anyone involved in the incident should it lead to criminal charges. There is no due process or 1-800-HELP number.

"Yeah," I said, trying to recount the ten most extraordinary days of my life. I flashed back to Raz's words in the classroom on August 21. "I think we got a job." I peered through my rifle scope as Randy Weaver, Sara Weaver, and Kevin Harris dodged trees and rocks and buildings, running from my marksmanship. I watched Mark duck and cover amid a crescendo of garbage can racket during Lester's infamous wagon wheel patrol. I shivered through the long, semiconscious nights watching the infrared ghosts marching back and forth through the windows.

And I heard the banshee wail Vicki loosed in a death reflex floating high over 100,000 acres of Idaho wilderness. Her voice rose up through the wooded mountains, meeting my own nightmares somewhere just beneath those endless stars.

I stared into the cabin when we walked up to begin processing the crime scene, surveying the modest room they'd pulled around themselves as sanctuary. Bloody blankets and clothing lay in stale piles of death. I counted a dozen guns in plain view. I looked through my mind's eye into Sammy's wounds and Vicki's mangled face, past BR-1 standing perfectly creased in front of his Dr. Pepper cases, and out over the magnificent wilderness.

A large hand-painted sign, just to our left, welcomed visitors to Randy Weaver's herb farm. "Every knee shall bend," it read.

"Go ahead," I told the investigators from D.C. "Ask me anything you want. I'll tell you what I remember."

BOOK FOUR

*All in the wild March-morning I heard the
angels call;
It was when the moon was setting,
and the dark was over all;
The trees began to whisper, and the wind
began to roll,
And in the wild March-morning
I heard them call my soul.*

Alfred, Lord Tennyson

"The May Queen"

16

WACO

The six months after Ruby Ridge passed quickly. Our training regimen fell back into a daily grind of firearms drills and CQB. I had put in a year and a half at that point and earned the seniority to branch out into specialties like rock climbing, which I'd loved since childhood. Word trickled down from Headquarters that the shooting review board found no negligence in Hooch's actions. It looked like he'd be all right, despite the bad press. Life returned to normal.

Even at home, where my weeks on the road had raised signs of trouble, things improved steadily. My first year with HRT had inflicted more than a little hardship on my family. The kids had long since stopped talking about "the big one" with anything approaching enthusiasm. Every time my pager went off, Mickey ran to me in a panic, asking if I was going away again. Missions like the L.A. riots, the Horning manhunt, and the Ruby Ridge standoff never came with an itinerary. I couldn't tell the boys that I'd be home in a day or two or even a week. If and when I even got the opportunity to talk to them before leaving, it was just long enough to hug them and lie.

"I'll be home before you know it," I said. Mickey nodded optimistically, but Jake was old enough to know the truth.

"We gonna see you on the news?" he'd ask. That was the only reference point that made sense to him. There were no personal calls from potato fields in northern Idaho. He knew as well as I did that once I left, he probably wouldn't hear my voice until I got home.

Rose put on a brave face. "Just a couple more years," I told her in bed at night when we talked about the pressures my job placed on her. She'd endured several moves already in our years together, but this was definitely the hardest. While I was away, she had to juggle a full-time job, the house, the bills, day care arrangements, and two little boys who wondered why their daddy lived at HRT.

On top of that, she knew about the danger. Most wives welcome their husbands home with a casual "How was the office today?" Rose knew that my "office" usually hovered seventy-five feet in the air, waiting to drop us down fast ropes into the shooting house for a little live-fire run and gun. Whether I was home or on the road, the threat of losing me stuck to her like a low-grade fever.

Fortunately, Headquarters kept the Team in Quantico for several months after Ruby Ridge. Rose and I took advantage of the time-out to go with the kids to my parents' house in New Hampshire for Christmas. They played in the snow, got to know their cousins, and learned to skate. More important, they forgot about the beeper, my unpredictable absences, and the look on their mother's face every time I said good-bye.

The break must have helped, because nobody seemed to mind when February rolled around and I set out for Tucson with the climbing team for a week on the vertical beach. Maybe the fact that this was a training trip and that I was only going for a short while lulled them into a false sense of security.

By the time we arrived at the crags, the third week in February, Ruby Ridge seemed a million miles away. I pulled on my climbing shoes and started up a moderately difficult crack route called Stoner's Boner. The violent business of hostage rescue had fallen into a vague, distant distraction. All I cared about was the warm sun on my back, the high mountain air, and a soft breeze wafting through the tamaracks. Life seemed perfect.

"Climbing," I said.

Trailer Court, a soft-spoken former Seal Team Six operator, played out a fifty-meter climbing rope and checked his belay plate.

"Climb on."

Up I went, leading the first pitch through a majestic slab of limestone, high above the Tucson valley. Had I taken the time, I might have looked all the way back down to that cold desert where Doug Bob's BORTAC troopers had led me through my first international dope raid. I could probably see Davis-Monthan Air Force Base, where we trained several times a year in the aircraft graveyard. I might even spot the Cactus Moon, a local nightspot where we blew off steam with Bud longnecks and shots of tequila. But there was no time for sightseeing, now. My entire world was constricted to the vertical chess game that would take me to the top of this 600-foot cliff in about three hours.

Rock climbing had become one of many interesting fringe benefits of a job that made every day an exercise in commitment. Most people wouldn't think a team like HRT would need climbers, but then again, they wouldn't think much about how to reach the top floor of a skyscraper during a terrorist takeover, either. Whether rappelling down from above or climbing up from below, HRT operators depended on a cadre of capable rope men who didn't mind hanging their butts out over large amounts of elevation.

Climbing was just one of many areas I worked hard during my first year. I now shot top scores with all fourteen weapons in my arsenal. I felt at ease in the shooting house. I had even grown back most of the weight I'd lost for selection. From ability to endurance, I had adopted the air of invincibility that had so impressed me when I first saw it in HRT operators during my Academy training. My days as an FNG were over.

"No need to run it out," Trailer called up as I climbed. I had a bad tendency to scatter my protection a little too far apart, and he wanted to keep me from getting careless.

Encouragement also seemed a big part of life on HRT. Though competitive to the point of absurdity, HRT operators still celebrated accomplishment among their peers. Whether navigating parking garage pylons in forklift races during the L.A. riots, fighting for bragging rights during inter-team competitions, or shooting flies with rubber bands, we cheered the winner in every contest. Every day brought new opportunities to win.

I remember the time Walt found a briefcase made for diplomatic couriers. Its designers had installed an electronic capacitor that would deliver a heart-stopping shock to anyone who picked it up improperly. After a couple of pranks and a few laughs, talk turned to challenge, and half a dozen guys lined up, betting they could hang on to the wretched device longer than anyone else. I stood back and watched as they screamed and yelled, eyes bugging out of their heads. The electric charge tore through their bodies, but they held on. I'm sure someone eventually won.

Competition was part of the ranking process, a backroom

career path to a team leader slot. HRT made up its own promotion schedule. Each eight-man sniper unit and seven-man assault unit took its orders from a team leader and his assistant. The team leaders reported to an assault or sniper coordinator, and they reported to their respective Blue or Gold section supervisors.

This command structure did not exist in any FBI career development manuals. HRT had crafted it in military fashion to manage its unique mission. Whereas most FBI managers rise through the ranks through administrative "career boards," HRT's leaders ascended by virtue of balls and ability. Fifty alpha males caged in a highly secure compound tend to itch. That itch turns to scratch, and soon becomes aggression. When you add a five-day-a-week diet of extreme violence, a job description that focuses specifically on killing bad guys, and a regimen of life-or-death consequence, you build an environment with very special interpersonal dynamics. Call it pecking order or social stratification: it breeds a "run with the pack or die at the side of the road" psychology. The people who lead this kind of team don't try to fake leadership. They win it.

At that point in my career, I harbored no illusions of rising anywhere but straight up the beautifully posted climbing route. A brilliant desert sun warmed my back as I jammed, smeared, and edged the steep face, placing cams and nuts as I moved. The rope played out behind me and I rose higher and higher off the ground. My forearms pumped full of blood. My feet settled into the ultratight shoes that stuck to the rock like Velcro. Memories of climbing the Cannon cliffs as a teenager brought back the subtle moves that come with experience.

"Trust your equipment, trust your belay," my dad cautioned through the years. The higher I climbed, the more I understood. Thin air washed the soles of my boots, threatening to pull me off into the hundreds of feet of sheer nothing. Fatigue, frustration, lack of creativity, poor planning — all the things that make men fail — grew more and more ominous as the height increased. But the thought of falling barely fazed me, because I knew Trailer's belay hand wouldn't waver. If I fell, he would catch.

I knew that when I ran into a burning room full of terrorists, Metz would cover my right and Raz or Boat would cover my left. We knew each other's strengths, our weaknesses, our needs, and our dislikes better than anyone else on earth. We knew things wives would never think to ask, saw things no one else would ever understand, and bared things no one else would want to see. Words like *brother* and *partner* paled, really, because in many ways, we worked on a level of trust few people ever know. If Raz pulled his trigger a microsecond too soon, he might tap my skull. If Trailer dropped his belay, I might fall to my death. If Boat slipped off a fast rope, he could pull me with him off the parapet of a thirty-story high-rise.

Climbing felt like a perfect metaphor for HRT's team concept. We succeeded because we trusted in each other: a hundred hands with one heart. Work together and live. Fragment and die. The rules seemed so elegantly simple.

We finished our climb just before noon and hooked up with the rest of the team for a scenic drive back to town. I felt absolutely full on the ride down, switching back and forth through the winding mountain pass, recounting stories of near disaster and great success. I felt full of the camaraderie that made me better than I ever could get on my own. I felt full of a life aimed at virtually limitless horizons.

We pulled into a burger joint called Dirty Charlie's just before one o'clock for lunch.

Beep beep beep.

Chuck, the Hotel team leader and HRT's only PhD candidate, reached for his pager.

"It's the office," he said, checking the call screen. "Let me get this. I'll meet you inside."

❖

One hour later, eight of us checked out of our hotel, boarded a plane, and headed east toward what would soon be known as the biggest massacre in law enforcement history.

"Waco?" I asked Mark, as we waited for our Southwest Airlines flight out of Tucson. None of us had ever heard of David Koresh or a religious cult called the Branch Davidians. "What the hell is in Waco, Texas?"

Mark had lived in Houston and earned his Marine Corps commission as an A&M Aggie. I thought he might have some inside perspective on the Lone Star State.

"Raz is from Waco," he said. "I think he played football at Baylor."

Thanks, Mark.

Goldie Hawn and Kurt Russell stood in front of us at the ticket counter as we shuffled our black kit bags of gear through the line. I thought it ironic that everyone around us made a commotion about two movie stars, but had no idea that the eight guys standing behind them were running code three to what would become the biggest drama of the year.

We touched down in the tiny Waco airport just after dark. Our view from the air was less than impressive. As far as I could tell, the home of the Texas Rangers (the ones with badges) consisted of a river, lots of unremarkable architecture, and broad stretches of empty pastureland. If the pristine wilderness of northern Idaho dazzled me with its beauty, Waco struck me as benign. It looked like one of those places about which people say "I can't believe this happened here."

Eight of us landed with nothing but the Browning Hi-

Powers on our hips, a couple dozen carabiners, and some 10mm climbing rope. Though first on the ground, we held little hope of driving Koresh out of Mount Carmel by ourselves.

A slightly overwhelmed FNG from the Waco Resident Agency met us at the airport, loaded our bags into a van, and drove us to an empty aircraft hangar at Southwest Technical College. The rest of the Team was due in early the next morning, but the Dallas Field Office had already poured itself into the building. Logistics people set about building a command post while technicians dragged phone lines, electricians wired in extra outlets for the computers, and secretaries began hammering out the paper mountain that ultimately rises around every crisis.

SWAT teams from Dallas and San Antonio rolled in, prepared to hold a perimeter around Mount Carmel until HRT took over. Several agents sat quietly at small desks, drafting the operations strategy necessary to assign and direct the hundreds of law enforcement officers streaming in from around the country.

"What's this all about?" I asked one of the electronics technicians as we sat in the hangar, helpless to do much but wait. My cumulative knowledge of the crisis came from what we'd heard from airport television and Chuck's two phone calls back to D.C.

He led us into a side office near the nascent command post, crowded us around a small television, and popped a video into the VCR. It was carnage. A team of ATF agents executing a search warrant on a religious cult outside of town had been ambushed, he said. Four agents were dead and several more had been wounded, some of them pretty badly.

"Poor bastards," someone whispered, as the news cameras closed in on survivors carrying out the dead. It looked more like war than law enforcement. "Poor bastards."

The rest of the Team rolled in early the next morning with all our gear. We unloaded the box trucks in the hangar, dressed out, and headed for the crisis site.

Luck, in any investigation, can mean the difference between standing in the batter's box and sitting on the bench, so Metz and I thanked our stars when Lester assigned us the only real sniper position overlooking the compound. No one had dared move inside firing range once ATF pulled out of the firefight, and the wide expanse of empty grasslands made productive observation posts hard to come by. Fortunately, the Dallas SWAT team had secured an empty ranch house about 600 yards to the south. Metz and I yanked a Barrett .50-caliber sniper rifle out of the weapons truck and hauled ass out to man what would for a short time become HRT's only eyes on Koresh.

What I saw when we got there shook me. Mount Carmel loomed huge but eerily quiet on the horizon, sprawled across the plains like a wide brown stain. Bobby climbed up on the hood of our Chevy Suburban and pushed the butt of a Barrett up to me as I fought to hold my balance. The thirty-mile-an-hour wind rattled my Gore-Tex parka and sent shivers up my spine.

I pulled the heavy rifle up to the ridge and leaned it toward the compound. I hadn't fired the thing for more than a month, but it never ceased to amaze me with its long-range accuracy and punishing effect. Its ten-round magazine could spit out 750-grain armor-piercing bullets at 2,900 feet per second, as quickly as one could pull the trigger. Even with its anemic ten-power Leupold scope, a halfway decent shooter could drop a man at more than a thousand yards. At that distance, the bullet would reach the target almost a half second before the ear-splitting crack of its supersonic vapor trail.

"Geez, what's up with this wind?" Metz asked as he crawled up beside me. I had already set the big .50 on the crest, tucked close against the chimney, with its heavy bipod resting on the far side. I wore full rain gear, polypro underwear, BDU utilities, and a wool sweater, but the wind cut right through me.

Bobby keyed his radio and called our position in to the sniper TOC: 187 degrees magnetic, back azimuth, at approximately 600 yards. Our view spanned the entire playing field, from EE highway on our right, where military armor waited on low-boy trailers, to gently rolling fields on the left. The media circus had stormed in behind us with everything from satellite trucks to portable soup kitchens. Black Angus beef cattle meandered about, grazing in the knee-deep fescue beneath us. A big black bull paced a fence line, prompting Metz to take note. He'd never seen one in the wild.

Despite our view of virtually everything around Mount Carmel, we had no particular role except to provide intelligence on the crisis site. The likelihood that anyone inside the compound would reach out with any kind of long-range sniper fire seemed remote. Intelligence reports indicated the ATF agents had probably inflicted some casualties of their own, and most of us pictured a bloody scene inside the buildings. Negotiators had opened lines of communication with Koresh, or Howell, or whatever the hell he called himself, and it seemed unlikely that they'd start any new hostilities. Despite my end-of-the-world weaponry, the only shooting I expected to do was a few 35mm glossies.

I settled down behind the Barrett and drew my crosshairs on the front door of the sprawling complex. This wind made calculating trajectory a little risky.

"Holy cow, will you look at the size of that place!" Metz

said, as he benched his CAR-16 and stared out over the open pasture. Bobby seldom swore.

Half a mile south, just distinguishable against the off-season wash of dead rye, a royal blue flag danced wildly, waving its white Star of David like some holy admonition. Mirage roiled through the reticle of the Leupold scope as I swept for targets. Even though the .50-caliber round I'd chambered weighed six times more than a .308 bullet, the wind would make it dance at this distance. Pulling the trigger now would be a complete gamble.

"Got anything?" Metz asked, as he leaned into a 40× spotting scope.

"Nah," I said. "They're probably hunkered down, waiting for us to make the first move."

The scene felt so much like Ruby Ridge after the shooting that I wanted to bring it up for conversation. Vacuum follows conflict, in everything from playground fistfights to gun brawls. The air grows quiet, as the adrenaline cools and the pain starts to flow in. There's a period of assessment when you sit back and test your limbs to see what works and what doesn't. The dull ache starts to sharpen. Sounds and smells and peripheral observations creep back. Then everything floods into focus. Metz and I had crawled in on that slow, confusing time after the fight when everyone sits around wondering what the hell comes next.

"Could you believe that stuff on TV?" he asked. His ruddy complexion glowed red in the March wind.

I steered the .50's muzzle back and forth across the Davidian compound, trying to map landmarks along the way for my range card. Sniper school taught us to pick objects at various distances to help read trajectory.

"TOC to all Sierra units. Stand by to copy."

Metz reached into his pocket for a government-issue notebook and a pen. "Stand by to copy" usually meant something was just about to happen: At that point, I had no idea what it could be. No one I had talked to knew much of anything about a resolution strategy. The assault teams had contained the perimeter with armored vehicles that were arriving by the hour from Fort Hood. The command element was sitting around phones at the command post, juggling a dozen or more local, state, and federal agencies while Koresh yelled in one ear and Headquarters yelled in the other. Some of the voices surely advocated restraint and negotiation in light of the Ruby Ridge shootings. Others pointed to the Talladega prison rescue as proof positive that HRT could resolve the crisis tactically.

The Branch Davidians sat quietly inside their building and nursed their considerable wounds.

"Here we go," I said. "Sierra Two, ready to copy."

Lester broke squelch and relayed the plan in brief sentences. Negotiators had convinced Koresh to give up, he said. Plans called for him to emerge from the building within the hour. All we were waiting on was a brief radio address Koresh wanted to issue over a Christian broadcast network. Once that was done, he was coming out. The rest of the Branch Davidians would follow him out and surrender in a peaceful capitulation.

"My butt," Metz said, still writing. "Nobody's coming out. We're gonna be here awhile."

I nodded. This one just felt different.

Early the next morning, about twelve hours after Koresh reneged on his first of many promises, HRT moved in close. I'd never been to war, but sitting inside a Bradley Fighting Vehicle with five other Gold snipers, dressed in full assault regalia, gave me a pretty good sense of how it might feel. The Bradley's big diesel whined like a jet turbine as we rolled east toward Mount Carmel at fifty miles per hour. My primary weapon, a CAR-16 with an Aimpoint sight, rested between my knees, cocked and locked, muzzle pointing up for no particular reason. If that thing had gone off, the round would have caromed off the hardened steel facets, turning all of us into very expensive hamburger.

The thought bothered me just a bit, because intelligence reports indicated that Koresh had two .50-caliber Barretts of his own. No one had verified that the Bradleys could withstand a .50 strike, and I didn't relish the idea of dodging a red hot slug as it ricocheted through the Bradley.

I had packed light for the close-quarter fighting some predicted: four extra thirty-round magazines, a Browning in a tactical holster on my thigh, and another on the trauma plate of my body armor. A belt pouch held eight flash-bang grenades. My Kevlar helmet kept me from splitting my skull on the jagged edges inside the machine, but it wouldn't do much good against long guns. Earplugs reduced everything to a dull roar. All I could see was the olive drab door in front of me. I was first man out.

"Hang on, boys, we've got a little obstacle up ahead." Matty, a Hotel team assaulter, leaned down from the turret gunner's seat with a big smile on his face.

We all knew the "obstacle" was a small red sedan owned by some newspaperman who supposedly had compromised this thing to begin with. We'd heard he'd abandoned it during the firefight, in the middle of EE Highway, just outside the driveway leading to Koresh's courtyard. Nobody had the keys or the slightest interest in getting out to move it.

We were going right over the fucker.

Jordan, our driver, slowed considerably, then revved the engine and powered forward. We mounted the subcompact with twenty tons of tracked vehicle. It proved no match at all. The armored personnel carrier lurched nose up, settled back down, and bounced softly, as if we'd just navigated a parking lot speed bump.

Everyone yelled out with satisfaction. We believed that four good men had died as a result of this bastard's quest for a front page story. Maybe we could get the Texas Rangers to charge him with littering.

Our mission was simple. After a full day spent swallowing Koresh's bullshit, the command element had finally loosed us to establish an inner perimeter. It didn't matter to me that the front office had forgotten to call Metz and me in from our rooftop observation post the night before. I hardly even cared that they'd split Gold snipers into groups for shift work. For the first time in a long time, I was working a day shift that didn't involve weeds, water, or weather. This felt like the action I'd been waiting for.

Aerial surveillance photos showed a cinder block garage 300 yards behind the main building. Blue snipers had already occupied the residence ATF had used for long-range cover fire during the initial raid, but we needed a reinforced position to contain the rear. That cinder block garage looked like the perfect parcel of real estate. All we had to do was clear it and make it ours. Unfortunately, ATF snipers thought several of Koresh's men were holed up in there with automatic weapons. We had to go in and clean them out.

"You gotta get out that door fast, Whitcomb," Gunny yelled, over the screaming engines. He sat right next to me with enough experience to know what he was talking about. "They catch us in the door and we're all going to bleed."

Bleeding seemed to be the easiest part of this job. Bradleys are cold, angular vehicles designed to keep troops alive, not comfortable. The insides are cluttered with sharp steel edges that tend to pop skin open like ripe fruit. I'd cut myself twice already and this was just the commute.

Fortunately, the Bradleys ride like Cadillacs once you get

them up to speed. At forty miles per hour, they plane out, smooth as a ski boat, oscillating slowly up and down as the diesel turbine screams. Jordan drove very well, considering the unfamiliar terrain and his limited view through a small bulletproof prism that served as a windshield.

I moved forward in my seat, preparing to bolt through the hatch once we hit the garage. Images of Branch Davidian bullets ricocheting around inside, and Koresh's threats to blow us to hell with a LAW (light antitank weapon) rocket made a quick exit all the more attractive.

"One minute!" Matty called down from the Bradley's turret.

"One minute!" everyone called back in unison.

I didn't have time to check for facial expressions from my buddies. I knew what they were thinking: Stay low, move fast to the building, maintain fields of fire. If the Bradley drivers positioned their vehicles properly, we'd have plenty of cover against snipers inside the compound itself. Hopefully, our overwhelming force would neutralize any threats inside the garage before they knew what hit them.

"Stand by!" Matty called down. The massive vehicle stopped, pivoted on one skid, and backed about ten feet.

"Go!"

No time for good wishes here. Raz broke open the hatch and I dove out into the gray spring sky. Operators were already bailing out of the other two vehicles on our flanks when my right foot hit the ground. Unlike most assaults, this one hadn't been rehearsed. No time. Gold snipers, acting in an assaulter capacity, headed for the line of buses, junk cars, and trailers lining the building's east side. Echo and Hotel teams stormed the building and cleared it of potential threats.

"Metz, Junior — check out that bus!" Gunny yelled out.

Though officially our assistant team leader, Gunny really ran the show. Considerable experience as a Marine Corps gunnery sergeant gave him the braced calm men respect in combat. This was our first mission with him, but I could see from the way he carried himself to the way he nodded his head toward the buses that he knew just what the hell he was talking about.

I walked my CAR-16 through a line of ghetto Lincolns, clearing for threats. Just a dry hole. Echo assaulters had already started emptying junk out through the garage's corrugated double doors to claim the space inside by the time we got back.

Suddenly, a voice tore through the group.

"Freeze! Freeze, or I'll blow your fucking brains out!"

I spun right, flipped off the safety, and fingered the trigger without a conscious thought of why I needed to react. The voice sounded tinny and overdrawn, like a dachshund threatening a grizzly.

"Drop 'em!"

I followed my muzzle up and left, in the direction of the voice. My right eye picked up the front sight as it rose on target. My cheek met the collapsible stock just below horizontal. My left knee bent slightly to accommodate the spin, the way a second baseman turns to scoop up the double play.

"Hey, hey, easy!" someone yelled.

Then I saw him, standing beside me, dead center between my flash suppressor and the two-man team Gunny had just sent to clear a culvert. One of the ATF snipers, whom the front office had sent along in the spirit of cooperation, was aiming his assault rifle right between Raz's Waco-born eyes. His finger staggered on the trigger.

The guy's eyes were bugging so far out of his head, I thought they might fall out and roll down his sallow cheeks.

"It's okay, man," I whispered.

He looked so wired, I thought the sound of my voice

might push him over. "Easy. Easy. It's the good guys ... they're with us."

Half a dozen men froze death-warrant still, waiting for this guy to gather up his shit and tune back in to our world. I'd seen the look before, the time a friend of mine notified me he'd found Jesus in a box of Cracker Jacks. Wacko. Zonked. Gonzo. Out of touch with reality. Whatever the hell you call it, this poor bastard was flashing back forty-eight hours to the firefight that took a bunch of his friends.

"Freeze ..." he said, mumbling more than yelling now. You could see rationality dripping back into his eyes, which glowed red hot. He started to shake, then lowered his weapon and cried. No sobbing. The simple tears that come when the whole world is spinning just a little too fast to ride any more. They looked like they were leaking out through the skin on his cheeks.

"It's okay, bud," Gunny said. He put his hand on the agent's rifle barrel, ensuring that he couldn't raise it back up.

This man no longer looked like a warrior. He looked lost and alone.

"Better get somebody out here to pick this guy up," Hick, the Echo team leader, said. "Whoever sent him out here ought to have his ass kicked."

Made sense to me. Images of brave ATF agents falling burned in my mind. I couldn't for the life of me understand why any commander would send survivors right back into the line of fire.

Raz and Metz walked up to me as Gunny steered the embarrassed, crumbling agent back to one of the Bradleys.

17

COME THE BABYLONIANS

Things slowed considerably after our initial raid on the cinder block garage. Lester designated the garage "Sierra Two," and broke Gold snipers into two four-man groups to staff the observation post in twelve-hour shifts. My group included Gunny, who had just transferred over from one of the assault teams; my partner, Bobby Metz; and Junior.

Blue snipers moved into Sierra One, a small ranch house overlooking the front of the Branch Davidian compound. The assault teams were divided among the two bases of operation also. Charlie and Echo teams came with us. Golf and Hotel went to Sierra One. From those two positions, we could keep close ties on the compound, establish a secure perimeter, and fortify fighting positions should hostilities resume.

Almost immediately after establishing our beachhead, we set about clearing Sierra Two of improvised explosive devices, booby traps, and the possibility of tunnels or trapdoors. Our intelligence cell reported that Koresh had built an elaborate series of tunnels leading out of the compound, and we wanted to make sure that none of them ended up in our midst. Every loose rock, board, and hubcap got a boot check, just to make sure. The only thing we turned up was a handsome pair of diamondback rattlesnakes in hibernation. Joey Two Butts, an outdoorsman of some repute, shoved the lethargic vipers into a box and proclaimed them our new mascots. No one came up with names. Like the mongrel dogs Weaver kept chained outside his Idaho cabin, they never really felt like pets.

Metz and I took the first shift on-rifle, playing countersniper to Koresh's self-styled Mighty Men. We watched them as they watched us through the scopes of their own rifles. Someone had taught them well how to build sniper hides, but we could see their barrels and the glimmer off their optics. I caught an occasional face hidden by a curtain, or a small child held up as a human shield, but most of the images appeared as shadows, deep enough in the rooms to keep us guessing.

That's how I met David Koresh — through the crosshairs of my sniper scope. He appeared, briefly, in the tower, peering around the edge of the window, assuming correctly that a whole lot of the heavily armed men outside wanted to put a bullet in his head. The Prophet of Mount Carmel wore a light blue T-shirt that read "God Rocks." Sunlight reflected off his Coke bottle glasses. We knew from the negotiators that he'd been hit during the initial firefight, but he looked strong enough to me.

In fact, Koresh had already mustered enough strength to begin working his magic on the FBI negotiators. By day three, he was spinning his yarns and talking that downhome, aw-shucks drawl all over anyone who would listen. I'd heard the tapes of his surrender promise, and shook my head at how sincerely he phrased his lies. All he wanted was a little time to pray, an opportunity to get his side of the story out to the Christian world, and a guarantee of safe transport to jail, he said.

"Shucks, fellas, I want to cooperate with ya, if you'll just give me a little time." He spoke with a confidence and charm that could have won him Salesman of the Month at any car lot in Waco.

After that first day, things settled quickly into monotony. We constructed an "urban hide" behind an open window in the front wall. Late at night, after Mount Carmel had settled behind the watchful eye of three Davidian sentries, we sneaked outside and hung a black cloth screen over the window. We built a plywood platform for our rifles and spotting scopes behind it. Later in the week, a bunch of trusties from the county jail reinforced our little redoubt with seven layers of sandbags and three layers of half-inch boilerplate steel. Everyone knew Koresh's .50-caliber Barretts could hit us with devastating effect if we didn't take proper precautions. Four feet of sand and steel seemed like reasonable insurance.

I actually found observation duty interesting for a week or so. First, we mapped Mount Carmel's windows and doors, giving them names so the TOC would understand where we saw movement or substantive activity. The process works pretty simply, along a military model. The first floor is designated alpha level, the second is bravo, the third, charlie. The building's four sides get colors: red for the front, blue for the right, yellow for the left, and white for the back. All doors, windows, and openings get a number, beginning with the furthest port to the left. From our observation port in Sierra Two, I would call movement to the TOC by saying, for example, "White bravo three," meaning the third window on the second floor of the back side.

We extended the same logic to people. Each face got a nickname. Whenever possible, we'd match faces and names,

using driver's licenses or some other identification, but nicknames remained the identifier of record during all intelligence reporting. The rules were simple: First sniper to see a
new face got to name him.

Beef distinguished himself there. Three or four nights
into the siege, he called the TOC to report a man in a doorway, carrying a weapon.

"I've got a white male, approximately five foot ten, a
hundred sixty pounds, with dark hair and a mustache," he
said, covering the vital statistics. "He's wearing a black T-
shirt, blue jeans, and white tennis shoes."

"Got a name?" someone in the TOC radioed back.

"I'll call him . . ."

The radio transmission broke for a while as Beef labored
over an original handle.

"I'll call him 'White Tennis Shoes.' "

Nice job, Beef.

I got to name a couple of the faces myself. One guy had
muttonchop sideburns, so I called him Elvis. One of the
women looked a lot like an old girlfriend of mine, so I
named her Michele. And there was the guy in the red parka
who held a little boy up in front of himself as a human shield
every time he came to the window. The little fella stared
back at me, paralyzed with the terror that would come with
confronting the devil himself. That's surely what Koresh
told him, just before one of his Mighty Men decided to use
him as a bullet trap. Somebody else got to name him, because all I could come up with was Asshole.

Unfortunately, nicknames and window numbering held
our attention only so long. After that, life in Waco settled
into a 7/8 rhythm, lurching just a beat off the meter of lives
we all brought to the place. Days came and went with no real
sense of mission or strategy. Everyone knew Koresh and all
his followers had to leave before we did, but after that, any

sense of schedule fell in the "how should I know?" file. In fact, almost no information of any kind reached the operators. Every once in a while we'd hear something vaguely promising, but those morsels trickled down like droplets in a Chinese water torture.

We stayed busy, of course. Gold snipers watched the compound and fed intelligence back to the TOC, while Charlie and Echo teams ran the Bradleys back and forth to the fork in the road known as the Y intersection. They ferried personnel during shift changes, delivered hot meals at dinnertime, carried fuel, supplies, building materials, just about anything we needed.

Our days fell into a simple, predictable routine. Every morning, my team met in the hotel parking lot, sporting camouflage BDUs and Igloo coolers filled with lunch. We climbed into a white Chevy van. Gunny drove. Junior sat in the passenger seat. Metz and I worked the crossword puzzle in the back.

After a brief drive out to Mount Carmel, past the T-shirt vendors, protesters, and stand-in prophets, through the Texas Ranger checkpoints, where law enforcement patches, hats, and pins traded like currency, past the news media who tried to snap our photos through the smoked glass of our van, past the cows indifferently chewing their cud, we checked in at the forward TOC. Bobby picked up new radio batteries while Junior and I pulled our war gear out of a Ryder box truck. Gunny checked in with Lester to see what we'd missed the night before. From there we drove to the Y intersection, climbed aboard a Bradley, and made the Great Crossing to Sierra Two.

Once we got to Sierra Two, it usually took about five minutes to stow our gear, roll out our sleeping bags, and climb out of our body armor. The only thing on my mind most days was finding a comfortable spot to sit and making sure the kerosene heaters had enough fuel to take the edge off the cold Texas winter. Nothing about Sierra Two offered any warmth. The gray cinder block walls and oily concrete floors colored any sunlight dun. Lanterns were not allowed for fear of backlighting our position. With the exception of an occasional flashlight beam, the place felt viscerally dead.

Duty came in two-hour segments. One of us would set up his rifle behind the front wall and put eyes on the compound. Though we quickly grew bored with visual surveillance, none of us let our guard down. The one sniper on duty had to keep watch for Koresh's .50-caliber rifles. Predictability was not one of the Prophet's qualities, so none of us ever took peace for granted. Sierra Two appeared as a broad white wall from the front, but any of his men could have slipped a .50-caliber round right down our throats if they'd wanted. At 300 yards, I'd probably get just enough time to register the muzzle flash before the round hit. We all hoped the sandbags would stop it, but most of us knew in the back of our mind that the only call to arms we'd muster would sound like "Oh shit." The only thing separating us from Koresh's sharp-shooters was a black sheet of tight-weave muslin and the grace of God. The real one.

Security outside the front room faltered pretty quickly, as most of us mistook inactivity for invulnerability. Despite the American flag flying from Sierra Two's low pitched roof, we didn't own the property the way we thought we did. Koresh had garnered celebrity status in the outside world, and every loser with a hard-on for government seemed hell-bent on getting close to him. All it took to get us to consider the threat seriously was a reminder of the stiff we'd found in the locust grove down by the pole barn. ATF caught a Davidian fighting his way into the building on day one. He came up behind Sierra Two with a Glock 9mm and a serious lack of gunfighting skills. He got a couple of rounds off before his pistol stovepiped, rendering the other ten bullets in his magazine worthless, but he paid. The holes in his face showed me all I needed to know about the importance of good weapon maintenance.

Shift changes came at six and six. Each outgoing shift would brief the new guys on where Koresh's men had cut firing ports in the walls of their building during the previous twelve hours. Most of this activity came at night, so those of us fortunate enough to work the day shift ended up with very little to report. I liked that particularly well, because a quick shift change meant a quick trip out of that shithole and into a cold beer.

Unfortunately, shift change also meant riding shotgun in a new game that had escalated to the point of war between the assault teams. HRT operators tend to starve for competition when it's not presented in training, so daily life at Waco quickly evolved from rock-throwing contests and push-up marathons to braver enterprise.

The Bradley races started each day at shift change.

"Let's go, boys! It's Miller time," someone would yell. To the unsuspecting ear that proclamation sounded innocuous enough. To the rest of us, it meant "Get on the fucking train, because this is your only chance of getting out of here today." It also became a thinly veiled reference to the race from the back door of Sierra Two to the Y intersection. Only the assaulters got to compete. The snipers had to sit back and endure the ride. Rules called for an equal load in each vehicle and the snipers served as ballast.

Every competition has rules, and this was no exception.

Each assault team had to front one driver. Each driver got one run per day. A member of another team had to keep time with an officially sanctioned watch. Since several operators wore Rolexes, the sanctioning committee went with the highest common denominator and limited official runs to calculation by Swiss chronograph.

All runs started from a dead stop, doors closed, engine running. Time started on command and stopped at a thin yellow line painted on a tree just far enough from the Y intersection to permit safe braking.

BR-1 would have erupted if word of the races leaked out, so everyone talked in code.

"Charlie Four to Sierra Two," I heard through my radio earpiece. "I got a full boat inbound."

"Copy, Charlie Four. Stand by."

That meant the timer was checking his watch.

"Night shift's *ready* . . ."

I never found out if the guys monitoring radio traffic in the sniper TOC figured it out.

"Our gear is *set* . . . you're a *go*."

Wham. The monstrous machines would leap forward, juggling their silent crew of empty-spirited snipers. The first stretch was a full-out drag, down past the pole barn, through the cattle crossing, out to Elk Road. A sharp turn there brought the speeds down considerably, but the good drivers learned to cut the corner, jump a culvert, and power through without backing off much at all. From there it was another flat-out drag to the yellow line and a shot at the record.

As the weeks wore on, the original route changed so radically, races were called off and the records sealed. The early trips had steered wide of the compound for fear of antagonizing the Davidians and setting off another confrontation. After negotiations stalled, though, drivers were allowed more and more leeway in tightening the perimeter. Part of the reasoning came from a security perspective. No one had moved close to the building since the ATF firefight. We had no way of checking access routes other than the driveway, which offered ample opportunity for Davidian gunners to walk their rounds in on us. Koresh had bragged to negotiators that he had enough ordnance to blow us to hell, and none of us felt compelled to give him a predictable target.

Another part of the reasoning came from a behavioral perspective. The closer we got to the building, the less Koresh felt sovereign over his property. We worked like a crawling weed, climbing into his sense of domain, choking off his personal space. I imagined him watching through the windows, locked rigid in frustration as we closed in, his self-proclaimed deity fading in the diesel exhaust.

Screw him, I thought. I had listened to his religious ramblings and utter hypocrisy until they made me sick. Lying repeatedly in the name of epiphany looks bad on the son of God. Claiming exclusive husbandry over the wives of your disciples doesn't look too good either. Having sex with twelve-year-old children on your record seems like it might be a real problem at the Pearly Gates.

By the end of the first month, days had settled into a foggy malaise. Lester switched the shift schedule to twenty-four hours on and twenty-four off, hoping to give everyone more of a break. Time off changed almost nothing. The world I used to live in had faded away into four slightly worn photographs and a daily phone call to Virginia. Rosie and my parents sent letters when they could, care of the Waco Holiday Inn. I knew my life had changed when the mail carrier saw a return address from my sister in Vermont one day and asked if I had found a new pen pal. Getting to know the mail carrier on a first-name basis while living in a motel seemed strange enough. Having him memorize the return addresses on my correspondence bordered on sad.

Things at home weren't going much better. Rose ran out of excuses to explain my absence, and the boys dreamed up their own ideas of what had happened to Dad. Jake drew pictures in art class, depicting me and the Branch Davidians shooting it out in front of a big brown building. Mickey stood up in class during a current events discussion and pronounced that his father was a sniper sent to Texas by the FBI to kill all those "Wackos."

The school counselor called Rose in to talk about it, but there was nothing Rose could do. She had tried to give them a sense of my life away from home by huddling them in front of the television every night to watch the news, but this only created more confusion. Most broadcasts showed file footage of the ATF shoot-out over and over and over, and they just assumed all that violence was meant for me.

This created a dilemma. If she turned off the television, they would wonder why I'd disappeared altogether. If she left it on, they'd continue with their terrible visions of their father caught in an endless gun battle. Neither of us could come up with a decent solution.

We eventually decided the news was worse than the mystery, so their days came and went with no more images of Mount Carmel. I tried to call them every night, after they'd had their bath and bedtime story. We talked tentatively, about small things that had nothing to do with how we really felt. You try to maintain distance after a while, because it hurts too much to invest yourself in moments that won't last. It's easier to pretend everything is fine, tell each other "I love you," and promise it will all be over soon.

"Good-bye" became an easy word.

Something in their voices changed when they talked to me over the phone. During the first few weeks, they asked when I was coming home, but after a while, they just stopped asking. It affected them.

It affected me, too. Working toward a goal can sustain a man, but no one even peripherally connected to the siege could offer me any estimate of how long the standoff would last. We had no goal. Whenever I asked someone, I got a look of utter contempt. "How the hell should I know?" was the usual reply. The SAC in charge of the operation conducted daily press conferences. The negotiators talked, or didn't, depending on Koresh's mood. The academics argued theology in banter that never amounted to shit. HRT operators grew more angry and bitter every waking moment. Everyone drifted into coping mechanisms.

My particular survival strategy included reading a novel a day, playing cards, and writing poetry in a little notebook that I kept hidden from the other guys. That worked for a couple weeks, but boredom and frustration eventually outfoxed my muse, so I broke down and bought a brand-new Fender Stratocaster electric guitar. It had a sunburst finish with a maple neck and a whammy bar. I carried Sierra Two's only musical device back and forth in the Bradley along with my lunch cooler and CAR-16 machine gun. SWAT team members from other divisions asked about its odd-looking case, but I told them it was a special HRT weapon that we couldn't talk about. They nodded their heads, and whispered speculation.

The only person who knew its real value was the salesman at Heart of Texas Music who gave me a hell of a deal when I explained that I needed some kind of distraction out there on the frontiers of reality. Card games and push-up contests made work feel just a little too much like prison. The new instrument reminded me of life outside the glass walls that seemed to close in around us more each day. It felt like reason.

Unfortunately, reason had run from Waco. After a time, even music lost its charm. All I could muster in the way of productivity was a series of hangovers and a substantial bar tab. I barely drank prior to Waco, but after a few weeks in a lonely motel room, that changed. Days off usually meant a quick nap, a trip to the gym, a shower, and whatever drink specials we could find at various local watering holes. We drifted in packs through the bars at night, comparing notes and trying to maintain a little perspective.

By the time Easter rolled around, I felt lost.

Easter Sunday had always been a time for family outings in northern New Hampshire, when at the end of a long winter of snow and rime ice, people poked their heads out of hibernation to the possibility of warmth. Easter meant egg hunts at Cannon Mountain, where we could ski in jeans and light flannel shirts. The snowmaking crew would hide brightly colored treasures at the edge of the slopes, forcing us to space our turns, hunting along the margins for special treats. Echo Lake sprawled beneath us, its borders darkening with thin ice. New life hung in the air, just a suggestion of the growing season.

Easter meant Tuckerman's Ravine, a hike-in-and-ski headwall off the back side of Mount Washington. Every lunatic in northern New England went to try his luck on the steepest slope in the East. I remember walking up the face my first time, skis strapped to my back — I could actually reach out and touch the wall in front of me.

I remembered Easter in Malaga, on my college sojourn through Europe, waking up in a town focused on the resurrection of Christ. Tens of thousands of devout Catholics lined the streets, high on the optimism of redemption. Women in white dresses with embroidered lace shawls and rhinestone combs danced in circles with children by the armful. Church bells filled the air. Men dressed in immaculate suits hoisted tons of wood, papier-mâché, and flowers on their shoulders and walked the floats past the feverish mobs, celebrating, for all the world, the beauty of one man's remarkable sacrifice.

Not in Waco. The Messiah of Mount Carmel wore a two-day beard and a handgun. Easter was just a day, another chalk mark on the wall, twenty-four more hours alone in a dull trance. I walked outside after sunset and stared off toward the lights of Waco in the distance. I imagined children asleep in their beds, dreaming of tall baskets full of cellophane grass and chocolate bunnies. My kids went to bed wondering about a dad they knew only through pictures now. Normal parents shuffled about in the dim light of a table lamp, trying to figure out the bills, or how to come up with the money for braces. Normal parents. Normal. The concept escaped me.

The job itself wasn't bad. We worked two hours on the scope, then had six hours off. When my turn in the rotation rolled around, I moved into the observation room, set up my rifle and a forty-power spotting scope, and began my search. It felt like a kid's game, really — hide-and-seek with Koresh's men. Every night when they thought we couldn't see them, they'd carve new firing ports in the outer walls. During the day, they'd go about their daily business as if we weren't even there. I'd watch them as they skittered past windows or poked their heads out the doors to feel the sun on their faces. I studied the building's features, trying to commit them to memory so I'd notice changes as soon as they made them.

That's the way I found the Barrett. I had just begun my sweep one day, working left to right across the compound from white alpha one, past the storage barn, up to an area we called the doghouse, through the courtyard, past the boarded-up cafeteria, around the silo, and over to the green side of the main building. I counted firing ports the Davidians had cut out of the various walls, confirming intelligence reports from Boat's shift. I checked the known sniper positions, waiting at each until I caught the glare of light off their optics. We knew all their positions. Sometimes I even admired the skill with which they'd set up their concealment. Hiding in plain sight is no small feat, yet Koresh's Mighty Men had built urban hides that would have won Staff Sergeant Morton's respect.

I had just about ended the day's first tour of Ranch Apocalypse when movement caught my eye. Second story, far right side of the building, in the dead space between green bravo one and two. The firing port door rattled and then fell back into the room.

I trained my scope on a one-by-two-foot opening in the wall. Something moved around inside, deeper than I could penetrate with the high-magnification lens. Something moved toward me, black and shiny in the oblique sun. It poked out through the hole, downward toward the ground and then up again, a long gun-steel barrel fluted down its flanks and stunted with an arrow-shaped tip.

"Sons of bitches," I whispered.

The barrel moved awkwardly, eighteen inches outside the T-111 siding, then settled into position. I stared into the half-inch hole sticking out the end as the scope collected light and reflected glare right back into my searching eye.

"Hey, Bobby," I yelled into the back room. He was probably playing cards. "Bobby, come here!"

He pulled back the crinkly vinyl tarp covering the door way and stepped up behind me.

"What?"

"Look at green bravo three and tell me what you see."

I slid off the barrel and motioned to the spotting scope, which I'd trained on the area. Something hastened my heartbeat — not adrenaline; something subtler, like discovery.

Metz focused the scope to fit his eye.

"Shit, that looks like a fifty to me."

Good. I wasn't seeing things. Barrett .50-caliber sniper rifles kick so heavily, they need a muzzle brake to control rapid-fire shooting. This factory-installed feature channels muzzle gases back toward the shooter at a forty-five-degree angle, making recoil manageable. It also made identification easy, because nothing else in the world looks quite so intimidating as the big delta-shaped muzzle on a .50-caliber Barrett. Anyone who knew its profile would not mistake it.

Metz adjusted the focus ring, trying to compensate for the effects of mirage through a high-magnification lens. "Better go and get Gunny."

Everyone knew Koresh had .50s, at least two of them. Assault teams circling the compound in Bradleys knew Koresh could probably punch holes in their armor with them. Snipers in Sierra One and Sierra Two saw them as the single greatest threat. Prior to this moment, none of us had any damned idea where he kept them. Finding the rifles and setting up on them could make the difference between "Oh shit" and homecoming.

"That's a Barrett, all right," Gunny said, after we'd fetched him to verify our little discovery. "I'd say somebody's feeling a little squirrelly."

I felt a little strange myself as I hunkered down on my own rifle. Koresh's sniper and I stared at each other, sharing the same mixture of power and exasperation. There is no distinction between fair fight and cheap shot in a duel like this. When push comes to shove, one man gets the first shot and the other man dies. He had a .50. I had a .308. Shitty odds.

"Better call it in to the TOC," Gunny said. "We'll want that in the log."

Finding the rifle felt like a bittersweet success. On one hand, we could take it out if given that option. That was very important to us, because we couldn't fight what we couldn't see. Koresh had finally shown us his trump card.

On the other hand, we would have to stare that sonofabitch in the eye every day, knowing full well that action is faster than reaction. It was like finding the hawker during a sniper school stalk: You have identified the threat, but he's still a threat. In this case, the enemy we could see was better than the enemy we couldn't. Locating that Barrett gave us a distinct advantage.

Thirty minutes later, everything changed.

"You hear that shit?" Gunny asked. He shook his head and spat as we just stood there, barely able to believe our ears.

"Unbefuckinglievable," Junior chimed in with his Alabama drawl. "What the hell is wrong with those guys?"

The TOC had just radioed information none of us wanted to believe. Our own negotiators had called in to the compound and told Koresh we knew where he kept the Barrett. "Move it," they said, "or we'll cut off the milk deliveries."

"Wait, wait, wait a minute," we yelled out loud. We'd worked hard to find that Barrett. We'd called it in to the TOC, like we were supposed to. Now our own people were diming us out to the bad guys.

"What the hell are they thinking?" I asked. I felt weak in the knees. Betrayed.

Hostage negotiations struck me as an odd and cumbersome process. Something in the play of events just didn't make a whole lot of sense. It seemed that the only people coming out were the people too young, old, or infirm to fight. Every time Koresh made a deal, he got some concession and we got his problems. Sure it was good to get anyone possible out of that building, but not at the expense of substantive progress. Most of the guys out in the trenches saw this as a clever move on Koresh's part and needless capitulation on ours.

This process led to grumbling at first, then open hostility.

Hostage negotiations may sound complicated, but they boil down to a simple process of building rapport, allaying fear, mitigating consequence. People negotiate every day, buying a car, working in committee, trying to decide who gets the first shower in the morning. We do it instinctively, without any real training, because it is simple human nature. Two parties want different things, so they argue back and forth until both sides get what they think makes them whole.

We had no problem with that. We wanted negotiators to bring Koresh and his followers out of the compound just as much as anyone else did. What we didn't like was the way they were going about their haggling. Koresh worked the negotiators from day one, when he promised to come out if they'd just give him the radio address.

"Sorry," he said when he got what he wanted, "but God just came to me and told me to stay inside a while longer."

Okay, so he changed his mind. The self-proclaimed Son of God should have that prerogative, right? Well, what about the second lie, and the third lie, and the twentieth? At some point, you had to ask him if that Bible of his wasn't missing a few pages.

We listened day after day as he set up rules just to break them. Every time he got away with something, he got stronger. David Koresh was a salesman in the grandest tradition — a bullshit artist. I imagined him as a time-share pimp, selling chunks of salvation. First he gives you a free weekend at Ranch Apocalypse, just to get you to listen to his spiel.

"Sign away your soul, and I'll take care of the details," he argues.

Then he sells you the service option: "Give up your money, your children, your wives. Sign on the dotted line. Invest yourself in me."

Unfortunately, none of the negotiators or FBI decision

makers traveled out behind Sierra Two to look at the trailers full of personal possessions his followers had left behind when they bought in to his lifestyle infomercial. None of them thumbed through the photo albums full of lives, lives entire families had sworn off to his charm. We did. We saw that Koresh's entire empire — from the dozens of go-karts and motorcycles parked outside to his guitar collection and prepubescent harem — screamed of selfishness and manipulation.

Everything David Koresh had ever wanted came to him during the siege at Mount Carmel. He already had all the women and guns he could desire, long before we arrived. What he didn't have was exposure. We gave him the big pulpit. A global audience. More minds to shape. A whole new flock of sinners. The guy was a master, and we were too arrogant to admit it.

By the end of the third day everything we knew about negotiations had flown out the window. Our guys talked and talked and talked. Koresh healed, refortified, regrouped, and sat back on his couch watching television as national broadcasters turned him from plowboy preacher to international celebrity. HRT stared down rifle barrels. The ATF buried their dead.

"What a bullshit artist," everyone grunted. "How long are we going to put up with his crap?"

Casual grumbling turned to open disgust. Conversation soured to fury when anything resembling negotiations filtered into a card game. A lawyer named Dick DeGuerin had entered the compound, in violation of everything anyone knew about negotiations and crisis management. We had actually allowed a criminal defense attorney to walk inside the crime scene, handing him a full view of and access to the only evidence against his clients. If Koresh wasn't smart enough to clean up the telltale signs of murder, his attorney sure as hell should have been.

Every broken promise felt like a thorn in our side; not because of Koresh — we expected that from him — but because our own people bought his limitless lies. Day after day, we waited through another edict of impending surrender only to have a potential resolution fade off into silence. No one even called us when the deadlines turned into another letdown. It felt like no one believed we'd care.

"Better check this out," I said at the end of my shift.

Gunny peered through the spotting scope to where they'd cut the firing port.

The Barrett's big muzzle bobbed up and down a couple of times as if waving good-bye, then shrank back into the building and disappeared. A gloved hand pulled the trapdoor shut.

The weapon was gone. None of us believed we'd find it again, until it flashed.

18

THE DORIAN MODE

Spring came late. After seven weeks of rudderless drifting, Sierra Two had become an outpost at the edge of the world. I sat in the observation room one night, wondering how and when this thing would ever end. Joey Two Butts had taken our rattlesnakes out back earlier in the day and cut their heads off with a jackknife. Their mottled skins hung on boards just inside the door, like tribal omens to anyone visiting from the outside world. Klieg light drifted aimlessly through a low ground cover, framing Mount Carmel in a nimbus of incandescent spite. Echo team ringed the perimeter in their Bradleys, tending the concertina wire and chasing Branch Davidians back into the building when they came out just to test us.

Loudspeakers blared the sounds of Tibetan monk chant played in reverse. Chills tiptoed up my spine. The nightmarish sound effects loop reminded me of something between

Linda Blair's *Exorcist* monologue and Vicki Weaver's death aria.

I leaned into The Truth, pressed my eye against the scope reticle, and began my sweep. Miles Davis played a mournful trill through the two-inch speaker on my battery-powered radio. Ten HRT operators lay asleep behind me. Charlie team was supposed to have a sentry out back, but I wouldn't have bet on it. We'd installed motion detectors during the early weeks, but cows ambling through the surrounding fields set them off so often, we disconnected the whole system.

No one really worried about intruders sneaking up on us at that point. No one in his right mind would want to sneak in to Mount Carmel, and it seemed obvious that no one else wanted to come out either. That left us sitting calmly in Sierra Two all by ourselves.

I dreaded early morning most: the hours between three and five. Life slows to a crawl, tempting gentle sleep. It's that biorhythm thing. Your body temperature drops, your mind retreats, and thirty thousand years of sleep cycle conditioning kick in. I thought back to countless nights over the past two years when I'd found myself in the exact same position, fighting my eyelids. At least I wasn't cold.

Three minutes on the scope, two minutes off. That was my plan. Miles launched one of those eighth-note arpeggios I liked so much. It's strange how beautiful a jazz trumpet can sound juxtaposed against the guttural chant of Tibetan monks. With the fog and the light, this would have made a wonderful Stephen King set. You could almost hear the demons laughing. For a place consumed with talk of God, it sure seemed a lot like hell.

I shook my head and rubbed sleep out of my eyes. I hunkered down on The Truth, settling my right shoulder over the rubber butt pad. My left arm folded beneath my chest, allowing my hand to squeeze the beanbag just behind the trigger assembly. My cheek rested against the leather stock pad, setting just the right distance from the sharp edges of the Unertl scope. Move too far forward and the rifle's recoil will lay your skin open for stitches. Too far back and shadows around the reticle will throw off your aim. Eye relief is vital.

I sniffled against the spring air. My nose ran all the time.

White alpha one. Warehouse. Tower. Silo.

I panned left to right, across the doors and windows, like a beat cop, checking for anything unusual. Klieg light flickered off the concertina wire. The Branch Davidian flag snapped in the wind. The firing ports all looked closed. Same as usual. None of Koresh's sentries stayed up late anymore.

I pulled my eye off the scope to wink out the fatigue. Someday this is going to end, I thought. Someday after they all come out and the crime scene investigators have their run at the evidence, they'll let us in to see what lay behind those damned walls. I wondered about what we'd find in there. Would they stack all their weapons in one room or spread them out so we'd have to search? Surely their attorney had told them we could match bullet casings to the weapons that fired them. The lab guys make cases that way all the time: they simply hold up the weapon and the casing, point out similarities between firing-pin marks and firing pins, extractor bites and cartridge rims. All they need to make a murder conviction is a fingerprint on the gun.

Juries love forensics experts who can walk up to the stand, swear out long careers of expertise, and talk out their case. Add a few charts and some blown-up photographs and it would be a piece of cake — one of those cases where you don't even have time for lunch before the jury calls you back in for the verdict.

Surely they'd cleaned up all the blood, but what about the bullet holes? How could they alter the building, which read like a blueprint of the February 28 shoot-out? Forensics experts could determine which holes showed rounds going out and which showed rounds going in. News video had captured the ATF agents under fire. Even if the Davidians' attorney coached them on what would look bad in court, we still had the building. They'd have to burn it down to change that.

I thought about the hundred men, women, and children still crowded inside. What would they bring with them when they came out? Maybe a photo album or a family keepsake or a favorite poem. I knew many of the women — Elvira, Candy, Blondie — by sight. They'd become regular personalities in the narrow world of my sniper scope. I recognized them the way neighbors know each other in bakeries and coffee shops, faces in passing.

I knew the Mighty Men almost casually at that point as well. Elvis waved to us as he sat on the windowsill, his leg cocked up under him like a fraternity brother scanning the horizon for distraction. He liked to eat his lunch while enjoying the warming sun and the sight of HRT assaulters tending the electric generators. Any hostility during the early weeks had matured into mutual indifference. We were there to keep him inside and he was here to keep us out. That's what two months of standoff had turned into. Life during wartime had worn us all out.

The children. I knew just a few faces, those the men held up as tiny human shields. One boy came to a window in the tower from time to time, by himself. His blond hair danced in the wind, against the light blue curtains in white charlie two. He'd stare out into a yard full of camouflaged men in armored vehicles, tracing the outline of a rainbow decal someone had stuck in the window during happier times.

"Sleep tight, buddy," I whispered the first time I saw him. "Maybe this is the last night you'll go to bed afraid."

I was wrong, of course. There was no tomorrow at Mount Carmel. The days rolled together in one big long never. I wanted to believe that one day we'd get him and his brothers and sisters out of that dump. That's why we were there, why we had come to begin with.

I thought back through the process that had brought me. First I saw the crowd roiling around the president on the floor of the House of Representatives the night of the State of the Union speech. *Justice,* I thought. That's my cause. Four years of twelve-hour days chasing shitheads through the hills of Missouri. Selection. NOTS. Sniper school. Missions. Watching my kids grow up in postcards. All the "I'll be home for your next birthday" promises. Breaking them.

Every member of HRT stood ready to sacrifice his own life — to jeopardize his family's future — just for the opportunity to save that one little kid in the window. Every one of us sat there in that shithole for almost two months, hanging on the outside chance that some spineless puke back at Headquarters would give us the chance to do good.

No more nightmares, no more terrible stories about the devil waiting outside. The little girls wouldn't have to take Koresh's sex. The little boys wouldn't have to take Koresh's beatings. Those poor little bastards who knew nothing of the world except what their sick fuck father told them.

"OHHH-SO-LETTED-DEEERAAY-ASHEEB . . ."

The loudspeakers to my right echoed off the building, drowning out a Coltrane melody. The distraction came in waves, sometimes, bouncing around, swelling and moaning like a giant Leslie organ speaker. I thought about going to the front office and asking if I could hook my guitar up to the monstrous preamp. Koresh might not mind the sound of Tibetan monk music, but I knew what would really torture his soul. We shared two things, he and I: birthdays in 1959, and a love of guitars. Nothing would needle him more than listening to me murdering a raucous Jimmy Page solo.

Just ten minutes, I told myself. Just ten minutes alone in

the gravel lot behind Sierra Two, playing a 180-decibel lead for the Ranch Apocalypse Orchestra. I knew I'd never become a rock star like I'd dreamed in college, but this one show would have been the greatest performance of my life. I could see them pulling Koresh out of the building in a straitjacket as he screamed for an amplifier and a chance to play me down.

"Screw the theologians and all the scholars," I whispered, sitting there in Sierra Two that morning. The key to yanking Koresh's chain wasn't the Bible; it was his ego.

I never got my solo. The best I could manage was a couple of hours each day practicing scales in the Dorian mode through a battery-powered amplifier. Amazingly, none of the guys even complained.

"White bravo one, two, three . . . nothing." I counted windows aloud, trying to keep my eyes open.

Nothing changed much anymore. They knew we posed no more threat than pollen blowing through their open windows. Our guys got a rise out of Koresh when they bulldozed his pride-and-joy Camaro, but he got over it. They bitched when T.J. accidentally bumped the building early one morning with a Bradley while trying to clear debris from the red/white corner. No harm, no foul. The diesel fumes and the camouflage-covered men with assault rifles were just part of the scenery at that point.

"White charlie one. White charlie two, white . . ."

I stopped.

White charlie two. Someone stood in the window staring out at nothing in particular. His hair fell down both sides of his face, around the edges of chrome-framed glasses with lenses thick enough to distort his eyes. Heavy stubble darkened his expression. His hands hung at his sides.

"Well, hello, Vern," I said.

The meeting surprised me. I hadn't seen Koresh in quite some time.

I stared at him through a long breath. He couldn't see me, but he knew someone was watching.

I gathered his features in my scope: long, thin face; sea captain's eyes; drawn chin. This was the reason we'd stumbled slowly into a fetid cesspool of indecision and waste. This man was the reason so many people had died in the ATF shoot-out. This one man had proved beyond a shadow of a doubt that with big enough balls, you can take on the world.

Theologians flocked to him, publicly berating the FBI for misunderstanding his intentions. Academics weighed in with everything from thumbnail behavioral assessments to sociological profiles. Politicians danced around the edges, afraid to say anything for fear of what voters would remember when it was over.

I paid none of them a moment's attention. The siege had changed me fundamentally, in ways I'd never felt vulnerable. Nothing made sense any more, because rules I had vested my life in suddenly flew right out the window. Things like the validity of federal legal authority had been dragged through the same black mud that never really scraped clean off my boots. The gold FBI badge that I'd vested my life in no longer worked.

"Fuck yourself," Koresh hissed into the night. "I'll just call myself God, tell the world to kiss my Bible-thumping ass, and hang out until I figure a reasonable solution. Try something — I dare ya."

Koresh was a junk collector, nothing more. He gathered the flotsam and jetsam society had no place for and stacked it in piles, waiting to be restored. But he never restored it. He never finished anything. Not the building. None of his cars. Not the seven seals. Not a single broken life.

I held my crosshairs on the bridge of his nose, touching

the trigger just enough to feel the consequence in my balls. What would happen? I thought.

Gunny Patterson whispered a marksmanship lesson to me. "Bone on bone. Take muscle out of the equation — it will flinch and throw off the shot."

Thirty-mile-an-hour wind at 296 yards. Tough shot, but not impossible.

Staff Sergeant Morton barked out orders. "Don't lie there shivering like a dog shitting razor blades, man, take the shot."

I was a risk taker. Always had been. I squeezed the bean-bag with my left hand and adjusted my cheek on the cool leather rest. Sierra Two snored behind me, on the other side of a concrete block wall, oblivious to my encounter. They were wearing earplugs against the loudspeakers that shook the night. My barrel jutted out the front edge of the building. The wind suddenly died down to a light caress.

I laid my index finger along the ribbed plane of the trigger. Koresh smiled and winked. I squeezed the trigger a little harder.

"Aim for the brain stem," Gunny Patterson instructed. "He won't even twitch."

I thought about the children. Little kids, hungry and tired and cold. So much pain and suffering from just one man.

"Do it," he whispered. "Make me a martyr." I could almost see his lips moving.

My crosshairs settled where the glasses met his nose.

"End it," he begged. "Give me my destiny."

I felt myself slipping away with his guile.

"I'm tired. Send me home."

I wanted to listen, to oblige, to end it. This place would die without him, just crumble for lack of will. They were appendages, those Davidians, followers of anyone who dared reach out and offer direction.

I could hear the children crying for one single dawn without horror. I could hear Sanity pleading "Enough." I could hear my own heart bleeding. "Do it."

But, suddenly, there were other voices, too.

❖

"You're nuts, man!"

Gary Braun, a chunky twelve-year-old with cheeks red as cherry bombs, locked both his arms around a steel girder and peered 250 feet down into the Ammonoosuc River. His eyes bounced and swelled from the height, but he didn't move.

"Come on, Whit. Get down off there. You're gonna kill yourself!"

Andy Tabbott, a short kid with the jet-black hair of a Plains Indian and the brilliant blue eyes of his French-Canadian father, shook his head and watched for the afternoon train.

"Don't make me climb out there and get you!" he threatened.

There was no need to turn and look. It was just false bravado — kid talk. Andy was smiling. I could feel the warmth of his encouragement on my back. He would have been out there, too, if I hadn't beaten him to the mark. Those were the rules. In order to "claim" a bridge or trestle, you had to run the tracks and touch the center riser first, then yell "Rights!" That entitled you to first shot at the edge.

My legs reached considerably longer than Tabbott's, and I found it easier to set a rhythm, running from tie to tie, watching the river flash below me like frames in a slow movie reel. One missed step could have meant a broken leg or the ultimate penalty, a fall through the gap.

This made our sixth bridge since September. It was the tallest, a real trophy. Tabbott had walked it a dozen times, measuring the steps on his way home from school every day, practicing to gain an advantage on me and claim it for himself. But that day I saw it first as we rounded the long corner deep in conversation about Barbara Miles and Erin Godbout. I broke for it and ran hard, just ahead of him, all the way to the girder.

"Rights!" I yelled, tagging first. My voice echoed out over the river as I sucked in the cold January air and pushed out clouds of pearl white mist.

"Rights!"

Life clouds, we called them, those plumes of frozen breath that rise on cold mornings when winter creeps inside your jacket and hardens your resolve. Life clouds turn the inside of a tent to a crystalline wonderland at twenty below zero. They turn a ski mask white around the mouth and nose holes. But most important, they measure the size of your heart and the depth of your soul. Life clouds show themselves on the coldest days of winter because that is when the life force stands out most starkly against the untenable void of day-to-day existence. They live briefly within us, these clouds, until forced to show themselves, then they drift away into the vastness of the universe like smiles and anger.

The bigger your life cloud, the legend says, the bigger your spirit. Only those capable of exhaling extraordinary weather have any chance of doing anything remarkable in life. That's why we fought so hard to prove ourselves through daring. We dreamed of climbing Mount Lafayette faster than anyone in the North Country or posting a new route up the Cannon cliffs or of skiing the Tuckerman's Ravine headwall in a single reckless schuss. This was our chance at breaking away from the anonymity of youth.

Braun couldn't stomach the heights. He ran with us to the edge, then clenched up those fighting fists and squinted his eyes, drawing a little distance as we climbed. His heart wanted to follow, but his body just couldn't.

"How high am I, Gary?" I asked, exhaling a life cloud the size of Manitoba. I didn't care about the answer, but I wanted to know he was considering the fall. I loved the fear in his voice, that foreign misgiving I knew nothing about.

"Three hundred. Maybe four."

"Three hundred? That's bullshit." Andy laughed. "What do you know about heights, Braun? You piss your pants standing on the curb." True.

"Maybe . . . but I got no problem kicking your ass when we get off this thing!" Also true. Tabbott was no fighter.

"This was your idea, Tabbott." I eased the words out as I shuffled my feet slowly along the smooth beam. The dark green paint had cracked and bubbled around rivets the size of bottle caps. I could feel them underfoot as I moved.

"It was your idea to walk home this way. This could have been your bridge."

"Well, hurry up and do it, then," he said. "It's goddamn cold out."

Gary said something, too, but I couldn't hear a word. This was the tricky part, where the support span juts out from beneath the trestle. The cross member was ten inches wide, like the one I stood on, but it was also three feet lower and terminal; just a truss butt sticking out from someplace underneath the bridge. The climb down to it looked tricky, and there were no handholds or guy wires. Just air.

I stretched a hand down to my right as I slowly lowered myself to the crossbeam, concentrating on the step, finding the balance. A knot burned in my stomach from anticipation, not fear. This wasn't where I was going to die or how. I knew that.

My left foot found the beam. Then my right.

"You're fucking nuts," Braun muttered, "both you guys. Come on back up. I'll give it to you."

I stood there.

I heard his voice, but the words melted into the wind and fell away. That view was just too much to compromise with conversation.

I shuffled both feet the final step out onto the trestle brace and steadied myself. The air felt cold. Maybe twenty degrees. What little snow we'd picked up in the last storm had melted, then frozen hard, leaving long winter shadows and gun-steel clouds to color the rocks and ice below. A gust of wind cut through my Johnson jack-shirt, clinging to the sweat under my arms and at the base of my spine. The smells of damp wool and rusting steel filled my nose as I sucked in a cleansing breath and shook my head.

The risers and ties of the railroad trestle towered above me, whistling into the wind like lanky workmen, content just to watch three twelve-year-old boys playing at men's games. My feet barely fit on the end of the ten-inch girder. Beneath me, the most delicious day passed effortlessly by. I loved this cold, pristine winter — the thick lonely air that threatened snow.

Braun had exaggerated the height, like he always did. It was no more than a couple hundred feet down into the iced-over Ammonoosuc. Birds flew below me, blackbirds and grosbeaks and crows circling silently. Winter birds never call out on the wing.

"Toes over, Whit," Tabbott insisted. That was the inviolable rule. You couldn't claim the bridge unless toes on both feet dangled out into space. You had to get your toes over the edge.

I squinted the wind out of my eyes and let the tears freeze on my cheeks. My hands floated up from my sides, out like the wings of the creatures lilting below me. My left foot slipped forward just enough, and then my right. And I stood there, still as angels' breath, air all around me: above, below, beside. There was no vanity or regret or restraint. There was just consequence.

I imagined the waters beneath the ice, so far down below. I'd been through the ice before, out on Echo Lake, where the cold fills you, more emotion than sensation. Experience slows. Your fingers disobey. Your judgment clouds. You get out of the water then, or you pass slowly into it, all the heat of life seeping back to nature.

We never stayed too long in the water: just enough for a few screams and bragging rights. We were New Hampshire boys, after all, outdoorsmen bred of pilgrims and mountaineers. This was our inheritance, this wilderness of granite, maple, and birch. It sustained us in lives our children might consider crude.

I held my hands out to my sides and lifted my head up high. The cold pricked at my heart. The winds rushed in to watch and mumble, the voices of all souls waiting for company should my balance fail or the river rise up to take me. The shy northern sun peeked through for a moment, brilliant and clear, but then passed, afraid that even a suggestion of light might wake me from this exquisite trance.

I needed that place, where risk held me and coaxed me to reach a little further, just past the tips of my fingers, as far out as I could stretch them. A life cloud drifted high, away from me, out among the coming snows.

This was my youth, and I knew with unquestionable certainty that it would not kill me. Years from now I would look back with a smile, knowing this was practice for something important. I'd tell my grandchildren about young life in a simple place full of promise.

Someday this would matter.

"Morning."

Bobby Metz pushed the tarp out of the way and emerged

from the back room. He blew his nose on the floor. "What you got?"

I blinked with the distraction, and Koresh was gone. Just an empty window.

"Hey, bud," I said. Another shift on-rifle, done. Number 297 in the series. Last peep show of the night. Shift change.

"Anything going on?"

Maybe I dreamed him. Maybe I didn't. It doesn't matter. Lots of faces come in the middle of the night. Some smile, some don't. It's the ones like Tabbott and Braun that sustain me.

Metz stretched his arms and yawned sleep out of his eyes. The morning air felt wet, cool to the touch.

"No," I said. "The place is dead."

19

THE WIND

I remember the flames.

An overcast sky hung lifeless and gray over the compound as I aimed The Truth north toward white bravo 13. I waited. White bravo 13 was the midpoint in my sector, the thirteenth window of the second floor on the Branch Davidian building's south side. I'd grown used to movement there during the previous seven weeks. Deep within the shadows, behind the sky-blue curtains where David Koresh's men had constructed a sniper hide, I'd seen the unmistakable reflection of a scope reticle. Behind it, staring at me, someone aimed the stainless steel bore of a sniper rifle right between my eyes. There was a finger on the trigger, a toxic hatred festering behind it.

White bravo 13 was a sniper position, as surely as I was there to neutralize it, and I sat ready that hazy April morning for muzzle flash to tell me that David Koresh's Mighty Men had decided to try their luck.

My range card indicated 297 yards to Koresh's back door. Sandbags seven layers deep stood between me and my target. The Truth lay obediently beneath my shoulder, awaiting the lightning-bolt signature of the big Barrett. Koresh's riflemen might get off the first shot, but they damned sure weren't going to get a second.

That final morning, the sandbags felt thin as tissue paper as I leaned into them and pulled the stock into my shoulder. Metz waited quietly to my left. Junior and Gunny scoured assigned sectors from their positions off to my right. The four of us lay within whispering distance, but none of us talked. We concentrated all our attention on the building, searching for muzzle flash as the four assault teams circled the compound in Bradley Fighting Vehicles. I could hear the hollow *thump, thump* of tear gas rounds being lobbed into Koresh's refuge.

My watch read 11:55 A.M., but the view had not changed much in the previous six hours. The skies lightened at dawn but never allowed any sun. A strong Texas wind howled across the flats between us and Koresh, pressing down the tall grass and tugging at the bright blue Branch Davidian flag. I watched his Star of David dance and flutter, using its movement to judge the wind speed and calculate my aim.

A head shot at this distance would be no great challenge for any of the six Hostage Rescue Team snipers in Sierra Two, but the incessant thirty-mile-an-hour winds added an element of risk. Long-distance precision shooting depends on a number of factors other than a steady hand and good eyes. Humidity, elevation, temperature, angle of incidence, and wind all can wreak havoc on a bullet. All those stories about Kentucky farm boys making the best snipers are just stories. The world's best marksmen are technicians who have mastered physiological discipline, trajectory formulas, and timing.

I turned a calibration wheel on the turret of my sniper scope, adding a half minute of angle to compensate for the shifting wind. Then I laughed to myself at the irony: The Branch Davidians thought they were flying their flag as a symbol of defiance, but to those of us ringing the compound, it simply told us where to hold our crosshairs.

The room felt cold and damp around me. The sweet, musky scent of diesel fumes hung in the air as the Bradleys lurched back and forth through my field of view. Four teams of HRT assaulters had been working hard since dawn, lobbing tear gas cartridges into the building. I searched for targets as they went about their work, hoping for muzzle flash that would mark Koresh's snipers and let me do my job.

❖

April 19, the last day at Mount Carmel, began well before dawn with an operations briefing and enormous anticipation. My team had rotated off duty the day before, but Roberts called us in at 6:00 P.M. for an unscheduled shift. We knew what this meant. After nearly two months of mind-numbing frustration, Headquarters was finally handing us the reins.

All four assault teams and the Gold sniper section reported to Sierra Two just before dinner. Everyone settled in, staking out sleeping space and room to stow their gear. Golf team delivered dinner in styrene boxes — chicken breasts with mashed potatoes and peas. We ate heartily, wolfing down our last meal before what we hoped would be our final day in Waco. Despite the lack of detailed information, everyone knew why we'd been called in for the extra shift. It was time to end this cluster fuck.

Sierra Two fell asleep early. The team leaders had announced a 4:00 A.M. wake-up on the 19th, and everyone climbed into their sleeping bags full of the anticipation children feel on Christmas Eve.

Metz woke me at 3:45 with a well-placed boot. The rest of the Gold snipers rustled around me, moving through the dim shadows like apparitions, gathering a few gulps of water as they pulled on their camouflage utilities and loaded bullets into their magazines. Outside, the loudspeakers blared that seemingly endless effects loop of ringing phones, slamming doors, and rabbits being slaughtered.

HRT supervisor Steve McTavish arrived by armored vehicle just before 4:00 A.M. and assembled his agents in a broad semicircle. We listened impatiently as he read the marching orders. Steve talked slowly and clearly in the hushed glow of a penlight.

The plan sounded simple enough: Two armored combat engineering vehicles (CEVs), piloted by Homey and T.J., would approach the building and insert CS gas (a highly noxious chemical irritant) through nozzles attached to steel booms. Four Bradley Fighting Vehicles manned by HRT assault teams would circle the compound and wait to assist if necessary. Should Koresh and his flock open fire, the assault teams would escalate the tear gas delivery with projectable canisters from M-79 grenade launchers. HRT snipers would divide the building into sectors and provide long-range precision fire to cover the assault teams' movements.

The rules of engagement — the conditions under which we could use our weapons — stipulated that we could return fire only if we had visually identified specific human targets and determined that they posed an imminent threat to FBI agents inside the perimeter. Seeing muzzle flash from a window in the early morning darkness might tell us where to look for a shooter but it would not, in itself, be enough to shoot at. We needed unmistakable identification and a clearly defined threat.

When Steve finished his briefing, an indescribable energy filled the dank gray space. Two dozen men stood silently around him, fighting to contain their excitement. After fifty-one days of frustration and indecision, fifty nights of going to sleep with no idea in the world when we'd go home, someone had finally made the call to end this thing.

The assault teams gathered their gear and mounted the Bradleys while the Gold snipers readied firing ports at the front of Sierra Two. I took my position at the center of the north wall and aligned my rifle barrel through a six-by-six-inch hole cut in a plywood sign advertising "Ranch Apocalypse." One of Koresh's people — I never found out who — had painted the wall-size mural in bright colors, depicting the four horses of the Apocalypse. I stared out at the Branch Davidian complex, a ghostly white mirage in the klieg-light mist, through the eye of the gray horse. David would have enjoyed the irony.

It seemed like time paused in a long, slow yawn as I leaned forward into the stock of my rifle. The dawn skies hung grudgingly around the Branch Davidian building. An anemic sun rested just below the horizon, as if trying to decide whether or not this day should really happen at all.

Everything felt so heavy. The weight of the sandbags. The weight of the air. The weight of lives hanging in the balance. All I could hear was the roar of the Bradleys' big diesel engines, the beat of my heart, and that incessant Texas wind.

The tear gas insertion began at 6:00 A.M., just as outlined in BR-1's operations order. On command, T.J. and Homey stormed down EE Highway in their loud machines, turned right into Koresh's huge circular driveway, and roared at full throttle straight at his front door. Koresh probably thought nothing of the commotion during these last moments before dawn. We'd made a habit of violating his space during the previous seven weeks, and he must have assumed that this was just another harassment tactic.

Some howl of alarm surely echoed through Mount Carmel, however, when the negotiators called in with word of the gas delivery. As Koresh and his lieutenants scrambled to battle stations, T.J. took aim at the front door and rammed the front end of his sixty-ton tank right through the bullet-riddled skin of Mount Carmel.

Koresh and his Mighty Men unloaded with everything they had. Hooch spotted the automatic weapons fire first and called "Compromise" in a loud, clear voice over the encrypted radio network.

None of us returned fire. Koresh's riflemen hid deep within the building and hosed the CEVs with small-arms fire, but we knew their weapons would not penetrate the hardened steel plates. We scoured the sprawling compound for targets of opportunity, but the Davidians had built their sniper hides carefully. They had moved their rifles inside the rooms and hung dark cloth to cover muzzle flash.

None of the six snipers in Sierra Two called out targets, and no one fired a round. Unless Koresh's band of assholes cranked up their big .50-caliber Barretts, their small-arms fire posed no imminent threat to any of us. I could see the bullets ricocheting off the CEVs' thick armor like cow piss on a flat stone, but all I could do was wait.

Inaction should not imply lack of intent. I'd already laid out extra ammo for my sniper rifle and prepared a range card, sighting landmarks to calculate my aim. My big .308 would serve nicely outside 100 yards, and I had more than enough ammunition to accommodate the fight. But if Koresh's men got outside the razor wire, I'd move to a fully automatic M-16 lying on the sandbags to my left. Behind me on the concrete floor of Sierra Two sat an M-60 and a .223-caliber squad automatic weapon (SAW), both belt-fed machine guns. Insurance.

Most of the snipers in Sierra Two fully expected the Davidians to come rushing out with guns leveled and death in their eyes — a massive suicide-by-cop assault. There were six of us, and fifty or more of Koresh's Mighty Men inside the main building. We knew they had weapons every bit as devastating as our own and that they had trained extensively with them. The ground between us was riddled with ruts and trenches that would make any frontal assault an even and pitched battle.

Once they started shooting, I held the butt of my rifle just a little tighter and scoured the no-man's-land between us a little more closely. Koresh may have been clever enough to dance the negotiators in circles, but he wasn't going to gain any ground on Sierra Two. If there was to be a fight, I sure as hell knew who was going to win.

In the meantime, HRT's Gold section assault teams (Echo and Charlie) opened up on the back side of the building with their M-79 grenade launchers. These shotgun-style weapons can walk a fist-size tear gas canister 100 yards with reasonable accuracy. The canisters resemble huge plastic bullets, but they detonate like brittle-shelled water balloons when they hit something hard, such as an interior wall. We could hear the hollow *thump* of the M-79s and watched as the rounds sailed through the windows or drifted off target and smeared the building's brown siding in splotches the size of tablecloths.

❖

Around 10:00 A.M., the compound grew quiet for a while. Word spread that FBI commanders had called a news conference and put the gas insertion on hold. This brief mid-morning cease-fire gave our mobile teams time to restock their supplies and the sniper teams a chance to rotate off their scopes for a few minutes, but an edgy skepticism spread through Sierra Two. Some sat and talked about whether this would actually be the end of a siege that seemed to have no end. Others argued that this was just another in a long series of capitulations that would allow Koresh more time to jerk the negotiators around and resupply his shooters.

BR-1's tactical plan had always been controversial, and many of us suspected that this indefinite cease-fire was the beginning of a power play against him. Attorney General Janet Reno was new to her job in April 1993, and despite years of experience with criminal prosecutions, she lacked familiarity with operations of this scale and desperation. Waco had become a national obsession at this point, and despite all her advisers and their expert testimony, the gravity of committing arms must have been enormous.

Those of us inside the perimeter knew Reno had been weighing the tear gas option for weeks. Tactical advisers had considered every imaginable alternative including flooding the compound with water and spraying it with a giant "goo gun." All plans carried downsides. They were tactical operations, after all, and everyone knew that Koresh would likely meet any act of aggression with further aggression.

But Waco had, at that point, already been infected with aggression. Anger and resentment and hatred spread like a contagion with each passing day. They crowded the air like bilious Texas storm clouds, threatening to tear us all apart at any time. A virtual war had been brewing within FBI ranks between negotiators and tactical personnel. Fifty of the best-trained tactical operators in the world sat idly by, day after day after monotonous, agonizing day, waiting for something to happen. Nothing happened. The negotiators went for what seemed like years without speaking to Koresh's people at all, and when they did speak it was only to accept more of his lies.

"Wait him out," everyone said. It became the FBI motto.

For the warriors among us, talk had become tiresome. We all knew Koresh would never give up of his own volition. Inside that compound he was a rock star prophet infused with the immutable power of God. Outside he was just another con man who would be found guilty of murder and rot in jail for the rest of his anonymous life. Anonymity was a sentence he could not accept. We all knew he'd push and stall and promise as long as he could get away with it, then he would fight. He had no other option.

We had watched Mount Carmel for fifty days and nights. The sun had risen and fallen on us with little more than rumor and resentment to mark its passage. No one in this vast sea of law enforcement seemed to have a plan or to know what was going on.

Lines of communication between the command staff and the front line troops had crumbled. Though we operators should have been regularly apprised of developments in the standoff, we gleaned most of our information from local newscasts. We received regular printed intelligence reports, but they seldom included information about the overall plan. The most valuable data reached Sierra Two through the two-inch speaker of a transistor radio.

We widely ridiculed what we felt were spineless decision makers back at FBI Headquarters. Director William Sessions's sole contribution to the crisis, for example, had been a highly publicized offer to visit Waco and talk Koresh out

"Texan to Texan." His naïveté seemed an affront to our professionalism.

Never, not once in the history of civilian law enforcement, had anyone gained so much control over his own captors. For nearly two months, the best-equipped and most highly trained law enforcement agency in the world had been frustrated to the point of begging by a charlatan with an electric guitar and a good rap.

Every expert with a voice chimed in with an opinion.

"Give him time," they argued. "Let him finish the seven seals. Let him tell all the lies he wants. He's running the show. Give him his curtain call."

But all of the best minds in the world — and the world was surely involved by the seventh week — differed on one point. All of their academic examination and soul searching came down to just one thing: Would Koresh come out or would he fight? For those of us who had watched him murder federal agents and thumb his nose at the world for two months, the answer seemed banal. On April 19, 1993, David Koresh was coming out of that compound, one way or the other. None of us there gave a rat damn about how.

The gassing resumed just after eleven. The CEVs steamed back toward Koresh's stronghold in their monstrous armor and began peeling chunks of siding off the compound's flimsy walls. Homey wheeled around back and opened a wide, ragged scar in a barnlike storage area. He pushed his CEV's boom deeper and deeper into the structure with each pass, exposing mounds of packing boxes, old furniture, and the junk that piles up around stagnant lives. One of Koresh's observation posts, which we had nicknamed the Doghouse for its distinctive shape, came crumbling down directly on top of Homey's CEV, but the relentless machine never even slowed. It simply coughed a cloud of black smoke and continued its destruction.

I'd watched the Doghouse for two months, wondering what lay behind its thick curtains and plywood walls. Now it gaped open like a wide sore, nothing more than an empty hallway leading to Koresh's old bedroom.

The adrenaline of those early morning hours had long since worn off by the time the walls came down. The great edifice I'd scoured day after day was suddenly, gracelessly crumbling. It seemed like one great overwhelming anticlimax.

My neck ached from crouching over the rifle since dawn. My eyes throbbed with fatigue from staring through the scope.

Conversation cracked the cold dark silence inside Sierra Two. "What the hell is going on in there?" someone asked.

We speculated about what it was like inside, what insanity could keep those people there. We'd pumped huge quantities of tear gas into the building and nothing had happened. Not a single soul had emerged.

I thought about the children. Could they have escaped the noxious fumes, climbed down into a bunker beneath the building? I imagined their bewilderment and hysteria, running through gas-clouded rooms, screaming for their mothers as their eyes swelled shut and their lungs fought to bursting for a clear breath. I saw their small faces contorted in terror as their parents fired deafening weapons out the windows and screamed directions from one part of the house to the other. I imagined Koresh's stories of the White Devil marching after them in this end-of-the-world struggle. Surely he had prepared them for our assault with promises of salvation at his own hand.

Scenes of the Jim Jones massacre in Guiana flipped

through my head: bodies piled on top of each other, linked in a simple embrace.

Where were they? Why didn't they come out? It was over.

Then we saw it.

Smoke.

Just a puff, near white alpha 14 — the first breath of conflagration.

It started as a dark gray shadow drifting from a boarded-up window near the dining area, dark and out of place in the hazy noon sun.

"What the hell is that?" someone asked.

"Smoke?"

We stared across the 300 yards through high-powered spotting scopes, focusing and refocusing, trying to decide what we were watching. But within seconds, we knew. Off to the left, 100 feet upwind, near where Homey had torn down the Doghouse, we could already see the flames.

Black smoke rolled out of white alpha 14, the kind that chokes you when you light the grill with too much starter fluid. Petroleum smoke, acrid and thick. Flames followed like a refrain, licking at the tinder-dry siding and dancing through the mirage in our optics.

"We've got fire showing," someone called out over the radio.

My partner said, "Well, they've got to come out now."

I remember a dryness in my mouth, the sarcasm in his tone. Fire was an option I'd never even considered. Surely they'd have to come out now: human wave, gun battle, mass suicide, even surrender. But fire?

I knew there were people inside. Human beings. I'd seen their faces every day for seven weeks. David Koresh, Steve Schneider, Linda Thompson. I'd identified them from driver's license photos and other pictures. Elvis. White Tennis Shoes. Bones. Elvira.

I remembered Koresh's face, the way the sunlight reflected off those glasses. I remembered the power of knowing that he was mine if I really wanted him. Prophet, rock star, international celebrity, God — it didn't matter to me; I could have made him bleed like any other flesh.

I saw Mount Carmel before I went to sleep at night and when I woke up in the morning. I watched the Mighty Men smile as they ate their lunch, sitting in the windows and holding up the dishes to show us they had better food than we did. I watched the women dump five-gallon buckets full of human waste out the windows like medieval housemaids. I watched the helpless looks of fear in the eyes of toddlers, whom the Branch Davidians held up in front of themselves like shields when they stood at the windows to watch us refuel the generators.

I knew these people like members of some grossly dysfunctional family, full of mistrust and resentment and hate. Time had tattooed their faces in black and white designs on my mind.

But it was the building I knew best. I knew every crack and corner, every broken pane of glass, the color of every curtain, the size and location of every firing port. It was that scarred, brown, sprawling building that I saw every time I closed my eyes.

And now it was burning.

❖

The flames spread quickly, raging in monstrous gulps and towering black gusts. I leaned into my rifle, half standing and half lying on the wall of sandbags as Koresh's Ranch Apocalypse sign towered over me. Within seconds, it seemed like the whole of central Texas was burning. A strong spring gale hardened the fire like a heavenly bellows. The shaft of my rifle scope kept darkening with loss.

"Holy shit," someone said.

The sounds of gunfire changed. Instead of the sporadic prattle of automatic weapons fire, I heard spaced, almost rhythmic shots, as if we were back on the HRT ranges running steel drills. *Pop. Pop. Pop.*

"They're killing themselves," I said out loud. The other snipers were moving now, anxious to do anything but lie there and watch the flames. *Pop. Pop. Pop.* The methodical, distant gunfire sounded effete, almost whimpering.

I stuck to my assigned sector for five, maybe ten minutes, before realizing the odds of identifying any threat bordered on nil. Smoke had obscured most of the white side. Radio traffic indicated a couple Davidians had spilled out the front, but no one emerged from the back. The windows they could have climbed through darkened, then turned brilliant shades of red and yellow and orange, bright as the sun I imagined above that prescient gray.

"You getting this?" Metz asked. As coordinator of the surveillance photography program, I had the lenses and equipment to get very close.

"Hang on," I said. I backed off my rifle and grabbed a Nikon A-1 with a 600mm boomer. The shutter clicked and whirred as I swept the viewfinder right to left, pulling back and closing in on the conflagration.

I could feel the heat, 300 yards from Mount Carmel. The flames rose in the tinder-dry wood, sending ash out across the greening fields. Such profound waste.

Gunny and I moved away from our rifles, out through the empty main room of Sierra Two, into the backyard. Echo team had set up a squad automatic weapon in a sandbagged stronghold just off our southwest corner, and I thought it might offer a good vantage point for photographs. Gunny stood beside me as I lifted the camera and started to shoot. Both of us were exposed above the sandbags and just left of the building.

SNAP! SNAP!

"Holy shit!" I said, hitting the ground before the third syllable passed my lips. "Where the fuck did that come from?"

I worked day in and day out with a gun in my hand. Sometimes it was a .308 sniper rifle shooting movers at 500 yards. Sometimes it was with a 10mm MP-5 in a 737 fuselage, practicing airliner rescues. I knew the feel of bullets passing close by. You get the vapor bulge before the sound. Bullets move through the air like a ship at sea, building bow pressure and leaving a wake. You feel it on your cheek or the back of your hand when the projectiles pass close enough. Gunny and I both knew the feel of bullets missing, barely.

Two rounds fired from somewhere in that raging inferno came within inches of blowing our heads clean off.

"Some fucking way to die," I said, crawling back behind the building. "We wait fifty-one days out here with a gun in our hands and get whacked taking a couple of snapshots."

Echo team hunkered down beside us. Without a scope on the SAW, they had nothing to shoot at.

"Come on," Gunny said.

We ran back to our rifles. If they could still see us well enough to shoot, maybe we could return the favor. But in the seconds it took to dive back behind our guns, simple combustion had finished a job none of us could do. A mushroom cloud erupted, roiling high into the sky until the flames cooled and the sloppy black smoke blocked out what was left of the sun. I stood over my rifle wondering who had taken the shots.

Elvis, maybe. Or White Tennis Shoes.

Perhaps one of them recognized me through his scope,

holding on to spite or anger as the flames came for him. He must have fought the smoke, trying to steel his nerve against the heat as his whole world melted behind him. Maybe he heard God calling to him as he cycled his bolt, slamming a large-caliber round into battery. Maybe he wondered about the violence that would punctuate the final moments of a life turned so terribly wrong. All the sermons and the prayer and the blind faith boiling down to this?

Somewhere on that desolate plain two voices called out. One was the devil. The other was God.

I stared into the devastation and wondered about the shooter. At that point, he must have known the difference.

❖

By one o'clock I was walking through the embers. Metz, Junior, Gunny, and I loped out across the field that for two months had seemed a whole world wide. Small pieces of paper drifted across the new grass. I gathered up a few out of curiosity. They were pages from a prayer book, marked in pen and pencil with Koresh's teachings. The explosion had thrown them high into the air and scattered them among us like confetti in a ticker tape parade.

I saw BR-1 as we neared the remains of the building. He stood with his hands on his hips, surveying the rubble. He wore a ballistic helmet with tanker's goggles and carried his Hi-Power in a low-slung tactical holster. The red and yellow embers reflected off his pallid skin.

I took my camera and followed Hotel team as they moved through the smoking debris, clearing for survivors. The thought of anyone living through this devastation seemed preposterous until one of the Davidians emerged from the silo, slightly toasted but very much alive. No one else would share his luck. Golf team with attachments had already fought their way down into an underground bus, searching for the children we hoped Koresh had spared. Half a dozen assaulters waded into a tunnel, oblivious to the likelihood of improvised explosives or booby traps. They rushed down through a pitch-black sewage lagoon, up to their knees in human excrement, rotting body parts, and rats. They found no children. The bus was empty.

I walked through the glowing coals that one hour earlier had been a rambling building filled with almost a hundred lives. Everywhere I stepped, my foot landed next to a half-cremated body. Some of the corpses still wore flesh, striated muscle on bone, beneath skin and fat that had cooked off in the slow roast. It smelled different than I expected, not like singed hair — more like barbecue.

I photographed a skull, perfect in symmetry except for a small hole above the right eye and a big hole above the left ear. Bullets make wounds like this: small when they enter and big when they leave.

I walked over thigh bones poking up like broken chair legs, backs and bottoms and legs and arms of all shapes and sizes. Some lay atop the chalk-colored rubble. Others stuck up from beneath it, emerging in death to fresh air for the first time in two months.

Everywhere, literally everywhere, I could reach out and touch a weapon. AR-15 barrels in rows, AK-47 receivers, bipod-mounted machine guns, handguns, the two big Barretts. Boxes filled with ammunition in numbers I couldn't even estimate. I walked up to photograph the concrete bunker that stood above everything else in the rubble. Empty bullet casings filled the room almost to my waist. I later learned there were so many rounds, investigators had to weigh them to approximate numbers. They said it was more than a million.

Bullets cooked off all around us, harmless without a gun.

Hundreds exploded in the flames, presenting no more danger now than the man who had bought them.

The fire department arrived when everything had cooled to afterglow. My teammates and I wandered the scene for a time, comparing notes and learning what had happened in the Bradleys and at Sierra One. That's when I heard about survivors. More had escaped than I had realized. Some came voluntarily, emerging from the windows, stripping off their war gear and throwing their arms up in surrender. Others did not.

I started to collect the stories.

Big Bob told me how Scarhead, a living legend on Hotel team, had left the cover of his Bradley and gone after one woman. She had emerged from the building, decided she wanted to die in the blaze, and run back toward the compound. Despite the barrage of small-arms fire, Scarhead sprinted across the open field and actually climbed inside the building after her. The fire was so close around them, her clothes ignited and she had to be put out like a flaming s'more.

"I kept screaming at her, 'Where are the kids, where are the kids,'" he told me later, over beers. "She just looked at me with this blank stare and said nothing. She wouldn't say a fucking thing."

Less than an hour later, we climbed atop a Bradley and powered away from Sierra Two for the last time. I rode with the rest of my team, finding space to sit just forward of the gunner's hatch. Emotion boiled within me, filling my heart with happiness at finally going home and the inconsolable loss of no longer knowing where that was.

If I have dreams of that place, they will glow red, the way fire simmers, hot coals and embers. In them, I can hear the whispers and hot breath from a voice I never wanted to recognize.

The kids are all dead. Souls searching for a place to sleep.

Skulls and half-eaten flesh stick up through the ashes, rude suggestions of humanity. Guns everywhere. Bodies huddled around them — femurs and skulls and fingers stripped of flesh, robbed of the feeling that ran from this place long ago.

I see my shadow dancing in the coals. I hear the voice of evil.

It's me.

20

TOES OVER

Mount Carmel wasn't the only thing that perished in the fire on April 19. In many ways, the FBI died right along with it. It took a while for the effects to show themselves, but they came with a vengeance, ripping away at the organization as methodically as T.J. and Homey had torn down that building.

None of us noticed at first. Everyone just sort of walked away from the rubble, glad to be done with the whole damned mess. There was no wild celebration like after the Danny Ray Horning mission, no drunken wrap-up like after the Ruby Ridge standoff. Though HRT tended to play as hard as it worked in those days, we stayed in our rooms after the fire. I simply shuffled back into the Holiday Inn, tossed my flesh-covered boots in the trash, and fell on the bed. I couldn't sleep. I couldn't stay awake.

The overwhelming sense of loss I felt is difficult to explain even now. I hadn't known a whole lot of failure in my life, yet that moment made the whole thirty-four years seem like a waste. It gripped me as the single greatest mistake of my life. Just being there. For seven weeks, we'd focused all our energy on bringing those people out of that building alive. We'd invested ourselves in the process of freeing those people and putting the murderers of four brave ATF agents behind bars. Then, within the course of twelve hours, it all went away. All the work. All the sacrifice. All the prayers.

My mind flipped back through every lesson the FBI had taught me, from the legal instruction on the Constitution to the Hostage Rescue Team's motto: "To Save Lives."

We were the good guys, right? The riders in white hats who showed up near the end of Act I to run all the shitbirds out of town. I stared into the mirror at the foot of my bed and looked for something, someone, anything, to tell me I was right. All I could see was that poor little kid in the window, tracing the rainbow decal with his finger, waiting to die. I didn't have the balls or the energy to ask any of my buddies how they felt, but I knew. We weren't that different. They picked us alike.

Two days later, we packed our gear and flew East. It had been winter when I left. Now the trees were budding and the flowers were in full bloom. Rosie and the boys met me at the airport with lots of hugs and smiles. I saw Mickey and Jake first when I entered the terminal. Rose had gotten them brand-new flattop haircuts, like I'd worn when I left.

"Daddy! Daddy!" they yelled.

I buried my face in the smell of their spring jackets and tried to breathe. Emotion, something I'd never been terribly good at, surged through me like a giant nausea, threatening to burst out and flood the American Airlines gate with laughter or rage or tears. I had no fucking idea what I felt. I felt everything all at once, the whole human response chain hammering at the walls of my heart in one jagged "I've missed you."

I conjured up the best smile I could fake, and kissed Rose. Mickey looked up at me, trying to figure out what to say. I shook my head, trying to hold the corners of my mouth up. Little boys shouldn't have to worry about things like what to say. That's the beauty of youth: spontaneity. They should spill out whatever moves them.

None of us spilled. Rose hardly spoke a word. Mickey and Jake looked at me with caution, like they might believe what they'd seen on the news two days earlier. Surely, the kids had talked about it at school. They must have remembered Mickey's pronouncement about his dad, the FBI exterminator.

"What did you bring us, Dad?" Jake asked. He and Mickey reached for my bag, like they used to — two little kids waiting on any dad coming home from the road. Finally, some honesty.

I tried to stand up, but my legs just wouldn't straighten. I felt lost, like the first time I got separated in the woods from my own dad. I'd been gone a little more than two months, dwelling on their faces with every waking thought. I'd spent days' worth of hours wondering what they were doing, whether they were happy. I sang them bedtime stories by myself, some nights, just to remember what that felt like.

"Easy, guys," Rose said, sensing my defeat. "Let your dad relax a little. He just got here."

I understood then that Waco might weigh on me a little longer than I'd thought. During my lifetime at Mount Carmel, I'd strolled the years of my life, guessing, believing, regretting, hoping. I'd read thirty books, written seventy-eight poems, composed eighteen songs, and consumed who knows how many gallons of beer, all in hopes of getting home with my head in one piece.

I just knelt there in that airport with a little boy's hand in each of mine and a wrenching sadness in my gut. In all that time, I'd never found the occasion to buy them so much as a gumball.

I lay awake the first night in my own bed with the sounds of armored vehicles raging through the house. Faces appeared on the ceiling in a slow but steady procession. Children mostly. Toddlers. I started to sweat for no reason at all. Eyes open or closed, the view never changed. The smell of barbecue filled my nose. My muscles cramped. Anger consumed me.

Two days later I climbed on my Harley and rode west, hoping I could make Waco before it rained. The place begged me to return. Nothing pleased me. Nothing made sense.

Staff Sergeant Morton and Gunny Patterson from the sniper school, friends now, rode with me. My buddy Rick Crabb, close as a brother, rode point. He stretched us out through the back roads of Virginia, alone except for the wind and a bond I can't quite describe. We rode into the mountains, up high enough to see the past in all directions.

When we got to the top of the Blue Ridge Parkway, Rick pulled over at the side of the road and shut down his engine. He had a real knack for framing deliberation.

"Look around," he said.

I stared out to the west. It was just more ground. Earth. Same to the north and south.

"We'll take you anywhere you want to go," he said. "But it's not going to make a whole lot of difference. There's no place you haven't already been."

Right then, I knew what lay ahead. What I had to do. I could barely stand under the weight of what I carried in my head and my heart, but I realized that falling down wouldn't help. Lots of other people depended on me. I could run on that motorcycle as far as I wanted, but the real destination lay inside me.

"You might as well get used to the voices," Gunny Patterson said. "They're going with us."

❖

Waco played no favorites in handing out defeat. Americans take pride in assessing blame, and since the real culprits in the Branch Davidian crisis were already dead, it was only a matter of time before they ganged up on the survivors. Washington took the first salvo. The newspapers and magazines and broadcast journalists stepped back for a few days, like everyone, trying to read the tea leaves, then tore in.

First they went after the brand-new attorney general, who had made the call to start gassing. When she stood all six feet three inches of her own bad self up in front of the cameras and took full responsibility, they did what any self-respecting journalist would do. They went after her boss. Unfortunately, he never had half the balls she did. He let her take the blame until the polls showed America respected her candor, then he tried to stand under the flag with her.

FBI Headquarters was not nearly so bright. Unfortunately, bureaucracies are only as strong as their director, and ours just wasn't cut out for this sort of thing. As a former federal judge better suited to grand juries than grandstanding, he just didn't understand how to fight for the troops.

My strongest personal recollection of Director William Sessions is from a visit he paid to the Team just after the fire. BR-1 assembled us in the HRT classroom, dressed in our formal white rugby shirts and best behavior. No one said a word as Sessions entered with his driver and two lackeys.

I sat in the back row, shaking my head at his total lack of presence. The Director always wore his gold FBI shield pinned to the front pocket of his dress shirt. As a man who well remembered Eugene Brodie's distaste for improper display of the badge, I couldn't help but snicker.

"Who the fuck is that? Marshal Dillon?" Shelly mumbled. Half a dozen operators snickered loudly enough that BR-1 started to flash red.

"I want to tell you all how very pleased your Director is with your effort," Sessions began. The Director always referred to himself in the third person, unless referring to himself as "Alice," his wife who, many argued, really called the shots.

Our Director proceeded to recount salient features of the Waco standoff, at least from his perspective. These recollections made no sense to us, but we understood his distraction. Everyone knew that the rest of FBI Headquarters had worried so much about what he might do if given the chance, they steered him far clear of day-to-day operations.

I soon found out why. Midway through a sentence about something totally unrelated to Waco, our Director lost his train of thought and started to stumble. He twitched and squirmed for a second or two, then turned to BR-1, who stood against the wall, awaiting praise.

The Director remembered the day in question, but not his whereabouts or the reason for mention.

". . . and last Tuesday, when I was, when I was . . ." He turned to BR-1, as if asking about the weather. "Last Tuesday — where was I, Dick?"

Poor BR-1 had planned for every eventuality, from serving the Director's coffee with two sugars to clearing a special parking space outside, but he hadn't planned on reconstructing his appointment schedule in front of the boys. Neither man gained much from that visit.

Things quickly soured for HRT and the FBI in general. First came the Ruby Ridge investigation. Despite the initial shooting review board's findings that Hooch had acted within the scope of the law and the letter of FBI policy, Headquarters bowed to congressional pressure for a deeper probe.

FBI internal investigations come in two forms: First is the administrative inquiry — usually conducted by the Office of Professional Responsibility. If unfortunate enough to find himself in such a situation, the employee is compelled to answer any and all questions. Lack of candor is a firing offense. No lawyers. No due process. No rights. You sit in a chair and you answer all the questions they ask you, without exception. They can ask you absolutely anything, and the chips fall where the Bureau decides they should fall.

The second type of internal investigation is criminal. The investigator is supposed to tell you about this up front, but due to the gut-wrenching bewilderment in finding oneself in such a situation, no one really knows where he stands. I know, because in the two years following Waco, I found myself facing both.

"Look, Special Agent Whitcomb," a field supervisor said, sitting me down at a long conference table. His partner sat quietly beside him. "We all want the same thing, so just tell us what really happened up there and this will turn out just fine."

Of course, I thought. I'm an FBI agent. That's what I do.

"Can the information I provide be used against me in a civil case?" I asked.

They looked at each other, trying to decide how much I should know.

"Under Fifth Amendment protections, nothing you say here today can be used against you in court."

"Can what I say be used against anyone else?"

Another pause.

"Yes."

I guess it was my responsibility to figure out the agenda.

❖

The Waco and Ruby Ridge investigations took up a good deal of our time in the two years after the fire. I answered questions or provided sworn statements to government investigators no less than seven times in the first year alone. It got to be routine after a while: a new set of faces, a fresh subpoena, a bigger mandate. Ultimately, Congress came calling. They waited until the political fallout settled before taking their stand, but they came.

"This committee will now proceed," I heard on my first trip back to Capitol Hill since leaving my job with Congressman Conte. Senator Arlen Specter sat higher than the rest of us on September 14, 1995, like an inquisitor in the British courts. As chairman of the Terrorism, Technology and Government Information Subcommittee, he could sit anywhere he liked.

I knew we were in for a long day from the time the FBI lawyers paraded us down the hallway leading into the Dirksen Building committee room. I saw a sound mixer big enough to sleep on. Video dubbing machines, preamps, editing equipment lit up the control room just off to our left as if we were walking into the broadcast studio at CBS News. This committee room wasn't built to help senators ferret out truth. It was a sound stage built to get them votes.

"We will have two panels today," Specter said, "the eight sniper/observers from the Federal Bureau of Investigation and then the pilot of the helicopter, together with the deputy U.S. marshal who was in that helicopter."

Ruby Ridge, Waco — it didn't make much difference to me at that point.

Specter spoke softly, trusting the microphone in front of him to convey his intentions to the American people in the televised hearings. Broadcast cameras guarded the exits. Technicians recorded every word. Still photographers lined us up from left and right, snapping visuals for the front page headlines.

I sat third from the right with Boat and Mark, just the way we'd lined up on the ridge above Randy Weaver's cabin three years earlier. Three years? I stared across the room, past copies of my four sworn statements, my name plate, and the half-empty glass of water they'd left me. I'd endured three years of internal investigations, grand juries, criminal trials, civil suits, and second-guessing. Three years of business-as-usual workdays while lawyers in fine suits postured and planned and panicked over a way of life they could never really understand.

Senator Fred Thompson stared down at us, quietly sizing up our veracity. As a former prosecutor and big-screen actor, he probably knew how to watch for the subtle facial gestures and tapping fingers that give away deception. His lips curled up under his nose just the way they did in *The Hunt for Red October.* I considered myself a fan of his drama, even in the hearing.

"It's my understanding that it's the seven counsel who have been provided by the Department of Justice and one of the sniper/observers here is without counsel. And which one is that?"

Specter looked up from something he was reading. I raised my hand and nodded. Fuck lawyers. I was there for myself.

"And Mr. Whitcomb, why have you elected to appear without counsel, if I may ask?" he said.

The question surprised me.

"It just didn't seem necessary," I said.

"Didn't seem necessary?" He cocked his head and lowered an eye, like an elementary school principal preparing to scold an impertinent pupil. He sounded shocked that someone would show up representing the Federal Bureau of Investigation with nothing but a sworn oath.

"You just want to put that on the record." He motioned to the court recorder. He looked me in the eye as if offering a last chance. "I know you've been informed that you can have counsel if you want."

"Yes," I said. I had been informed.

Lawyers, I thought to myself. That's what everything ultimately comes down to. The FBI had decided early in the Ruby Ridge inquisition that despite our employment and the fact that we had acted in performance of official duties, shelling out for lawyers would look bad to the public.

"How could the Department of Justice fund an internal investigation and offer defense counsel in the same budget?" one Headquarters geek once asked me. The appearance of propriety is usually more important than propriety itself among these people. If we wanted lawyers, we'd have to pay for them ourselves.

That bothered me. When the FBI gave me a gun, it came with certain disclaimers. I knew that I alone was responsible for its handling, storage, and care. That made perfect sense. If I used it in the line of duty, I alone was responsible for exercising good judgment. That still made good sense.

What confused me was how, even when everything went according to plan, they could cut us off at the knees and leave us to bleed. After going to the Agents Association for help, we finally got the Bureau to offer $60 an hour to retain legal representation. Where I lived that wouldn't pay a plumber.

❖

HRT stayed home in 1994, hunkered down while the firestorm of derision from Capitol Hill eroded public confidence in law enforcement. During the Waco hearings and the

Ruby Ridge investigations, we plodded through the motions, day after day, training like we always did, but realizing in the back of our mind that no one had any intention of sending us out after real work. Though HRT took its share of the heat, it was Headquarters that suffered most during the Dark Years. BR-1 fell on hard times, almost from the start. Though a rising star within the FBI just after the Talladega prison rescue, he had become a bit of a pariah.

Controversy over the Ruby Ridge rules of engagement turned ugly. BR-1's superiors at Headquarters claimed they had never seen them or signed off on any approval. Bullshit. Eleven HRT snipers waited four hours in the pouring rain that day for Washington to sign off on the new deadly-force policy. Dick Roberts would not have held us back four seconds without someone hamstringing his intentions.

The Justice Department started its own inquiry into why the FBI, the Assistant U.S. Attorney's Office in Spokane, and the U.S. Marshals Service had such difficulty following the trial judge's orders regarding evidentiary issues. More trouble. Who approved the unusual rules of engagement stipulating that snipers could and "should" use deadly force if adult males were seen with weapons? Why did the U.S. Attorney's Office visit the scene and play a role in the investigation?

Headquarters, that heretofore faceless assemblage of power brokers, began to crumble. An Assistant Director took a letter of censure for his part in the alleged misconduct, but the Director took his word that nothing else had happened and moved him up to the number two slot on the seventh floor. An SAC took two years of paid administrative leave, early retirement, and a book deal. Another top official took jail time. Roberts stepped down for a dead-end job uptown. Within a year, he was back working cases as a street agent in Phoenix. Sessions resigned under the weight of his own financial scandal. The SACs in charge of the siege retired. And on and on.

Virtually everyone associated with the FBI's command and control element at Ruby Ridge or Waco was banished from the kingdom. Even Hooch, who eventually won Headquarters backing and a taxpayer-funded attorney, lost his right to carry a sniper rifle. We were helping the San Juan Field Office with a kidnapping investigation in 1995 when word came down that he was no longer a shooter.

"You can go and watch, if you want," they said, "but from now on, you're not allowed to carry a rifle." He still carried team leader status and responsibility for six other men, but he couldn't play with sharp objects. They might as well have cut his balls off.

Bodies fell along the way like possums on an East Texas farm road. Even some of the guys on the Team began to show effects of the stress. I saw changes in behavior at first. Not everyone. Enough.

One operator started wearing hooded sweatshirts in August. Virginia gets hot in August, hot enough for people to notice that sort of thing. Others stopped working out or called in sick. Guys started getting hurt more than usual. Nobody talked. Nobody laughed.

I felt it on my skin, itching, rubbing every day raw. Angst. Depression. I didn't know what to call it. I turned from people, friends who saw it in my eyes but walked away rather than confront me. Every word I spoke reeked of derision. Every thought became darker and emptier, leaving me one emotion: anger. Uncontrollable, vicious rage.

First came the nightmares. I seldom remembered details, but I'd wake up yelling, drenched with sweat, staring into the dark and wondering how the hell to turn on the lights.

Rose tried to explain to the kids, but they weren't old enough to understand. All they knew was that there was something wrong with Daddy. My behavior changed radically. I started taking absurd chances, where I had previously calculated risk. When we practiced fast roping evolutions, for example, I would hang my body out the helicopter, testing gravity. We always sat on the cargo deck of our Hueys with our lower legs hanging off the edge. There were no safety lines, so you rode the friction between your butt and the deck, into the sticking point in every turn, beyond which the chopper would spit you out like a caraway seed. I tested the limits, leaning into the edge until I could feel myself losing contact.

I spread out my protection on rock climbs, tempting gravity to pull me back to the hard ground. I rode my motorcycle on its sidewalls, scraping the floorboards through sweeping turns up and down the Blue Ridge Parkway, out west where the mountains broke toward the distance.

Wherever I went, I found the highest possible structure to climb and tempt. Going "toes over" became a personal trademark which I built among my friends — the people I dared bleed in front of. All ten toes over the edge. No safety line.

I tested skyscrapers in New York, bridges in West Virginia, towers in New Orleans, cliffs, rooftops, anything high enough to draw me. *Consequence,* I thought — I needed something tangible in a life that no longer carried any sensation. Something had changed my perspective on penalty.

"What the hell's up with you?" Metz asked one day, as I borrowed his shoulder to get my feet up on a handrail. He turned his back as I climbed, so he wouldn't have to look at the height.

I couldn't explain what I felt. I just felt numb, like I was floating in some flat emotionless haze, waiting for small moments I could feel. Only risk gave me sensation.

"You know what the greatest feeling in the world is?" I

asked, balancing over a long fall one day. "Knowing you're going to die . . . and surviving."

Though I can't speak for any of the other operators, I suspect my misery shared company. Six months after we returned from Waco, Headquarters advised us that a group of "mental health professionals" would visit Quantico the following week. All training would be canceled that day. Attendance was mandatory.

The operators erupted with a chorus of invective. "We don't need any fucking headshrinkers coming in here and feeding us some bullshit, touchy-feely drivel. Leave us the fuck alone." Those are my words, but the sentiment seemed common. Even though we stood one step from self-immolation, it was no one else's damned business.

Not according to BR-1. The psychiatric SWAT team came, and we went.

Fifty men gathered in a second-floor classroom at the Academy just after the daily 8:00 A.M. meeting. A pedantic little man with wire-rimmed glasses and a whippoorwill voice told us he'd been sent by Headquarters to assess an anger management problem.

"Anger management," I hissed under my breath. They were right that I had an anger management problem, but I didn't need a shrink. All I needed was some bean-counting asshole from Washington to come down and explain why the organization I had joined to save the world couldn't find its ass with a shit taster. Veins popped out of my neck. My ears rang. My heart just thumped and thumped until I had to breathe hard at the exertion.

"We're going to split you up into two breakout groups," the lead psychiatrist said. "We'll meet again this afternoon to discuss our findings."

Breakout groups or break dancing, no one in our wolf pack had any intention of joining this party. None of these brain experts had any idea what it meant to win a spot on a team like this. Vulnerability is anathema. Weakness might as well be bubonic plague. Everything we did boiled down to ability. Every characteristic of success folded on misgiving and trepidation. To walk into a room and lay any sort of emotional problem down in front of other Team members sounded patently absurd.

But the front office said "March," so we marched down to classroom 314, a windowless space that closed in around us. We sat in a circle, staring at the floor, as a female PhD talked.

No one responded.

She prodded.

No one responded.

She begged.

No one responded. Finally Cordy, a deeply introspective former Marine from St. Louis, tossed a stone into the pool. In a soft, measured voice, he touched several wounds I hadn't finished licking. Emotion rose in my throat. One emotion. Hatred. I hated the way I felt, the way Koresh came to me in my dreams, standing in that window, mocking me. "Do it," he said. "Do it."

I hated the way I felt about investing myself in an organization that from its Manual of Investigative and Operational Guidelines to its Legal Handbook stood on rules and regulations that applied to everyone but the people who wrote them. I'd given up a good life for this one because I firmly believed I could make a difference — swim right-out in the middle of the storm and snatch back the drowners. But there was no organization in any of this. There were just people who made decisions and ran from them with all the conviction of a midway hawker.

We stared at each other for two hours, then broke for lunch.

"You know what I realized this morning," the therapist

said when we returned. She looked beaten by the weight of our entanglement. "It hit me while I was eating my salad." Another pause for drama. I couldn't tell if she planned it or not. "This is real. You know? This is real."

"You got to be shitting me," Scarhead mumbled. He knew real. He was the guy who had charged into the burning building to drag out one of the Branch Davidians.

"Real." She said it over and over.

If only by accident, her provocation pricked the thin scab covering our infection. Seething hatred oozed out. No yelling, no hyperbole. Men in the room spoke disturbing words in conversational tones. We showed her just enough "real" to knock her right off her academic polemic. And it scared the shit out of her.

When they brought us back together at the end of the day, the lead psychiatrist walked up to a lectern at the front of the room and arranged some papers.

"I think it is only fair to tell you," he said, without looking up to engage a single set of bloodshot eyes, "what we have found here today and what we will convey to Headquarters. You seem to have a significant issue with anger. I think it is very dangerous, and . . ."

"Anger! You want anger, you motherfucker!" One of the Team members lurched from his chair, red the shade of open wounds. "I'll show you some fucking anger . . ."

Guys on either side of him reached to keep him from pouncing. Only a faint recollection of honor kept him from surfing down the tiered lecture hall seats and ripping this man's throat out.

I'll never forget the look on the shrink's face. He grabbed his stack of papers and ran out the door. That was the full extent of the FBI's post-traumatic-stress counseling. We never heard from any mental health professionals again.

Things just got worse after that, as if I'd seen a rescue

vessel passing at night and lost my flare. Darkness descended. The tunnel narrowed. The night sweats soaked my bed.

Later that year a drunk driver hit me on my motorcycle. Shortly after I recovered, I contracted Rocky Mountain spotted fever and spent a week in the hospital. I blew out my shoulder on the bench press, trying to push 320 for two. The investigators came. I tried to remember, though all I wanted to do was forget.

Journalists wrote condemning stories based on what they read and heard from those who would talk. Unfortunately for us, the only ones who would talk were defense attorneys like Dick DeGuerin and Gerry Spence. Randy Weaver talked. Branch Davidians talked. The FBI said nothing.

"Don't worry about it," the front office said. "Americans don't believe everything they read. They know we were just doing our jobs up there. They know we were right."

I bought that until my dad called one afternoon to tell me he'd just seen the latest copy of *American Rifleman,* one of the National Rifle Association's periodicals.

"Better look it over, Chris. They wrote an article about Ruby Ridge and you're in it. They call you a coward."

I told him I didn't care to look, but he sent it just the same. A manila envelope arrived from New Hampshire a week later, and I opened it. I could hardly believe what I read. I'd worked as a newspaper reporter myself. I knew the game. They had no idea what happened up there, but that didn't matter. They had an agenda, and that agenda included a government they perceived as a threat. In order to neutralize the threat, they had to chop at its strongest weapons. One of those weapons was HRT.

What surprised me most was that prior to Ruby Ridge, I had agreed with most of what the NRA stood for. Though my official membership had lapsed, I still believed strongly in the right to bear arms. I had even thought seriously about going to work for their public relations office in 1987, had the FBI Academy not come calling.

But something had changed. The people I felt closest to politically were working overtime to paint me and my friends as threats to the integrity of the American way. From Charlton Heston to Paul Harvey to Fred Thompson, the conservatism I had embraced since high school was kicking my ass. It simply baffled me.

And then, two weeks after my dad sent the article, I received another envelope in the mail. This one came from the NRA, and it contained a membership application. It was addressed to me, by name, at the HRT building, FBI Academy, Quantico, Virginia. Someone must have had a good laugh at my expense. I didn't get the humor.

The skepticism extended beyond the news media. Our counterterrorism counterparts in the Army and Navy asked us disturbing questions about our motives and what "really happened" in Waco. Friends and family members tried to sound sympathetic, but with every exposé and critical article, their support seemed less convincing.

No one spoke up from Headquarters. No one defended us publicly. No one offered anything to give people a reason to believe that we did precisely what we were supposed to do in impossible situations, with badly flawed information. Hindsight is 20/20, and we were looking right down the barrel of public opinion.

Slowly, the blood settled. HRT hires strong souls and trains them well. We went back to our jobs. Generation Ten, the first NOTS class post-Waco, arrived in the spring of 1995 with the fruits of two selections: seventeen new operators. They came like duende, breathing new optimism into the squad rooms and equipment cages. So many guys had left after the fire, we needed every body we could recruit, just to bring our numbers back to full strength. Metz had moved to a SWAT team leader job in Florida. Raz and Matty went to Headquarters. Boat went to HRT's front office. Yoda picked up a promotion as assistant legal attaché, Tokyo.

We started getting work again. Small jobs at first, utility missions that pushed us back into the world. BR-1, once a rising star in the FBI galaxy, handed the reins over to an infectiously optimistic ASAC from the Richmond division named Roger Blake. Blake had been one of the founding voices behind the Team back in 1982 — one of a handful of Special Operations and Research Resources supervisors who had chanced career damage by pitching the concept to Headquarters. HRT meant everything to him, because he believed, with the conviction of a street agent, in the power of fifty badges and a cause. The Director picked him from a deep pool of applicants, and he saved us.

The first change Blake brought to the Team was respect. The new commander opened the door to his office and announced during his first morning meeting that he had nothing against anyone with a bitch as long as they brought it to him first. Nobody trusted him then, but after a time, the back room warmed.

First we got some missions. He started with a series of high-risk drug raids in Puerto Rico. I lay behind The Truth with real people in my crosshairs again, and started to breathe. Amazing, I thought, how something as simple as trust can restore purpose. Perhaps it was a small step, but it was the first.

Next came a Team realignment. Whereas snipers had long been treated as bastard stepchildren, Blake doubled our numbers, created two new units, and gave everyone identities. Whiskey, X-Ray, Yankee, and Zulu sniper teams. Seven men each. That gave us parity with the assaulters and a whole new dynamic.

I drew a slot on X-Ray and a new Generation 10 partner out of the San Diego office. He introduced himself as "Buck" and quickly distinguished himself with a rifle. Despite his pedigree as a certified public accountant from Connecticut, he shot like a world afire.

A soft-spoken Naval Academy graduate named Quinny stepped up to the team leader slot, enlisted what he considered the six best talents, and whipped us into an enterprise worth investing ourselves in. The darkness started to peel away like clouds passing in a summer breeze.

More missions. First came the dignitary protection details. We picked up a steady stream of foreign judges like Giovanni Falcone, the scourge of Italian Mafia, and high-risk government witnesses like Sammy "the Bull" Gravano. Everything went flawlessly. No headlines. No problems.

It got better. We branched out into a whole new type of mission, rounding up some of America's most wanted international fugitives. Although most of the details remain classified, we began reaching out in small, fast-moving teams to let terrorists know we could come for them virtually anywhere they tried to hide.

Watching the expression on a former hijacker's face when you bust down his third-world hotel room door, slap on the cuffs, throw a bag over his head, and whisk him away to life in an American prison is enough to raise anyone's spirits.

"Renditions," Headquarters called them — high-risk international fugitive pickups, part of the Director's new international expansion initiative. We called them "grabs," but under any name, bombers and assassins, drug lords and hijackers from Trashcanistan to Peru found fewer and fewer places to hide. Our creel began to swell with trophy catches.

Just about the time HRT began to hit its stride again, a bunch of socially dysfunctional extremists called the Freemen threatened to kill a judge in Jordan, Montana. HRT put together a plan in which five operators would infiltrate the group, wait until we had the upper hand, then execute a "grab what you can" arrest. I jumped at the chance for an undercover assignment and promptly started growing my hair down to my shoulders, and a ZZ Top goatee.

The Undercover Safeguard Unit conducted psychological testing one afternoon to determine who among us would best suit the needs of the mission. About a dozen guys assembled in the classroom and began taking a series of tests. As often happened, the pack mentality kicked in and guys started discussing answers, just to make sure they all fit in the same box.

After a few minutes, one of the Hotel assaulters noticed that an Echo guy was copying off his paper. He covered his paper with one arm and said, "What the hell's wrong with you, man? This isn't the SATs. Get your own personality."

Humor started to trickle back among us, too.

Those of us selected for the Montana mission never got to execute the plan, but that worked out for the best anyway. Headquarters originally called for a frontal assault that almost surely would have led to the dissolution of HRT. Only a last-minute power play of sanity by our commander prevented another Waco. Ultimately, even the staunchest hawks at Headquarters came to realize that it was best to wait eighty-one days to bring those idiots out. No corpses. No fires. No lawsuits. No congressional inquiry. Times were definitely changing.

Slowly but surely, we pulled ourselves up by the proverbial bootstraps. The Team remembered itself.

Things improved at home, too. The lack of missions in the year immediately after Waco gave me time to reacquaint myself with two little boys who needed a full-time dad. Though it took a while to find that man among my demons, I eventually learned to deal with the rage. Rosie's master's degree in psychology and years of work as a family counselor didn't hurt. Pride and a fear of losing my security clearances kept me from getting the professional help I could have used, but she knew how to work around the edges.

I rediscovered the value of bedtime stories. We went camping, just for the hell of it. The boys took me fishing again, and rock climbing and mountaineering. I volunteered to coach their soccer teams and their baseball teams and their hockey teams. I even took a couple of days off just to follow them around school, so I'd know what they were talking about. Life started to twist back into focus.

Then one night in 1995, just before the Team's first Puerto Rico trip, I went up to tuck the boys into bed. Mickey called my bedtime serenades "story songs," and he demanded that I play one. When I finished, I kissed them each on the cheek and broke the news that I had to go away for a few days for "business."

He immediately started to cry.

"Hey, easy, buddy," I said. "Just a few days. I promise. I'll be home before you know it."

"That's what you said last time, Dad."

Jake didn't make a sound. He usually let his younger brother do all the heavy lifting.

"No, that was different, Mick," I promised. "This time it's a couple days. I'll make sure I don't forget the present this time."

"I don't want any present," he said. The tears rolled down his cheeks. His voice got high and broken.

"Come on, buddy," I countered. "This isn't Waco. I'll be . . ."

"I miss you, Dad! Please don't go." The tears came in earnest.

I leaned close and spoke softly with words a little boy could understand.

"Mick, read my lips . . . three or four days."

I waited for an answer. I could see him looking up at me through the dim light, tears sparkling in his little eyes.

"Come on, Dad," he said. His lip started to quiver. "You know I can't read."

Rose started laughing outside the door. I started laughing. Jake joined in. Mickey choked on his tears, trying to figure out what he'd missed. That's when I realized that things could get better.

We could heal.

BOOK
FIVE

The way a body weightless in a lake
Remembers shore, the way a body pays
For Buoyancy with breath. It's a mistake,
The nurses say, but when cool waves erase
The ragged shore and when the fresh mud rises
Beneath light fissured on the water's skin,
Even the moon impatiently undresses.
It breaks to heal, heals to break again.

TOM HAWKS

21

FINDING THE
PULSE

By early 1995, the lights had come back on. Shortly after William Sessions's scandal-driven retreat from public service, a New York judge named Louis J. Freeh stormed into Washington like a force of nature. He was a former agent — the first true FBI man to become Director since Hoover — and he knew that what the Bureau needed more than anything in the world was a new sense of itself. He started by launching a series of initiatives so wide-reaching and brazen, no one had time to sulk.

First, he took a wrecking ball to the place. He instituted a two-phase plan in which he offered office-of-preference transfers to virtually anyone at Headquarters who would volunteer to go. Lots of people raised their hands. In fact, more than three hundred management-level agents cleared their desks and headed back to gainful employment in the field. The very fact that the FBI had that many managers speaks volumes about how top-heavy the organization had grown. Virtually every agent who wanted to work his or her way up the career ladder had to serve time in Headquarters along the way. Louis Freeh found more than a thousand waiting for him when he got there, all supervisory level or higher, most just taking up space. Out they went.

Next, he realigned the Bureau's investigative priorities to better reflect what the Uniform Crime Reports were showing. The massive white-collar-crime initiatives launched during the savings and loan crisis had run their course. Violent crime and drugs now needed attention, as did a fairly new concept called domestic terrorism. The Oklahoma City bombing proved that the FBI had to re-zero its sights away from international hooligans, toward homegrown Armageddon. Suddenly it wasn't some Libyan zealot in a head wrap we had to worry about. It was Billy Bob in a John Deere cap. America found itself vulnerable to anyone with a truckload of fertilizer and a couple gallons of diesel fuel.

After pruning headquarters and realigning investigative priorities, Freeh marched up Capitol Hill and took on a phalanx of politicians who had turned FBI-beating into a cottage industry. Freeh's predecessor hadn't left him much of a leg to stand on, but that didn't matter much to the new Director. His lack of political skills seemed almost refreshing to people on the Hill. They saw him as an honest, tell-it-like-it-is leader of an agency that hadn't stood up for itself in some time. As the Republicans and Democrats squared off over Clinton, Gingrich, and scandals ranging from Travelgate to Filegate, Freeh thrust his Jay Leno jaw in front of the whole Congress and stated the obvious: The FBI are the good guys.

It was about time.

Not everything ran smoothly. Starting a reconstruction project with a hammer as big as Louie's can cause some grumbling. Fortunately, he came in with a sense that he was still one of us, and his rap sheet looked good. Former colleagues praised his work as a New York field agent and as a federal prosecutor. People who knew him swore he was fair and honest and focused. On top of that, he knew better than to wear his badge on the breast pocket of his shirt. He didn't take agents along to carry his wife's shopping bags. He came up with original ideas that made sense. And best of all, he listened.

Most agents came to see Louie Freeh as their first true leader in a long time. The budgets grew, the resources improved, cases got bigger. He restored a sense of pride. You could almost feel the darkness lifting.

HRT got a break of its own around the same time, when Roger Blake took over the Team during a change-of-command ceremony worthy of mention. BR-1, in a Hall of Fame demonstration of hubris, assembled the Team, their wives, children, janitors, and everyone else he could find in one of the Academy's auditoriums. While everyone looked on, he formally relinquished control of HRT and handed Roger the "commander's pistol." This might seem like a reasonable tradition to start in a military unit, but HRT is law enforcement, not military. Blake promptly threw the gun into a drawer, never to be seen again.

After the ceremony, BR-1 rolled out a big cake and cut it with a chrome cavalry saber. That turned out to be a whole lot more pomp than HRT's famously reticent operators could handle. The guys offered him a civil handshake on his way out, but that was all.

Another of the new Director's first initiatives involved cleaning up lingering doubt about the Bureau's ability to handle large-scale crises. When Freeh took over, HRT still fell under the administrative purview of the Washington Field Office. Negotiators and the behavioral assessment experts (profilers) in the Behavioral Sciences Unit worked for the Training Division at the Academy. Headquarters oversaw small, disparate specialty cells like the explosives unit and evidence response teams in the laboratory, as well as transportation specialists and logistical support.

The concept of adding integration to the business of crisis management hadn't really dawned on anyone at that point. When major events rolled around (and there hadn't been many), respective field divisions dealt with them by mustering whatever resources they could pull together. If things really got out of hand, they reached out through Headquarters to individual units such as the Hostage Rescue Team. Everyone brought their own toys. The fact that none of them talked to, interacted with, or understood each other didn't really seem to bother anyone.

Louis Freeh changed that, too.

In April 1994, after getting stung by a highly critical report from Congress, he formed an entirely new division called the Critical Incident Response Group (CIRG). This sort of thing just didn't happen very often within the FBI, and it turned a lot of heads. Field divisions work crime by geography. Headquarters divisions work crime by classification. Everything falls within carefully delineated realms of responsibility and prescribed territories.

The CIRG concept introduced a whole new way of looking at crisis management. No one had ever thought about starting a free-roaming band of hit-and-run specialists trained to fight high-profile crime wherever it occurred. Though it sounds like common sense now, it sounded like anathema then. The Critical Incident Response Group became the first outfit of its kind in civilian law enforcement.

In order to honcho this revolutionary idea through a skeptical and well-entrenched command structure, Freeh needed a personality of considerable strength. He found that in a hard-talking, head-banging former Marine named Frank Gleason, who recently had served as SAC of the Portland

Field Office. Gleason arrived April 19, 1994, a year to the day after the Branch Davidian fire, and started building the new office from scratch.

He pulled the negotiators and the tactical people together and laid down new ground rules. Law enforcement had changed since Mount Carmel went up in flames, he said. HRT would still get the call when the end of the world rolled around, but the FBI's new line of frontal attack would go straight through a negotiator's phone line. Negotiations almost never start fires or shoot the wrong person. Tactical operations were out. Talking was in. That's just the way it was.

To everyone's surprise, the concept thrived.

CIRG borrowed administrative office space from the Academy, pulled the negotiators and profilers up from the basement beneath the gun vault, dragged HRT out of their fenced-in compound, and made everyone shake hands. I remember how huge that first step felt. Even a year after Waco, I still had to turn around and walk the other way when I saw a negotiator coming at me, for fear that I might reach out and knock him on his ass. That sort of mentality was ridiculous, of course, but a fundamental lack of communication had kept us apart. Until that point, no one had ever sat down and talked about Waco or the distance that split tacticians and negotiators when we got back.

Cross training helped roof the walls. I joined most of the other operators in taking the Hostage Negotiations in-service. For two weeks, I sat in a classroom waiting for someone to fire up the warm soapy shower and start singing "Kumbaya." Never happened. Everything I saw and practiced made perfect sense. The negotiators wanted to put the bad guys in jail every bit as much as we did. The only difference was that they could do it without explosives, long-range-rifle fire, and helicopters. That sort of thinking does several things for an organization like the FBI: It saves money, limits the likelihood of agents' dying in the line of duty, and dovetails modern expectations of the American public.

Not everything about this new paradigm thrilled me. During the in-service, I listened to a presentation about a recent hostage situation in Hawaii. A very large Samoan had taken a very small hostage at gunpoint inside a building and threatened to kill him. The Samoan called his girlfriend and said he was going to kill him. He told the cops he was going to kill him. He called a radio station and told the entire listening audience that he was going to kill him. Then he started counting backward from 100 down to 1. When he got to the loneliest number, he was really going to kill him.

Street cops and tactical teams surrounded the building. Snipers took positions of cover. Everything went according to plan. Then the Samoan emerged into the parking lot with the muzzle of a shotgun taped to the poor bastard's neck. He started counting. Everybody with a gun pointed it at him. Snipers lined him up in their sights with clear shots at his brain stem. Instant neurological termination. No twitch. Easy pickings.

The negotiators talked, yelled, implored. The counting continued for more than two minutes.

"... nine ... eight ... seven ... six ..."

Suddenly, the hostage wrenched his head to the side and grabbed the shotgun barrel in both hands. The gun went off, blowing the tape off the guy's neck and freeing him from a follow-up coup de grâce. At that point, uniformed officers ran in and shot the Samoan to death in a hail of bullets.

The lights came up. The video ended. Everyone sighed. I raised my hand.

"When were we going to shoot him?" I asked.

The instructor looked at me strangely. "Shoot him?" The rest of the class sat silently in their chairs.

"Yeah, how far were you going to let the big guy count

down before our snipers whacked him? I mean, you had to know this guy was serious."

The instructor looked at me like I was nuts.

"Shoot him? We weren't going to shoot him. What if the shotgun had discharged accidentally? We would have been liable."

I realized at that point that I didn't want to be a hostage in the post-Waco era. Times had surely changed. When push comes to shove, this country still needs a bunch of heroes waiting to stand in the fire. We can speak softly all we want, but from time to time, it's still advisable to haul out that big stick.

In March 1997, word came down from Headquarters that the Director was planning a historic trip to the Middle East and needed someone to ride shotgun. I'd already traveled in fourteen countries, but the thought of an all-expenses-paid trip to the Holy Land struck me as a junket worth explaining to the kids.

International relations had not always been one of the Bureau's fortes to that point. When I first joined up, I still believed that the FBI worked within the United States, and the CIA worked the world. Not true. In addition to its fifty-six field offices around the country, the Bureau also maintains satellite offices or legal attachés (Legat) from Islamabad to Seoul. FBI agents, working closely with the State Department, carry jurisdiction in virtually any matter where an American suffers a criminal loss. With a shrinking globe and an expanding business environment, Americans are suffering losses in a whole lot more places.

Unfortunately, the Legat program had not grown to match consumer demand. Director Freeh recognized this problem early in his tenure and set about expanding the program to build new offices in dozens of developing countries. Establishing a new post in Tel Aviv made perfect sense, due to the threat of terrorism and the strategic importance of U.S.–Israeli relations. What really turned some heads, however, was his insistence on extending an olive branch to Yasser Arafat and his newly born Palestinian homeland. The trip's itinerary listed a courtesy call on PLO headquarters in the Gaza Strip. The fact that just a few years had passed since Arafat was considered a terrorist on par with Osama Bin Laden was lost on no one. The peace process was suffering daily failures at that time, and sending America's top crime fighter to the land of car bombs didn't make a whole lot of sense.

Regardless, once Louie Freeh set his mind on something, it usually happened. HRT got the protection detail, and immediately started planning for a whole new kind of mission. Up to that point, the Team's only state visits had included things like BR-1 hosting a shooting-house tour for the commissioner of the Philippine National Police.

Traveling overseas as an FBI agent is tricky. While on official business, we have to carry red passports which identify us immediately to foreign customs agents, as well as to curious terrorists. To make matters worse, we can't carry weapons. Agents are *required* by FBI policy and federal law to carry their handguns on domestic flights, but they can't climb on an international plane with so much as a pocketknife. I'd already learned that lesson the hard way.

Just six months earlier, I'd traveled to Rome as part of a six-man competition/training team. Our Italian counterparts were hosting a twentieth-anniversary celebration, and had invited counterterrorism teams from all over the world. The French GIGN came, along with the German GSG-9, and the Spaniards, Israelis, Brits. We jumped at the opportunity to show our wares.

The six of us drove up to National Airport, like we'd all

done a hundred times, and climbed on a Northwest 747 bound for points east. We looked the same as everyone else, except for the red passports in our pockets and the black Haliburton travel case we carried on and stowed in a stand-up closet. Inside that box rested six MP-5 submachine guns, half a dozen .45-caliber competition pistols, flash-bang grenades, and enough ammo to take on half of Europe. No one suspected a thing.

Members of the Italian NOX met us at the airport, whisked us through customs, and proceeded to show us two weeks of Rome's finest hospitality. Everything went like clockwork, from the flight, to the competitions, to the way we held our own with some of Europe's premier beer drinkers. Just for the record, nobody can hold a candle to the Germans. With the exception of an occasional nap on the bus to training sites, they never slowed down for thirteen days. And they shot like robots.

When it was over, the whole crew celebrated with a formal dinner and a bar crawl unlike anything I'd seen since my fraternity days. International relations is a sensitive process of tact and diplomacy, so we didn't want to make the FBI look bad. For five hours, we slammed, chugged, and guzzled everything any country could throw at us. I don't remember who won the overall competition, but I damned well know who won the party.

We finished just in time for a convoy of carabinieri to shuttle us to the airport and rubber stamp us through customs. A shy, introspective NOX operator named Primo badged us through the gate and escorted us to our seats. The box of guns went into the closet, just like before. There was no paper or discussion with the pilot. No conference with the flight attendants. No one on board seemed to have any idea at all what we'd just carried on. At that point, none of us cared. This was Italy and they seemed comfortable with the arrangement. When in Rome, do as the Romans do, right?

Wrong. About an hour after takeoff, the plane started its descent into Geneva, Switzerland. The flight attendant told us that we, in fact, had not boarded a nonstop hitch to Washington. We had to deplane and switch aircraft.

Oh shit.

Our options seemed pretty limited at that point. The only thing we could do was wait until the entire plane emptied out, then grab our carry-on luggage, including the doomsday box, and head for our connecting flight. Unfortunately, the plane unloaded all passengers out on the tarmac, so we had to drag our box of guns into the airport and through a bank of metal detectors to get to the next flight. That's where things started to look glum.

None of us spoke Swiss or French or whatever the hell they were jabbering at us. We had no paperwork explaining our official status or our cargo. The box in our possession held what to the uneducated eye would have looked like a do-it-yourself hijacking kit, and we were severely hungover.

After about twenty minutes, one of the security supervisors approached us and explained something about airport protocol. At least that's what I think he said. All I knew was that he looked pretty pissed when none of us moved.

We tried to explain our situation in sign language without creating a panic, but the Swiss pay no one to be patient. He wanted us out of the hallway and through the metal detectors, now. There was no arguing the point.

Finally, we did what any self-respecting FBI agent would do in a situation like that. We badged him. He looked at us like we were nuts. FBI doesn't mean a whole lot to an airport guard in Geneva. Louis Freeh and his international expansion initiative hadn't really caught on there yet.

Two hours and some very tenuous moments later, we got

the box through Swiss customs, and onto a flight to Reagan National. After all the yelling and broken English, we ended up shaking hands and exchanging phone numbers. Cops find a way to work things out. All except for Primo, that is. I have no doubt that the poor bastard hit the bricks on his ass a short time later, trying to find work as a taxi driver.

Armed with that experience, HRT hired charter aircraft to ferry the Blue section and all its gear from Quantico to Tel Aviv. Four X-Ray snipers and several members of Hotel team climbed aboard a private Gulfstream G-4 executive jet and set out for Israel, via refueling stops in Gander, Newfoundland, and Shannon, Ireland. Seven of us rode first class on the chartered plane, enjoying the leather seats, finger sandwiches, and fully stocked bar.

"Ain't this some shit?" Antman grunted. As a former Army Ranger, he was used to canvas bench seats in a C-141. Missions weren't the only thing looking up for HRT. The way we got to them was improving, too.

The Middle East struck me as a world away from anything I'd seen before. The drive from Tel Aviv to Jerusalem gave us a fascinating look at a country defined by war. Burned-out tanks from the Ten-Day War sat at the side of the road as reminders of the threat that country faces every day. Military vehicles and soldiers popped up everywhere, just part of the scenery. Everyone carried a gun, from the sixteen-year-old tour guides at the Wailing Wall to the army sentries at bus stops.

After two days of preparations, HRT locked down a hotel near the old city and made preparations for the Director's arrival. We rented an entire floor of rooms, posted sentries at all points of entry, mapped out medical evacuation routes, cleared protocol with the ambassador's office, checked all travel stops, and met with Israeli security agencies. By the time the Boss arrived, we'd covered virtually every imaginable contingency from how to honor the Sabbath to where he could get the best deal on a set of rosary beads.

What we didn't count on was Louie Freeh's uncompromising discipline. As an avid runner, he didn't want to miss his morning workout, so just three hours after he arrived, at five o'clock in the morning, we hastily put together a four-mile route, strapped on the Nikes, and hit the pavement.

Twenty-one hours later, after a full day of meetings, business lunches, formal dinners, courtesy calls, and visits to holy sites, we whisked him back to the hotel to wrap up the day. It all flew by in a frenzy of motorcade traffic, guard duty, and language barriers. What amazed me was how well he handled the jet lag, lack of sleep, and the general frenetic nature of the official visit. All we had to do was watch for trouble and drive. He had to talk government business with high-ranking officials, pimp his new Legat initiative, and try to look interested.

The really impressive part came at the end of the trip, when he ordered food and Heineken for the whole crew. Lots of bosses write letters of commendation or throw around bonuses. Not many of them toss back a cold one with the boys at two o'clock in the morning after a long day of shaking hands with prime ministers.

I don't know what kind of impression he left with the Israelis, but he damned sure left a mark on us.

"Can I get you a cup of tea?" A tall, skinny Arab sporting Vietnam-era fatigues, vinyl zipper boots, and a Marlboro belt cocked his head, awaiting my reply. He also wore a red beret, two days' growth of beard, and some serious body odor. A Soviet-made AK-47 with a collapsible stock dangled from his right hand. Even indoors, his finger rested on the trigger.

"Sure," I said, "that would be nice."

After three days with the Israelis, we pointed our motorcade east toward the Gaza Strip. PLO headquarters.

Our protection detail performed like clockwork within Jerusalem, but no one knew what to expect once we left Israel and ventured into Gaza. To the uneducated eye, we may have looked impressive, but car bombs and suicide gunmen are a much greater concern in that part of the world than in ours, and a dozen men armed with MP-5 submachine guns and .45-caliber pistols aren't much of a match for state-sponsored terrorism.

Fortunately, the detail worked flawlessly. X-Ray snipers rode point in a black Suburban as we raced from one meeting to another. The Director, a guest or two, and three personal security operators rode in the middle vehicle. A blocking vehicle pulled up the rear with four more heavily armed operators aboard.

On top of that, we sent advance teams to all sites and coordinated routes with Israeli security specialists who provided everything from intelligence reports to police escort. As any security specialist knows, the guys with sunglasses and lapel mics are mostly for show. If a bad guy gets close enough that protection detail needs to get dirty, someone else has fucked up. The real security on a jaunt like this takes place behind the scenes, where the average person wouldn't think to look.

On day four, we gathered up the Director, fired up the Suburbans, and headed out to Yasser's place for a little chat. Though not a great distance by car, Gaza is at least one world removed from modern Jerusalem. In order to get there, you have to pass through a no-man's-land buffer zone between two groups of people who have killed each other for thousands of years.

Our Israeli escorts dropped us off at the west gate to the

border crossing and left us to our own devices. The Palestinians picked us up on the other side in Jeeps topped with belt-fed machine guns. Johnny drove. Eddie sat up front. Buck and Antman and I sat in the back with the subguns.

Though just a rocket-propelled grenade's attack away from Israel, Gaza might as well have been a parallel universe. I felt like we'd entered some kind of time portal. Within half a kilometer, we moved from European luxury to pony carts and camels. Leather-skinned men in traditional garb tended garbage fires along the sides of what could be called roads. Filthy little kids played in mud puddles and threw rocks at stray dogs as our motorcade of black Chevy Suburbans and Peugeots raced toward the sea at eighty miles an hour. Yasser's tour guides led us through every street in the city, sirens blaring, horns blasting, announcing that America had come to him this time, and recognized his authority.

I'm not sure what I expected PLO headquarters would look like, but even my fervent imagination couldn't have done this place justice. Yasser Arafat's new seat of government looked nothing like the White House or 10 Downing Street or Red Square. PLO headquarters was a rather trendy-looking two-story beach house with an ocean view. The Mediterranean stretched out the western wall, filling the sliding glass doors with a magnificent seascape of cerulean skies and small fishing skiffs drifting in a midday breeze. Neighbor buildings outside ranged from new construction to entire blocks of rubble.

My shock at the architecture paled by comparison to my surprise at the hospitality extended by the Palestinian security forces. Our Israeli hosts had barely spoken to us, despite their excellent English. The State Department had warned us prior to departure that the Israelis would toss our drawers when we left our rooms, follow our every off-duty move, and install mics and television cameras wherever possible. I didn't really believe the warnings at first, but standing in a service corridor one night, outside a diplomatic dinner, my impressions changed. I waited there for three hours, just an arm's length from an Israeli bodyguard who spoke perfect English. We shared the same duty, protecting bosses who sought common ground. Our countries are close allies. Three hours, he stared straight at me. Never said a word.

The Palestinians, however, made a point of offering every courtesy, from tea and biscuits to friendly warnings that the volleyball court out back would be a poor place to stretch our legs. Though it looked placid enough, running down to the ancient sea, it was actually a minefield. Yasser Arafat hadn't lasted all these years by sunning himself while his people played beach games. Though this seaside bungalow would look quite nice along Malibu's billion-dollar coast, it was just another place Arafat didn't dare stay too long.

X-Ray snipers waited patiently as the bosses met upstairs. Eddie, Buck, Antman, and I sat on two brocade couches facing each other in the middle of the room. A table leaned against the wall to my left. A vase of plastic flowers colored the otherwise blank walls. There was no other furniture.

Mr. Arafat arrived minutes later in a black 600 series Mercedes sporting an AMG package, gold hubcaps, and a Dukes of Hazzard spoiler on the back. The only difference between it and an East St. Louis pimpmobile was the small Palestinian flags flying left and right of the gold three-point hood ornament.

His personal security detail wore anything they could throw together. Their uniforms consisted of a vague theme in olive drab and lots of quarter-grown beards.

"Can you believe this place?" Buck asked me. "We're in PLO headquarters, drinking tea with Yasser Arafat. Five years ago, they would have given us a medal to grease these assholes."

Our machine-gun-toting host returned just as Buck finished shaking his head. He handed me a demitasse filled with gritty liquid and motioned me to drink.

"This stuff's pretty tasty, huh?" Antman asked. It put Starbucks to shame.

Johnny came in from the hallway outside and sat beside us.

"You won't believe this," he said. The look on his face piqued my interest.

"Believe what?"

"See that guy over there?" He pointed to one of the AK-toting PLO soldiers pulling a black plastic garbage bag across the floor. "You know what he's got in there?"

It looked heavy, but I had no guess about its contents.

"Money. It's full of cash. American."

"Huh?" I asked. Something about the place reeked of absurdity, from the volleyball court minefield to the pimped-out Benz and the guard wearing a red and white Marlboro belt. Now some guy was pulling a bag of greenbacks across the floor like he was taking out the garbage.

"What the hell's he doing with that?"

"He told me Arafat's going to Russia after we're done," Johnny whispered. "I guess being a new country is kind of tough. They don't have their own currency. They don't have any credit."

"No shit," Antman chimed in. "Kind of like having a ticket you can't use, huh?"

That's when I remembered another experience with a Palestinian. My mind slipped back to a crowded train, twenty years earlier, during my junior year abroad. A nosy Palestinian sat next to me as we rattled toward the Basque, trying to pass on one of those prescient truths fortunate souls find once in a lifetime. How could he have known that I'd end up here, lost since my Waco experience, without a clue where to look for answers? How could he have foreseen something so utterly absurd?

I slumped in the couch and shook my head at the irony. Almost two decades had turned since I sat on that train, but they came back to me in a moment.

"Where are you from?" the old man asked.

I was nearly done with *Doctor Faustus* — I'd come to the part where Mephistopheles returns for Faustus's unrepentant soul. It just seemed like a poor time for conversation.

"You look American."

American? I hadn't eaten a bite of food in more than two days. My clothes resembled something out of a Goodwill grab bag. My hair hung almost to my shoulders in a painfully Caucasian attempt at dreadlocks. On top of that, I smelled like a pungent mixture of wet leather and bad cheese. I didn't look American. I probably didn't even look completely human.

"Yes, American," I said.

If it weren't for the fact that I'd waited six hours to get that seat, I would have bolted for some peace and quiet.

"I'm Palestinian," he said, suggesting a little pride. He stared forward when he talked.

Palestinian meant nothing to me. As an English major studying Elizabethan drama, I went to great lengths to avoid matters so pedestrian as international affairs. As far as I was concerned, the only politics worth discussing died with the Tudors in 1603. Unless this guy wanted to talk about dream allegory in *The Tempest,* I didn't have time to bother with him.

"I'm sorry, but I don't really know what that means," I confessed.

He continued to stare straight ahead, clutching a black and white Adidas bag between his legs.

"It means getting on this train at night and waking up in the morning with no place to go."

No place to go? I was a twenty-year-old college kid working his way home to London after a five-week tour of Europe. As far as I was concerned, "no place to go" meant the bars were all closed.

I looked him over, now that he'd interrupted my moment. The white stubble on his chin stood out in stark contrast to his deeply tanned skin, which glowed in the evening sun with the texture of lap embroidery.

"Could we talk about this later?" I held up the book to show that I was almost finished.

He nodded dejectedly and stared out the window as the long flatland between Barcelona and the Basque flashed behind us.

"American," he mumbled.

I read the next scene three times before my sense of nationalist pride pushed Mephistopheles out the window and forced me to engage.

"You got some kind of problem with that?"

I didn't want to pick a fight with an old man, but despite my appearance, I felt somehow obligated to defend my country.

"No problem. You read your Marlowe and tell me what you've learned when you finish. We have a long night together, you and I."

Excellent English. Reasonably well read. Open challenge. Okay, he had me.

"What did you mean by that?" I asked.

He shrugged his shoulders and stared out into the passing

idyll. This old man struck me as lonely, bored, and disillusioned, in that order. Unfortunately, he was also spoiling for distraction: me.

"Really, I want to know," I said. "You say you are Palestinian. I don't know what that means. I've never woken up with no place to go. Why don't you tell me?"

I spat the words at him. Now he had to bite.

"It means sitting down next to a wise-ass teenager who thinks he's seen the world and knowing that no matter what I say or do or wish or believe, I'll never have the opportunity you have today. Not in the rest of my life."

Whew. I took a deep breath and regrouped. I was no rich kid, by any stretch of the imagination, but I'd never wanted for anything, either. Though I imagined myself the starving poet, I could have solved most any problem with a simple phone call home. Perhaps it was just that lifeline that gave me the courage to hang my toes over one foolish adventure after another.

Spring vacation, midway through my junior year abroad, had started as a lark. Most of my friends had flown off to Greece during the Easter break for an Aegean romp. Knowing I had a grand total of $200 to last me through the five-week holiday, I declined their demands to join them and did the only logical thing. I spent $110 on a train pass that would provide unlimited travel throughout Europe, then tucked the other $90 in the front pocket of my faded jeans and headed for the Continent.

The train ticket provided coach lodging and transportation as long as I wanted to stay on board, but there were no taxi rides, museum admissions, beer garden tours, or hot meals included. If I wanted to see Europe, I'd have to make it on fumes.

No problem. I worked my way up through the north of Europe and down through Germany to the Mediterranean. I arrived in Monaco with the equivalent of about $150 in my pocket, feeling very industrious for having raised money with my guitar at the Marienplatz in Munich, the underground in Zurich, and numerous other smaller venues along the way.

Though lonely, my trip felt like great adventure. I had nearly drowned myself at the Hofbrau Haus with all the other tourists, slept with fleas on fetid mattresses and showered with hairy-legged Scandinavian girls, gotten kicked off the train in Italy, been thrown up against a wall and slapped around by Louvre guards in Paris and run out of the Eiffel Tower before I could climb it and lay claim to Europe's grandest spire. Andy Tabbott and I would never have imagined, all those years before, that someone would put up screening to keep madmen from jumping off. I remember staring out over Notre Dame and the Arc de Triomphe, mourning the fact that there was no way I was ever going to get my toes over any of those magnificent trusses.

Near the end of the third week, I took a small, sparsely furnished room in Torremolinos, overlooking the Mediterranean through shuttered windows with no glass. The old city reached down to the Costa del Sol, with winding, narrow streets of white stucco and red tile. Northern Europeans traipsed through tourist shops while whole families of Gypsies worked the streets, selling trinkets, running shell games, and begging. Brilliant smells wafted out of local kitchens, enticing me with tastes I couldn't afford.

I wandered, just the same, through the crowded streets, living at the edge of a poet's bacchanalia, thriving on the energy. I spent the days swimming and lying in the sun and the nights writing short stories with pencils and paper purloined from the front desk. The sounds of KC and the Sunshine Band drifted down from clubs on the hill, inciting the feral cats who fought over trash piles in the alleys behind me.

Sometimes they interrupted my dreams long enough for me to open the shutters and drink deep breaths of the same sea breeze that powered Cleopatra's barges and Odysseus's warships.

This was the most perfect place I had ever visited. If I could have written my entire life in that place, nothing would ever have changed. But of course it did. I ran out of money — really completely out of money. I broke two strings on my guitar trying to raise more and couldn't even afford to replace them. The friends I'd made left for other sunsets. It was time to go.

So I threw my last few pesetas into a filthy shawl near one of the Gypsy beggars, knowing the crumbs they would buy me couldn't help for long. And then I walked to the station and boarded a train headed north for London.

I spent the first night standing, watching grape fields and ancient farmhouses pass by the open windows in a slow, unruly stupor. The Spanish military moved its troops by commercial rail, and it seemed like everyone with a uniform wanted to return home on the same day. Soldiers with entire families, young tourists, and smug commuters all pressed belly to back in passenger cars built to accommodate half as many. I leaned against the walls of the narrow hallways until someone pushed through, then wrestled my day pack and guitar case out of the way. Eventually the hypnotic rhythm of steel wheels on wooden ties carried me back into my trance.

The train rambled north through Barcelona, past the turnoff to Catalonia, where Orwell wrote of dreaming about a cup of coffee during the Spanish Civil War. I felt his longing as mothers unwrapped huge home-cooked meals for their families, spilling torturous smells and sights among those of us who had nothing.

And so I found myself sitting next to this Palestinian at

three in the morning, lost in contemplation of the life that had brought me to him.

"Look, I'm sorry," I said. "Let's start over. You got me at a really important part of this book, and I . . ."

"Books never lose the moment," he sputtered, "but conversations come and go or they're lost forever."

Great, a philosopher. He shuffled the bag in his lap and turned to face me.

"You like your books. Maybe you fancy yourself a writer, huh? Well, let me pose you a question and I won't bother you any more."

I nodded. Though I hadn't noticed at first, this man wore a tarnished refinement, like a finely made blazer paraded through just a few too many parties. Something about the way he carried himself suggested a lifetime I needed to know more about.

"Shoot."

"Jalal ad-Din Rumi was a thirteenth-century mystic poet. Persian. Do you know him?"

I shook my head.

"He wrote about many things wonderful, but one of my favorite characters of his is a bit of a rogue called Nezradene. Nezradene is ready to set out on a great journey one day, but he can't find his ticket. He looks everywhere — under his bed, in his drawers, through his letters. Nothing.

"'But Nezradene,' one of his friends interrupts, 'why don't you look in your coat pocket? That's where you usually keep your most important things.'

"Nezradene shakes his head and rubs his exasperated eyes.

"'I know,' he says, 'but if I look and it isn't there, I'll be just devastated.'"

The old man smiled. I smiled. Good story.

"So what's my question?" I asked.

"You're a young man consumed with young man's things. One day you'll grow older and find yourself looking for something you've lost. So where do you look? Do you search in circles for all the places you might find it? Or do you tempt irrecoverable loss by going straight to the one spot you know it should be? One quest is easy. The other is hard. All because of consequence. When you invest all your trust in one solution and your trust goes missing, you have nothing else to fall back on but despair."

He shrugged his shoulders and stared me straight in my eyes.

"How much do you believe in your own sense of destiny?" he asked. "Where do you look?"

The question stuck in my mind, framed by sleep deprivation and a complete lack of the life experience necessary to answer. Suddenly, Faustus's perdition took a back seat to my own sense of fate.

"Don't try to answer it now," he said. "Life is perspective, and perspectives change. Some day you'll wake up in a world without reference and feel lost. That's when you'll remember me." He whispered in perfect English and smiled through rotten teeth.

"That's when you'll remember."

"You all right?" Antman asked. "Looks like that tea is making you sick."

I stared across the room at men who had dedicated their entire lives to an organization that even now had to pay for diplomatic travel with another country's currency. I remembered that train from Torremolinos and what an old man told me about standing up to the consequences of failure.

The years since Waco flashed in front of me in less time than it takes me to write it here. In that moment, I remembered what it was that made me join the FBI to begin with. Justice. A cause. If that cause is not meaningful enough to withstand the test of a couple falls, then it isn't worth investing your life in. You can't just give up and die the first time someone knocks you down.

At that moment I realized how I'd lost myself.

It didn't really have much to do with Waco or Ruby Ridge or this trip to the Middle East. It had to do with me. I'd stood too long in the HRT model of invincibility. Selection bred it. NOTS grew it. Years on the Team made it part of my inner self. But invincibility is just a myth. Sometimes the strongest men fail, even with the best intentions.

God has given me many gifts. One of them is weakness. Another is the ability to accept it.

"Yeah, I'm fine." I told Antman. "I just found something I've been looking for for a long while."

"What, another crossword puzzle?" He started to laugh.

I saw no reason to explain. Life's deepest revelations are hard to share.

22

BACK
TO BASICS

In May 1997, after nearly six years on HRT, I walked into Roger's office, sat down in a red leather chair, and called it quits. I had nothing left to prove with a rifle.

Every operator has his reasons for leaving. Mine seemed simple enough. I had already outlasted all but one member of my NOTS generation. My family had suffered through more than I cared to think about. I had just turned thirty-eight years of age in a world designed for younger bodies, and chronic problems with my back and shoulder made the physical commitment tougher every day.

Most important, I still felt that burning desire I'd first discovered looking down from the viewers' gallery in the House of Representatives more than a decade earlier. I wanted to make a difference in society, to wake up in the morning with a sense that I was doing something tangibly good. Working cases had never really fulfilled that desire, because I'd let the virtually limitless dimensions of crime overpower me. Serving on HRT left me unfulfilled to a certain extent also, because I realized more and more that saving lives is a whole lot more complicated than bursting through a door with a brave heart and a lot of cool toys. Besides, politics was rapidly becoming HRT's fifty-first member.

I knew that I still had something to offer, and that the next step lay beyond the realm of Flexlinear door charges and ceramic trauma plates. There had to be something else.

My decision came one morning as I shot 200-yard movers on a Marine Corps rifle range. I simply pulled the trigger, cycled the bolt, and realized that it was over. Just like that. No bells or whistles or soul searching. The call felt as natural as if I'd just decided to mow the lawn. I'd punched holes in enough targets. After six years, all that talk about marching in with a ball bat to kick ass and take names just seemed kind of foolish. It was time to move on.

Accepting the decision and calling it easy are two different things. I'd watched other guys stand up at their final morning meeting and make their good-byes. Big strong men choked down the emotion that came with swearing off the biggest single achievement in their lives. HRT operators bond like valences, in a world that stands two or three steps removed from the commonplace. Most come to the Team at their absolute physical peak. Breaking away means more than saying good-bye to a job; it means saying good-bye to a stage in your life. It means admitting age.

I didn't fully understand the ramifications when I went to Roger with my decision. All I knew was that it was time.

"All right, where do you want to go?" he asked. Roger Blake is one of those rare leaders who respond to challenge as opportunity. He'd already helped a dozen or more of my old teammates find gainful employment after HRT. Now it was my turn.

Unfortunately, the decision to leave the Team had struck so swiftly, I hadn't thought much about where I wanted to go. Diversity of assignment is one of the Bureau's greatest strengths, but I didn't really know where next to direct my energies.

The possibilities seemed endless. Though every Special Agent starts out working cases, career paths can take a three-year veteran anywhere from a door-knocker slot on a field SWAT team to DNA research in the FBI laboratory. Agents can accumulate expertise in more than three hundred criminal classifications, or sign up for coordinator duty in behavioral assessment, legal, negotiations, recruitment, media, Equal Employment Opportunity, or counseling programs, among others.

Those who want to work their way up the career ladder can apply for field supervisor jobs, overseas assignments in the legal attaché program, inspection duty, or a tour at Headquarters. Anyone who can't find something that interests him in the FBI job pool just isn't swimming hard enough.

I had lots of options. Several SWAT team leader jobs waited around the country. Grabbing one of those wouldn't have been difficult. If I'd wanted to try the career development path, I could have found something at Headquarters. Raz and Matty and Scarhead had already paved inroads for us up there. The commute would have sucked, but at least it would have been more money.

If worse came to worst, I could always burn my office-of-preference transfer and take my one-time pass to a retirement office virtually anywhere I wanted to go. The FBI tries to offer senior agents one discretionary transfer to let them settle someplace closer to home, and with ten years on the job, I qualified.

None of those choices really jumped out at me. When I drew a blank, Roger suggested a teaching job across the street at the Academy. He knew I'd taught high school English at a Massachusetts boarding school, and he knew about my media and public speaking experience on Capitol Hill. On top of that, he knew the chief of the Law Enforcement Communications Unit and felt comfortable calling him for a favor. Regardless of what party-line bureaucrats will try to argue, the FBI career path is an old-boy network. The only trick to advancement is figuring out how to be an "old boy."

"Academy?" I asked.

The idea hadn't really occurred to me. On HRT I'd taught FBI agents everything from SWAT tactics and combat marksmanship to photography and sniper craft, but none of those courses appeared in any Academy curriculum. Moving from a Nomex flight suit in the shooting house to pinstripes in a lecture hall seemed like a pretty challenging leap.

"Give it a shot," Roger said. "You two are a perfect match. You just don't know it yet."

Rose and I talked it over that night. No more road trips. Banker's hours. A GS-14 promotion to supervisor with about $3,000 more paycheck every year. I'd lose my government car and have to replace the suits that I hadn't pulled off the hanger in more than half a decade, but the benefits seemed obvious.

Besides that, I had always enjoyed teaching. A good friend of mine on Delta had just moved to their training cadre, to "recharge the batteries" after surviving the famous street war in Mogadishu, Somalia. If it was good enough for him, it had to be good enough for me.

Six months later, I found myself standing in classroom 211 — the very same place I'd started my own FBI career ten years earlier — teaching interview and interrogation techniques to a New Agent Training Class. Their enthusiasm awakened me.

Though the fact was not widely advertised, the FBI

stopped hiring new agents for two years during the early 1990s. When they opened the doors again, in the wake of the Branch Davidian standoff, entrance requirements had changed. Incoming Director Louis Freeh still required applicants to sit for a written examination and a standardized interview panel, but the overall format had evolved considerably.

Applicants now have to take a polygraph as part of their comprehensive background investigation. This added scrutiny has been offset by a loosening of drug restrictions. Because many of President Clinton's political appointees couldn't gain security clearances under the old policy, the executive branch eased the rules to allow use of virtually any illegal substance as long as it occurred more than seven years prior to application.

What the Bureau ended up with in 1994 was a remarkably accomplished wave of new agents, and lots of them. The first New Agent Class I taught included lawyers, accountants, linguists, military academy graduates, pilots, academics, business executives, even a forensic psychiatrist. Every one of them had traded a career of accomplishment to vest himself in the same altruism I'd felt a lifetime ago. Every one of them stared wide-eyed into a life that would change him as much as it had changed me.

"Guy comes up to the office the other day, looking for a job," I said, introducing myself to the class. "So I ask him if he has any qualifications — you know like lawyer, CPA, minority status. But the guy shakes his head and says, 'No. In fact, I'm disabled.' "

I doubt my introduction to FBI humor packed the same punch Ray Venable's did in that Kansas City bathroom. But then again, there's only one Ray Venable.

From that moment on, forty-seven new believers and I dove into a seventy-five-hour course on the art of interview/interrogation and the detection of deception. To the casual observer, this might not seem terribly exciting compared to midnight helicopter assaults on ships under way. But then again, most people don't know much about the thrill of manipulating human behavior.

The FBI and certain other intelligence-gathering agencies have become proficient over the years in the field of behavioral assessment. They have studied developments in everything from proxemics (manipulation of interpersonal space) to neurolinguistic programming (studying eye movement) and rolled those elements into a very effective means of influencing behavior. By finding commonality in human behavior, we can convince people to do things they might not otherwise do, like tell the truth.

This isn't some top secret mind alteration process dreamed up in a military lab. This is a commonsense amalgam of physiology, operant conditioning, and good old-fashioned intuition. If you learn it well and focus properly, you can ferret out deception and get people to tell you just about anything they've ever done.

Magicians know this process, as do hypnotists, car salesmen, and real estate agents. They understand that human beings give off all kinds of indicators without even realizing it. They also realize that getting people to give you what you want can be very rewarding.

I started one of my classes with a favorite example. My sophomore year in college, a well-known illusionist and psychic came to school to put on a show. As chairman of the programming committee, it was my job to pay him. I sat in the audience with my mouth open as he read minds, bent spoons with the stroke of a finger, and performed other amazing feats. When he was through, he walked to the edge of the stage and announced that his last trick of the night would be the most difficult. We, as an audience, could hide his paycheck anywhere in the theater. If he couldn't find it, we wouldn't have to pay him.

"I've got to see this," I mumbled. I had his rather large payday in my pocket and he was going to have to get past me to collect it.

Two of my buddies accompanied him to the green room in the basement and stood guard. I took the check and gave it to another trustworthy friend sitting in the bleachers. He slipped it under his baseball cap. All two thousand people in the room knew where it was, but my friends downstairs made certain the performer never saw or heard a thing.

Up he came.

"First I need a helper," he announced.

He chose a person in the audience and told the student (whom I also knew) to walk where he directed him. With that, the two ambled around the room for a few minutes, eventually finding their way to my buddy in the ball cap. As everyone looked on in silence, the performer waved his hand over the baffled check holder and stopped.

"I believe you have something that belongs to me," he said. With that, he reached out, removed the cap, and collected his check.

Twenty years later, the FBI taught me how he did it.

"Did you ever play Red Light, Green Light when you were a kid?" one of my colleagues asked me my first week in the Law Enforcement Communications Unit. "What we do here is just about the same thing, only we get our feedback in a slightly more subtle way."

I got it. In the children's game, the other players use words to tell you you're getting close. In the adult game, the clues come wrapped in layers of subterfuge. Sometimes a criminal wants to confess, but just doesn't dare. Guilt wears on him subconsciously, to the point where he gives off clues that can lead you to a confession. Unwrapping truth from this cloak of deception is no different from finding a check in a crowded auditorium. All you have to know is how and where to look.

The FBI version of this trick starts in a classroom with an instructor and a bunch of skeptical students.

"What I'm going to teach you here you already know," I told my classes. "Most of you can tell when someone is lying to you. In your old lives, this might have led to an argument or some kind of dispute. In this business, it has to lead to a conviction. Our goal is to work past suspicion to confession."

I started by explaining that most humans lie poorly. No matter how hard we try to disguise deception, we still give off clues of doubt, fear, or stress that can be read with proper training. That's how that magician earned his living. First he established a baseline, so he'd know what to expect from his audience in terms of behavior.

How do they act when they feel calm and unthreatened? he asked himself. His two-hour performance gave him all the time he needed to jerk people around in circles. Set up a trick and everyone perches quietly on the edge of their seats. Resolve it and watch them collapse in applause and amazement. How do they sit? When do they move? What expressions do they show? From the stage, he had a perfect view.

Next, he created a sense of consequence to stimulate behavioral anomalies. By setting up a contest between the audience and himself, with a substantial check hanging in the balance, he gave every member of that audience a reason to get involved.

Finally, he needed a human divining rod: someone who knew where the check was hidden. Someone who would tense up when he got close to it and relax when he walked away. The rest the performer did himself, using skills refined to the point where he got paid $10,000 a night to show them off.

The more that audience tried to keep him away from that check, the more they pointed the way. He had them right where he wanted them from the time he walked through the door.

"If you want to succeed in this business, you've got to learn to understand interpersonal dynamics," I told my classes. "Don't worry, we're still going to give you a gun and all the ammo you can shoot. Just bear with me a little while, and we might get to the point where you can avoid using it."

We began with listening. Most people process thousands of bits of information each day without really paying attention to any of it. We focus on what interests us and on what offers us direct benefit. Everything else, we put off or shut off with subtle gestures, like a shake of the head, a rubbing of the eyes, or an outright "Look, I just don't have time for this right now."

The net result is a culture that hears and tolerates but never actually listens. FBI agents need to know the difference.

That sensitivity begins with an open-ended question, the kind that can't be answered with a yes or no. Let the person talk. Mirror his behavior without being obvious, affirm what he says with a nod of the head or a subtle smile.

"Show them you give a damn about what they have to say and eventually, they'll tell you anything you want to know."

I told them the story of a Southwest Missouri State University student who claimed to have seen a man running from a building and yelling that he had just planted a bomb. We evacuated the campus, and called in an Army bomb unit from Fort Leonard Wood. After talking to the witness for an hour or so, I realized that his answers didn't add up. Something sounded wrong.

After I'd listened and agreed and consoled until I was sick to my stomach, he finally took a deep breath and said, "Okay, man, you got me. There's no bomb. I just didn't want to take that test."

Never asked him a single question. I just let him talk his way through it.

"An interview is a conversation with a purpose," I told my classes. "And our purpose, as an investigative agency, is to gather information. Ask a question properly and you can put the devil himself on the ropes. Screw up once, and you might as well become the applicant coordinator."

From there, it always degenerated to war stories of personal experience. I resurrected tales about Karen the extraterrestrial orgasm victim, Red Ryder 749, James and Billy Jenks, Bobby Matthews, and a dozen others just as memorable. I told them about things that aren't in any curriculum, like how I got a bank robber to confess by convincing him that our lab could chemically peel the mask off his face in the surveillance camera photos.

"You can't do that," he said.

"Of course we can," I argued. "How do you think we busted Al Capone?" Hey, the Constitution offers no specific protections for morons.

Contrary to what we tell Congress in our budget proposals, very few of the FBI's greatest achievements have come down to high-dollar technical devices or high-speed tactics. The biggest convictions can usually be traced to one or two exceptional agents who knew how to influence behavior with a couple of basic techniques and a good rap.

Getting what you want in a conversation begins with good preparation. Checking criminal histories, informant information, FBI files, NCIC warrants, and other basic background can make or break the day. To illustrate my point I recounted a background investigation I once conducted on a new agent applicant. Cases like these are way too boring to spend much time on, so I skipped the preparation part and went out to knock it down on my way to lunch.

Thirty minutes later, I found myself staring down the barrel of a .30-06 bolt gun, into the delusional eyes of a whacked-out meth queen. She kept yelling, "Fuck you, Frank! Fuck you!"

A little preparation would have revealed that the woman I was looking for had moved out. The new tenant — the one with the rifle — had just celebrated her release from a halfway house with a speedball and a bottle of muscatel. That apparently made her paranoid about some guy named Frank, which sucked for me, because she thought I was Frank.

Fortunately, this Frank was trained in the Big Al school of personal defense. Talking isn't the solution to every crisis.

Step two in the interview process is a firm handshake, good eye contact, and some humanity. Benny taught me that on a stolen truck case out of Neosho, Missouri. Two brothers had made a living out of boosting reefer trailers and chopping them up for the salvage weight of their aluminum. When we took them down, Benny waited for the hottest day of the summer, then let his personality walk. Something about a blue suit and an Arkansas drawl just seemed to hammer the locals.

"Too hot for fishing, ain't it, boys," he said. They knew he was FBI, just by the way he held his shoulders. "I damned sure don't know why you work so hard at stealing when there's good money in honest labor."

I think they confessed just to get out of the midday sun.

Third step: rapport. I learned the art of small talk from a legendary detective with the Springfield Police Department named Truly Ashton. Sporting a name like Truly, a man either learns the art of self-deprecation or commits himself to a career making floral arrangements at the local Food Lion.

"Hello, my name is Truly," he'd say, introducing himself to the toughest felon. "I know what you're thinking, but I love my momma just the same."

Never saw a bad guy that didn't break out in a smile. From there on, he had them by the short hairs. Crime fighting isn't always serious.

Questioning is the meat and potatoes of law enforcement work, but it adds up to no more than step number four in the overall process. You want to focus on the facts, then prod a little around the edges, looking to see where they flinch. No one asked questions like Big Al. Every once in a while he stooped to physical persuasion, but most times he relied on creative phrasing and a good old-fashioned taunt.

One morning he and I took down a trio of bank robbers in a local five-star called the Silver Saddle Motel. Two brothers, one wife. The details . . . well, they were pretty gross.

We took the woman down to the police department, which had better interview rooms, and gave her a chair. After letting her stew for a minute or two, Al turned her over to me, hoping I'd land my first real confession. When I entered the room, I found a 5'2" Cruella sitting lotus position in a swivel-back morris chair. Her hair hung down in front of her face, halfway to the floor.

"Hi, I'm Chris Whitcomb with the FBI," I said. "I'd like to talk to you about the bank robbery earlier today." That pretty much ran the gamut of my experience with interviewing. I still spoke with a little too much New England accent to pass as down-home.

Not a word in response. She never even told me her name.

After an hour or so on the ropes, I gave up and handed off the baton. Big Al slapped me on the back and pulled the door closed behind him. He emerged twenty minutes later, looking for a pen and paper to take her written statement.

"How the hell did you do that?" I asked. "I never got through the hair."

"She's a simple little thing," he said, struggling with his eternally untucked shirttails. "All it took to lure her out was one question."

"What was that?"

"Well, it's pretty obvious she's humping both o' them boys. I just asked her who got to climb on top first, the one carrying the gun or the one driving the getaway car."

Crime fighting isn't always delicate, either.

Unfortunately, law enforcement doesn't net a whole lot of veracity. When an interview leads to answers that don't make sense or to just a bad feeling in your gut, you might decide to move on to that bright-light-in-the-middle-of-the-empty-room favorite: the interrogation.

Interrogation is an enormously gratifying yet very difficult technique to perfect. Whereas the interview revolves around interpersonal skills, tact, and witty repartee, the interrogation comes down to who can be the biggest asshole.

In order to begin an interrogation, as the FBI defines it, you have to know in your head that the subject is lying to you or is flat-out guilty. Interrogation is a point-of-no-return proposition, and you don't want to make an allegation and spend the next four hours yelling at the guy if you're not damned sure he's going to confess.

Determining whether or not he's lying becomes the key element. They'll almost always tell you whether they're lying or not, but you have to pay close attention.

People lie in two primary ways. They either lie by commission, meaning they come right out with a real flyer, or they lie by omission, meaning they simply dance around the whole truth. Both versions of deceit carry certain clues that a good investigator can use to his or her advantage.

Vocal clues can be very obvious, such as stuttering, stalling, or adding false emotion (in the O. J. Simpson, Susan Smith, Bill Clinton tradition). They can also seem fairly innocuous. Swearing to God used to throw me. I just figured that no matter how bad the offense, no one would lie in God's name. Wrong again. Every shitbird I ever arrested swore to God at some point in the process. The guiltier they were, the more they swore — on anything or anyone.

Benny taught me to translate.

" 'I swear to God on my poor mother's eyes!' means 'You got me, you son of a bitch!' " he said.

After a while, I learned to reach for my car keys every time I heard those words. I knew we'd be done in half an hour.

Some people lie well verbally, but rat themselves out in the way they move. Nonverbal indicators of deception are actually a whole lot more fun to work with than words. Most of us learn this sort of behavioral assessment intuitively, through years of relationships, raising kids, or dealing with spineless bosses. People just "know" when someone is lying to them, even if they can't put their finger on a reason. Gut feelings don't get much respect in federal courtrooms, so we taught new agents to look for specific indicators.

First, accept what a person shows you over what he tells you. Every time.

I had an informant called Chubb who never had much use for the truth. Every time I asked him a critical question, he'd say yes but shake his head no. Sometimes he'd reverse it, just to show off.

I tried it myself a couple times, just to see if I could do it. It's hard to say yes and shake your head to the converse. The body naturally wants to match the two responses. When they don't match, go with the head.

Second, humans are mammals, and mammals have responded in the same way to stress since God showed Adam he was naked. In a classic fight or flight scenario, your body prepares to wage war or run from it. Either way, blood and adrenaline start pumping through your veins, changing your body chemistry. Blood shunts to core organs, cutting oxygen to the brain, making the skin cool and blanch. Adrenaline quickens the heart rate, increases respiration, accelerates digestion. Your glands start secreting lubricant to keep other mammals from grabbing hold of you.

You can tell when the process kicks in, because the person you are talking to will lighten in complexion, his stomach will growl, and his mouth will dry up, making conversation difficult. With a decent nose, you can even smell the stress-induced secretions. They give off an odor different from sweat. They smell like fear. (Working in the Ozarks made it difficult to fine-tune this particular part of the job. I came across a whole lot of unique smells out there before stumbling on proper calibration.)

Finally, establish a baseline. All of us have mannerisms and idiosyncrasies that define us as individuals. In order to assess behavior, you have to look at clusters of behavior and differentiate between what is normal and what is not.

Watch a person sometime during conversation. Really watch him. What does he do with his hands? His feet? The tip of his tongue?

Now, yank his chain a little and see what happens. "Hey, buddy, I hear you got caught in the closet with the new boss the other day. I never took you for that kind of guy."

What happens? What behaviors does he show you under stress? How do these behaviors differ from his calm demeanor?

Ferreting out deception is like probing the enemy's armor, looking for holes. You know you've hit the right spot when you see him twitch.

❖

When an interviewee shows signs of lying, and you think it's time to lean in for the kill, certain things have to happen right off the bat. First comes the "car salesman interlude." Anyone who has ventured onto a car lot knows this step. You walk in knowing you'll pay a certain price for a certain model with certain features. The salesman hits you with a perfectly executed handshake, shows you your dream car, and escorts you to a quiet space for a little chat. He jots down a couple of notes on a piece of paper while you summon your toughest "I'm not coming off this price no matter what you do" face, and then you make your offer.

"Geez, buddy," he says, "I want to work with you, but you've got me bleeding on the table here."

He leans back in his chair, assesses your reaction, just as he's been taught in sales seminars, then he hits you with the oldest trick in the book.

"Tell you what I'm gonna do. Let me take this offer back to my sales manager. I'm just not authorized to give up this kind of money."

Off he goes to grab a cup of coffee or head for the bathroom or call his buddies to laugh at your expense. There is no sales manager. The real boss is out chasing bigger deals than yours.

The point in leaving is that it gives you time alone to do what he can't: break yourself down. You sit there and stew over how much you're willing to pay for the car he has just let you drive, feel, smell, love. Nobody wants that car as much as you do. Nobody deserves it more.

By the time the salesman comes back in, you're ready to

offer him more than sticker. Good salesmen know how to turn the screw. That's how they afford all those nice polyester ties.

Interrogation isn't much different. After hanging around Big Al and Benny long enough, I just knew when things were falling apart for the subject. Sometimes the bad guy would come right out and mess up verbally, telling me he had committed the crime. Sometimes I'd have to read it in his behavior.

It didn't really matter. When I sensed deception and decided to make my play, I used the same techniques salesmen have used for centuries. The only difference is that an FBI agent has to try and sell jail time. That's not an easy go.

"Can you excuse me a minute?" I'd say when the moment came to make the break from our cordial little conversation and move into hammer time. "I've got to make a quick phone call. Can I get you a Coke?"

I'd walk out, all nice and friendly, and check the weather or the stock quotes or call home to see what was for dinner. The subject would sit there, trying to decide whether or not I'd bought his load of crap.

When I thought he'd had enough time to work on himself, I'd reappear a changed man.

When I came back in, the gloves came off. No Coke. No rapport building. No questions. You start with a formal accusation, cut off his denials, and make him believe you know exactly how he committed the crime. Along the way, you offer reasons to confess. Rationalize his role in the crime. Project blame on everybody else. Minimize the downside to confessing.

I interviewed a man in the Republic, Missouri, jail one time who had bragged to another inmate about robbing a bank in my territory. I drove out to the jail, read him his rights, and proceeded to use every trick I could think of to build a decent working relationship. Even though he knew exactly why I was there, we were still two human beings engaged in conversation. He knew what he wanted. I knew what I wanted. Somewhere in between lay common ground we could work with.

When I decided I'd seen enough, I excused myself to take a leak and left the interview room long enough for him to stew in his own lies. That's the poetry in the process. They can lie all they want to your face, but once they're alone, it's just them and the God they falsely swore to. Most of the time, the voices in their heads are a whole lot more persuasive than yours.

When I returned, I made my accusation, cut off his denials, and assured him I had plenty of evidence to put him in federal prison long enough for his muscle-bound roommate to change his name to Suzy.

He asked for a cigarette, and I knew I had him. The Big Sigh is the number one gesture of resignation, but firing up a Marlboro runs a close second. Once my man lit his smoke and leaned back in his chair, I was ready to call the AUSA and fill out my FD-515, claiming another solved case.

"Okay," he said. "You got me. I did it."

Problem was, he shook his head no when he said yes. That was a new one.

Two weeks later, after digging through all the evidence, I figured out that he'd confessed just because he thought federal time beat three to five in the state prison at Jefferson City.

Sometimes people are too smart for their own damned good.

Teaching gave me a whole new perspective on the FBI and my role in it. The Academy had changed quite a bit since my new agent days. Administrators had extended the curriculum from thirteen to sixteen weeks. They added a week-long Bonduron-style driving school during the first week to teach new agents how to respond code three to bank robberies. They switched Bureau weaponry from the old .357 Smith and Wesson wheel guns to .40-caliber Glocks with fourteen-round magazines. New agents seldom wore business attire and could sport blue jeans almost at will. Poor J. Edgar kept rolling and rolling.

The real change, however, came with creation of a whole new instructional model. The Assistant Director in charge of the Academy had come up with an idea to integrate all sixteen weeks of New Agent Training into one extended scenario. This new curriculum would teach the skills necessary for the job while giving new agents a sense that they were working a real investigation from inception to prosecution. Decent idea.

For some reason, the Academy asked me to put together the script, and I jumped on the opportunity. Six frenetic months later, we rolled out the Integrated Case Scenario (ICS).

This scenario, dubbed NACBOMB (major FBI investigations get code names), started during the third week of training with a phone call from a concerned citizen. Fourteen weeks later, the case ended with a series of arrests and a moot court prosecution. In between, new agents learned how to conduct interviews in my class so they could use the information to draft search warrant affidavits in Legal I. Over at Hogan's Alley they learned how to clear rooms without losing tactical advantage, then slapped on the cuffs with techniques learned in Defensive Tactics. While conducting surveillances, they could even query a specially prepared database, just as they would check FBI indices. All along the way, they gathered information on fictitious bad guys and a supposed plot to topple the Washington Monument.

Each new agent worked at building a case as if working an investigation in a real field office. Every time the investigation required a new job skill, the agents received it during some aspect of their academic and practical applications training. Though complex and time consuming to create, the ICS functioned like a three-month guerrilla theater production in which the characters interacted with the audience. Professional actors played the roles. New agents put them behind bars.

The result was Academy graduates who left Quantico with more than the basic skills necessary to their jobs. They left with a sense of what it felt like to work cases in the field and call themselves professionals.

New agents weren't the only people changing in 1998. My life just took off. First, Rosie and I found a hundred-year-old Victorian house in serious need of renovation. Instead of spending all my time on the road, I spent it wiring, painting, roofing, sanding, and plumbing with her and the boys.

The time at home must have had some kind of mystical effect on me, because five years after I'd had a vasectomy, Rose found out she was pregnant. That wasn't exactly what we had in mind at that point in our lives, but it turned out to be one of those blessings God saves for special occasions. Eight months later, we tucked a new daughter named Chelsea Marie into her crib for the first time. She looked so good in there, we decided to have another. Collin came the following September.

As if four kids and a 5,000-square-foot money pit weren't enough to keep me busy, I went back to school to earn a master's degree in adult education. A cohort of seventy-two Academy personnel started the program. Seventeen finished. Along the way, I learned more about myself than I could have discovered in a thousand hours of counseling. The experience reinvigorated an intellectual curiosity I'd misplaced over the years. It felt like some kind of divine gift.

My job expanded my horizons, too. I got to work with lots of outside agencies, including teams of United Nations arms negotiators who needed a little help with their interviewing skills for upcoming trips to Iraq. I taught effective communication to Bureau executives as part of our Executive Development Institute. I taught field in-services, Equal Employment Opportunity counselors, even college students during an occasional guest lecture. I read and learned and reinvested myself in a new FBI that was changing for the better on an almost hourly basis.

And then one day, a year and a half into my two-month stay at the Academy, Roger found me walking toward the library. He'd been promoted to SAC of the Critical Incident Response Group and he had a proposition. CIRG included virtually every asset necessary to help manage and resolve the most extreme criminal crises. Within one completely self-contained organization, they had gathered the talent, resources, and experience to support field offices with all facets of crisis resolution. What they lacked was a way to manage strategic information flowing into and out of the organization.

"I want you to start a whole new program," he said. "You can build it any way you want. I'll give you whatever you need. But it's time to come back across the street."

I felt like the prodigal son, going home.

23

THE NEW
MISSION

Two weeks after Roger called me back to CIRG, I got a message on my office voice mail.

"Hope you don't have anything planned this summer," he said. "I need you to pack your gear. We're going to Kosovo."

Kosovo? My heart started to race. I hadn't taken a mount-out call in almost two years. Just the thought of joining my old teammates for an international rescue mission seemed like manna from heaven. The fact that the UN still considered it a war zone made it even better. Teaching interviewing and interrogation brought moments of fulfillment, but now that my batteries were recharged, I couldn't wait to jump back into the fray.

The word *Kosovo* carried a good deal of emotion in the summer of 1999. The hot war between Slobodan Milosovic and the ethnic Albanians had barely cooled. Pictures filtering out through various international relief agencies and media sources showed devastation beyond anything the West had seen in a long time. The United Nations had just indicted Milosovic and several of his top generals. They'd even formed an International Criminal Tribunal for the Former Yugoslavia (ICTY), to gather evidence of widespread atrocities.

That's where the FBI came in. Though some Americans would argue the merits of sending agents off to investigate war crimes abroad, no one inside the government seemed bothered. Louie Freeh's foreign expansion initiative had grown to include Legats in more than sixty countries. Bureau communications arrived almost weekly advertising vacancies in lands most agents had never even heard of.

The FBI's crisis response plan had also been expanded to include rapid deployment response to the four corners of the earth. Just months before, agents from Headquarters, CIRG, and various field offices responded to the embassy bombings in Dar es Salaam, Tanzania, and Nairobi, Kenya. Nobody really talked anymore about the FBI being taken over by the United Nations and flying around snatching personal liberties in black helicopters. Although Headquarters actually made HRT paint its black helicopters mediagenic colors, they didn't shy from jumping on the ICTY bandwagon.

On June 22, 1999, more than sixty members of a handpicked team touched down in Skopje, Macedonia. We included highly trained evidence recovery technicians from five field divisions, a security detachment from the Hostage Rescue Team, two caseworkers representing Physicians for Human Rights, as well as two pathologists, a criminalist, and a forensic anthropologist from the Armed Forces Institute of Pathology in Washington.

The team arrived in C-5A Galaxy transport planes with all the gear we'd need for up to a month in-country. Our 100,000-pound payload included everything from four-wheel-drive vehicles (HRT's own Humvees and Chevy dual-axle pickups) to satellite communications equipment, tents, food, electric generators, and a portable morgue. We brought our own shovels, picks, decontamination chemicals, medical supplies, hazmat suits, and ammunition. Two enterprising HRT operators even found a way to rig a shower facility out of an air compressor, some garden hose, and a bunch of big blue tarps. All the comforts of home.

After a day gathering our bearings at Camp Bond Steel, just south of the Kosovo border, most of the team flew north in U.S. Marine Corps helicopters to a large Albanian city called Gjakove. The HRT operators caravanned the vehicles and equipment north along narrow, badly damaged roads clogged with bombed-out vehicles and thousands of refugees.

I thought I'd seen tragedy, but I was wrong. This country had been destroyed. Whole towns were leveled. Entire communities gone. Every house was burned. Cows and pigs and human beings lay where they had fallen along the road, bloating in the summer sun. No matter how far or how fast you drove, you couldn't escape the smell of death. It was everywhere.

It's funny how a single image strikes you as a symbol of an indescribable event. Mine is a tired old man walking north from the refugee camp. He shuffled slowly along in filthy, tattered clothes, carrying a white plastic shopping bag in one hand and a rusting chrome car bumper in the other. Life is pretty desperate when the only commodity worth clinging to is a beat-up old car part.

If the politics of FBI involvement sound complicated, at least the mission seemed simple. Our job was to find, exhume, and determine cause of death in bodies identified by ICTY investigators at scenes of mass executions. No one knew exactly how many people had been killed at that point. Survivors told stories of mass executions and common graves, but no one had documented them to the point where evidence could be taken to court. That was our job.

❖

Day three, site four. A short, fat man wearing pants cut for even larger girth led us down a narrow path. Mountains stretched in bright yellows and shadowy blues to the north and east. A light breeze ruffled the overgrown grasses and cedar branches.

Our guide led us toward a cemetery at the edge of town. Most of the graves looked freshly dug — small mounds of red loam marked by short planks of wood. Some of the markers carried names. Most were blank. They stood quietly, offering no suggestion of the violence that had raised them.

People in town call him "Schindler" because of what he did when the Serbs came. After killing the city's men by the hundreds, the soldiers placed him in charge of corpse disposal. They burned what they could, but some of the victims — those killed in open fields or alleys — had to be taken out and bulldozed to prevent disease.

Schindler earned his name in an unlikely act of heroism. Instead of disposing of his former friends and family in mass graves as instructed, he secretly moved them to this graveyard and kept detailed records of who lay in which hole. This seems a simple gesture, but in the terror of war, he risked his own life just so those who returned could erect cairns to their past. Schindler struck me as a perfect symbol of how far this place had fallen: they defined their heroes less by whom they saved in life than how many they saved in death.

"Over there." The translator pointed toward a crowning meadow, just a couple hundred meters from Gjakove's easternmost subdivision.

Schindler pulled a crumpled piece of paper out of his

pocket and checked some hastily jotted words as if collecting his bearings on a treasure hunt. He claimed to have buried the remains of a couple hundred people in this one field. The freshly tilled earth seemed to lend his claim credence; graves filled the open field, reaching left to right from the road to the crest of a far hill.

The land looked scarred with the remnants of rampant slaughter. I imagined this is what towns look like after great battles: Megiddo, Gettysburg, Verdun. The sounds of warfare had faded off in the wind, leaving quiet, sullen plots of ground, full of loss.

"Look at that," Jimmy said. He pointed off toward the mountains at a light gray Marine Corps helicopter diving to the right, almost out of control.

"He just dropped chafe, see that? Must be taking surface-to-air fire."

It was a CH-53, one of the big transport choppers that had ferried half our crew from Camp Able Sentry in Skopje, Macedonia. The awkward gray birds sat in rows there along the macadam after returning from troop transport and supply sorties to the north. It seemed strange, climbing into the web seats, past a young Marine door gunner who pointed his M-60 barrel toward the ground and waited until we lifted off to charge it.

Jimmy followed the chopper's evasive maneuvers with his hand, as if flying the bird himself. He would have known what to do. Prior to joining the Bureau and HRT, he flew Blackhawks with the Army's Task Force 160. In fact, he won the Silver Star for flying into the Mogadishu street battle during the ill-fated Delta operation. Amazing, some of the people who join HRT.

We waited for a moment, watching for the vapor trail of Russian-made SAMs. Nothing. The chopper leveled off and disappeared to the south, evidently free of whatever it was that had spooked it.

"Can you believe this place?" Johnny asked. He walked beside me in body armor and camouflage. A CAR-16 assault rifle dangled from his right hand like a cold steel prosthesis. "The fucking smell."

Whether standing there in a graveyard or walking through the town square, we found the sweet, skunky breath of decay overwhelming. Yesterday we had driven out toward another cemetery east of town to clear it of land mines. We rode more than ten kilometers into the countryside and never breathed a mouthful of fresh air the whole way. The place held the stench of roadkill the way clothes hold smoke after a night in a bar. You just couldn't get it off.

Johnny and Jim and the rest of my old sniper team moved off to secure the perimeter. Most of the shooting had died down at that point, but we still got intelligence alerts warning of snipers. In camp at night, the sounds of gunfire and explosions filled the air. The glow of homes burning provided the only light, since electricity had died months earlier. Back in the city or out there in the fields, Kosovo felt primitive. If not for the clatter of tanks, the place would have seemed medieval.

"All right, let's get to work." Art, an FBI laboratory director, marshaled the rest of the troops around a black Chevrolet 3500, full of picks, shovels, and body bags. A tall, balding agent with a thick goatee reached into a box for a white hazmat suit. He pulled it on over his blue jeans, leaving a big bulge where his .40-caliber pistol jutted out from his hip. A dozen other evidence response technicians from the Pittsburgh, Newark, Philadelphia, Washington, and Boston field offices followed his lead, preparing for another day of nightmarish labor.

As the song goes, "The job was simple, but it wasn't

easy." We went there to gather evidence of war crimes, but in reality, we recovered bodies and body parts from a wide array of graves. I pulled my T-shirt up over my face in hopes of filtering the air, but nothing worked. I tried cigars and Vicks under my nose and a half-dozen other ploys, but they just added aftertastes of Cuban seed and eucalyptus. It seemed almost negligent to waste a nice Dominican robusto in a cloud of shit flies. Sometimes the flies got so bad, people used the white cotton masks just to keep them out of their mouths.

When HRT moved off to the perimeter, I walked toward a crew of Gypsies whom Schindler had hired to help open the graves. One of the men had been there long enough to scoop out a hole just deeper than his knees. He dug earnestly against the nightmare of this whole place until, suddenly, he dropped his shovel, walked over to a tree, and puked his guts out. One of his buddies followed suit, then another, and another. Within ten minutes, the whole crew waved off a day's wages and quit. They had a reputation in that part of the world for doing the work no one else would, but this was too much even for them.

An evidence response technician from the Washington Field Office picked up the Gypsy's shovel and pushed it into the soft soil with the heel of her boot. A dark brown pony tail stuck out the back of her FBI ball cap. The smell barely fazed her.

She dug down into the earth, two, maybe three feet, until the tip of her shovel retrieved a chunk of flesh rotted to the consistency of tapioca.

"Need a bag over here," she said. The words sounded distant and garbled through her mask.

One of the Gypsies looked on, trying to gather himself to rejoin the dig. Just then the wind shifted and doubled him over again. The noise of his retching made me smile. I didn't really understand why. Maybe I felt stronger than him for enduring the horror of it all. Maybe I was simply transferring emotion. They told us it happens sometimes, in places like this.

❖

Two days later, I accompanied one of the Physicians for Human Rights psychologists to the home of a woman named Ilya. The remains of her small white house stood at the end of a long dirt alley in the oldest section of Gjakove. Just a few days earlier, we'd exhumed the bodies of five men, all relatives.

"They came late in the night," the woman whispered, tears welling in her eyes. "Five men, or six. They pulled us out of our beds and took us outside to the garden."

She sat on her knees in the sparsely furnished family room. An oak entertainment center on the far wall held a television, silver candlesticks, and a copy of the Koran. Colorful Isfahan rugs covered the floor. A long, cushioned couch lined three walls.

"The children cried because of their guns," she said. "I tried not to show my fear." Her English sounded educated, almost Midwestern in accent.

Ilya's three sons, ranging in age from four to eleven, sat on their hands, across the room. The middle boy, maybe eight, smiled nervously at me as his mother continued her story.

"These men screamed at us and pushed us around with their rifles, like we were criminals, but we did nothing wrong."

Ilya had not cried in the five days I'd known her. She told me she didn't dare, because if she started, she'd never be able to stop. This woman had lost her husband, her father, two brothers, and an uncle. Their photos leaned against the wall along the back of the couch, like paper-thin gravestones in a makeshift plot. The bodies were gone now. We'd taken them three days ago to our camp for autopsy.

I looked at the color images, trying to match them with the corpses that lay on plywood tables back at our morgue. The evidence technicians had delivered them wrapped in black plastic tarps — a thick, noisy garment that opened in layers, filling the room with a caustic stench.

One of the men stared out from his photo, as I recalled how the doctors had cut his skin at the back of the neck, where his collar would have touched his hairline. He pulled the man's face forward, down off the bone, until the vaguely human features slumped in wrinkled tufts beneath his chin. Without turning to explain, the doc handed his autopsy knife to one of the HRT operators who had lugged the corpses in from the trucks. Dr. Frank, a forensic anthropologist, motioned toward the five other bodies. His intentions seemed clear enough. There were lots of cadavers, and this was not exactly skilled labor.

The dissection saws made thin, whining noises as the doctors cut open the skulls. The criminalists, forensic anthropologist, and pathologists reached down into the soupy brains to retrieve the bullets. That's why we'd come. To retrieve the bullets.

These men looked different in repose. In the photos and among the surviving family, I saw color and spirit and a suggestion of dimension. Back at the morgue, I saw spoiled flesh, a line of carcasses empty in death — no longer full of blood that rages, muscle that moves, and vanity that we parade around, then bury. I felt glad that these boys of Ilya's never came to the morgue. Something passes in death, something they didn't yet need to see: more than the life force. Maybe it's grace.

Ilya's family room steeped quietly in grief. Half a dozen

family members, including Ilya's elderly mother and her brother's family, sipped Turkish coffee and smoked dark tobacco. The strong, sweet brew rolled down my tongue, leaving pebbly grit between my teeth.

"They took our men." She sighed, trying to gather herself. The words came with resignation, as if she were describing how the rain had washed away a flower bed. "My husband and his father and his brothers. They took them to the courtyard outside. And they shot them."

The boys watched as she hung her head, still fighting the tears. Ilya's mother-in-law wrapped a shawled arm around her and rocked back and forth on her folded legs. The old woman pointed to the photographs of her dead, and whispered something in her own language.

One of the four widows in the room translated.

"They made these children watch," she said, pointing toward the boys. The kids looked on, somehow distant from the mourning. "They made them watch so they would tell everyone what happens to us if we don't leave this place."

I sat there for a time; maybe minutes. My eyes had always found places to settle at times like those, when the air gets fat, heavy. Twelve years of work as a criminal investigator had led me through murder scenes, tragedy, confessions. I'd interviewed victims so traumatized they couldn't pronounce intelligible words because of the tremors. I always tried to keep it clinical, hiding inside myself from their emotion, distant enough to avoid it in personal terms. I needed to assure myself it was just someone else's pain, to keep it from growing under my own skin.

My defense mechanism is simple: I pick a spot on the floor or in a painting on the wall, anywhere to fix my gaze. That way, I can listen without looking into their eyes.

Hard as I tried, though, I just couldn't find a spot in that room.

One of the boys stared at me, smiling. His name was Latsiva. Just weeks earlier, police had wakened him from a sound sleep, kicked him out of a little boy's dream, and forced him to witness his father's murder. How the hell was he smiling?

He stood up, balanced behind a curiosity so torturous his bare feet moved ahead of his body like walking sticks in front of a blind man. Latsiva made his way over to where I posed on the couch. His movements looked animated in contrast to the slow, funereal gestures of his family.

I nodded, motioning for him to sit down.

"Ef Bay Ee," he said.

Though less than perfect, it was the first English he'd offered.

Everyone stared as he tested me, searching for something brighter than what I'd brought in. I was not family. I was not Kosovar or Albanian. I represented distance.

He pointed to the credentials I'd showed when we arrived, then reached out and tapped my thigh where I had placed them in the side pocket of my cargo pants.

"Ef Bay Ee."

His older brother made his way across the room to join him on the couch. The little one still didn't trust me.

"FBI. Yes," I said. I pulled the credentials out of my pocket and handed them to him. A worn plastic cover obscured a photo of a younger man. I should have had it changed a long time ago, but it reminded me of the optimism I'd felt when I joined.

He weighed the old leather case with reverence, as if assessing the gravity of our presence.

I had to smile. I didn't even know what to call his language, let alone how to make it work. But I knew his wonder. I remembered it in my own kids' eyes when they first grew old enough to understand that I carried something more powerful than cash in my pocket. I remembered the way it felt in my own gut when I took my credentials from an Assistant Director after thirteen weeks of FBI Academy training. That simple piece of paper represented something good even there, in a country so ravaged by death and violence the stench filled the air, broad as winter.

I smiled back at Latsiva and his brother as they juggled my FBI credentials between them, entertaining the whole room with their excitement. One of them opened the worn black wallet, revealing the FBI identity I'd carried since 1987. At various times I had pressed it into fugitives' faces or walked behind it into bank robbery investigations. I'd stared at the credentials myself on occasion, mentally sorting all the things they stood for. It amazed me, as I sat in that mourning room, how often I still felt the same sense of excitement Latsiva could barely contain.

"FBI," he said again, adding inflection to his small English. It was the best he could do, but I understood his eyes. He wanted to tell me more about his life in Gjakove. Old men clogged the streets, pushing mule carts and tractors through the garbage, hauling what they could find of their lives back to some place they remembered. Children stood at the sides of the road as we drove by, waving behind timid smiles and yelling "NATTO! NATTO!" They recognized our vehicles, which were crudely stenciled with the KFOR (United Nations Kosovo Forces) logo.

Something in their impossible optimism filled me with humility. Most of them had never heard of the FBI, much less the Critical Incident Response Group or the Hostage Rescue Team, but they knew by our posture that we were the first men in camouflage who hadn't come to shoot at them.

"That's the first time I have seen his teeth in a long time," Ilya whispered. She talked softly, as if the sound of her voice might wake her son from some pleasant dream. Tears stood in her eyes, dancing. Any words I could have offered stuck in my throat. I had children too, and I prayed that they'd never have to bring tears to my eyes with a smile.

The boy held up my wallet for the others to see. He pointed his index finger in the air with his thumb cocked, wielding the imaginary handgun that seems to go with the fantasy. He lowered the knuckled barrel and pointed to my belt line where he imagined I carried it. A thin T-shirt hung over the grip. Poor camouflage.

No one tensed up, like I would have expected. The simple fact that he would want to see any kind of weapon amazed me. Guns had killed the men depicted in the photographs along the back wall. Guns had almost destroyed his culture. What could he possibly find intriguing about this blue steel lump on my right hip?

"Pistole?" he said. "FBI pistole!" He could convey just two things in words I understood: One of them meant life, and one of them meant death.

"Pistole," I said, nodding. He pointed, hoping I'd pull it out to show him, but that wasn't going to happen. He'd seen enough guns. I felt bad for bringing it.

I leaned back into the couch and raised my hands in the universal sign of surrender. "I give up, FBI man," I said.

Ilya translated, as her son bolted to his feet and waved the credentials in my face. He said a bunch of words that didn't make a bit of sense, but his intentions seemed clear. In the time it took most children to say "Tickle Me Elmo," he had grown from timid little boy to international peacemaker. Something about the small piece of paper in his left hand gave him the authority to change lives, at least his own. The FBI had come to Kosovo representing justice, and even small boys recognize hope.

Amen.

❖

The next day, we traveled north to Pec, an alpine village near the Albanian border. Our Italian hosts led us in armed escort toward the British sector, pointing .50-caliber machine guns into oncoming traffic. I rode in the back of the big Chevy as our ten-vehicle convoy ambled past carcasses of bombed-out vehicles: Mercedes sedans and military halftracks and school buses. Every kilometer or two, we'd pass long stretches where the Yugoslav army had buried lasting reminders of their visit. Yellow ribbon and red stakes marked where KFOR scouts suspected land mines.

Occasionally, a car of refugees veered off the rutted narrow roads and tripped a tank mine. You could tell the difference between it and an antipersonnel mine because all that settled back to earth was a chunk of chassis or an engine block. And the smell. Tank mines cut and tear and kill. The bodies aren't even worth going after.

The destruction got even worse as we drove north. Bullet holes, rocket strikes, fire damage. Out through the suburbs, into the country, everywhere we went the view remained the same. Beautiful forested mountains towered over communities of large two- and three-story houses, all vacant. Their brown brick walls were crumbling. The red tile roofs bared gaping holes where flames had eaten through them.

A year ago, this place would have looked Old World charming to wandering tourists. Now it looked like a postcard from hell. Bedrooms opened out to the mid-morning air, their walls fallen to rockets and conflagration. There was no furniture, no window glass. What the Yugoslav army had left behind smoldered in ragged piles. Cattle lay dead at the sides of the road, bloated and crusted in mud. A brood of piglets tried to suckle a rotting sow.

I snapped photographs until I realized that I was wasting film. All I needed to remember that place was a single frame. It looked the same from every angle.

We arrived in Pec just before 9:00 A.M. and parked the vehicles around a fountain in the town square. The Brits had established a command post in a former tourist hotel along the river. In better days it would have made a nice stay, but now old mattresses and baby carriages and dark, matted clothing clogged the river. The roads rattled the wheels off our trucks where the tank treads had eaten up the pavement. All visitors wore camouflage and carried long guns. Concertina wire and portable barricades cordoned off the hotel from the rest of the village, giving the place all the charm of a black and white World War II newsreel.

Art assembled our team at the back of an Italian-troop carrier and told us about the morning's mission. ICTY investigators had directed us to a mountain farm outside Studenica, where Milosovic's soldiers had allegedly killed nine members of a single family. Our entourage now included my old HRT sniper team running security, a dozen FBI investigators, two pathologists, a well-known author stringing for *Vanity Fair,* two German photographers, and a *60 Minutes II* camera crew. If anyone had observed that this whole scene was turning from the sublime to the ridiculous, I would not have argued.

After twenty minutes of organization, we divided the equipment, mounted the vehicles, and started out for Studenica. We would have made good time except for the car bomb that stopped us along a narrow alley for nearly an hour. Once ordnance disposal techs had cleared the road, we drove another forty-five minutes, wending our way into the mountains along a potted dirt road until it emptied out into a breathtaking Tyrolean pasture. A ragged mountain ridge rose high above us to the north. It looked for all the world like Mittersill, a chalet community three miles from my childhood home in Franconia.

I sat back and stared at the landscape, weighing it against

other scenes I knew and searching for rationality. Though
the names had changed, this place could have come straight
out of my youth. The grass looked the same. The homes
looked the same. Even the air tasted familiar this high above
the death-riddled lowlands. That's a strange thing about this
job: Bad things happen in the most beautiful places.

An old man met Art outside a crumbling two-story house.
They stood above us as we waited for them to agree on
terms. Despite a United Nations mandate, it is difficult to
knock on a man's door and ask him for permission to exhume his murdered relatives. Negotiations like this take
time, particularly when the good guys come with a press
pool in tow.

We stretched our legs next to the vehicles, observing orders not to stray out into the surrounding hay fields. The area
had been heavily mined, and no one wanted to go home with
a plastic leg for a souvenir.

"Mount up, guys! We're on," one of the HRT operators
yelled after ten minutes. And it began again. First the photographers documented the crime scene. In this case, it was
a large home scarred by rifle bullets and incendiary
grenades. The roof had collapsed into the top floor. The
barns had been burned, too. Several other houses smoldered
in the town below us. The last flames of a fading war spun
dark clouds up into the crystal clear sky.

Then the evidence techs moved in to gather physical
proof of the butchery. Two months after this particular
killing, the yard still looked like a landfill, littered with
clothing, shoes, children's toys - the material things that
define us in life. One of the agents lifted a brown corduroy
jacket and poked a black government-issue pen through several bullet holes. Another picked 7.62mm rifle casings off
the front porch. A third sifted through the carcass of a small
car parked in the driveway. All that remained inside the

burned hulk were the seat springs and a melted steering wheel. It sagged like something out of a Salvador Dalí painting.

Down below, at the edge of what could have been a lawn, Art and the doctors brushed the last earth off a man buried in a shallow grave. He was seventy-six years old when they shot him, a survivor said. The survivor was his brother.

They pulled him out of the hole, still wrapped in clear plastic sheathing, and laid the body face up on a bright blue tarp. Nine people had died here, just like the UN said. Yugoslav soldiers had driven up to the house and killed everyone, from a two-year-old child to the great-grandfather. They'd stuffed the bodies down a two-by-two-foot well to foul the water for those who returned. Four generations died in the same hail of bullets. Only this old man had stayed on his land, now part of the soil. The others were taken to a family plot down closer to town.

Two dozen or so people watched as the doctors performed their autopsy right there on the sky-blue tarp. They peeled the plastic away, just like they did with Ilya's family back at our camp. One of the doctors cut the scalp at the back of the neck, pulled the face forward, and removed shards of skull. I watched as a gloved hand reached down into the pocket and rummaged around until it found the bullet. This man was easy, because the bullet had done plenty of damage.

When he'd finished, the senior doctor nodded to Art, who draped an arm over a middle-aged observer. This man was a brother who was away when the killing occurred. He came back to find the devastation and no family. Only after picking through the rubble did he realize what they had done with the bodies. He'd had to lower himself down into the cold dark well and pull them out, one at a time.

No one spoke. There were no walls to stare at out there,

no simple way to avoid the emotion. All of us were used to death and to tragedy, but not on this scale.

When the docs finished, they pulled the man's face back up over his skull, restoring a modicum of humanity. The gesture struck me as almost touching.

Perspectives change in a place like that. Emotions that hang in the shadows of day-to-day life emerge and wrap around you, trapping judgment and rational thought. We tried to help these people. We lived in their world for a few weeks, then left for something starkly better. But the survivors couldn't leave. They had to struggle on under the weight of immeasurable loss. In most cases, there was little food, no housing, no simple conveniences like a hot cup of coffee or indoor plumbing. Winter would come soon. That's when they'd start to grieve: once the snows settled in and they had nothing to do but wonder about how something so inconceivably devastating could happen to them.

I had already started back toward one of the trucks when a quiet old man pointed to me and lowered his head. His eyes spilled tears down cheeks tanned the color of field rye. White stubble poked out of his cheeks. He stopped to hug me. I could feel the bones of his shoulders through his wool sweater.

Maybe this is it, I thought.

All the years I had been chasing a sense of righteousness came to a head in that moment. There in that beaten, empty place, many thousands of miles from anything I knew to be real, we found people who understood what we risked our lives for.

Peace. Safety. The hope for justice.

I held on to him long enough to remember his smell. He was life in a land full of death. He was the reason we came.

24

BACK IN
THE SADDLE

I had only been back in the States a few months when my beeper signaled the next mission. I was driving south on I-95 one Friday night after work when that familiar buzz made me reach for my belt.

"Shit," I mumbled as I hit the recall button. Another call I'd have to return when I got to the house. The months since Kosovo had been tied up with administrative work, meetings, business trips, and training sessions. It seemed like I never got off the phone.

When I looked at the number, though, my eyes lit up like streetlights. There in the dim glow of the LCD window stood those magic three digits.

888.

I hadn't seen them in more than two years.

Work. Job. Mission. Time to get busy. Some things you just never get tired of.

I hit the brakes, yanked my beat-up old Chevy Caprice to

the side of the road, and called back to the office for a situation report. Rioting Cuban inmates had taken over a jail in rural Louisiana, they told me. Several violent felons had used homemade knives and clubs to overpower guards. They'd already seriously injured the sheriff, taken four guards hostage, and threatened to kill them if their demands were not met within seventy-two hours. Roger wanted a seven-man advance team to be wheels up and southbound within two hours. I had a seat on the plane.

I knew the rest of the drill by heart. Crisis management had evolved dramatically since my days on the Team, but the response logistics hadn't changed much at all. CIRG stood at the center of a fast-spinning hub, and the wheel was really gaining speed.

Before CIRG gets called into any acute-onset operation, several things almost always have to happen. First, the local law enforcement agency responsible for resolving the crisis has to reach out for help. That call usually goes to the next agency up the chain, in this case the Louisiana State Police. If the state decides it doesn't have the resources, manpower, or jurisdiction to handle it, it calls the FBI and any other pertinent federal agency.

In this case, the governor called the Special Agent in Charge of the New Orleans Field Office. The SAC there realized he could use a hand, so he put out an all points bulletin to FBI Headquarters and other regional offices like Houston, Dallas, and Little Rock. As soon as Headquarters read the details, they fired up the Strategic Information Operations Center (SIOC) and deployed CIRG.

By the time all of this rolled downhill to a beeper call on I-95, hundreds of people were already gearing up.

I called Rose to tell her I'd be a couple of weeks late for dinner, spun the car around, and headed north for the airport. One hour and forty-eight minutes later, seven CIRG assessment team members, two pilots, and a flight attendant lifted off from a small Northern Virginia airport in CIRG's own DeHaviland Dash 8 aircraft. I sat in the second row of seats, behind Roger Blake and the ASAC, strategizing with representatives from the Crisis Negotiations Unit, the National Center for the Analysis of Violent Crime, HRT, and the Crisis Management Unit.

The collective experience on that plane covered virtually every major American investigation of the past twenty years. From serial killers like Ted Bundy and John Wayne Gacy to hostage negotiations in the jungles of Colombia to tactical assaults in Talladega, Alabama, CIRG personnel have earned their bones in the biggest and toughest cases. I can think of no other place on earth where one could find such a concentration of expertise.

I looked out the window as we climbed over the Blue Ridge Mountains and thought about the huge juggernaut gearing up for this mess down below. CIRG had grown considerably in the past few years to include eleven separate units. In addition to those represented on the plane, we also staffed the Rapid Deployment/Logistics Unit, the Aviation and Special Operations Unit, the Special Detail Unit (the attorney general's protection detail), the Child Abduction and Serial Murder Investigations Resource Center, the Behavioral Assessment Unit, the Operations and Training Unit (national SWAT program), and the Violent Criminal Apprehension Program.

Each of these highly specialized components brought a different eye to bear on a critical incident. Every one of the 280 agents and support staff assigned to CIRG had already proved themselves somewhere in the FBI. We had no first office agents. No FNGs.

Though not even part of the official staffing chart yet, I represented something very different from what most people associate with crisis response. Since Cain killed Abel, violence and the business of resolving it have fascinated people. This fascination has spread, in the Information Age, to a phenomenal interest in true life drama. Americans define things now in terms of what they see on television or the Internet. They expect images with their news, like scones with their chai tea. Events either happen on television, or they end up as sidebars in *U.S. News and World Report.*

That's great for viewers at home, but it creates a good deal of difficulty for those trying to free hostages. Decision makers realize that every call they make will show up as a graphic on CNN within the hour. That's not just a problem for career climbers. It's a problem for the guys in the trenches trying to get people out alive.

In order to cover this gaping hole in the government's crisis response plan, Roger asked me to create a strategy for managing the critical but noninvestigative information that flows through a crisis. The FBI, with all its considerable resources, had never adequately addressed issues such as mass communications, evacuation notification, emergency information, and media strategies.

The consequences of not building such a program could be disastrous. No matter how much careful investigation and hard work we devote to a hostage situation, a single negligent news bulletin could bring it all crashing down. Negotiators can't work their voodoo if the bad guys are watching live updates on cable news. Tactical personnel can't sneak up for an emergency assault if camera crews are piping live footage into the crisis site.

The problem is not limited to media reports. In any crisis, public perceptions can directly affect the FBI's resolution strategy. A terrorist bomb threat in Times Square, for example, could necessitate cancellation of a Rangers game in Madison Square Garden. The problem then becomes twofold: How do you tell 30,000 New Yorkers their tickets are no good without tipping your hand to terrorists? And how do you keep the media from discovering the real story, which could create a panic? Even if the bomb turns out to be a hoax, the panic to get out of Manhattan could kill thousands of people.

On top of that, crisis management is a multi-agency effort these days. A simple barricade situation in Los Angeles could quickly involve a dozen agencies from the L.A.P.D. and L.A. County Sheriff's Office to various fire departments, the health department, public works, and others. When the state and the feds get involved, it can get really complicated. All of these agencies need to work together to bring widely disparate resources to bear on the problem without gumming up the works.

And there are other considerations. Will school bus routes take hundreds of unsuspecting children through the blast apron? What major events could put additional people in harm's way? What about traffic patterns, power plants, flashpoint civic issues, and other considerations? They can each have a dramatic impact on how the command element shapes its investigation.

The days of rolling into town with HRT and a couple of negotiators are long gone. The FBI now looks at every imaginable consequence of each move as a giant chess match against the bad guys.

My seat on the CIRG advance plane required that I jump on three primary issues the moment we touched down. First, I had to provide an incident assessment, which means collecting, assimilating, and disseminating strategic information about the crisis. This data helps the command element avoid the tunnel vision that can come with a fast-moving criminal investigation.

Next, I had to establish an emergency information management cell. Emergency information is a new field being developed by the military to identify and predict the effects of critical incidents on large groups of people. Researchers have found, for example, that approximately eight people will report to a hospital emergency room for every one real casualty in the event of a chemical incident. This kind of knowledge can be crucial to the command element as they prepare contingency plans. My responsibilities included conceptualizing various outcomes of an incident and offering strategies to help the command element plan its resolution.

Finally, I had to address the pipeline for most information: the media. Crisis media operations just don't exist in this country. Virtually every agency bigger than the dog pound has a public information officer or a public relations staff, but they deal with day-to-day issues like ribbon cuttings, arrest announcements, and public service events. Even on the federal level, no one outside the military has put together any kind of multi-agency media protocol for crisis situations.

That became obvious the moment we touched down outside St. Martinville, Louisiana. About a dozen violent felons had executed a takeover, using homemade knives and clubs. They controlled more than a hundred other inmates and four badly shaken jail guards. The sheriff had taken a chair to the face while trying to intervene, and no one in law enforcement had any clear plan of how to resolve the situation.

On top of that, Channel 10 News had a camera crew inside the jail as the prisoners rioted. Satellite feed trucks surrounded the jail so closely, the fire trucks couldn't get through.

The inmates had taken over the asylum in more ways than one.

Within hours of our arrival, more than three dozen local, state, and federal agencies swept in to help quell the revolt. FBI agents from the New Orleans office met with the sheriff to try to delineate responsibilities. Anyone who has spent any time in Louisiana probably understands that the local sheriff reports to no one except God himself, and that's just a courtesy call. Even though the local boss man had requested federal assistance, nothing happened without his express say-so.

Special Agents in Charge sometimes take the same attitude. In this case, the sheriff of St. Martin Parish and the SAC of the New Orleans office hit it off nicely and concentrated more effort on resolving the situation than marking turf. That worked to everyone's benefit, because rapid deployments can cause confusion in the early hours. Everyone wants to help, but no one knows precisely what to do. Integrating a multi-agency response can become vital.

That's where CIRG comes in. The Crisis Management Unit hits the ground first with a logistical framework called a Joint Operations Center, or JOC. In theory, this JOC offers a central processing facility to all participating agencies. In reality, it's an air-mobile backbone that can be set up and operated in virtually any environment. The Louisiana package arrived early the next morning from Quantico with a load of laptop computers, information management software, and all the office equipment necessary to support hundreds of investigators working an end-of-the-world scenario. Fortunately, all we needed at the prison riots was a few computers and a fax. Most of this crisis was limited to Cellblock C.

We set everything up on the second floor of the county courthouse, just across the lawn from the jail. It was close enough to offer quick access to the jail, yet far enough away to provide security should something happen inside.

Other assets arrived by the hour. HRT rolled in with two assault and two sniper teams. They immediately obtained blueprints of the jail, built a full scale mock-up, and began planning for emergency and deliberate assaults. Breaking out of jail is pretty tough, but breaking in is even tougher. The hostage takers controlled the whole facility, so any attempt at a rescue would require sophisticated breaching tactics. The command element probably wouldn't use HRT except as a last resort, but if the Cubans started killing guards, shit was going to happen.

The Crisis Negotiation Unit brought in three talking heads and set up a Negotiation Operations Center to oversee local efforts. Initial reports showed that the hostage takers had few demands. They wanted news media, cigarettes, and safe passage to one of three foreign countries: Libya, Syria, or Hawaii (yes, I know). The initial anxiety spike had passed. It seemed like a good time to listen to their bitching, reiterate positive aspects of the situation, and cull out a leader. It's always better to deal with one bad guy than a whole brood.

Behavioral analysts (profilers) from our National Center for the Analysis of Violent Crime started workups on the individuals inside. They looked at criminal histories, recent expressions of violence, interpersonal dynamics, and a number of other factors in determining that these guys presented a very real threat to the hostages. If we didn't resolve this matter in the near future, they said, someone was likely to die.

I concentrated on building an information strategy that would help negotiators work their magic. We knew everything we gave out to the media would pass directly through the jail television to the hostage takers. That became a valuable tool. Hostage takers will usually accept the word of a local television reporter over the word of an FBI agent, so passing information through press conferences and interviews can be quite effective. We used our techniques to modify their behavior without giving anyone an idea what we were up to.

When the hostage takers screamed out loud about something they had just seen on television, it was because we wanted to let them vent. When they saw something that backed up our promises, it was because we'd planted the verification. Though we never lied about anything, we went to great lengths to pass strategic information, knowing it would influence their behavior much more than any one-to-one conversation. In many ways, we simply applied the techniques of behavioral manipulation I taught at the Academy.

While some of us strategized, I asked the locals to move the camera crews and reporters away from certain parts of the jail to predesignated vantage points. These new positions afforded full view of certain parts of the jail, but gave us three primary avenues of approach that the cameras just couldn't see. The media seemed very pleased with the access we offered but had no idea what we were really up to.

By day three, things had turned decidedly in our favor. HRT had practiced its assault plans thoroughly. Negotiators had established good rapport and a clear sense of who was who inside the jail. The profilers had developed a clear vision of what types of personalities we were dealing with. Even luck started to go our way. When two of the hostage takers left the control room to grab a shower (hey, they'd been in jail together a long time), half the inmates escaped. Just ran right out. Actually, they simply traded one jail cell for another. They still had time to serve.

The original seventy-two-hour deadline came and went

without further mention. The only significant downside was that the hostage takers moved five female inmates and the jail guards into the warden's office and chained the door shut. SWAT and HRT personnel took back the majority of the jail and set up shop just a few feet from the bulletproof glass of the warden's office.

To get a sense of how dramatic even a relatively small crisis like this can get, you have to understand violence. Human beings are much more prone to hurt someone under stress, and situations like this can get extremely stressful. Sitting back on the couch with a couple of beers on a cool fall day and watching golf doesn't usually get the blood boiling. Spending two days locked in a ten-by-ten-foot office with fifteen other people and no bathrooms while a bunch of guys with machine guns stare you down does.

When you throw in the fact that almost all the hostage takers had convictions for murder, rape, or violent assault, things got more than a little edgy. On top of all that, the hostage takers were actually illegal immigrants being held in "excludable alien" status by the Immigration and Naturalization Service. They had already served their jail sentences for crimes committed inside the United States. Cuba wouldn't take them back, so the INS was keeping them locked up ad infinitum, pending yearly file reviews.

Bottom line: These guys had absolutely nothing to lose.

Big problem. Every time negotiations slowed or the tactical guys made a move the inmates didn't like, they flipped out. Several times, we had to stand by and watch as they bounced the hostages against the glass or held knives so tightly against their throats a sudden gasp would have sprayed blood everywhere. Just to make things really tough, eight male hostage takers held six female hostages. Every time things heated up, we anticipated the possibility of a violent assault. Every time things quieted down, we worried about the possibility of rape. We walked a very thin line.

Unlike Waco, where nothing seemed to happen for weeks at a stretch, St. Martinville buzzed with activity twenty-four hours a day. SACs from Little Rock and Houston came in to help with the twelve-hour shifts. SWAT agents and officers arrived in hordes. Ambulance crews, fire trucks, and media vans clogged the streets. Even the governor stopped by on his way to a hunting trip, just to say hello.

Electronics technicians worked their magic with microphones and other eavesdropping devices. Negotiators worked toward resolution with a specific and aggressive strategy. HRT operators positioned themselves inside the jail for an emergency assault if things turned dire. A team of agents and sheriff's department personnel cut their way in through the back of the building to evacuate the remaining prisoners. By the end of day four, a wild and violent riot had been whittled down to one roomful of trouble and a whole bunch of cops.

Everything remained fairly stable until day six, when the hostage takers grew much more aggressive. Part of that was probably due to their wretched living conditions. Fifteen people were using a couple of buckets for a toilet. They had no food and little water. No one had slept in days. The prospects of getting a free trip to Libya or Hawaii didn't look too good.

Violent tempers started to flare. HRT stood ready to go if given the word. Negotiators searched for answers.

Most crises spin on a singular event that no one anticipated or strategized. We caught Danny Ray Horning when an insomniac looked out her window and saw a strange man sneaking around in her backyard. Bo Gritz pushed Randy Weaver off dead center. Waco . . . well, maybe Waco is an example of what happens when things spin the wrong way.

In this case, the pivotal factor came in a taxi around lunchtime. I was walking back to the courthouse from a local restaurant when I noticed several camera crews swarming around two women. When I moved in for a look, I found a pair of overwrought strangers, trying to find someone to speak Spanish in French Louisiana. One of the reporters told me they had come to see the older woman's son. He was inside the jail and she wanted to talk him out.

Bingo, I thought. This was the magic ingredient we'd been looking for. Negotiators like to find viable third-party intermediaries who can convey the law enforcement message without carrying all the associated stigma. If we could get these women to convince one of the leaders to come out, the resolve of the others might fracture and they'd follow right along.

Our plan started with the media. When the hostage takers had cloistered themselves in the warden's office, they lost access to television. Negotiators provided news updates, telling them that Cuban Americans throughout the United States had rallied to their cause. We showed them coverage of the two women arriving in town to seek an end to the stalemate. We even offered to allow a camera crew inside the prison to document their safe surrender.

This slowed their degeneration into violence, but it didn't win any resolution. That came just after dinner on day six, when the two women accompanied a female chaplain into the jail and went face to face with the gang leader.

Up to that point, I wouldn't have believed that a mother's wrath could outdo fifty men with machine guns. But I would have been wrong.

"If you don't stop this nonsense and come out of there now, I will no longer consider you a man!" the tiny woman yelled. "You are no longer my son!"

That's pretty much all it took. That and a letter from the

attorney general authorizing passage back to Cuba as part of a hush-hush State Department deal with Castro. Fortunately for us, the Elian Gonzalez mess was brewing in the background and politics opens lots of doors, even in prison. Forty minutes later, HRT operators ushered in a reporter and her photographer to witness the surrender. The hostage takers walked out of the warden's office with their hands in a very familiar posture, and surrendered to INS custody. The hostages emerged unhurt. The warden came out last. He secured what was left of his jail and climbed into an ambulance for a checkup at the local hospital.

No shots fired. No fires. No lawsuits. Even the press coverage looked good.

Holy shit, I thought as I tossed back a cold one at the after-action celebration. We've come a long way since the last time I worked this gig.

While most people left St. Martinville to catch up on Christmas shopping, CIRG dove right into preparations for a Y2K counterterrorism initiative. Though the much heralded apocalypse ended up slipping by with a pronounced thud, the U.S. government prepared for the worst in a multi-agency stand-up of historic proportions. As the primary investigative organization in the event of a terrorist incident, the FBI had to commit considerable assets to the effort.

Everyone in CIRG stood by their beepers on New Year's Eve waiting for three eights. A skeleton crew staffed a local command post, and another handful of agents went to SIOC at Headquarters to monitor trouble. On top of that, CIRG sent a team of specialists to Germany as part of an international strike force, prepared to respond in short order to virtually any crisis in Western Europe.

Under provisions of an executive directive, the FBI has

been designated lead law enforcement agency in a weapons-of-mass-destruction event or domestic terrorism incident. This designation assigns the FBI primary investigative responsibility for managing all aspects of a crisis to include operational response, infrastructure planning, negotiations, tactical resolution, and information flow. Virtually all local, state, and federal agencies involved in a large-scale crisis will work at the direction of FBI on-scene commanders.

In responding to this executive directive, the FBI has charged CIRG with the responsibility of assisting both the field and Headquarters in planning, implementing, and managing an interagency response to crises ranging from overseas evidence-gathering missions (as in Kosovo and the East Africa embassy bombings) to major criminal investigations, terrorist attacks, fugitive apprehensions, and high-risk arrests. This response often integrates widely diverse local and state agencies as well as federal components of the Domestic Emergency Support Team and/or the Foreign Emergency Support Team.

When January 1, 2000, came and went with nothing more traumatic than a global hangover, all talk turned to a huge congressionally mandated terrorism training exercise called TOP OFF. This sort of thing is nothing new to CIRG. The Crisis Management Unit stages simulated disasters around the country every couple of months to give field commanders a sense of what to expect in a real-life crisis. Creative writers put together elaborate scripts, complete with fiendish terrorist plots, defined characters, and potentially violent climaxes. Everyone gets to play, from tactical units and negotiators to the office management.

I started working with the FBI's National Press Office to spread my Strategic Information Management Office (SIMO) concept to other organizations in hopes that it would help coordinate the diverse protocols. What I found in my first TOP OFF meeting really surprised me. Representatives from more than thirty federal agencies sat around a huge conference table and admitted that the federal government had no crisis management plan for dealing with public information and media affairs. We had clearly aligned all other assets, but no one had ever taken the time to address issues such as mass evacuations, incident assessment, or emergency information strategies.

Perfect, I thought. An opportunity.

For the next two months, I worked with the Federal Emergency Management Administration (FEMA), the Justice Department, the Department of Defense, the Department of Health and Human Services, the Environmental Protection Agency (EPA), and a couple dozen smaller agencies, trying to come up with an integrated approach toward crisis information management. The SIMO plan had worked well in Louisiana, but large-scale operations bring widely disparate interests into high-pressure situations. Making the wrong call in a terrorist incident could throw a city into panic. Just as a cry of "Fire!" could set off a stampede in a crowded nightclub, one ill-conceived comment could bring a city to its knees.

TOP OFF planners set up mock nuclear, biological, and chemical crises in three American cities. Portsmouth, New Hampshire, would take the first hit with a mustard gas contamination at a local 10K road race. Denver would follow a short time later with an intentional release of pneumonic plague. Washington, D.C., would receive the final blow — detonation of a low-order nuclear dispersion device — a day later.

Virtually every federal agency was scheduled to play. Ultimate decision makers would include the attorney general, the Secretary of Defense, and the National Security Council at the White House.

My role in the TOP OFF exercise grew each week as the FBI plan for integrating strategic information efforts became the new model. Suddenly I was attending top-level meetings at the Pentagon and strategy sessions at Justice, where we wrote or changed policy for the entire government. Most of the things we discussed had never been considered before. On most previous missions, I'd carried a sniper rifle into the weeds. Now I carried the authority to make decisions that affected a whole new set of variables. The transition sometimes felt pretty dramatic.

Two months later, I sat in the cargo hold of a Marine Corps CH-53 helicopter, worrying about something a little more dramatic than authority: my life. The pilot had just aborted his second attempt at a landing, and having spent lots of hours in a chopper, I knew things weren't looking good for orbit number three.

I have never trusted helicopters. Though I love to fly in them, the idea that two or three wands of spinning steel could hold so much weight in the air just doesn't make sense. The first time I ever climbed into one, it flashed a master caution light 1,000 feet in the air and promptly crash-landed. This time, we were flying blacked out, with the pilots using night vision goggles. With no depth perception and few references on a tiny island smack dab in the middle of the Atlantic Ocean, landing can get a little tenuous.

I sat in my webbed seat among three dozen fully outfitted SWAT guys as the prop wash filled the cabin with dirt and flying debris. A Navy combat swimmer lay on the tailgate, hanging his head out into the night, trying desperately to find a reference point for the pilots. The giant chopper bounced up and down as they fought to control a hover. I pulled my shirt over my mouth so I could breathe through the flying debris. Thirty-eight lives hung in the black void of a Caribbean sky.

"I don't think he's got it," I said. The guy next to me shook his head back and forth.

With that, the pilot pulled pitch and we bounced upward like a cork, back around for another try.

This flight seemed like a damned good metaphor for a mission that just couldn't seem to find its legs. In May 2000, the FBI went in to a small island off the eastern tip of Puerto Rico called Vieques. The Navy claimed it needed the island because of its strategic training importance for overseas deployments, but the local population wanted it back.

That sounds easy enough. All we had to do was sneak a couple of teams of HRT snipers in during the night, wait until the protesters fell asleep, and hook them up. The total operation would have required twelve round-trip plane tickets, a boat ride to the island, and a few local cops to write up the trespassing tickets. These were misdemeanor offenders trying to regain land that legally belonged to them. If they didn't want the Navy strafing their island, so be it.

That's not the way Washington saw things.

After six months of preparation, including meetings reaching all the way to the Oval Office, the U.S. government stood poised to launch an armed incursion unlike anything since the Panama invasion of 1989. The Navy waited offshore with two helicopter carriers full of Marines. The Coast Guard ringed the island, enforcing a Magnuson Act embargo, which gave them the legal authority to seize and keep any approaching vessel. The United States Marshals brought in their Special Operations Group to transport prisoners from the arrest sites to a holding area, and then back to the main island, where they would be released. The local police ferried dozens of officers to Vieques to provide crowd control at entrances to the bombing area.

And that was just the support agencies. The attorney general had designated the FBI lead agency, so we came with everything we had. Actually, HRT had to stay home, with the exception of a few advisers, because the seventh floor decided they'd look a little too heavy. Instead, we flew in SWAT teams from six American cities. CIRG came with a C-17 cargo plane full of troops and gear. Headquarters sent an Assistant Director in Charge (ADIC) to oversee the on-scene operations. We even brought our own helicopters.

Hundreds of federal agents set up cots on the Roosevelt Roads naval complex. Base commanders closed down the gates and tripled security. The mood grew somber. H-hour approached.

Wait, wait, wait a minute, I thought as the big helicopter banked hard left on approach for his fourth and, I hoped, final attempt at a night vision goggle landing. Intelligence reports indicated that our subjects would include grandmothers, Catholic priests, children, and a bunch of old men. The only legitimate threat involved a local fisherman with a slingshot who had launched an old spark plug at a Navy guy.

What the hell were we doing?

The answer was actually pretty simple. One element and one element alone turned the Vieques inconvenience into Operation Just Cause.

The media.

Those protesters knew what every halfway intelligent protester knows in this Information Age: Images sell sentiment. They could have sat out on that beach tanning in the

Caribbean sun until George Hamilton came to visit, and no one would give a damn. As soon as the Navy and the FBI showed up with their black suits and machine guns, all bets were off. News footage of these peaceful protesters getting dragged away in chains would play on every television set in Puerto Rico, launching street protests, marches on the governor's mansion, and a nationalist sympathy strong enough to bounce the United States Navy all the way back to Guantánamo Bay.

Smart people know how to use the media. These were smart people.

Unfortunately, they almost won. When I first flew in to Puerto Rico with a representative from the FBI's National Press Office a week earlier, our orders were clear. According to Headquarters, we were not supposed to talk to anyone from the media. We were not to interfere with the arrest plan. We weren't even supposed to let anyone know we were there. Our jobs boiled down to providing information to Washington and providing bullets for the press release when it was all over.

I didn't know much about Headquarters, but I knew they were wrong. Prior to rejoining CIRG, I hadn't spent much time wondering about what actually happened there. I just did my job and left the tough calls to people with bigger badges. All that changed, however, once TOP OFF swept me into its vortex. For the first time in my career, I got to look behind the curtain at the way things really get done. From the Director's suite, which is protected like Fort Knox by an inner circle of advisers, to the National Press Office and the Office of General Counsel, the seventh floor might as well be called Oz. Every edict, pronouncement, and directive issued to the field bears the fingerprints of some inner-circle string puller.

Fifteen minutes into the operation, I knew that the string

pullers in Oz needed to round up Toto and click their heels together three times. Intelligence reports showed almost as many media representatives on the island as protesters. Someone had leaked virtually every minute detail of the operation to CNN. The protesters all knew exactly when we were coming and how. On top of that, arrest teams were given orders to prone out and cuff reporters just like the protesters. Cameras and broadcast equipment would be seized and given back when it was all over.

Bad idea. Vieques was a media event. Period. Kicking sand in a bunch of journalists' faces wouldn't help the Navy's cause one bit. On top of that, Janet Reno's last foray into public relations with the Hispanic community had ended up on the front page of every newspaper in the country: a terrified Elian Gonzalez with an MP-5 to his head. That made for a bunch of pissed-off congressmen, Capitol Hill hearings, a disillusioned public, and a pretty decent potential for violent protests in San Juan, New York, and Miami.

All that over a handful of beach bums listening to Jimmy Buffett music? Some perspective had gotten badly skewed.

Well, career advancement has never been a priority of mine, so I took a chance and tried to do the right thing. Danny Milar, the representative from the National Press Office, and I went to the incident commanders with a slightly revised plan. If the protesters wanted a media event, why not give it to them? we asked. The only way this was going to turn confrontational was if we made it. Give them their camera time, their stand-ups. Let the news crews shoot their video as long as they didn't get in the way. All the FBI's good work would show through clear as day. No one would be able to claim strong-arm tactics, poor planning, or a big government cover-up. Put everything out in the open and show the good things we do for a change.

"Makes sense," the ADIC said. Main Justice agreed. The National Press Office backed us. Everyone thought it made perfect sense, so Roger and the ADIC placed a conference call to Oz, just to clear it through to the top.

"You've got to be shitting me!" was the first reaction I heard. For the next twenty minutes, the Director's play callers recited reason after reason why the news media should be tagged and bagged just like everyone else who had thumbed their nose at government authority.

"These people are illegal protesters," they yelled. "We can't give them special treatment just because they have cameras in their hands."

"They're the reason we're here," I pointed out. "This isn't an arrest. It's a photo op."

Fortunately no one on the seventh floor had ever heard my name before, so I feared no immediate retribution.

"We're going to do this right," I argued. "Why not let the American people see it?"

Eventually they did. Roger and the ADIC convinced them that we were wading into Gilligan's Island, not Normandy. CIRG rewrote the tactical plan to dress SWAT agents in khaki pants and T-shirts instead of black fatigues. We pulled media representatives out of the command post and put them on helicopters with the tactical guys and teams of on-scene negotiators. Instead of marching in with assault weapons at ready-gun, the new plan called for SWAT to establish a perimeter while the team leader, a negotiator, and a media rep walked down into the camp alone.

That's when I knew we had evolved. It may not seem like much when boiled down to synopsis, but that call represented lots of constructive thinking since 1993, when two CEVs loaded with full tanks of CS gas had rolled down a Texas farm road. Crisis resolution isn't a rigid, violence-driven science anymore. The FBI is moving forward with a whole new bag of tricks. Some of them reach to the edges of technology. Some of them involve behavioral assessment techniques we are just now learning to understand. Some of them involve better tactics and smarter negotiations.

And some of them come down to what Eugene Brodie taught me in a small Midwestern RA fifteen years ago. Treat people with a little dignity and most of them will do anything you ask.

The chopper pilots finally put us down in the field, just before midnight. SWAT agents from all over the country lumbered off the bird, marched a half-mile to a bivouac site, and hunkered down for the night. The Southern Cross lit up the sky around us as we made last-minute plans and refined our strategy.

At dawn the next morning, my old partner Bobby Metz (now head of the Jacksonville SWAT team), a negotiator named Dennis Connerton, and I walked side by side into one of the protester camps and made history. This isn't the stuff that stands out in textbooks. If I didn't write it here it would probably never even make a footnote. But what happened on May 19, 2000, represented a fundamental shift in the way the FBI looks at crisis resolution. The days of leading with a heavy right hand were over.

For the remainder of the morning, we moved about two hundred protesters onto trucks and handed them to the Marshals Service for transportation off the island. Those who wanted to get cuffed for the six o'clock news got white plastic flex cuffs wrapped so loosely around their wrists, they had to hold their hands up to keep them from falling to the ground. One man refused to move, so we let him roll around in the hot sand until he looked like a sugar cookie. He eventually realized no one really cared, and climbed sheepishly aboard the transport vehicle. The whole thing looked more like a Boy Scout Jamboree than a law enforcement crisis. Nothing wrong with that.

While the Marines waited just offshore on their ships, the helicopters circled overhead, and the decision makers paced holes in the carpet back at Oz, I turned to my old HRT sniper partner and smiled.

"Ain't this some shit, buddy?" I asked. "Who'd ever believe, five years ago, that we'd end up in a scene like this?"

"Yeah," he said. "Who'd a thunk it?" Bobby seldom swore.

25

THE FUTURE

The FBI's New York Field Office has just received a small manila envelope threatening a biotoxin attack on the United Nations. Under normal circumstances, this would not raise particular concern; threats like this dribble in several times each month. But something about the enclosed vial of murky fluid and the Cyrillic handwriting on the note gets their attention.

At 4:28 P.M., the Assistant Director in Charge of the New York office rushes back in to 27 Federal Plaza and rides the elevator to his office suite on the twenty-eighth floor. First, he calls in Evidence Response Team technicians to secure the vial and fly it via Bureau plane to the FBI's new $100 million laboratory in Quantico, Virginia. Next, he calls his criminal division Special Agent in Charge back from vacation, dedicates twenty agents to a preliminary investigation, and calls Headquarters with a weapons-of-mass-destruction threat advisory.

Perhaps he's moving a little too quickly on a small glass vial and a piece of paper. On the other hand, the island of Manhattan hosts almost 8 million people during a typical business day. If this letter is legitimate, the panic to escape alone could kill one in ten.

Two hundred and thirty miles south, in a gray-brown building between Pennsylvania Avenue and I Street, North West, the Assistant Director in Charge of the FBI's brand-new counterterrorism division hangs up one phone and grabs two others. With one call, he deploys the Critical Incident Response Group to coordinate a multi-agency response. With the other, he activates the Domestic Emergency Support Team, an interagency task force made up of the Department of Defense, FEMA, the Centers for Disease Control, Department of Energy, and the EPA.

Within minutes, his national 911 is rippling out through the most sophisticated network of crisis resolution experts on earth. Every conceivable kind of specialist, from molecular biologists to behavioral assessment profilers, stands up for a long night of decision making.

Crisis resolution has become an art in this country. That's good, because terrorism is coming. You don't need an army and a big bankroll to lay siege to a country anymore. All you need is a couple hundred bucks' worth of commercially available chemicals, access to the Internet, and some balls. Oh, yeah, and the media. A few dozen bodies and a big explosion mean nothing without video footage.

Lots of political and religious zealots understand this process. They can't afford a seat at the United Nations, but they can buy themselves a prime-time introduction to the world with a five-dollar pipe bomb and a crowded public place. The World Trade Center bombing in 1993 was etched into the collective memory by home video that CNN aired over and over. Remember the footage that tourist shot of the panic following the Olympic Park bombings in Atlanta in 1996? Would you have the same vivid memories without it?

Those images burn brightly in a nondescript office building six miles south of the FBI Academy in Quantico. Inside, the linchpin of this enterprise crosses a wide-open bull pen full of workstations toward the office of Roger Blake, former commander of the Hostage Rescue Team and current Special Agent in Charge of CIRG, who asks his secretary to issue a division-wide page notifying everyone of a potential emergency.

Three numbers go out to 230 beepers:

888.

The days of learning about missions through rumor or speculation have ended. Information flows through CIRG like high voltage through ten-gauge wire. CIRG was designed and built to respond at a moment's notice, and this response begins immediately.

Three Crisis Management Unit supervisors bow out of a domestic-security-preparedness meeting at the Pentagon and dive into rush hour traffic. Fifty-seven members of the Hostage Rescue Team scramble from separate training exercises in Key West and Tucson. Eight hostage negotiators interrupt a field in-service and hurry for their jump kits.

The National Center for the Analysis of Violent Crime gears up its bull pen of behavioral analysts and profilers. The Violent Criminal Apprehension Program stands by for queries to its enormous serial-offender database. Six Tactical Helicopter Unit pilots strip rotor caps and tie-downs from three Bell 412 twin-engine choppers that sit ready, just east of the HRT building. Technicians prepare communications gear, logistics planners organize a military airlift out of Andrews Air Force Base. The Operational Training Unit readies nine enhanced SWAT teams for potential call-out.

All in all, more than 175 of CIRG's 280-person staff react

to the call. Within one hour. The other 105 phone home to tell their wives and husbands and kids they'll be working just a little late. Though the overall New York mount-out could involve more than 2,000 individuals by morning, someone will have to stay behind and mind CIRG's other responsibilities.

Just before 5:00 P.M., Blake and seven supervisory members of the Crisis Assessment Team board a brand-new $42 million Gulfstream G-5 executive jet.

Blake grabs a seat in the front row, picks up an encrypted satellite communications phone, and calls the Strategic Information Operations Center at Headquarters for an update. SIOC, the FBI's crisis management nerve center, occupies a large chunk of the fifth floor at the J. Edgar Hoover Building. During burgeoning crises like this, SIOC becomes the Bureau's sanctum sanctorum, a highly sophisticated communications center equipped with everything from secure worldwide communications to mainframe computers and an espresso machine.

Agents pour into a holding room outside the shielded grotto, where a security officer checks access badges. FBI credentials and a Headquarters security badge do not guarantee access to SIOC. Only those with mission-specific clearances pass down the long corridor toward a suite of rooms unlike any other in the world. Several dozen people wait their turn in line as a likeness of George W. Bush looks down from his dedication plaque on the wall. Green glass and fluorescent light make the large anteroom feel more like a sushi bar than a command post.

Inside, the shift commander receives information from Denver that the Department of Energy may have discovered an anomalous radiation signature in a suburban warehouse. They've found no known connection to the New York threat, but they're looking into the possibility. A preliminary run of the Bureau's automated case-support system, criminal indices, and various threat-assessment databases shows references to potential terrorist groups in virtually every U.S. city. Criminal analysts begin combing through the data, trying to cull out pertinent leads.

Back on the plane, Blake works the phone as two CIRG pilots clear the tower for takeoff and point the sleek G-5 north toward La Guardia. His ten-member advance team hunkers down over cell phones, IBM laptops, and response protocols, preparing for an indefinite stay in the Big Apple.

"Maybe this'll blow over in a hurry," one of them says hopefully.

He still has a ticket connection from his days in the Bureau's biggest field office. Maybe he can take in a show if they have to lay over.

At 6:27 P.M., a black and red executive jet touches down at a small private airport and taxis to a civil aviation terminal. Three smoked-window Excursions wait with engines running as the eleven-member advance team climbs off the plane and hurries through a light snow squall. Blake's staff includes the head of the Hostage Negotiations Unit, who will meet with New York's negotiators to discuss strategy. It also includes a criminal profiler, who will analyze the demand note, compare it against information gained during virtually every other incident during the past twenty years, and make suggestions regarding the man (and invariably it will be a man) who wrote it.

An HRT supervisor will secure rehearsal space and staging areas for the full Team, which is due in by 9:00. A computer expert, crisis management coordinator, and Rapid Start logistics coordinator will begin setting up the command post.

Two eighteen-wheel tractor trailers full of equipment left Quantico almost immediately after Roger took Headquarters' call. They should arrive in Manhattan within the hour.

Conversation is all business on the way in to town. Marked units from the New York Police Department help part rush hour traffic along the Brooklyn Bridge, as the Team speeds across the East River to Center Street. Cabbies honk and other drivers bitch like they would at any other motorcade. What they don't know is that these five vehicles could determine whether or not they ever get to bitch about anything again.

By the time the CIRG advance gets downtown, the New York office has already done considerable homework on its own. They have received a corroborating threat from a little-known cult outside Spokane, Washington. No one in New York has ever heard of them, but a grizzled old GS-13 working Indian reservations out of the Coeur d'Alene, Idaho, resident agency has. He knows them as a harmless bunch of militia wacks, led by a former cattle rancher named Evan Payette. The agent thinks New York's assessment is just a big mistake.

Could be. But with stakes this high, the Director himself has scrambled half the FBI agents west of the Mississippi just to prove him wrong. Agents from the Salt Lake City and Portland offices gear up to surveille Payette and find all they can about him without compromising the investigation. A preliminary check of research labs, National Institutes of Health contractors, and universities by the Centers for Disease Control indicates that twelve different sites store active Marburg virus. Only one, a research lab in Raleigh–Durham, North Carolina, has received nongovernmental inquiries during the past six months. Two weeks ago, they sent a live Marburg culture to a research epidemiologist at Boise

State University. So far, no one has established any connection.

By 9:30 P.M., the ADIC of the New York office has pulled a hundred more agents in from home and canceled all leave. One of them, an investigative analyst from Hoboken, is monitoring the FBI Web page when he sees an e-mail from someone claiming to have sent the Marburg sample. This e-mail demonstrates two dramatic developments: One, it shows that the bad guys possess the sophistication to hack in to the official FBI Web site, and two, that they have a new demand. From now on, all communications will be conducted in cyberspace, using an obscure chat room serviced by a "no-log" server. The e-mailer calls himself Luke.

At first, no one knows why the putative terrorists selected this mode of communication. That changes quickly. Systems analysts at the National Infrastructure Protection Center explain that modern Web-based communications make it easy for people to reach out from around the world with the punch of a button. Sophisticated specialists in Internet technology can hide a coded message in a photograph downloaded from a porno site. They can route communications through anonymous servers, cleaning themselves with electronic double-backs and cover drills. Talking on the Internet has become the modern-day equivalent of meeting someone in a dark alley. Only better.

One thing becomes clear early in the investigation: The bad guys seem familiar with New York City and the FBI's response plan. That shouldn't surprise anyone. Vast amounts of information about the FBI, other law enforcement agencies, and their techniques are readily available through books, television broadcasts, and mainstream media outlets. A free society always walks the thin line between educating the public about its protections and giving up the farm to shitheads who want to bring it down.

That's all right. The FBI keeps a few secrets for special occasions.

Regardless of its origin, the new e-mail message spells out a distinct problem. Somewhere on the island of Manhattan, terrorists have hidden twelve aerosol dispersion devices capable of spewing enough aflatoxin into the air to crash the population. The demand is simple: They want all United Nations diplomats out of the country by close of business tomorrow. If not, the devices cough and New York dies.

Fearing the terrorists may have thought to surveille the New York office, the ADIC routes Blake's advance team to a benign-looking warehouse in the meatpacking district between Greenwich Street and the Hudson River. Inside the 30,000-square-foot space, agents from C-12, the New York office's domestic terrorism squad, watch the motorcade pull up. They open double doors allowing everyone to drive inside, then close it back up. Just another warehouse.

Within fifteen minutes, the New York office begins a transformation, turning the "off-site" into a technologies-rich Joint Operations Center.

A large room off the right wall will serve as the Strategic Information Management Office, controlling communications into and out of the JOC. It has three specific missions: incident assessment, emergency information, and media strategy. These three areas pose significant challenges at this point in the investigation. Operational security seems paramount right now. If word of this crisis leaks out, the command element will face a firestorm of trouble.

Terrorists who think they're negotiating in secret will accuse the FBI of breaching confidence and threaten to detonate the devices. The United Nations will turn this bomb scare into an international event of potentially devastating consequence. The general public will storm the tunnels and the bridges, trying to escape and setting off riots, looting, com-

plete civil disorder. Consequence-management models predict that more than 60 percent of the public health and emergency response professionals will join in the panicked
evacuation, leaving everything from hospital emergency
rooms to squad cars and fire trucks with no one to run them.

We're all human. No one wants to die.

Within two hours, the warehouse will become a home
away from home for up to a hundred agents and support
staff. These negotiators have never worked in a cyber environment before, but if they don't learn quickly to upgrade
their expertise, America is about to face its first weapons-of-
mass-destruction meltdown.

By 10:30, the advance has done its job, and CIRG personnel are rolling in by the busload. Everything has been set
up before they arrive.

The Rapid Start/Crisis Management Information System
(CMIS) has established an automated data management
component in the Joint Operations Center. With hundreds of
investigators chasing down thousands of leads, it gets very
easy to drown in information. Knowing the answer is sometimes easier than figuring out that you know the answer. The
CMIS data loaders and systems analysts provide the command element with the tools they need to mine useful information from a mother lode of data.

Another room in the warehouse will be set aside for the
Joint Interagency Intelligence Support Element, which coordinates intelligence gathered by various local and state agencies. Despite the FBI's extensive database, we don't have
everything. Letting the home team play is more than
liaison — it's necessity.

As the FBI coordinates the criminal investigation, FEMA
sits down with the Consequence Management Group to begin weighing options. Representatives from the New York
Department of Health, the Centers for Disease Control,

Health and Human Services, and a dozen other public health agencies consider all options. Hazardous-material-disposal experts fly in from all over the country with everything from hazmat suits and decontamination equipment to pharmaceuticals and possible antidotes from national reserves. We have no cure for Marburg, but manufacturing enough to wipe out New York would not be as easy as the terrorists want us to believe. They may have a small sample of the virus and something less lethal in all those aerosol dispersion devices.

While investigators and crisis management specialists labor away inside the city, the Hostage Rescue Team off-loads its gear in a Queens warehouse. Three Bell 412 helicopters and an MD-530 Little Bird wait in an adjacent parking lot. The neighbors think the building is a New York Police Department storage facility. The choppers and the men in black suits won't be a problem until tomorrow morning, if anyone even notices the activity at all. This is New York. People mind their own business.

Back at the Joint Operations Center, dozens of local, state, and federal agencies gather in conference rooms, trying to coordinate their considerable resources. The FBI's crisis resolution protocol relies on a three-tiered response. Incidents like this begin with the most appropriate local agency, then get bumped up as the threat level increases.

Most terrorist incidents will probably start with a local beat cop stumbling onto a package that just doesn't look right. He'll call in the bomb squad, if his department has one. They'll call in the state. The state will call the local FBI office. They'll call FBIHQ. Then the phones will ring at CIRG. By the end of the day, everyone in the chain ends up working in concert to figure out what the hell they're going to do next.

The general opinion among those in charge here is that this particular crisis is quickly rising through the roof.

Everyone from the New York Fire Department to the Transit Authority to the Department of Public Safety shares a role. Firefighters break open hazmat equipment they have never even seen before. While their battalion chiefs draw up contingency plans and work with FEMA to coordinate evacuation plans, the rank and file will gear up for Doomsday.

America has never been so well prepared for an event like this, but after weighing all the facts, the command element faces the devastating conclusion that the best way to save the greatest number of lives might be simply to tell them to run.

Just before midnight, I stand on a balcony overlooking our midtown command post as the world's most sophisticated antiterrorism task force races to prevent a catastrophe. Every conceivable angle on this crisis, from legal considerations to how and where to hold the first press conference, is being handled somewhere in this space by some FBI expert.

The attorney general has been pulled out of bed. The White House situation room is up and running. The National Security Council is just beginning a conference call. The CIA and Interpol are scanning for potential leads.

The Hostage Rescue Team, my old mates, wait for permission to strike two potential targets in the Bronx. The Domestic Emergency Support Team works frantically to hook up experts at the Centers for Disease Control in Atlanta with a harried battalion chief from the New York Fire Department. FEMA struggles to draft an evacuation plan for Manhattan. A fearful press, tipped off by a cabbie pissed about late-night traffic, circles outside, clamoring for a statement.

I have just started down the hall toward the Joint Operations Center when the on-scene commander emerges from a conference call with the Director and the attorney general. He pulls me aside and tells me the preliminary investigation looks ominous. This group in Idaho has the expertise and the resources to pull off what they threaten. Washington wants answers. New York wants answers. Two hours from now, the whole country will want answers.

"I need a plan, Chris," he says. "What the hell are we going to say?"

I suck in a deep breath and gather my thoughts. Even in the FBI, moments like this don't come around very often.

I search back over the years for clues as to how I got here in the first place. More than fifteen years of investigations, tactical missions, overseas excursions, and adventures roll through my mind like murals on some huge, seamless wall. They reach out left and right, through ten lifetimes of experience, calling me to pick a scene that might make a difference.

I see a small boy in New Hampshire trying to guess at the world outside, testing his courage on railroad trestles, hoping the adventure might help him get there. There's the pride in my dad's eyes the day I swore an oath to defend this country and its Constitution. I look back on a sunny afternoon in Kansas City when I drew my gun for the first time. That woman in the housecoat with the broom. Wayne the applicant coordinator, James Jenks, selection, the color of Bobby Matthews's boots.

Years have passed since flames consumed David Koresh and seventy-eight of his followers on a windy Texas plain, but I can still smell their charred bodies, hear the gunshots, feel the heat of the blaze. I see their faces in the windows of Mount Carmel. The memories come to me when I least expect them, hanging just on the edge of consciousness like old bullies, taunting and racing off before I can catch them.

I see Randy Weaver and Kevin Harris running through a cold Idaho rain. The crosshairs of my rifle scope dance just ahead of them as they crouch beneath dark hoods and scramble back toward their cabin. Fog from each breath gathers in front of my eyes, obscuring the scene like mist on a cold window. I track them just like I've been trained, but I never catch them and I never fire. I pull on the trigger, but the bullet just won't go.

I see myself lying in the jungle above Villa Pilar, trying to come to terms with the whole process. I watch the young sentry through my rifle scope, realizing what awesome responsibility we wield in holding the power of life over death. He juggles the Ruger in his hands as my teammates race toward him with their drug warrants. His eyes grow wide, caught between the machismo that tightens the grip on his assault rifle and the basic instinct all humans share to survive. My finger touches the trigger, waiting for him to make the call.

I hold my breath when he swings the rifle toward my teammates. I set my crosshairs. One press against the cold blade and he dies. My heart pounds rhythmically, steeled with years of experience now to pump blood for concentration without shaking aim or intention. The world crowds to the periphery, outside the dark barrel of my scope.

Children's voices. Dogs barking. Women screaming.

Everything fades into the jungle I have grown into. It's just me and him. This moment. All the choices you make in a lifetime summarized in one immeasurable consequence.

I commit to the shot, pulling . . . pulling . . . pulling . . . until he drops the Ruger and turns away. That quickly, it's over. I breathe. Sometimes the most important shot is the one you don't take.

My mind turns to Bobby Metz and Scarhead and Spuds, Big Al and Benny — all heroes in their own way. There's Eugene Brodie teaching a wide-eyed FNG how to work his way into a whole new life without getting himself killed. There's Buck and Antman and Johnny, dragging me back to a world that made sense. There's Roger, showing me the way toward something better.

And in every picture, something pulls me deeper into the moment, a greater truth. I see Rosie and four patient kids waiting for me to come home. Their smiles sustain me, no matter how difficult the scene or painful the recollection. They save me when I fall.

The scenes glow in my mind's eye, red and glorious, like night over Washington all those years ago when I first guessed at how I might make a difference.

That's when it hits me. The FBI is not some nameless, faceless organization lurking in the shadows of American justice. It is men and women with strengths and weaknesses who get up in the morning and go to work because they believe in something greater than themselves. These people aren't jackbooted thugs and baby burners looking to steal away this country's God-given freedoms. They are ordinary people like me, with an extraordinary calling to save a way of life they still believe in.

"Well?" the Boss asks.

Andy Tabbott and Gary Braun call me back to that railroad trestle over Ammonoosuc. "Toes over, Whit," they say. "That's the rules. You gotta get both feet over the edge."

I push out with my toes until I can feel the tips of my well-worn loafers. A giant life cloud drifts out of my lungs, filling the huge room with every dream and aspiration and conviction I've ever summoned. This is the life I've dreamed about. This is why it matters.

"What do we tell them?" he says.

And I know.

"We're the Federal Bureau of Investigation, Boss," I say. "Tell them it's going to be all right."

ACKNOWLEDGMENTS

I could not have written *Cold Zero* without the help of many kind souls. I would like to thank my friend Peter Berg for convincing me I had a story to tell and encouraging me to find it. I would like to thank the Stone brothers, Web and Rob, for their insight and guidance in breathing life into a stack of loosely bound recollections. And I would like to thank my agent, Suzanne Gluck, for her optimism, her tenacity, and her friendship. I can't imagine a better business partner.

I am most grateful to Michael Pietsch and everyone at Little, Brown for giving me the opportunity to realize this lifelong dream. Michael's editorial wizardry and endless patience turned my initial ramblings into a book that I feel proud of. Peggy Freudenthal, Heather Kilpatrick, and Anne Montague taught me the power of revision. Mario Pulice and Scott Levine did a wonderful job on the art work. Ryan Harbage and Lauren Acampora made sense of it all.

Thank you.

I would also like to thank the FBI for allowing me to tell this story about the remarkable men and women who fill its ranks. Pat Solley and everyone in the prepublication review office provided considerable guidance and I appreciate their help.

Though it goes without saying, I want to express profound appreciation to my friends and colleagues on the Hostage Rescue Team. A few lines of acknowledgment, here, will never convey the gratitude I feel for their camaraderie and unyielding dedication to excellence. HRT operators are prone to understatement, so I'll just say "thanks."

I can't help but mention a few of the friends and family who make up a life worth remembering. My Mom and Dad, of course; my brother and sister, and my Uncle Mike and Aunt Sheila. Thanks to Rose, Jake, Mickey, Chelsea, and Collin for endless support. To Ben Cagle, Al Stiffler, Bill Deal, and Tom DenOuden for showing me the ropes. To Fritz Goodman and Chris Gillooly for teaching me the importance of dreams. To Eric Hjelm, Gary Braun, and Andy Tabbott for helping me find my way. To Roger Nisley and Jim McGee for defining the term *hero*. To Marie Venable for making it all matter.

And finally, I want to thank two extraordinary friends: Joe Blake and Rick Crabb. Joe showed me that the journey is what matters. Everything for a reason. Rick showed me the importance of questions and where to find the answers. A simple thanks isn't much, guys, but I think you understand.

Look for Brad Meltzer's
New York Times bestsellers

The First Counsel
(0-446-61-064-X)

Dead Even
(0-446-60-733-9)

The Tenth Justice
(0-446-60-624-3)

"Meltzer is so good."
—*Entertainment Weekly*

AVAILABLE FROM WARNER BOOKS

hospitable

Ladies,

Here's a little going-away gift courtesy of the islands. It'll be sad to see you
a quick trip to
go, but I'm happy for you none the less

In the mere month that I've known you you've all been so kind and ~~hospital~~ that I could easily say you're the best friends I've had since coming to DC

So, best of luck with your new place and, when you get settled, ~~give me a call~~ I look forward to hearing from you.

Mahalo and Aloha